A GRAMMAR OF
MISHNAIC HEBREW

A GRAMMAR OF
MISHNAIC HEBREW

BY

M. H. SEGAL

CLARENDON PRESS · OXFORD

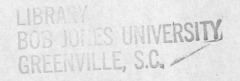

Oxford University Press, Walton Street, Oxford OX2 6DP
OXFORD LONDON GLASGOW
NEW YORK TORONTO MELBOURNE WELLINGTON
KUALA LUMPUR SINGAPORE HONG KONG TOKYO
DELHI BOMBAY CALCUTTA MADRAS KARACHI
IBADAN NAIROBI DAR ES SALAAM CAPE TOWN

ISBN 0 19 815454-2

First edition 1927
Reprinted 1958, 1970, 1978, 1980

Printed in Great Britain by
REDWOOD BURN LIMITED
Trowbridge & Esher

PREFACE

THIS little book has been written with a twofold object: first, to provide students of early Rabbinic literature with a fairly complete grammar of the dialect of that literature; and, secondly, to demonstrate the organic connexion of this Mishnaic dialect with Biblical Hebrew, and its relative independence of contemporary Aramaic, at least in the field of grammar. A good deal of material belonging to comparative grammar has, therefore, been introduced, and constant reference is made to the standard authority in the English language on the grammar of Biblical Hebrew, viz. Dr. Cowley's edition of *Gesenius-Kautzsch's Hebrew Grammar.* As that work is most familiar to English readers, I have followed it, as far as possible, in the arrangement and terminology of the present work.

The examples illustrating grammatical rules have been drawn mainly from the Mishna and, to a smaller extent, from the *Baraitot* and other Hebrew elements of the Babylonian Talmud, because these works are the most accessible to ordinary students. Other less accessible works, like the Tosefta, the Jerusalem Talmud, and the *Midrashim*, have been drawn upon only occasionally. The English renderings of the examples have been made as literal as possible, in order to exhibit clearly the construction and phraseology of the original.

As is well known, the text of Rabbinic works is in a neglected condition, and readings are often uncertain. In citations from the Mishna I have taken care to give only examples of which the reading is established as fairly correct by agreement between the Palestinian text of Lowe and the Babylonian texts of the current editions of the Mishna, and of the Mishna embodied in the Babylonian Talmud. I have refrained from troubling the reader with variant readings which serve no grammatical purpose. Occasionally, however, differences of reading have been indicated where they have a bearing on the grammar of the dialect.

It has not been found practicable to accompany the work with a general index. In order to facilitate reference to its contents, the Table of Contents has been made as detailed as necessary.

I desire to acknowledge my indebtedness to Professor Albrecht's excellent little book, *Neuhebräische Grammatik*, which has furnished me with numerous examples, and has thus lightened my labours in the preparation of this work.

I have also to record with gratitude the interest taken in the publication of this work by that good friend of all English students of Rabbinics, the late Dr. Israel Abrahams, ז״ל.

My friends Mr. Herbert Loewe, of Exeter College, Oxford, and Canon Danby, of Jerusalem, have read the proofs, and have otherwise helped me with corrections and suggestions. If the work be found free from typographical errors, it will be due chiefly to their help combined with the skill and vigilance of the readers of the Clarendon Press.

M. H. SEGAL.

THE HEBREW UNIVERSITY,
JERUSALEM.
September, 1926.

NOTE TO THE NEW IMPRESSION

IN this new impression a number of misprints and other errors have been corrected, but otherwise the book has been left unchanged.

Readers familiar with modern Hebrew who may wish to pursue further the grammatical study of Mishnaic Hebrew are recommended to consult the author's דקדוק לשון המשנה (Tel Aviv, 1936), which provides a fuller and more detailed treatment of the subject.

M. H. S.

THE HEBREW UNIVERSITY,
JERUSALEM.
January, 1957.

CONTENTS

	PAGE
LIST OF ABBREVIATIONS	xxxv
LITERATURE	xxxviii
ADDENDA	xxxix

INTRODUCTION

SECT.	
1. Four Periods in the History of Hebrew	1
2. The Name Mišnaic Hebrew	1
3. Name of the dialect in MH literature	2
4. Its Literary Remains	3
5. Differences between MH and BH	5
6. MH not an artificial language	5
7–8. Its Grammar derived from BH	6–7
9–12. Its Vocabulary	7–9
13. Its History as a spoken language	9
14–15. It is descended from colloquial Hebrew of Biblical times	10–12
16. Early MH	12
17–18. Use of BH, MH, and Aram.	13
19–21. The rise and decline of MH	14–15
22–23. Aram. in Jerusalem	16
24. Aram. chapters of Ezra and Daniel	17
25. The language of legal documents	17
26. The language of the Temple	18
27. Sadducees and MH	18
28. Trustworthiness of Rabbinic tradition	19

PART I

PHONOLOGY AND ORTHOGRAPHY

I. EVIDENCE FOR THE PRONUNCIATION

(*a*) **External.**

SECT.		PAGE
29.	Transcription from and into Greek and Latin	21
30.	Traditional pronunciation among the Jews	21
31.	Punctuation in MS.	22

(*b*) **Internal.**

32.	Vocalization by Vowel letters	22
33.	Mutation of Consonants	22
34.	Information in MH literature	23
35.	Analogy of BH	23

II. THE VOWELS

36.	Vowel changes from BH	23
37.	*e* and *u*	24
38.	Spelling with vowel letters	25
39.	Vowel letters	25

III. THE CONSONANTS

40.	Pronunciation	26

1. Gutturals.

41.	Distinction in Pronunciation	26
42.	Transcription from Gr. and Lat.	27
43.	Mutation	28

2. Palatals.

SECT.		PAGE
44.	Transcription from Gr. and Lat.	29
45.	Mutation	29

3. Dentals.

46.	Transcription from Gr. and Lat.	30
47.	Mutation	30

4. Labials.

48.	Transcription from Gr. and Lat.	30
49.	Mutation	31

5. Sibilants.

50.	Distinction between the various Sibilants	32
51.	Transcription from Gr. and Lat.	32
52.	Mutation	33

6. Sonants.

53.	Transcription from Gr. and Lat.	33
54.	Mutation	34

7. Semi-Vowels.

55.	ו	34
56.	י	35
57.	Doubling in Spelling	35
58.	Mutation	35

8. ב, ג, ד, כ, פ, ת.

59.	Distinction between *raphe* and *dageš*	36
60.	Not so marked as in modern Jewish pronunciation	36

9. Other Consonantal Changes.

SECT.		PAGE
61.	Metathesis	36
62.	Aphaeresis	37
63.	Syncope	37
64.	Apocope	38
65.	Prosthetic א	38
66.	Softening or Dissimilation	38

PART II

MORPHOLOGY

I. THE PRONOUN

1. The Personal Pronoun.

67.	First singular	39
68.	First plural	39
69.	Second singular and plural	40
70.	Third singular and plural	40
71.	Pronominal Suffixes	41

2. The Demonstrative Pronoun.

72.	זֶה, זוֹ, אֵלּוּ, &c.	41
73.	הוּא, הִיא, הֵם, &c.	41
74.	הַלָּז, הַלָּה, הַלָּלוּ	41
75.	אֵת	42
76.	The Article	42

3. Relative Pronoun.

77.	שֶׁ־ and אֲשֶׁר	42
78.	An ancient colloquial form	42

4. The Possessive Pronoun.

SECT. PAGE
79. שֶׁל 43

5. The Interrogative Pronoun.

80. מִי, מָה, אֵיזֶה, &c. 44
81. אֵילוּ as Interrogative 44
82. Origin of אֵיזֶה 45

II. THE VERB

A. General Survey.

1. Lexical.

83. Statistics of the MH Verb . . . 46

(A) *BH Verbs not found in MH.*

84. Rare or Poetical expressions . . . 46
85. Verbs common to BH and Aram. . . 47
86. Verbs frequent in BH; Denominative Verbs . 47
87. BH Verbs found in MH in cognate roots only . 47
88. MH equivalents for lost BH Verbs . . 48
89. Sources of new Verbs in MH . . . 48

(B) *MH Verbs not found in BH.*

90. MH Verbs found in BH in cognate roots, or with Metathesis 49
91. MH Verbs found in BH in derivatives . . 49
92. MH Denominative Verbs: (*a*) from BH nouns; (*b*) from MH nouns; (*c*) from Aram. noun; (*d*) from Gr. nouns . . . 50

SECT. PAGE

93. Old Hb Verbs not found in Aram. . . 50
94 Old Hb Verbs found also in Aram. . . 50
95. Old Hb Verbs found also in other Semitic languages beside Aram. 50
96. Verbs borrowed by MH from Aram.; from Gr. . 51
97. Onomatopoetic Verbs 51
98. Change of usage of the BH Verb in MH . . 51

(C) *BH Verbs with different usage in MH.*

99. Verbs more common in BH than in MH . . 51
100. Verbs more common in MH than in BH . . 52
101. Verbs with change of meaning in MH . . 52
102. Verbs with primary meaning in MH, and only secondary meaning in BH 53

2. GRAMMATICAL.

103. MH losses and gains in Morphology . . 53
104. MH losses and gains in Syntax . . . 54

(A) *BH Stems not found in MH.*

105. Rare formations in BH. . . . 54
106. Regular stems of rare occurrence in particular Verbs . 54
107. Qal of Intransitive Verbs . . . 55

(B) *MH Stems not found in BH.*

108. Quadriliterals: (*a*) by Reduplication; (*b*) by Augmentation; (*d*) Denominatives . . . 55
109. New Intensive Stem in Verbs ע״י, ע״ו . . 56
110. Application of regular stems to verbs in which they are lacking in BH 56

B. The Stems.

1. The Simple Stem.

SECT. PAGE

111. (1) The Qal. The Intransitive forms *Qaṭēl, Qaṭōl* . 57
112. Participle active. Formation of the Feminine . 57
113. Feminine termination in participles of intransitive verbs and in passive participles . . . 57
114. Feminine termination in BH and Aram. . . 58
115. (2) The Niph'al. Elision of ה in the Infinitive . 58
116. The infinitive of כרת 58
117. Origin of elision of ה 58
118. The feminine of the Participle . . . 59
119. Signification of Niph'al. (i) Reflexive and Tolerative. 59
120–121. (ii) Middle; (iii) Passive . . . 59

2. The Intensive Stem.

122. (1) The Pi'el. The spelling with . The Fem. participle 60
123. Signification of the Pi'el: (i) Intensive or Iterative . 60
124. (ii) Causative 61
125. (iii) Denominative. Privative . . . 61
126. (2) The Pu'al. Its occurrence in MH . . 61
127. Adjectival character of the Participle . . 62
128. The Fem. participle 62
129. Examples of the Participle . . . 62
130. Aphaeresis of initial מ 62
131. Cause of disappearance of finite parts . . 63
132. (3) Hithpa'el-Nithpa'el . . . 64
133. Occurrence of Hithpa'el forms . . . 64
134. Formation: (i) First radical a sibilant . . 65

SECT. PAGE
135. (ii) First radical a dental . . . 65
136. Signification of Nithpa'el: (i) Reflexive . . 66
137. (ii) Middle 66
138. (iii) Inchoative 66
139. (iv) Reciprocal 66
140. (v) Passive 67
141. (4) Po'el, Po'al, and Hithpo'el . . . 67

3. The Causative Stem.

142. (1) Hiph'il. Preformative א . . . 67
143. Infinitive: elision of ה 68
144. Fem. Participle. Jussive forms . . . 68
145. Signification of Hiph'il: (i) Causative . . 68
146. (ii) Inchoative. Internal Hiph'il . . . 68
147. (2) Hoph'al. Formation . . . 69
148. Examples of Hoph'al 69
149. (3) Saph'el 69
150. (4) Šaph'el 70

C. The Tenses.

151. Perfect second masc singular . . . 70
152. Perfect second plural 71
153. Imperfect second and third fem. plural . . 71
154. Pausal forms 71
155. Cohortative 72
156. Disappearance of Consecutive tenses . . 72
157. Consecutive tenses rare in colloquial language of BH times 73

D. Weak Verbs.

(1) Guttural Verbs.

SECT. PAGE

158. Phonetic changes in gutturals . . . 74
159–161. Examples of guttural Verbs . . . 74
162. The Verb שׁאר 74
163. (2) Verbs פ״א . . 75
164. The Verb הפך 75

(3) Verbs פ״י.

165. The three classes of פ״י Verbs. The Simple Stem . 75
166. The Intensive Stem 76
167. The Causative Stem 76
168. Verbs יעד, יתר, ילך and הלך . . . 77

(4) Verbs פ״נ.

169–70. The Qal 77–8
171. The Niph'al 79
172–3. The Causative Stem . . . 79
174. The Verb לקח 80

(5) Verbs ע׳ו, ע׳י.

175. Formation 80
176–7. (i) The Simple Stem . . . 80–1
178–9. (ii) The Intensive Stem. (*a*) Hardening of second radical into consonants ו and י . . 82
180. Analogies in BH 83
181–2. (*b*) Reduplication 83–4
183–4. (iii) The Causative Stem . . . 84–5
185. Interchange between roots ע״ו and roots פ״י and ע״ע . 85
186. The verb נוח 85
187. The verb נום, נאם 85

(6) VERBS ע"ע.

SECT. PAGE

188. General Formation compared with BH and Aram . 85
189–190. (i) The Simple Stem . . . 86–7
(ii) Intensive Stem.
191. Po'el, Po'al, and Nithpo'el . . . 87
192–4. Pi'el, Pu'al, Nithpa'el . . . 87–8
195. Reduplicated Forms 88
(iii) Causative Stem.
196. Hiph'il 89
197. Hoph'al 89

(7) VERBS ל"א.

198. Interchange with verbs ל"ה . . . 90
199–200. The Simple Stem . . . 90
201–2. The Intensive Stem 91
203. The Causative Stem 91

(8) VERBS ל"ה.

204. Interchange with verbs ל"א . . . 91
205–7. The Simple Stem. Participles in Adjectival forms (Qaṭel) 92–3
208–10. The Intensive Stem . . . 93–4
211. The Causative Stem. Denominative Hiph'il of עני . 94
212. The Verb היה 95

(9) VERBS WITH PRONOMINAL SUFFIXES.

213. Use of pronominal suffixes in MH . . . 95
214. Suffixes of the First person . . . 96
215. Suffixes of the Second person . . . 96
216. Suffixes of the Third person . . . 96

III. THE NOUN

1. General Survey.

SECT.		PAGE
217.	Special grammatical features of the MH Noun	98
218.	Lexical character	98
219.	Foreign Nouns	99

2. Formation of Nouns.

(1) *Nouns derived from the Simple Stem.*

220–2.	(i) Ground-form *Qaṭl, Qiṭl, Quṭl*	99–100
223.	Forms with root-vowel moved to second radical	101
224–6.	(ii) Ground-form *Qaṭal, Qaṭil, Qaṭul*	101–2
	(iii) Ground-form *Qaṭâl, Qaṭîl, Qaṭûl.*	
227.	*Qaṭâl*	102
228.	*Qaṭîl.* Verbal Nouns *Qᵉṭîla*; abstract Nouns *Qᵉṭîlût*	103
229.	*Qaṭûl.* Sharpening of third radical in Fem. forms	104
230–2.	(iv) Ground-form *Qᵒṭâl, Qᵒṭîl, Qᵒṭûl*	105–6
	(v) Ground-form *Qâṭal, Qâṭil, Qâṭul—Qôṭāl, Qôṭēl, Qâṭôl.*	
233–4.	*Qôṭāl, Qôṭēl*	106
235.	*Qâṭôl, nomina opificum.* BH and Aram. analogies	106
236.	(vi) Ground-form *Qûṭāl*	107

(2) *Nouns derived from the Intensive Stem.*

(i) Ground-form *Qaṭṭal, Qaṭṭil, Qaṭṭul.*

237.	*Qaṭṭal, nomina opificum.* Fem. abstract and verbal nouns	107
238–9.	*Qaṭṭil, Qaṭṭul*	108
	(ii) Ground-form *Qiṭṭal, Qiṭṭil, Qiṭṭûl, Qiṭṭôl.*	
240.	*Qiṭṭal, Qiṭṭil,* expressing physical defect	108

SECT. PAGE

241. *Qiṭṭûl*, verbal nouns; concretes; technical terms in plural; BH analogies . . . 109
242. *Qiṭṭôl* 110
243. (iii) Ground-form *Quṭṭal* . . . 110

(3) *Nouns formed by Reduplication.*

244. Reduplication of Third radical . . . 110
245. Reduplication of Second and Third radicals. Omission of third radical ל, ר . . . 111
246–8. Reduplication of the whole stem in roots ע״ו, ע״ע 112–3

(4) *Nouns formed by Prefixes.*

249. Prefix א 113
250. Prefix ה 113
251. Verbal noun *Haqṭel* 113
252. Verbal noun *Haqṭala*. BH analogies . . 114
253. Verbal noun of *Hithpa'el* . . . 115
254. Prefix י 115
255. Prefix מ 115
256. Ground-form *Maqṭal, Maqṭil, Maqṭul* . . 116
257. Ground-form *Miqṭal, Miqṭil, Miqṭul* . . . 117
258. Ground-form *Muqṭal* 117
259. Ground-form *Maqṭâl-Maqṭôl, Maqṭîl, Maqṭûl* . 117
260. Ground-form *Maqaṭṭel* 117
261. Prefix נ 117
262. Prefixes ס, שׁ 118
263–5. Prefix ת: Ground-forms *Taqṭal, Taqṭil; Tiqṭal, Tiqṭul; Taqṭîl, Taqṭûl* . . . 118

(5) *Nouns formed by means of Suffixes.*

266. Suffix ל 119
267–8. Suffixes ָן, ־וֹן. Mostly adjectives and abstracts. Sharpening of second radical . . 119

SECT. PAGE

269. Suffix ַי 120
270. Suffix ִי. Denominative adjectives; combined with suffixes ָן, וֹן 120
271. Suffix ִית, chiefly Denominatives 121
272. Suffix וּת, Abstracts and Verbal nouns . . 122

(6) *Formations by Sound-Insertion.*

273. Insertion of Vowel sound to form Diminutives . 122
274. Insertion of Consonantal sound ר, נ . . 123
275. (7) *Formations from Biblical Expressions in Technical Halaka* 123

(8) *Diminutives.*

276 Summary of Diminutive Forms . . . 124

3. Formation of the Feminine.

277. Termination ָה 125
278. Termination ֶת, ַת . . . 125
279–80. Terminations ִית, וּת . . . 126

4. Formation of the Plural.

281. (1) *Masculine Nouns.* The terminations ִים, ִין . 126
282. Irregular plur. formations: *Quṭl* forms; ע״ו nouns; ע״ע nouns; ל״ה nouns; *Qaṭîl-Qaṭûl* forms . 126
283. (2) *Feminine Nouns.* Nouns ending in ָה, ֶת; Segolate Nouns in ת; אַשְׁפָּה; עֶרְוָה . . 128
284–5. Nouns ending in ִית, וּת . . 128–9
286. (3) *Plural of Foreign Nouns* . . . 129
287. The termination ָאוֹת, ָיוֹת in Native Nouns . 130
288. Masc. Nouns with Fem. plur. termination . . 130
Nouns of the form *Haqṭel*; כָּרֵת . . . 131

SECT. PAGE
289. Fem. Nouns with Masc. plur. termination . . 131
290. Nouns which show the two plur. terminations with difference in meaning . . . 132
291. MH plur. of nouns without plur. in BH . . 132
292. MH singular of nouns without a sing. in BH . 133
293. **5. The Dual** . . 133

IV. THE PARTICLES

1. Adverbs.

294. BH Adverbs lost in MH. New MH Adverbs. Borrowings from Aram. . . . 134
295. Adverbs of Place 135
296–7. Adverbs of Time . . . 136–8
298–9. Adverbs of Manner . . . 138–40

2. Prepositions.

300. Derivation of MH Prepositions. BH Prepositions lost in MH 141
301. List of Prepositions 141

3. Conjunctions.

302. BH Conjunctions lost in MH. Aram. loan-words. New MH Formations . . . 146
303. List of Conjunctions 147

4. Interjections.

304. Pure Interjections. BH Interjections lost in MH . 148
305. Interjectional Expressions . . 149

PART III

SYNTAX

I. THE VERB

1. Tenses and Moods.

306. Comparison of MH with BH Tenses . . 150

(1) THE PERFECT.

307. The Tense of the Past . . . 150
308. Used in place of the BH Imperfect Consecutive . 151
309. As Pluperfect in relative clauses . . . 151
310. Use in hypothetical sentences . . . 151
311. Used beside the Participle in a temporal or hypothetical significance in descriptions of continuous or customary actions in the past . . 152
312. For actions of the Present . . . 153
313. As *futurum exactum* 153

(2) THE IMPERFECT.

314. The Tense of the Future . . . 153
315. Futurity emphasized by periphrasis with עָתִיד . 154
316. Used in place of BH Perfect Consecutive . . 154
317. In Hypothetical sentences . . . 154
318. As a Subjunctive 154
319. As Optative or Precative . . . 155
320. As Jussive 155
321. As *futurum exactum* in dependent clauses . . 155

(3) THE PARTICIPLE.

322. Twofold character of the Participle . . 155
323. Of the Present 156

SECT. PAGE

324. Of the Past as Frequentative or Iterative, with or without היה 156
325. Of the Future, with or without היה . . 157
326. For the Imperative, with היה . . . 157
327. For the Infinitive, with היה . . . 157
328. Without היה after certain expressions . . 157
329. Of customary actions without reference to a particular time 158
330. As Jussive 159
331. Retains its verbal character even when construed as noun 159
332. Adjectival character of Passive Participles . . 159
333. Difference between Passive Participles and Participles of Reflexive-Passive Stems . . . 160
334. Passive Participles in a Gerundive sense . . 160
335. Active Participles in a Middle sense . . 160
336. Passive Participle Qal in an Active sense: (i) in Intransitive verbs; (ii) in Transitive verbs; (iii) only apparently Active. . . . 160
337. Substantival use of the Participle: with the Article . 162
338. In the Construct State. . . . 162
339. Usual Negative אֵין. In short clauses לֹא, when negative follows immediately upon an affirmative, or when two or more Negatives follow one another . 162
340. Exceptions to this rule, as sometimes in BH . 163
341. Participle may precede its subject, usually for sake of Emphasis 163
342. May also precede its auxiliary . . . 164
343. The construction of the Participle with היה derived from old Hb. The Aram. construction of היה with the finite verb not found in MH . . 164

(4) The Infinitive.

SECT. PAGE

344. Most of the old BH constructions with the Infinitive lost in MH through natural decay . 165
345. Use of the Infinitive with לְ . . . 166
346. With מִן after verbs of preventing, and restraining . 166
347. The Inf. as Verbal Noun . . . 166
348. Expresses obligation, necessity; followed by עַל . 166
349–50. Its use with עָתִיד, סוֹף . . . 167

2. The Government of the Verb.

(1) *Subordination of Noun to Verb as Accusative.*

351. Direct Object after a transitive verb with אֶת; with לְ; without the *nota accusativi* . . . 168
352. Nominative as Direct Object . . . 168
353. Accusative after a Reflexive Verb . . 168
354. Double Accusative 169
355. Accusative of Time 169
356. Accusative of Place 170
357. Accusative of Manner. Substitutes for Accusative of Manner. Adverbial use of Nouns . . 170

(2) *Subordination of Noun to Verb by a Preposition.*

358. Use of Prepositions as in BH . . . 171
359. Special use of אֵצֶל 171
360. Special uses of בְּ: (i) of direct object; (ii) בְּ *essentiae*; (iii) of instrument, price, or measure; (iv) to limit verb; (v) in a local sense . . . 171
361. Special uses of לְ: (i), (ii) of Object; (iii) of Dative; (iv) of Genitive; (v) of Agent after Passive verbs; (vi) to limit verb; (vii) of Place; (viii) of Time . 172

SECT. PAGE

362. Use of מִן: (i) of Place; (ii) of Time; (iii) Partitive; (iv) Privative; (v) of Cause or Instrument . 173
363. Use of עַל: (i) of Object; (ii) After verbs of going, standing, &c.; (iii) of Addition; (iv) to limit verb; (v) of Cause or agent . . 174

(3) *Co-ordination of a Verb to another Verb as Auxiliary.*

364. The Auxiliary before the Principal Verb . . 175
365. The Auxiliary after the Principal Verb . . 176

II. THE NOUN

1. Determination of the Gender.

366. Gender of animate beings . . . 177
367. Gender of inanimate objects . . . 178
368. Change of Gender when used in a derived sense . 178
369. Feminine plural in ים—ַ construed as Masc. . . 179
370. Nouns ending in ת— 179
371. Change of meaning with change of Gender . . 179
372. Gender of Greek and Latin Nouns . . 179

2. Use of the Article.

373. Determination of Nouns . . . 180
374. Various usages of the Article . . . 180
375. Article with the Attribute of a Determinate Noun . 181
376. Noun without the Article, and Attribute with the Article 182
377. Noun with the Article, and Attribute without the Article 183
378. Standing expressions with and without the Article . 184

3. Expression of the Genitive.

SECT. PAGE

379. The various methods of expressing the Genitive in BH, Aram., and MH 185

(1) *The Construct State.*

380. Use of the construct state . . . 186
381. The plural of construct combinations . . 186
382. Construction of one *rectum* with more than one *regens*. 187
383. The Construct before a relative clause . . 188

(2) *Simple Circumlocution of the Genitive.*

384. By לְ־ alone, in BH and in MH . . . 188
385. By לְ־ with relative pronoun—שֶׁל־. Its origin . 189
386. Various uses of שֶׁל 189

(3) *Circumlocution of the Genitive with Anticipation.*

387. Only with Flexible nouns . . . 191
388. *Rectum* always determinate, but it never takes the Article 191
389. Anticipations also with Prepositions . . 192
390. Anticipation in Aram., in other Semitic languages, in BH 192

4. Comparison of Adjectives.

391. Expression of the Comparative: מִן, עַל, יוֹתֵר, פָּחוּת . 193
392. Expression of the Superlative: שֶׁבְּ־ . . 194
393. Expression of the Superlative by Repetition in the Construct state 194

5. Numerals.

394. (1) *Cardinals* 194
395–7. Construction of Numerals with the Objects . 195

SECT.		PAGE
398.	(2) *Ordinals*: 1–10	196
399.	Ordinals above 10	196
400.	Expression of the Days of the Month, and Hours of the Day	196
401.	(3) *Distributives*	197
402.	(4) *Fractions*	197
403.	Numerals in Verbal forms	198

III. THE PRONOUN

1. The Personal Pronoun.

404.	With Finite verb; with אַף	198
405.	Pronoun of the Third person as Copula. Its Position	198

2. Possessive Pronoun.

406.	Use of Pronominal suffixes. Substantival use of שֶׁל	199
407.	Adjectival use of שֶׁל: (*a*) on grounds of Grammar	199
408.	(*b*) On grounds of Style	200
409.	Analogies in BH.	200

3. Demonstrative Pronoun.

410–11.	Substantival and Adjectival uses of זֶה, זוֹ, אֵלּוּ	200–1
412.	Use of הַלָּז, הַלָּלוּ	201
413.	Use of הַלָּה	201
414.	הוּא, הֵם, contrasted with זֶה, אֵלּוּ; with הַלָּה	201
415.	Interrogative אֵיזֶה as Demonstrative	202
416.	Demonstrative use of אֶת before a relative clause	202
417.	Before a Noun. Analogies of this use of אֶת in BH.	202

4. Interrogative Pronoun.

SECT. PAGE
418. Use of מִי, מָה 203
419. Use of אֵיזֶה with הוּא, הִיא; אֵילוּ . . . 203

5. Relative Pronoun. The Use of שֶׁ־.

420. שֶׁ־ with clause; defining a subject or an object . 204
421. Defining Place or Time; with or without retrospective Preposition 204
422. Demonstrative שֶׁ־ after מִי, מָה, and אֵת . . 204
423. As Conjunction in object clauses . . . 205
424. Introducing *oratio recta* . . . 205
425–6. Before a Negative. Before a verb introduced by אוֹ . 206
427. To emphasize an Antithesis . . . 206

6. Expression of the Reflexive and Reciprocal.

428. The Reflexive expressed by the pronominal suffix . 206
429–30. By circumlocution with עֶצֶם; emphasized by כָּל . 206
431. Use of עֶצֶם in BH. 207
432. Reflexive expressed by נֶפֶשׁ, גּוּף, מֵאֵל . . 208
433. Expression of Reciprocity . . . 208

7. Expression of the Indefinite.

434. By אָדָם, emphasized by כָּל . . . 209
435. By כָּל with the Participle or with a relative clause . 209
436. By מִי; מִי with relative clause; strengthened by כָּל; מָה with הוּא, הִיא 209
437. By פְּלוֹנִי, מִקְצָת, כְּלוּם 210
438. By Cognate Participle 210
439. By simple verb without a subject, whether Participle, Perfect, or Imperfect. . . . 210

IV. SENTENCES AND CLAUSES

1. Nominative Absolute.

SECT. PAGE

440. Construction of the Nominative Absolute . . 211
441. With a Definite subject . . . 211
442 With an Indefinite subject . . . 212
443. Resumption of the Subject with הֲרֵי and a demonstrative Pronoun 212
444. The Subject of a Subordinate clause placed before the Principal Sentence . . . 213
445. Nominative Absolute left suspended, and the Predicate attached to a new subject . . . 213
446. A Complete Sentence as Nominative Absolute . 214
447. The new subject expressed by הֲרֵי and the Demonstrative Pronoun 214

2. Agreement between Subject and Predicate.

448. Agreement in number with Collective Nouns . 215
449. With Construct Expressions . . . 215
450. Agreement in Gender with compound subject . 216
451. Agreement in Gender with Grammatical form; or with the Sense 216
452. Impersonal use of the Verb before the Subject . 216

3. Sentences expressing an Oath or a Vow.

453. Use of אִם, אִם לֹא after an Imprecation . . 216
454–5. After קוֹנָם; after שְׁבוּעָה . . . 217
456. An Oath introduced by שֶׁ־ . . . 218
457. An Oath standing in Apposition after an Exclamation . 218
458. קָרְבָּן, שְׁבוּעָה followed by שֶׁ־ . . . 218
459. Construction of a Vow with קוֹנָם . . . 219

4. Interrogative Sentences.

SECT. PAGE
460. A Question expressed by emphasis of the Voice alone . 219
461. By הֲ, הֲלֹא 220
462. By וְכִי; also before another Interrogative Particle . 220
463. מָה in long Argumentative Questions (קַל וָחֹמֶר) . 221
464. שֶׁמָּא, כְּלוּם as interrogative particles . . 221
465. Indirect Questions 221
466. Disjunctive Questions, Direct and Indirect . . 221

5. Desiderative Sentences.

467. Expressions by Simple Imperfect . . . 222
468. By יְהִי רָצוֹן 222
469. By מִי and the Imperfect . . . 222
470. By הַלְוַאי 223

6. Negative Sentences.

471. With לֹא, אֵין, אַל 223
472. Use of בַּל, בְּלֹא in Biblical Quotations . . 223
473. Emphasizing a Negative . . . 224
474. Omission of a Negative in a Series . . 224
475. Use of שֶׁמָּא 224
476. לֹא joined with the Noun . . . 224

7. Relative Clauses.

477. Without שֶׁ־ 225

8. Circumstantial Clauses.

478. Circumstantial Clauses introduced by שֶׁ־, or with Prepositions 225

SECT. PAGE
479. Co-ordination of Circumstantial Clauses (i) without the copula; (ii) with the copula . . 225
480. Circumstantial Clause before the Principal Clause . 226

9. Causal Clauses.

481. Introduced by הוֹאִיל וְ 226
482. Introduced by שֶׁ alone; by שֶׁ combined with other Conjunctions 227

10. Conditional Sentences.

483. Construction of Conditional Sentences . . 227
484. Without Introductory Particle, when the condition is conceived as fulfilled . . . 228
485. With אִם when condition has been fulfilled in the Past . 228
486. When the condition is capable of fulfilment in the Present or the Future . . . 229
487. In Noun Clauses 229
488. Resumption of the Subject by הֲרֵי and the Demonstrative Pronoun 230
489. An Alternative Negative Condition: וְאִם לָאו . 230
490. Use of אִילּוּ, אִילּוּ לֹא 230
491. Use of אִילּוּלֵא, אִלְמָלֵא, before a verbal clause; before a noun clause 230
492. Other Hypothetical Conjunctions . . 231

11. Concessive Clauses.

493. Introduced by simple copula . . . 231
494. By Special Conjunctions: אַף and its various combinations 232

12. Comparative Clauses.

SECT. PAGE

495. Comparison by כְּ־ ,כְּאִילּוּ ,כַּיּוֹצֵא בְּ־ . . 232
496. By כְּמוֹת שֶׁ־ 233
497. By Correlatives 233
498. The Apodosis may stand before the Protasis . 234
499. An Argument to prove Similarity : אַף—מָה . . 234
500. Construction of an Argument from minor to major (קַל וָחֹמֶר) ; an Affirmative Apodosis ; an Interrogative Apodosis 234

13. Disjunctive Clauses.

501. An alternative expressed by the copula ; by אוֹ . 235
502. By Correlative Disjunctive Particles . . 235

14. Adversative, Exceptive, and Restrictive Clauses.

503. Antithesis expressed by copula ; by אֲבָל . . 236
504. Adversative use of אֶלָּא 237
505. Exceptive use of אֶלָּא 237
506. Especially after a Negative . . . 237
507. אֶלָּא strengthened by בִּלְבַד . . . 238
508. אֶלָּא after לֹא כִּי ; after כְּלוּם . . . 238
509. אֶלָּא with conditional force ; often followed by אִם כֵּן . 238
510. אֶלָּא followed by עַד ; אֶלָּא sometimes omitted before עַד 238
511. The Negative omitted before אֶלָּא in Questions . 239
512. Exceptive Clauses introduced by חוּץ מִן ; וּבִלְבַד שֶׁ־ . 239

15. Temporal Clauses.

513. Introduced by שֶׁ־ combined with various Conjunctions 240
Introduced by מִיָּד 241

16. Final Clauses.

SECT. PAGE

514. Purpose expressed by Infinitive with לְ־ alone, or preceded by עַל מְנָת ,כְּדֵי . . . 242
515. Purpose clauses introduced by שֶׁ־ combined with various Conjunctions 242

17. Consecutive Clauses.

516. Consecutive Clauses introduced by copula; by כְּדֵי שֶׁ־ . 242
517. Consecutive Sentences introduced by לְפִיכָךְ . . 243

INDEX OF BIBLICAL PASSAGES . . . 245

ABBREVIATIONS

Tractates of the Mishna, Tosefta, and the Talmuds:—

Ab.	אָבוֹת	(iv)
‘Ar.	עֲרָכִין	(v)
‘AZ.	עֲבוֹדָהזָרָה	(iv)
Be.	בֵּיצָה	(ii)
Bik.	בִּכּוּרִים	(i)
B^{e}k.	בְּכוֹרוֹת	(v)
B^{e}r.	בְּרָכוֹת	(i)
BB.	בָּבָא בַּתְרָא	(iv)
BM.	בָּבָא מְצִיעָא	(iv)
BQ.	בָּבָא קַמָּא	(iv)
Da.	דְּמַאי	(i)
‘Ed.	עֵדֻיּוֹת	(iv)
‘Er.	עֵרוּבִין	(ii)
Giṭ.	גִּיטִּין	(iii)
Ho.	הוֹרָיוֹת	(iv)
Ḥag.	חֲגִיגָה	(ii)
Ḥal.	חַלָּה	(i)
Ḥul.	חוּלִּין	(v)
Kel.	כֵּלִים	(vi)
Kil.	כִּלְאַיִם	(i)
K^{e}r.	כְּרִיתוֹת	(v)
K^{e}t.	כְּתוּבּוֹת	(iii)
Ma‘a.	מַעַשְׂרוֹת	(i)
Mak.	מַכּוֹת	(v
Makš.	מַכְשִׁירִין	(vi)
Mid.	מִדּוֹת	(v)
Miq.	מִקְוָאוֹת	(vi)
M^{e}g.	מְגִלָּה	(ii)
M^{e}‘il.	מְעִילָה	(v)
M^{e}n.	מְנָחוֹת	(v)
MQ.	מוֹעֵד קָטָן	(ii)
MŠ.	מַעֲשֵׂר שֵׁנִי	(i)
Naz.	נָזִיר	(iii)
Nid.	נִדָּה	(vi)
N^{e}d.	נְדָרִים	(iii)
Oh.	אֳהָלוֹת	(vi)
‘Or.	עָרְלָה	(i)
Pa.	פָּרָה	(vi)
Pe.	פֵּאָה	(i)
P^{e}s.	פְּסָחִים	(ii)
Qid.	קִידּוּשִׁין	(iii)
Qin.	קִנִּים	(v)
RH.	רֹאשׁ הַשָּׁנָה	(ii)
San.	סַנְהֶדְרִין	(iv)
So.	סוֹטָה	(iii)
Suk.	סוּכָּה	(ii)
Šab.	שַׁבָּת	(ii)
Š^{e}bi.	שְׁבִיעִית	(i)

Š^e^bu.	שְׁבוּעוֹת	(iv)	Ṭ Y.	טְבוּל יוֹם	(vi)
Š^e^q.	שְׁקָלִים	(ii)	ʿUq.	עוּקְצִין	(vi)
Ta'a.	תַּעֲנִית	(ii)	Ya.	יָדַיִם	(vi)
Tam.	תָּמִיד	(v)	Yo.	יוֹמָא	(ii)
T^e^m.	תְּמוּרָה	(v)	Y^e^b.	יְבָמוֹת	(iii)
T^e^r.	תְּרוּמוֹת	(i)	Zab.	זָבִים	(vi)
Ṭoh.	טָהֳרוֹת	(vi)	Z^e^b.	זְבָחִים	(v)

NOTE.—The figures after the tractates indicate the Order (סֵדֶר), or part of the Mishna, in which these tractates are found.

In citations from the Mishna, Tosefta, and the Jerusalem Talmud roman numerals indicate the chapter and arabic numerals the section or הֲלָכָה, thus: B^e^r. iii. 5. Citations from the Tosefta are marked by *t.* before the name of the tractate. Citations from the Jerusalem Talmud are marked by *j.* before the name of the tractate. In citations from the Babylonian Talmud, the folio is indicated by arabic numerals and the page or column by *a*, *b* thus: San. 75 b.

L.	The Mishnah on which the Palestinian Talmud rests, ed. by W. H. Lowe, Cambridge, 1883.
Ab. d^e^RN.	אָבוֹת דְּרַבִּי נָתָן
Gen. R.	בְּרֵאשִׁית רַבָּה
Ex. R.	שְׁמוֹת רַבָּה
Lev. R.	וַיִּקְרָא רַבָּה
Num. R.	בַּמִּדְבָּר רַבָּה
Lam. R.	אֵיכָה רַבָּתִי
Qoh. R.	קֹהֶלֶת רַבָּה
M^e^kil.	מְכִילְתָּא
Singer	*The Authorised Daily Prayer Book*, ed. Singer.
BDB.	*Hebrew and English Lexicon of the O. T.*, ed. Brown, Driver, and Briggs, Oxford, 1906.

Ges.-K.	Gesenius-Kautzsch's *Hebrew Grammar*, ed. A. E. Cowley, Oxford.
JQR.	*Jewish Quarterly Review.*
MGWJ.	*Monatschrift für die Geschichte u. Wissenschaft d. Judentums.*
ZAW.	*Zeitschrift für die Alttestamentliche Wissenschaft.*
ZDMG.	*Zeitschrift d. deutschen morgenländischen Gesellschaft.*
Aram.	Aramaic.
BH	Biblical Hebrew.
MH	Mishnaic Hebrew.
Gr.	Greek.
Lat.	Latin.

LITERATURE

A. Geiger, *Lehr- u. Lesebuch zur Sprache der Mischnah*, Breslau, 1845.

L. Dukes, *Die Sprache der Mischna*, Esslingen, 1846.

J. H. Weiss, משפט לשון המשנה, Wien, 1867.

C. Siegfried & H. Strack, *Lehrbuch d. neuhebräischen Sprache*, 1884.

L. Metmann, *Die hebräische Sprache*, Jersualem (no date).

K. Albrecht, *Neuhebräische Grammatik auf Grund d. Mišna*, München, 1913.

F. Hillel, *Die Nominalbildung in der Mischnah*, 1891.

H. Sachs, *Die Partikeln der Mischna*, 1897.

M. H. Segal, Mišnaic Hebrew and its relation to Biblical Hebrew and to Aramaic, *JQR.* (Old Series), vol. XX, pp. 647–737, and separately, Oxford, 1909.

Siegfried, *Zur Lehre von dem zus. gesetzten Satze im Neuhebr.*, Kohut, Semitic Studies, pp. 543 ff.

Albrecht, שֶׁ in der Mišna, *ZAW.*, 1911, pp. 205 ff.

J. Barth, *Die Nominalbildung in den semit. Sprachen*, 1894.

S. Stein, *Das Verbum in der Mischnasprache*, 1888.

A. Kohut, *Aruch Completum*, Wien, 1878–92.

J. Levy, *Neuhebr. Wörterbuch*, 1876–89.

M. Jastrow, *Dictionary of the Talmud*, 1886–1903.

S. Krauss, *Griechische u. Lateinische Lehnwörter im Talmud*, 1898–9.

ADDENDA

Sect. 2, note 2. So *Midrash Tehillim* (ed. Buber), ix. 3: שנו חכמים בלשון המשנה. The term is also frequent among medieval writers, e. g. Rashi on Gen. xl. 11. Menaḥem b. Saruq uses לשון משנה in contrast to לשון עברית, i. e. BH, cf. מחברת (ed. Filipowsky), p. 9. Abraham de Balmis uses it in contrast to לשון מקרא, cf. מקנה אברהם, ch. iv, Sect. פעלת.

Sect. 25, p. 18. Qid. iv. 1 is cited in Hebrew in Yᵉb. 85 a; cf. Grätz, *Geschichte*[4], iii. 711. That the *Kᵉtuba* was originally in Hebrew is shown by its Hebrew name (for the form cf. § 229 below, and Stade, *Heb. Gram.*, § 204 b. The Aram. כתובתא is a Hebraism). Cf. also its Gr. equivalent συγγραφή, Tobit vii. 14, and Grätz, *ibid.* 706.

Sect. 63. Krauss's suggestion (*ZDMG.*, 1919, 732) that ברבי should be pointed בִּרְבִּי, בִּיר + רַבִּי is improbable. It would have been spelt *plene*, בירבי.

Sect. 126. Another example of Pu'al is found in Pᵉsiqta R. ix. (ed. Friedmann, p. 33 a): נוּצַּחְתִּי, to prevail.

Sect. 134. A quadriliteral form of Nithpa'el is found in מִתְנַוְנֶה, fem. מִתְנַוְנָה to fail, decay, BQ 91 a; So. iii. 5; Ḥul. 57 b; also יִתְעַלְּפֶה to swoon, Šab. 9 b; Ḥul. 3 b. Cf. Kohut, vi. 209, and Ibn Ganaḥ, *Riqma*, 81, who explains it as an intensive.

Sect. 149. סרגל. Cf., however, Perles, *Festschrift für A. Schwarz*, 303, and Krauss, *ibid.*, 575.

Sect. 150. שלהב. Cf., however, Barth, *Etymologische Studien*, 49.

Sect. 168. יתוותרו. Cf. Ginzberg, *Festschrift für A. Schwarz*, 348.

Sect. 187. Cf. Barth's note in Petuchowsky's *Mischnajjot* (Berlin, 1922), iii. 89.

Sect. 191. Add מְסַתּוֹנֶנֶת, מְסַתּוֹנֵן to strain, refine, P^e^siq. R. 58 a.

Sect. 211. הרצתי. Cf. Fränkel, *ZAW.*, xix, 181.

Sect. 269. ברקאי, בורקי. Cf. also Ginzberg, *Journal of Jewish Lore* (Cincinnati, 1919), 202 f.

Sect. 282, p. 127. סממנים. Cf. Nöldeke, *Syr. Gram.* 74. The form may, perhaps, be a double plural, cf. Brockelmann, *Grundriss*, i. 451; also Bauer-Leander, *Histor. Gram. d. hebr. Sprache*, §§ 146, 160.

Sect. 298, n. 1. With pronominal suffixes the form דַּי alone is used, as in BH, thus: דַּיִי B^e^r. 24 b; דַּיֶּיךָ j. San. vii. 1; דַּיוֹ BQ 18 b; דַּיָּהּ B^e^r. 9 b; דַּיֵּינוּ 16 a; דַּיֵּיכֶם j. Š^e^bi. iv. 3; דַּיָּין (masc.) Šab. 31 b; דַּיָּין (fem.) Nid. i. 1.

Sect. 302. The use in Jewish Aram. of אבל, אלו, אפילו, אף על פי כן, and הואיל is borrowed from MH, cf. Levias, *Gram. of Aram. idiom contained in the Babyl. Talmud*, § 182. Cf. also Gen. R. 91: אבל לָשׁוֹן דְּרוֹמִי הוּא אֲבָל בְּרַם, is a southern expression for ברם verily. The Aram. ברם is also found in MH, e. g. Šab. 13 b.

Sect. 304. On הרי and ארי cf. also Barth, *Jahresbericht d. Rabb.-Seminars zu Berlin*, 1909–10, 27 ff.

Sect. 335. Cf. further כָּל שֶׁהוּבָא בְּחַמִּין = כָּל שֶׁבָּא בְּחַמִּין everything which has been put into hot water, Šab. xxii. 2. Similarly we find the active infin. used with a passive significance: צָרִיךְ אַתָּה לְנַדּוֹת thou shouldst be excommunicated, Ta'an. iii. 12; הָיָה בֵיתוֹ לִבְנוֹת גְּדֵרוֹ לִסְגּוֹר שָׂדֵהוּ לִקְצוֹר if his house had to be built, his wall to be closed in, his field to be harvested, N^e^d. iv. 7; cf. § 348.

Sect. 392. Cf. also זוֹנָה שֶׁבַּזּוֹנוֹת the worst of harlots, j. Šab. viii. 3; חָסִיד שֶׁבַּחֲסִידִים the greatest saint, j. K^e^t. i. 8.

Sect. 402. שמין. Cf. in a medieval text: שמין זהוב $\frac{1}{8}$ of a gold dinar, Mann, *The Jews in Egypt and Palestine*, ii. 188. The editor's correction is unnecessary.

Sect. 431. Cf. Frankel, מבוא הירושלמי, 10 a.

Sect. 435. Cf. Be. 3 b; Z^e^b. 72 a, where a distinction is drawn between אֶת שֶׁדַּרְכּוֹ לִימָּנוֹת and כָּל שֶׁדַּרְכּוֹ לִימָּנוֹת ʿOr. iii. 6, the first being definite and the second indefinite.

Sect. 437. כלום. Cf. also Schulthess, *Gram. d. christ.-paläst. Aram.*, § 65, 2. אחד also serves to express an indefinite subject: א״ל אֶחָד שֶׁאֵינוֹ נֶאֱמָן עַל הַמַּעַשְׂרוֹת some one, who was not to be trusted about tithes, said to him, Dam. iv. 1. 6; Ta'a. ii. 5; מַעֲשֶׂה בְּאֶחָד it happened of some one, Y^e^b. xvi. 4; עָמַד אֶחָד some one arose, K^e^t. xiii. 2.

Sect. 449. On כל אדם קורין cf. Frankel, דרכי המשנה (Warsaw, 1923), 273.

Sect. 502. On אחד . . . ואחד. So also with plur. nouns in the masc.: אֶחָד כֵּלִים גְּדוֹלִים וְאֶחָד כֵּלִים קְטַנִּים whether large vessels or small vessels, Miq. iv. 1; fem.: אֶחָד בְּתוּלוֹת וְאֶחָד בְּעוּלוֹת אֶחָד גְּרוּשׁוֹת וְאֶחָד אַלְמָנוֹת whether virgins or married women, divorced women or widows, Y^e^b. iv. 10; אֶחָד חֲקִירוֹת וְאֶחָד בְּדִיקוֹת whether cross-examinations as to circumstances or as to time and place, San. v. 2; sometimes, however, אחת is found with the fem.: אַחַת גְּדוֹלָה וְאַחַת קְטַנָּה Suk. i. 11. בין . . . בין is also found before nominal forms, but without -שֶׁ: בֵּין לַחִים בֵּין יְבֵשִׁים whether moist or dry, Šab. iv. 1.

Sect. 503. אבל may also introduce a co-ordinated noun clause: חַמִּים אֲבָל לֹא תַבְשִׁיל hot but not cooked; נוֹטְלִים אֲבָל לֹא מַחֲזִירִים (L ולא) one may remove but not put back, Šab. iii. 1.

Sect. 504. So אֶלָּא שֶׁבַּמְּדִינָה but in the province, &c., in contrast to the Temple, Tam. vii. 2. Cf. also Ginzberg, *Journal of Jewish Lore*, 1919, 279.

INTRODUCTION

1. The Hebrew language has been used for the expression of human thought, whether in speech alone, or in writing alone, or in both speech and writing, for some 3000 years. Its history may be roughly divided into four periods: (1) Biblical Hebrew (BH), from the earliest times to the end of the Biblical period, say about 200 B.C.E.; (2) Mišnaic Hebrew (MH), from about 400–300 B.C.E.[1] to about 400 C.E.; (3) Medieval Hebrew, from the redaction of the Babylonian Talmud, about 500 C.E., to 1700; (4) and Modern Hebrew, from the beginning of the eighteenth century to this day. The revival of Jewish life in Palestine through Zionism has brought with it a new efflorescence of Hebrew both as a literary medium and as a spoken tongue.

2. The present work is devoted to a study of the grammatical characteristics of the Hebrew language of the second period. We designate the Hebrew of that period 'Mišnaic Hebrew'[2] from the Mishna and its allied literature which form the sole literary remains that have come down to us in that particular idiom.

The name Mišnaic Hebrew is to be preferred to the name 'New Hebrew', by which the idiom is commonly known; for it serves to mark off this idiom both from the Hebrew of the first period, and also from the Hebrew of the third and fourth periods.

[1] The first period overlaps the second period, as BH continued to be used as a literary idiom long after the rise of MH. Cf. § 17.

[2] לְשׁוֹן הַמִּשְׁנָה, as in the late superscription to Ab. vi. 1. Cf. also Num. R. 1.

The term 'New Hebrew', on the other hand, distinguishes our idiom from BH only, but ignores the later phases through which the Hebrew language passed after the Talmudic age, or confuses these important phases with the particular idiom of the second period.

3. In earlier Mišnaic literature no distinction is drawn between BH and MH. The two idioms are known as לְשׁוֹן הַקֹּדֶשׁ, the Holy Tongue, as contrasted with other languages, which are described as לְשׁוֹן חוֹל, the common tongue. Thus, in So. vii. 1 ff. it is laid down that certain prescribed religious formulae may be recited בְּכָל לָשׁוֹן, which is interpreted as לְשׁוֹן חוֹל (B^e^r. 40 b; cf. also Šab. 40 b), and other formulae may be recited only בִּלְשׁוֹן הַקֹּדֶשׁ. These latter include passages from Scripture, like מִקְרָא בִכּוּרִים (Deut. xxvi. 3 b–10 a), חֲלִיצָה (xxv. 9 b), בְּרָכוֹת וּקְלָלוֹת (ib. xxvii. 15–26), which had to be recited in the actual words of Scripture, i. e. in BH. But they also include בִּרְכוֹת כֹּהֵן גָּדוֹל, which were composed in MH (So. vii. 7; cf. the commentaries, *ad loc.*), and the address of the כֹּהֵן מְשׁוּחַ מִלְחָמָה (Deut. xx. 3–4) which was amplified in MH (ib. So. viii. 1 f.). Cf. also: הָיָה ר׳ מֵאִיר אוֹמֵר כָּל הַדָּר בְּאֶרֶץ יִשְׂרָאֵל וְקוֹרֵא קְרִיאַת שְׁמַע שַׁחֲרִית וְעַרְבִית וּמְדַבֵּר בִּלְשׁוֹן הַקֹּדֶשׁ הֲרֵי הוּא בֶּן עוֹלָם הַבָּא:—R. Meir (*c.* 175 C.E.) used to say: 'Whoever dwells in the Land of Israel, and reads the Š^e^ma'[1] morning and evening, and speaks the Holy tongue, lo he belongs to the world to come,' Sifre, Deut. xxxii. 43; where certainly ordinary MH must be meant, like that used by R. Meir himself in this dictum. Again, מִכָּאן אָמְרוּ כְּשֶׁהַתִּינוֹק מַתְחִיל לְדַבֵּר אָבִיו מְדַבֵּר עִמּוֹ בִּלְשׁוֹן הַקֹּדֶשׁ וּמְלַמְּדוֹ תוֹרָה:—Hence they said: When a child begins to speak, his father speaks with him in the Holy tongue, and teaches him Torah, ib. Deut. xi. 19: אָמַר רַבִּי בְּאֶרֶץ יִשְׂרָאֵל לְשׁוֹן סוּרְסִי לָמָּה אוֹ לְשׁוֹן הַקֹּדֶשׁ אוֹ לְשׁוֹן יְוָנִית:—Rabbi (200 C.E.) said: in the Land of Israel why the Sursi (Syrian) tongue?

[1] Deut. vi. 4; Singer, p. 40 f.

Either the Holy tongue, or the Greek tongue, So. 49 b; BQ 83 a; אָמַר רַב יוֹסֵף בְּבָבֶל לְשׁוֹן אֲרָמִי לָמָּה אוֹ לְשׁוֹן הַקֹּדֶשׁ אוֹ לְשׁוֹן פַּרְסִי :— R. Joseph (*c.* 350 C.E.) said: In Babylon, why the Aramean tongue? Either the Holy tongue, or the Persian tongue, ib., where again MH must be meant, the language used by the speakers themselves.

Thus, also, BH is called עִבְרִית, as opposed to תַּרְגּוּם, the Aramaic portions of Daniel and Ezra, Ya. iv. 5 (תַּרְגּוּם שֶׁכְּתָבוֹ עִבְרִית וְעִבְרִית שֶׁכְּתָבוֹ תַּרְגּוּם); or as contrasted with לְשׁוֹן רוֹמִי, לְשׁוֹן אֲרָמִי, עַרְבִי, Sifre, Deut. xxxiii. 26; or with עֵילָמִית, Elamite, and גִּיפְטִית, Egyptian, Šab. 115 a; M[e]g. 18 a; but so is MH called עִבְרִית, as contrasted with יְוָנִית, Giṭ. ix. 8; and עִבְרִי, j. M[e]g. i. 11.

A distinction between BH and MH is found only in later times, when MH had ceased to be used outside the learned circles in the schools. Thus, R. Joḥanan (*c.* 275 C.E.) objects to the use in a *halaka* of the expression מְסָכוֹ, which he calls לְשׁוֹן תּוֹרָה, and insists on the use of מְזָגוֹ, which he describes as לְשׁוֹן חֲכָמִים, ʽAZ. 58 b. Similarly the same teacher demands the use of רְחֵלוֹת (לְשׁוֹן חֲכָמִים —), in the Mishna, Ḥul. xi. 1, instead of רְחֵלִים (לְשׁוֹן תּוֹרָה —), Ḥul. 137 b.[1]

4. The literary monuments of MH consist of the record of the teaching and sayings of the *Tannaim* and *Amoraim*,[2] as preserved in early rabbinic literature. These may be classified as follows:

(i) Tannaitic, in the following works which are exclusively in MH: Mishna, Tosefta,[3] Abot d[e]R. Nathan, Masiktot Q[e]ṭannot,

[1] So in Aram.: לִישָּׁנָא דְאוֹרַיְיתָא, contrasted with לִישָּׁנָא דְרַבָּנָן, Qid. 2 b.

[2] תַּנָּאִים, a Hebraized Aram. form of the MH שׁוֹנִים, repeaters (of the traditional law)—the Teachers of the Mišnaic period, as contrasted with אֲמוֹרָאִים, expositors (of the Mishna)—the Teachers of the post-Mišnaic, or Talmudic period.

[3] The Mishna is found in two chief recensions, (i) a Palestinian text, as given in the Jerusalem Talmud, and in the text edited by Lowe (L.). To this recension belongs also the text found in codex Kauffmann (K); see Krauss,

Mekilta, Sifra, Sifre, Seder 'Olam, and the *Baraitot*,[1] scattered over the Palestinian and Babylonian Talmuds. We must also include in this class the sayings of the Tannaim, as reported by the Amoraim in the two Talmuds and in the Aggadic Midrashim. In these works, though they are partly composed in Aram., the Tannaim are, as a rule, made to speak in MH, even in ordinary conversations, and with women and children: cf. for example, 'Er. 53 b (ר׳ יוֹסֵי הַגְּלִילִי, ר׳ יְהוֹשֻׁעַ בֶּן חֲנַנְיָא), Ned. 62 a, 66 b.

(ii) Amoraic. The teaching and sayings of the Amoraim, as recorded in the two Talmuds and in the Aggadic Midrashim.

The earlier Amoraim, especially in Palestine, used MH very frequently, though they are often found to speak in Aram. But even the later Amoraim, and even in Babylon, used MH exclusively for the following purposes: statements of the formulated *halaka*[2]; homiletical expositions of the Scriptures[3]; parables (מָשָׁל),

MGWJ., li, pp. 54 ff. (ii) a Babylonian text, as given in the Babylonian Talmud of the Mishna. With this the text found in current editions usually, but not always, agrees; cf. Frankel, דרכי המשנה (2nd ed., Warsaw, 1923), pp. 231 ff. Similarly the text of the Tosefta is found in a Palestinian recension, as represented by the edition of Zuckermandel (Passewalk, 1877–82), and a Babylonian text found in the current editions printed with the Alfasi. On these and other works named, cf. the respective articles in the *Jewish Encyclopaedia*; Schechter, Hastings' *Dictionary of the Bible*, Extra Volume, pp. 57 ff; Strack, *Einleitung in d. Talmud*.

[1] בָּרַיְתָא, Aram. for MH חִיצוֹנָה (מִשְׁנָה), the external Mishna, viz. the *halakot* not included by Rabbi in his standard Mishna.

[2] Even in popular addresses. Cf. the confusion by a popular audience in Babylon of the phrase, used by R. Matna (fourth cent. C.E.) in an address, מַיִם שֶׁלָּנוּ 'water *kept over night*' and '*our* water', Pes. 42 a. This confusion could only have arisen in MH, and not in Aram., which would have used different words for these two ideas, viz. דְּבֵיתוּ and דִּילָנָא; cf. Rashi, *ad loc.*, and also Wijnkoop, *JQR.*, vol. xv (1903), p. 29. Further the confusion by a popular audience in Palestine in the time of Rabbi of מֵי בֵיצִים and מֵי בְצָעִים (= בְּצִים = בְּצוֹת), San. 5 b. Contrast, however, the different account in j. Šebi. vi, 1; Giṭ. 1, 2.

[3] The evidence can be found on almost every page of both Talmuds, and

even in the middle of an Aram. conversation (cf. e.g. BQ 60 b; Ta'a. 5 b); and prayer (cf. B^{e}r. 17 a, 55 b, 60 a, b; K^{e}t. 8 b). The frame-work of the Talmuds is in Aram. So also the discussions about the *Halaka*, and the ordinary conversations of the Amoraim are in Aram. Tales and traditions about the Tannaim and past ages in general, are usually in MH, sometimes interspersed with later Aram. additions (cf. e.g. B^{e}r. 27 b; BM 59 b, &c.).

5. The differences between BH and MH are obvious and striking. They extend to grammar, vocabulary, and general style of expression. Some grammatical forms which are common in BH either have become rare, or have disappeared altogether in MH. Again, certain forms which are rare in BH have become the normal type in MH. Then as to vocabulary, we meet in MH large numbers of words which are rare or unknown in BH, but are common in Aram. Again, many words that are common in BH are absent in MH. Many BH words are used in MH in a changed connotation, usually as in Aram. Moreover, MH contains a large number of technical words and phrases which are unknown in BH. It has also borrowed a large number of names of objects from the Greek and Latin, which further help to detract from its Hebraic character. Finally, the diction of MH is quite unlike the ordinary BH style. Many familiar BH constructions are entirely absent in MH, whilst new constructions and usages have arisen in MH which are often similar to those known in Aram. or identical with them.

6. The similarities between MH and Aram., combined with the fact that MH has come down to us in works produced by the schools of the learned at a time when Aram. was used as a common vernacular among the Jews, have led many scholars to

also in the earlier Aggadic Midrashim. Cf., for example, the use of MH and Aram. in *halaka* in the first pages of BM, and in *Aggada* in the first pages of B^{e}r.

the view that MH was merely a Hebraized Aram., artificially created by the Schoolmen, like the Latin of the Middle Ages, and that it never had an independent existence as a natural medium of ordinary speech in the daily life of the Jews. This view rests, however, on a misconception of the whole character of MH. Far from being an artificial scholastic jargon, MH is essentially a popular and colloquial dialect. Its extensive literature does not consist of books composed by literary men in their study. It is rather a record of sayings, oral teaching, and discussions of men of the people on a variety of subjects, embracing, practically, all the manifold activities in the daily life of an organized civilized society. Its vocabulary and its grammar both bear the stamp of colloquial usage and popular development. Apart from the technical phraseology of the specialized *halaka*, not a single trace can be discovered in it of that artificiality with which it has been credited.

7. As to the alleged dependence of MH on Aram., a careful examination of the grammar and vocabulary of MH as presented in the following pages will show that, while Aram. has undoubtedly influenced MH in many directions, it would be an exaggeration to describe this influence as a dependence of MH on Aram. In its morphology, MH is absolutely independent of Aram., and largely also in its syntax. In its main characteristics, the grammar of MH is practically identical with the grammar of BH. Where it differs from BH grammar, the genesis of the difference can generally be traced back to an older stage in the language, out of which the new forms developed in a natural way. Forms that deviate from the regular type of BH are usually found in BH in isolated cases as grammatical irregularities. It is nearly always possible to trace the connexion of a MH form with a BH prototype, at least in later BH literature. If such forms in MH and late BH happen also to be found in Aram., they are usually also found in other Semitic languages, especially in a late stage of development. They are thus not Aramaisms, but grammatical phenomena common to the whole, or to a portion, of the Semitic family. On the other hand, MH has also a considerable number of forms which are quite unknown in Aram., and which could not have arisen if MH had been the artificial creation of men whose natural language was Aram.

8. It is chiefly in the sphere of syntax, particularly in the use of the tenses, the expression of the genitive, and the construction of the dependent clause, that MH deviates most from BH, and comes nearest to Aram. But this is due to the fact that, whereas BH is a highly poetical literary language, MH, like Aram., is a simple homely idiom, with no pretence whatever to poetical or picturesque expression. The refined, but often ambiguous, constructions of the poetical prose of BH could not have survived in the daily speech of the people throughout those centuries of violent changes which followed upon the golden age of BH literature. Refinement of expression had to be sacrificed to clearness and usefulness. Thus, popular Hebrew of daily use must have freed itself from the conventionalized literary forms of BH at a comparatively early date, if it ever had been subject to them at all. The simplification of Hebrew syntax in speech was in time reflected also in literature. It is possible to trace this gradual process of simplification in the later books of the Hebrew Bible, until we reach the severe plainness and baldness of MH. No doubt, Aram. exercised a powerful influence in that direction. But the tendency was inherent in Hebrew itself, and if left alone Hebrew would have developed on somewhat similar lines, though perhaps not so rapidly as it actually did under Aram. influence.

9. The evidence of MH grammar is strongly supported by MH vocabulary. It is true that MH has a large number of words which are common in Aram. But, on the other hand, it can also show a considerable number of words which are not found in Aram.

As is to be expected of two closely related dialects living side by side, MH borrowed extensively from Aram., but so did Aram., especially Jewish Aram., borrow extensively from MH, particularly in the sphere of religion and the higher life.[1] The presence of so many Aram. words and expressions in MH can affect its genuine Hebraic character as little as, for example, the numerical preponderance of the Latin element in the English dictionary can affect the genuine Teutonic character of the English language; or, let it be said, as little as the presence in Aram. itself of so many Hebrew and other foreign words and phrases can affect the Aramean character of the old language of Syria and Mesopotamia.

10. Moreover, a detailed examination and analysis of the MH vocabulary, such as is given below for the verb (§§ 83–102), reveals the fact that the Aram. influence on the MH vocabulary has been exaggerated in the same way as the Aram. influence on the MH grammar. It has been the fashion among writers on the subject to brand as an Aramaism any infrequent Hebrew word which happens to be found more or less frequently in the Aram. dialects. Most of these 'Aramaisms' are as native in Hebrew as they are in Aram. Many of them are also found in other Semitic languages. The lists given below show that of the 300 new verbs in MH only some 25 verbs can be described as undoubtedly genuine Aram. loan-words. The other so-called Aram. verbs are either ordinary Semitic words (§ 95), or are common to both Hebrew and Aram. (§ 94).

11. Further, the lists given there also show a group of over fifty verbs which are common to BH and to Aram. of the Mišnaic period, and yet are not found in MH (§ 84). If MH was merely a Hebraized Aram., or an artificial mixture of Aram. and BH, why did it not appropriate those verbs which belonged to

[1] Even the Christian dialect of Palestinian Aram. borrowed freely from MH; cf. Nöldeke, *ZDMG.*, xxii, pp. 513, 522.

both the elements of which it is said to have been composed? Again, the lists show a group of over thirty verbs of undoubted Semitic origin which are peculiar to MH, and which are not found even in Aram. (§ 93). How is one to explain the origin of these verbs, if MH was but an artificial mongrel, made up of BH and Aram.?

12. The same phenomenon appears in the other parts of the MH vocabulary. Thus, in the particles we have only a dozen or so loan-words from Aram., against a considerable number of new formations and adaptations from old Hebrew words and expressions (§§ 294, 300, 302, 304). The numerals are practically all identical with BH, and free from Aramaisms (§§ 394 ff.). So also the pronoun exhibits some interesting new formations, but is practically free from Aram. influences (§§ 66–81). In the noun, MH has borrowed much from Aram.; but it has also borrowed much from Greek, Latin, and other sources. On the other hand, the substance of the MH noun rests on the BH noun, not only in its grammatical, but also in its lexical character. Furthermore, as in the case of the verb, MH has preserved a considerable number of old Hebrew nouns not found in BH or in Aram., and, in addition, has coined from Hebrew roots many new names for objects and ideas produced by the changed conditions of life (cf. §§ 217 ff., and the nouns enumerated in 'Formation of Nouns', §§ 220 ff.).

13. It is clear from the facts presented by its grammar and vocabulary that MH had an independent existence as a natural living speech, growing, developing, and changing in accordance with its own genius, and in conformity with the laws which govern the life of all languages in general, and the Semitic languages in particular. It was greatly influenced by Aram., its close neighbour and rival, but it was not submerged by Aram. till after some centuries, when political factors made it impossible for MH to continue as a living speech. The home of MH was Palestine. So long as the Jewish people retained some sort of national existence in Palestine, MH continued to be the language of at least a section of the Jewish people living in Palestine. As Jewish life in Palestine gradually decayed, and eventually suffered total extinction, so MH was banished step by step from everyday life, and eventually, towards the end of the Mišnaic period, became confined to the learned in the schools and academies. With the ruin of these schools in Palestine, MH disappeared altogether from its native home, but continued to exist side by side with Aram. in the Jewish academies of Babylon, whither it had been carried by the Palestinian immigrants. When, in their turn, the Babylonian academies also decayed, towards the end of the Talmudic period, the last remnant of MH died out. The dialect continued a more or less fitful and precarious existence as a literary medium, until it passed into the new literary dialect of Medieval Hebrew.

14. We may now attempt to define more precisely the relation of MH to BH. In defining this relation we have to recapitulate the lexical and grammatical characteristics of MH, already briefly outlined above.

The bulk of the MH vocabulary is found in BH. This applies especially to the most necessary words, such as pronouns, numerals, particles, and the most common verbs and nouns. But a considerable number of BH words have been lost in MH, particularly words that were rare in BH, and used only in poetry, even though these were common and prosaic words in Aram. (cf. for verbs, §§ 84 ff.). On the other hand, MH shows a considerable number of words of undoubted Hebrew origin, which are not found in BH. This may, indeed, be due to a mere accident, in view of the scanty and fragmentary remains of BH literature. Nevertheless, the possession by MH of Hebrew words not known in BH establishes the important fact that MH was not derived from BH, but that it drew its lexical material from a source much wider than the literature of the Hebrew Bible. What was that source? Was it a literary source, more extensive than the Hebrew Bible, containing, in addition to the Bible, books discarded when the Canon of Scripture was fixed, and now lost, but familiar to the creators of MH (assuming again that MH was an artificial creation of the Rabbis)? This is hardly probable. For if those lost books were of such merit and value, that the Rabbis thought them worthy of the closest and most intimate study, and became familiar with their vocabulary as with the vocabulary of the books of the Bible themselves, then those books would not have been excluded from the Canon as of no value, or as of heterodox tendencies. It is much more reasonable to assume that the MH vocabulary was in the main drawn not from a literary source, but from the actual Hebrew speech of daily life which preceded the Mišnaic period, and which, of course, possessed many Hebrew words that did not find their way into the books of the Bible. If this assumption be correct, MH is the direct lineal descendant of the spoken Hebrew of the Biblical period, as distinguished from the literary Hebrew of the Biblical period preserved in the Hebrew Scriptures.

This explains also why MH has not preserved the poetical words and expressions of BH. These words and expressions were not used at all, or only rarely, in the colloquial Hebrew of Biblical times, which was the ancestor of MH. This also explains the homely and severely prosaic chracter of MH. It was a purely colloquial, one might say a vulgar idiom, directly descended from an older colloquial or vulgar idiom.[1]

[1] We use the term 'vulgar' in its original sense of popular. The explanation that the usual prosaic baldness of MH is due to the technical character of the *halaka* leaves out the extensive *haggada* which, though not technical, is yet

15. This view of the origin of MH affords also a satisfactory explanation of the grammatical characteristics of the dialect. As has already been stated above, MH agrees in the main with BH grammar. Its various differences from BH consist chiefly of BH irregularities which have become the regular type in MH. On examination these will be found to be colloquial and popular variations from the standardized literary idiom. Cf. below the discussion on the pronouns אֲנוּ, § 68; הַלָּלוּ, הַלָּה, § 73; שֶׁ־, § 78; the Nithpa'el, § 131; the consecutive tenses, § 157, &c. Some of these variations are probably due to differences of dialect in the Hebrew spoken in different parts of Palestine. Traces of the existence of dialects, especially in Northern Palestine, are found even in BH.[1] The concentration of all Jewish life in Palestine in and around Jerusalem, which began towards the end of the Judean monarchy, and which lasted throughout the period of the second Temple, must have introduced those dialectal variations into the speech of Jerusalem. From the spoken vernacular these irregularities found their way also into the literary dialect of the time. Hence the phenomenon that from the days of Jeremiah onwards, BH begins to show, in constantly increasing numbers, forms and expressions which are the normal type in MH, and many of which are also found in Aram.

16. It is not possible to trace the rise and development of MH, owing to the lack of early literary monuments in the dialect. The earlier *halaka* still shows a free and picturesque mode of expression, cf. נִסְתַּחֲפָה שָׂדֵךְ, לֹא מִפִּיהָ אָנוּ חַיִּין, Ket. i. 6; מוּכַּת עֵץ, דְּרוּסַת אִישׁ, 7; שׁוֹתֶה בַּעֲצִיצוֹ, iii. 5; כּוֹשֵׁל שֶׁבָּהֶן, ix. 2; הִנִּיחַ מָעוֹתָיו עַל קֶרֶן הַצְּבִי, xiii. 2; הַבָּנִים יִשְׁאֲלוּ עַל הַפְּתָחִים, 3; פָּשַׁט לוֹ אֶת הָרֶגֶל,

similar in its diction to the *halaka*. That the *halaka* was sometimes capable of picturesque expression, is shown by the examples cited in § 16.

[1] Cf. below, § 78; Stade, *Heb. Gr.*, pp. 11–14; Bergsträsser, *ZAW.*, xix, pp. 41 ff.; Sznejder, pp. 27 ff.

אֵשֵׁב עַד שֶׁיִלְבִּין רֹאשִׁי, 5; יִפָּרַח בָּאֲוִיר, 7; also BQ. i. 1, &c. Also the descriptive passages in Yo. i. 5, 7, &c.; Suk. iv. 4, 5; v. 4, &c.; Ta'a. iii. 5; So. i. 4, 6 f.; ix. 15; M^{e}n. x. 3 f.; Tam. i. 1 f.; N^{e}g. xii. 5 f.; Pa. iii. 1 f., &c. Contrast also the picturesque tale of Simon the Just, t. Naz. iv. 7; Naz. 4 b, with the style later developed in such tales (מעשיות). A characteristic specimen of the early historical tale is found in Qid. 66 a (§ 126, n.). No doubt many of the Palestinian apocryphal and apocalyptic books must have been composed in a similar style, as can be seen from the Hebrew fragments of such compositions that have come down to us.

17. But, nevertheless, BH, with a MH colouring, continued to be the principal literary medium long after it had died out as a living speech, as is shown by the later books of BH. There can be no doubt that the authors of Chronicles, Esther, Ecclesiastes, Daniel, Sirach, and the Psalms of Solomon did not use BH in their ordinary everyday life. BH was to them only a literary and artificial medium of expression which they had acquired in the schools from the study of the old sacred literature. That is why they sometimes show awkwardness in handling the old Hebrew idiom, and difficulty in expressing their thoughts with clearness and exactness. That is also why they often lapse into usages and expressions which remind us of MH or of Aram. What language did the authors of those late BH books speak in their daily life? Or, in other words, what was the language of ordinary life of educated native Jews in Jerusalem and Judea in the period from 400 B.C.E. to 150 C.E.? The evidence presented by MH and its literature leaves no doubt that that language was MH. Of course, those educated Judeans also understood Aram., and used it even in writing, but only occasionally, and not habitually—in the same way as the educated Boer in South Africa sometimes uses English, or as the Flamand in Belgium may often use French.

18. Thus, for a number of generations, the Judean Jews

remained Hebrews in their language, using the classical dialect—BH—for literary purposes, and the popular dialect—MH—as a medium of speech in their ordinary daily life, in the school, in the Temple and the Synagogue. Gradually, however, the influx into Jerusalem of Aram.-speaking Jews from the Eastern Diaspora, and also from Galilee, Transjordania, and Syria, established Aram. as a native tongue in Jerusalem. The native Jews then became bi-lingual, using both Aram. and MH indiscriminately in ordinary life, but MH exclusively in the school, and for religious purposes. Eventually, Aram. gained the upper hand, and MH, like BH, became a לְשׁוֹן הַקֹּדֶשׁ, a purely religious language; then, finally, at the end of the Mišnaic period it was reduced to a לְשׁוֹן חֲכָמִים (§§ 3, 13).

19. It is possible to indicate only approximately the probable dates of these linguistic changes. The rise of MH may be assigned to the period associated by tradition with the 'Men of the Great Synagogue'. The saying reported of them is already in pure MH (Ab. i. 1). They are also reputed to have been the authors of the oldest portions of the Jewish liturgy, which are likewise couched in MH (cf. Bᵉr. 33 a). That period may approximately be identified with the end of the Persian rule and the beginning of the Greek rule in Palestine, say 400–300 B.C.E. The BH books of the period all show distinct traces of MH, viz. Chronicles, Canticles, Esther, and especially Qohelet and Sirach, and also Daniel.[1]

20. MH seems to have attained the height of its power during the rise of the Hasmonean dynasty.[2] Its decline as a spoken language seems to have begun with the fall of that dynasty and

[1] Driver, *Introduction to Lit. of OT.*[9], pp. 474 f., 484 f., 539 f.

[2] Cf. Graetz, *Geschichte d. Juden*[4], III, i, pp. 81–2; Klausner, *Origin of Mishnaic Hb.*, Scripta Universit. Hierosol., Orientalia atque Judaica I, Art. IX.

the reign of Herod. The destruction of many of the native families in the bloody wars which accompanied the coming of the Romans and the establishment of the Herodians (whose original language was probably Aram.); the closer connexion between Jerusalem and the Aram. Jewries of Syria and the Eastern Diaspora which followed on the incorporation of Palestine in the Roman Empire; and the settlement of those Aram.-speaking Jews in Jerusalem, all tended to spread the use of Aram. at the expense of MH. But MH still remained a popular speech, as is testified by numerous passages in its literature. Thus, e.g., the Jewish damsels at their dances in the vineyards sing to the young men in MH (Ta'a. iv. 8); the taunt-song against the tyranny of the powerful priests is in MH (Pes. 57 a; t. Men. xiii. 21); popular vows are in MH (Ned. i. 1, &c.).[1]

21. Finally, the destruction of Jewish life in Judea after the defeat of Bar Kokba (135 C.E.), and the establishment of the new Jewish centre in the Aram.-speaking Galilee, seem to have led to the disappearance of MH as a popular tongue. In that age we find R. Meir pleading for the preservation of MH speech at least among the pious, just as he pleads against the emigration from the Holy Land, which then prevailed in consequence of the Roman oppression. The Aramaization of the Jews in Palestine was completed one generation later, when Rabbi complains of the exclusive use of Aram. in the Land of Israel (cf. § 3).[2]

[1] Cf. בנדרים הלך אחר לשון בני אדם, Ned. 30 b, 51 b and Rashi, *ad loc.*

[2] Nevertheless, Rabbi's words prove that MH was still thought of as a language of everyday life. So two generations later than Rabbi, R. Jonathan of Beit Jibrin says: אַרְבַּע לְשׁוֹנוֹת נָאָה לְעוֹלָם שֶׁיִּשְׁתַּמְּשׁוּ בָּהֶם לַעַז לְזֶמֶר רוֹמִי לִקְרָב סוּרְסִי לְאִילְיָיא עִבְרִי לְדִיבּוּר:—There are four tongues good for the world to make use of: the Foreign (= Greek) for song, the Roman for war, Sursi (= Syriac) for lamentation, and Hebrew for (ordinary) speech, j. Meg. iv. 4. So R. Joseph's saying (§ 3) proves that MH was known as a spoken language in Babylon in the fourth century C. E.

22. Before concluding this sketch, we may refer briefly to the evidence advanced for the view that Aram. was the exclusive language of the Jews in Judea during our period.[1] This evidence consists in the use of Aram. in Ezra and Daniel, and in *Megillat Ta'anit*; the use in the Synagogue of an Aram. translation (Targum) of the Scriptures; the use of Aram. in legal documents, like *K^e^tuba* (marriage settlement), *Geṭ* (bill of divorcement), &c.; the use of Aram. in inscriptions in the Temple; the reported Aram. sayings of some Rabbis in the Mishna and Tosefta, and of Jesus in the Gospels; the existence of Aram. proper names, and of Aram. words in Josephus.

The most that this evidence can prove is that during our period Aram. was understood and used in Palestine, a fact which nobody denies. It cannot, however, prove that Aram. was the exclusive vernacular of all Jews of that period. For against these remains of Palestinian Aram., there is the vast MH literature, including the MH liturgy; there is, further, MH itself, with all its popular and original elements, to prove that during our period Jews in Judea spoke MH.

23. It must be remembered that Jerusalem was more than merely a Judean city. It was the metropolis of a world-wide Jewry. Beside the native Judean majority, there were in Jerusalem also important colonies of Aram.- and Greek-speaking Jews, especially in Roman times. In addition to the Aram.-speaking residents, vast numbers of Aram.-speaking Jews visited the Holy City for the celebration of the Festivals of the Temple. It is not, therefore, surprising that there were Aram. inscriptions in the Temple, just as there were also Greek inscriptions (Šeq. vi. 5; iii. 2); that there were numerous Aram. proper names, just as there were numerous Greek proper names; that the Synagogue used an Aram. Targum for the benefit of unlettered Galilean and Oriental

[1] The evidence is collected by G. Dalman, *The Words of Jesus*, pp. 1–13.

Jews, or that the calendar of the *Megillat Ta'anit* (completed *c.* 70 C.E.), intended as it was for all classes of Jews, should have been composed in Aram.; or that certain legal documents of common and universal use should have been in Aram. Against the few isolated sayings of Hillel (a Babylonian!), and some other Rabbis, there are numerous sayings by the same Rabbis in MH.[1] So also Josephus cites Hebrew words in addition to Aram. (cf. *Antiquities*, iii. 7; x. 6). With regard to the language of Jesus, it is admitted that in the Roman period, and perhaps earlier, Aram. was the vernacular of the native Galilean Jews. But even in Galilee, MH was understood and spoken, at least by the educated classes.

24. The Aram. chapters in Ezra and Daniel, dealing as they do with Babylonian and Persian subjects, may have been the work of Jews of the Eastern Diaspora. This seems very probable, at least, with regard to the Aram. in Ezra. A Jerusalem Jew would not have said אֲזַלוּ . . . לִירוּשְׁלֶם (iv. 23), but אֲתוֹ . . . לִירוּשְׁלֶם. Again, a Jerusalem Jew would not have described the Temple repeatedly as בֵּית אֱלָהָא דִּי בִירוּשְׁלֶם (iv. 24; v. 2, 16; vi. 12, 18).

25. The same may be said of Aram. legal documents. It is possible that the formulae of the *K^etuba*, *Geṭ.*, &c., originated in Babylonia, and their Aram. was retained also by MH-speaking Jews, in order to give these documents the recognition of the Persian authority.[2] On the other hand, legal documents of undoubted Judean origin were composed in MH. So the *Prosbol*, instituted by Hillel (Š^ebi. x. 4), the קִיּוּם שְׁטַר (confirmation of a bill that has become illegible, BB x. 6), and scrolls of genealogy

[1] Note the express remark of the narrator: וּבְלָשׁוֹן אֲרָמִית אֲמָרָן ובלשון ארמית שְׁמָעָן;—he said (he heard) them in the Aram. tongue, t. So. xiii. 4–6, as if the use of Aram. by Samuel the Little (died *c.* 70 C.E.) and Simeon the Just called for a special explanation.

[2] Cf. Cowley, *Aram. Papyri*, p. 119. For early *K^etubot* in Aram. ibid., pp. 44, 54, 131.

(Yeb. iv. 13. In Qid. iv. 1 we have an extract of such a document in Aram., with, however, several Aramaized Hebrew terms: אֲסוּפֵי, גֵּרֵי, &c. This Mishna is attributed to the Babylonian Hillel, Yeb. 37 a). So also a special condition in the Judean *K*e*tuba* is cited in MH, as contrasted with the Jerusalem and Galilean *K*e*tubot*, which followed the established legal formula, and are cited in Aram. (Ket. iv. 12). Other special conditions in the Ketuba are also given in MH (ib. ix. 1, 5). So the *Geṭ* of divorcement and of manumission are cited in MH (Giṭ. ix. 1, 3).

26. The view has also been expressed[1] that the usual language in the Temple was Aram., and that it was only in the last few years of its existence that the Pharisees replaced the Aram. in the Temple by MH. This view is based chiefly on the report that on two occasions High Priests heard in the Temple *Bath Qol* speaking Aram. But, surely, the evidence of such an isolated legendary report cannot outweigh the evidence of innumerable passages in MH literature which prove that the Temple ritual was carried on in MH. No doubt, the Babylonian priests (Men. xi. 7) may have spoken Aram. in the Temple, as elsewhere; but it is incredible that in the Temple of all places, with all its reverence for tradition, Hebrew would have been banished in favour of a new and un-Jewish tongue. Hebrew has remained the exclusive language of the Synagogue to this very day. Even if we had not the evidence of Rabbinic tradition, we should conclude that such was also the case in the ancient Temple.

27. Further, there is no evidence whatever that the use of Hebrew or Aram. was a subject of controversy between the Pharisees and the Sadducees. Nor is there any reason to believe that the Sadducees preferred Aram. to MH. On the contrary, one would be inclined to infer from their exclusive, aristocratic

[1] Büchler, *Die Priester u. d. Cultus*, pp. 60 ff. The account of the Bat Qol is found in So. 33 a; t. So. xiii. 4–6.

character, and from their conservative political tendencies, that the Sadducees would have favoured the use of the old national language, rather than the foreign *patois* of the unlettered populace. The sayings of the Sadducees are all reported in MH, cf. Ya. iv. 6–8; M^en. 65 b, &c.; and a conversation between a Sadducee High Priest and his father, Yo. 19 b.

28. In conclusion, we must refer briefly to the linguistic trustworthiness of the Mišnaic tradition, which has been called into question by some writers.[1] Its trustworthiness is established by the old rule, older than the age of Hillel, that a tradition—which, of course, was handed down by word of mouth—must be repeated in the exact words of the master from whom it had been learnt: חַיָּב אָדָם לוֹמַר בִּלְשׁוֹן רַבּוֹ. This rule was strictly observed throughout the Mišnaic and Talmudic periods (cf. 'Ed. i. 3, with the commentaries; B^er. 47 a; B^ek. 5 a), and was, in fact, the basis of the authority of the Oral Law. So careful were the Rabbis in the observance of this rule that they often reproduced even the mannerisms and the personal peculiarities of the Masters from whom they had received a particular tradition, or *halaka*. This rule makes it certain that, at least in most cases, the sayings of the Rabbis have been handed down in the language in which they had originally been expressed. There were, of course, exceptions, as when heathens are made to speak in MH (Ša. 31 a; Ta'a. 18 a, b); but, nevertheless, the rule was strictly observed in all *halakot*, and also in Aggadic and other sayings which are reported as the *ipsissima verba* of the speakers. This linguistic faithfulness of the tradition is proved by the preservation of a number of sayings in Aram. (e.g. 'Ed. viii. 4; Ab. i. 13; v. 22, 23, &c.), and by the preservation of the text of *Megillat Ta'anit* in Aram., though the exposition of the text is given in MH.[2]

[1] M. Friedmann, *Onkelos u. Akylas*, pp. 86 ff.; Dalman, op. cit., p. 8.

[2] Cf. Ta'a. 17 b, 18 b; M^en. 65 a, and the special edition, Neubauer, *Medieval Jewish Chronicles*, ii, pp. 3 ff.

These Aram. traditions were not translated into MH, but were left in their original language. It follows, therefore, that MH sayings were originally spoken in MH. A striking illustration of the care which the Rabbis took to reproduce the actual language of their predecessors is afforded by the interchange between Aram. and MH in narrative passages. Thus, we often find narratives in MH which contain conversations in Aram. (e.g. So. 48 b; Ša. 31 a, &c.). Again, we find, even more frequently, narratives in Aram. in which the persons of the story are made to speak in MH (e.g. Pᵉs. 3 b; BM 83 b, 84 b, &c.). This change of language between the narrator and the persons introduced into his story is clearly due to a deliberate effort on the part of the narrator to reproduce the original speech of the persons he is reporting, whether MH or Aram.[1]

[1] Cf. also Ben Jehudah, עד אימתי דברו עברית, pp. 77 ff.; Sznejder, p. 54 (כב).

PART I

PHONOLOGY AND ORTHOGRAPHY

I. PRONUNCIATION

The evidence for the pronunciation of MH may be grouped under two heads:

29. (*a*) **External**:

(1) *The transcription of Greek and Latin words in MH.*[1]

(2) *The transcription of Hebrew words in Greek and Latin, viz. in Origen's Hexapla and in Jerome's writings.*[2]

This evidence has to be qualified by the consideration of the inequalities which exist between the Hebrew and the Greek and Latin alphabets, and their respective inability to express adequately each other's peculiar sounds. Thus, for example, MH was unable to transcribe correctly the Greek and Latin vowels. Similarly, Greek and Latin were unable to express the Hebrew sibilants, the Hebrew gutturals, and the variation in the sound of the letters, ב, ג, ד, כ, פ, ת.

(3) *The traditional pronunciation preserved among the Jews.*

30. This is a valuable witness, representing as it does a living and uninterrupted tradition reaching back to the time when MH was still a living speech. The value of this tradition is, however, discounted by the considerable differences in pronunciation which

[1] Cf. Krauss, *Lehnwörter*, i, §§ 1 ff., and, more briefly, Albrecht, §§ 5, 7–9, 10.

[2] Cf. Siegfried, *ZAW.*, iv, pp. 35 ff.

exist between the Jews of different countries.[1] Some of these differences are, no doubt, original, and go back to dialectal variations in Hebrew itself as spoken in different parts of Palestine. Others are the result of the influence of the various vernaculars spoken by the Jews in the Diaspora. Moreover, many errors must have crept into the traditional pronunciation. This tradition is, therefore, not to be trusted when it disagrees with the established rules of grammar.

31. (4) *The punctuation, complete or partial, found in some MSS. of the Mishna, and other MH works.*[2]

This is even less trustworthy than the living pronunciation. There never was an authoritative system of punctuation for the Mishna, as for the Hebrew Bible. The scribes were often ignorant, and never consistent. At best the punctuation in the MSS. can only serve as evidence of the pronunciation current in the time and the locality of the particular scribes.

(*b*) **Internal:**

(1) *The method of vocalization by vowel letters.*

32. This is helpful, but insufficient and often misleading, in view of the inadequacy of the few vowel letters to represent what must have been a fairly complicated vowel system. Thus ו represents no less than seven distinct vowel-sounds (*ô, ō, ŏ,* o ֳ; *û, ū, ŭ*), י represents six distinct sounds (*î, ī, ĭ; ê, ē, ĕ*). Cf. below, § 39.

33. (2) *The mutation of consonants.*

The interchange between various consonantal sounds affords evidence as to the relationship between these sounds, their similarities, and their differences. Cf. below, §§ 42, 44, &c.

[1] On the various systems of pronunciation among Jews cf. A. Z. Idelsohn, *MGWJ.*, vol. lvii 527 ff., 697 ff.; M. B. Sznejder, תּוֹרַת הַלָּשׁוֹן, pp. 117 ff.

[2] This punctuation, as also the whole of the MS. material of MH, still awaits special investigation.

(3) *Information in MH literature.*

34. The literature contains a few scattered notices which shed some light on contemporary pronunciation, particularly the guttural letters. Cf. below, § 41.

35. (4) *The analogy of BH, as represented by the Massoretic Text of the Hebrew Scriptures.*

This is undoubtedly the most valuable witness for the correct pronunciation of MH. The gradual fixing of the present text of the Hebrew Scriptures took place in the MH period. The men responsible for that text spoke MH, and the living MH speech must have been reflected to a considerable extent in the form given to the Authorized Text, especially in the vowels.

II. THE VOWELS

1. Vowel Changes.

36. In the absence of a trustworthy system of punctuation in MH, it is not possible to determine with any certainty the character and value of the MH vowels, or to ascertain what modifications they had undergone in comparison with the BH vowels. The spelling gives us no help. The three vowel letters א, י, ו, corresponding to the three Semitic vowels, *a*, *i*, *u*, are used to represent a large variety of modifications of these three vowels, both short and long, simple and composite. On the whole, it may be assumed, for the reason given in the last section, that the MH vowel system is identical with the latest form of the BH vowels, as represented in our consonantal texts of the Hebrew Bible, and in the system of punctuation elaborated in later centuries by the Massoretic Schools. No doubt, there must have been also a strong Aram. influence on the pronunciation of the MH vowels, but with our present knowledge of the subject, it is impossible to say what that influence was. Moreover, this Aram. influence would have been operative also on the contemporary pronunciation of the BH vowels, if not to the same extent. The various sources of external evidence enumerated above in (*a*) have, unfortunately, not yet been investigated and compared. But it may safely be said that that evidence would not materially modify this statement.

37. A vowel change which has no parallel in BH is found in the change of *ĕ* into *ŭ* in two nouns: אֵם mother, becomes אום in the derived significance of 'the matrix of a female, and of a millstone', Ṭoh. ix. 8, and then 'bulk', 'substance', Nᵉg. i. 5;[1] and שֵׁם name, becomes שׁום in the derived sense of 'subject', chiefly in later texts, and with the preposition מִן = מִשּׁום because, Pea i. 3. So also with other prepositions, e.g. עַל שׁום Pᵉs. x. 5, &c. But this latter is most probably an Aramaism due to the scribes.[2] Palestinian texts show also a change of *ă* into *ŭ*, as רַצְעָן — רוּצְעָן; קַרְדָּם — קוּרְדּוּם, cf. § 267. This vowel change is common in Palestinian Jewish Aram.

[1] L reads here אֵם. So Lev. R. 14 = matrix. In the original sense of 'mother' אום is found only once, j. Yᵉb. xi. 1. The change is due to assimilation with the labial *m*. Cf. the Assyr. *ummu*, and the Arab. أُمّ. This form is not found in Aram.

[2] L has usually שֵׁם, even with prepositions when other texts have שׁום. [So cod. K, Krauss, *MGWJ*., li, p. 452.] With the preposition לְ, it is almost always לְשֵׁם in all texts. L, however, has sometimes לְשׁום by the side of לְשֵׁם, e.g. Zᵉb. i. 2, 3. Cf. Assyr. *šumu*. Jewish Aram. has both שם and שום. Syr. only ܫܡܐ. See König, *Lehrgebäude*, i. 2, p. 512. See further, Weiss, מ׳לה״מ, pp. 14–15; Bacher, *Aelteste Terminologie*, p. 118; *Terminologie d. Amoräer*, p. 218. Albrecht's suggestion (§ 6) that שׁום is an artificial modification to distinguish this meaning of שֵׁם from its use for the Divine name is disproved by the great frequency of the use of שֵׁם in a secular sense. Moreover, the use of this form שׁום belongs to a later stage in MH, when the Deity was described by other terms, such as הַמָּקוֹם, הקב״ה, &c.

2. The Spelling of Vowels.

38. The vowels are represented in MH by vowel letters much more frequently than in BH. The vowel letters are, as in BH, א, ה, ו, and י.

א. The א is used as in BH to represent *ă* and *ā*: רָאשֵׁי heads, RH iii. 1, &c.; אֶלָּא but, B^er. i. 2; כָּאן here, ibid. i. 4;[1] at the end of a word in foreign feminine nouns: טַבְלָא *tabula*, MQ iii. 7; הֶגְמוֹנְיָא *ἡγεμονία*, Giṭ. i. 1. This is an Aramaism which is also found in BH.[2] א is found also after other vowels whenever it belongs to the root, קוֹרֵא, יֹאכַל, לֹא, אִלְמָלֵא if not, Ab. iii. 2. After *ā*, *ă*, when followed by ו, or in some texts by י, to indicate that the ו or י are consonants: לָאו not, B^er. i. 1; בַּנַּאי a builder, Kel. xiv. 3; גּוֹבַאי locusts, B^er. vi. 3; זַכַּאי innocent, San. iii. 6; רַשַּׁאי permitted, B^er. i. 7.[3]

ה. The ה is found as a vowel letter only at the end of a word. Its use is exactly the same as in BH.

39. ו. The ו represents not only *ŭ* and *ŏ*, but also *ū*, *ŭ*, and *ō*, *ŏ*, o$_{\text{ְ}}$: מְקוּבָּל accepted, B^er. v. 5; לוּקַּט gathered, Pea v. 1; כּוֹבֶד heaviness, B^er. v. 1; גָּובְהָן their height, רָוחְבָּן their breadth, עָובְיָין their thickness, ʿEr. i. 6; עָומְרֵי sheaves, Pea vi. 1; עֳומָרִים, vi. 5; חֳומָשִׁים fifths, T^er. vi. 4.[4]

[1] L. has always כן, cf. below, § 295.

[2] Cf. Ges.-K., § 80 h. L, however, retains a final ה also in such foreign words. Cf. also in native words: צְנִעָא, L צינעה, privacy; P^es. 1, 3 קַיָּימָא; L. קיימה, existence, Y^eb. iv. 1, שֶׁמָּא (§ 302), &c. מהוהא Kel. xxiv. 17; Ṭoh. ix. 9 (ed. מהוהה) has א at the end, owing to the presence of the ה twice before in the same word. Cf. נמהה, Kel. xxvii. 12.

[3] Cf. the plural forms רַשָּׁאִים, זַכָּאִין below, § 282. L. has usually יי for אי. See below, § 56.

[4] L has עמרים, חמשים. So elsewhere L. has the defective spelling, e.g. כתלו for ed. כותלו, BB ii. 4, &c. So cod. K, Krauss, *MGWJ.*, li, p. 325; but see below, § 282.

Similarly, the י is found also after ĭ, ĕ, and ĕ, e.g. מִידָּה measure, Ber. ix. 7; כִּיֵּן he directed, ii. 1; עֲבֵירָה transgression, i. 3; חֲבֶירְתָּהּ her companion, Šab. xi. 5.

Sometimes י follows ā before ו to indicate the consonantal character of ו: עַכְשָׁיו, עָנָיו, Ber. 6 b, on the analogy of such forms as דְּבָרָיו, בָּנָיו. Some Pal. texts have even לָיו for לָאו.

It must be added that this method of spelling is not always applied consistently, and that it often differs from text to text. But as a rule, the full spelling is more common than the defective spelling, particularly when the consonants might be read in more than one way.[1]

For the rendering in MH of Greek and Latin vowels, cf. Krauss, *Lehnwörter*, i, § 23 ff. (for MH and Aram.), Albrecht, § 7.

III. THE CONSONANTS

40. What has been said above on the pronunciation of the MH vowels is also true to a very high degree of the MH consonants. The pronunciation of the consonants was, on the whole, the same as in BH at the time of the Massoretic redaction of the Scriptures. The evidence of the other sources is, however, fuller in the case of the consonants than the vowels. In what follows we shall briefly summarize this evidence, and also tabulate the various mutations among the consonants.

1. The Gutturals א, ה, ח, ע.

41. The various BH gutturals were still distinguished in MH as late as the fourth century C.E. Thus we find later Amoraim discussing whether certain words in the Mishna should be pro-

[1] Cf. also below in verbs, §§ 122, 126; and in the plural of nouns, § 282. For isolated cases in BH, cf. Ges.-K., § 90. The full spelling is also usual in Medieval Hebrew; cf. ספר חסידים, § תתפ״ו; Güdemann, התורה והחיים, i, p. 153.

nounced with א or ע: גְּמִיאָה or גְּמִיעָה sipping, Šab. viii. 1; גַּרְאִינִין or גַּרְעִינִין kernels, vii. 4; אוֹמְמוֹת or עוֹמְמוֹת dim, Pes. 75 b; מְאַמְּצִין or מְעַמְּצִין shutting the eyes, Šab. xxiii. 5 (Šab. 75 a); מְאַבְּרִין or מְעַבְּרִין extend, ʽEr. v. 1; אַכּוּזוֹ or עַכּוּזוֹ[1] buttock, Bek. vi. 6 (ʽEr. 53 a, b); אֵידֵיהֶן or עֵידֵיהֶן heathen festivals (ʽAZ. 2 a). This can only refer to the pronunciation and not to the spelling in a written text, and proves that there was yet a distinction in the sound of א and ע. But this distinction was not universal. Thus we are told in a *Baraita* (beginning of the third century, Meg. 24 b) that people of certain localities, including Beth Shean and Haifa, could not distinguish between א and ע. The same is said of the school of R. Eliezer b. Jacob (end of second century, Ber. 32 a), and of the Galileans who are held up to ridicule for their slovenliness in speech, particularly in the pronunciation of the gutturals (ʽEr. 53 b). They, together with certain others, could not distinguish between any of the gutturals. Thus, חַרְדָּל mustard, they pronounced הַרְדָּל, and וְחִכִּתִי לה׳ (Isa. viii. 17) they read וְהִכֵּתִי, which was tantamount to blasphemy (Meg., loc. cit.).[2]

Jerome still heard a distinction in the various gutturals, though in his transcription, as also in that of Origen, the differentiation between the hard and the soft ח, the hard and the soft ע, was not copied from living speech, but rather from the older transcription of the LXX. (But note the mutation of ח and כ, § 43).

42. *Transcription from the Greek and Latin.*

א equals the Gk. *spiritus lenis*: אֲוִיר ἀήρ, Šab. xi. 3; אַפְרוֹדִיטִי = Ἀφροδίτη, ʽAZ. iii. 4. א represents the Lat. initial vowel, like אִיטַלְקִי *italicus*, Šebi. i. 2; but also initial H: אַדְרְיָאנִי Hadrianic, ʽAZ. ii. 3; and initial V: אֶסְפַּסְיָנוֹס Vespasian, So. ix. 14.

[1] Or עבוזו; cf. Kohut, *Aruch.*, i. 74; iv. 157 ff.

[2] Cf. also j. Ber. ii. 4, viii. 6; j. ʽEr. v. 1; j. ʽAZ. i. 2; Gen. R. 26; Lam. R. ii. 2. See Dalman, *Gram. d. jüd.-Pal. Aram*[2]., p. 57 f.; Berliner, *Beiträge z. heb. Gram. in Talmud*, p. 15 ff.; Frankel, מבוא הירוש׳, 49 a.

ה represents the Gk. *spiritus asper*: הֶגְמוֹנְיָא ἡγεμονία, Git. i. 1; הִילֵינִי Ἑλένη, Yo. iii. 10; rarely also the *spiritus lenis*: הֶדְיוֹט ἰδιώτης, Yo. vii. 5; הַכְלָסִים ἄχυλος, Ter. xi. 4.

ח equals *spiritus asper* in חִילָק ἁλικός (a kind of salt fish), 'AZ. ii. 6; also sometimes χ: חַלִיקוּפְרִי Χαλκοπάρειος, Makš. i. 3.

ע seems to represent the *spiritus lenis* in עָמִיל ἄμυλον, Pes. iii. 1 (but some texts have אמל, אמיל).

Mutation of the Gutturals.

43. א and ה. As a rule, Palestinian texts prefer initial א, and Babylonian texts ה: הֵיכָן, L.: אֵיכָן where, 'Er. x. 15[1]; הַגָּדוֹת, L.: אַגָּדוֹת *Aggadot*, Ned. iv. 3. Conversely, אוֹגֶן, L.: הוֹגֶן[2] rim, 'Er. viii. 6; Kel. xxv. 6; אוֹנָאָה, L.: הוֹנָאָה wrong, BM iv. 3; אֵילָךְ further, Ber. i. 2, and הֵילָךְ, Pes. vii. 13; אַזְהָרָה = הַזְהָרָה forewarning, Pes. iii. 1. Cf. below, §§ 249, 295.

א and ע: אוּמָּד and עוּמָּד, L., valuation, San. iv. 5; אִירוֹנִיּוֹת, L., עִירוֹנִיּוֹת urban, 'Ed. ii. 5; כָּאוֹר, BQ ix. 4, and כָּעוֹר, 'Ar. iii. 1, ugly; יִתְעַכֵּל, L., יִתְאַכֵּל to be digested, Ber. viii. 7. Cf. above, § 41.

ה and ח: חָרִיעַ, L., הָרִיעַ bastard saffron, Kil. ii. 8; הִידּוּק = חִידּוּק sticking,[3] Kel. iii. 5; מוֹחֶל, L., מוֹהֶל secretion,[4] Miq. vii. 4; מהה to be shabby, worn, Kel. xxvii. 12 = BH מחה.

ח and כ: לִכְלוּךְ soiling,[5] Miq. ix. 4 = לִחְלוּחַ, from לח wet. This shows that there was also a hard pronunciation of the ח, as in earlier BH.

[1] Cf BH. הֵיךְ (Dan. x. 17; 1 Chron. xiii. 12) with אֵיךְ (2 Sam. vi. 9).

[2] Cf. BH אַגָּנוֹת (Exod. xxiv. 6).

[3] As in Aram. Cf. Kohut, iii, pp. 185 f., 349 a.

[4] Cf. BH מָהוּל (Isa. i. 22). See Kohut, v, p. 109.

[5] Cf. Kohut, v, pp. 31, 40 f.

2. The Palatals ג, כ, ק.

Transcription from Greek and Latin.

44. ג transcribes the Gk. γ, and the Lat. *g*: גַּמָּא γαμμα, Mid. iii. 1: גֵּינוּסְיָא γενέσια, ʻAZ. i. 3; אַנְטִיגְנוֹס Ἀντίγονος, Ab. i. 3; גַּרְדּוֹן *gradus*, ʻAZ. i. 7. ג may, perhaps, also represent the Gk. κ in גִּימוֹן, Šab. v. 4, κημός. Combined with ז, ג represents ξ in גְּזוֹזְטְרָא ἐξώστρα, BB iii. 8. L., however, has here and elsewhere כְּצוֹצְרָה.

So Jerome renders ג by *g*. He does not distinguish the dageshed גּ from the raphe גֿ, most probably because the Lat. alphabet possessed no equivalents for these finer sound distinctions.

כ represents Gk. χ: כִּי the letter χ, M^e^n. vi. 3; also Gk. κ: כּוֹכְלְיָיר κοχλιάριον; כּוֹכְלַת κοχλίας, Šab. vi. 3. Also in combination with ס, the Gk. ξ: אַכְסַדְרָה ἐξέδρα, ʻEr. viii. 4; אַכְסַנְיָא ξενία (with prosthetic א, cf. below, § 64), Dam. iii. 1.

Jerome renders כ by *ch*. He does not distinguish between כּ and כֿ, for the reason stated above.

ק represents the Gk. κ: קוֹלְמוֹס κάλαμος, Šab. i. 3; דְּרָקוֹן δράκων, ʻAZ. iii. 3; rarely χ: אֶסְקְרִימִין ἐσχαρίτης, Ḥa. i. 4. Together with ס, it renders also the Gk. ξ at the end of a word: פִּנְקָס πίναξ, Ab. iii. 6.

ק transcribes the Lat. *c*: קַלֶּנְדָּס *Calendae*, ʻAZ. i. 3; קַסְדָּא *cassis*, Šab. vi. 2. Combined with ו, it renders *qu*: קוּסְטוֹר *quaestor*, B^e^k. v. 3 (L. Babylonian texts have קַסְטוֹר or קַסְדּוֹר).

So Jerome transcribes ק by *c*.

Mutation of the Palatals.

45. ג and כ: מזג to dilute, mix, Dam. vii. 2, BH מסך. Cf ʻAZ. 54 b, cited above, § 3. בגר to be of age, K^e^t. iii. 8, BH בכר. Cf. also גְּזוֹזְטְרָא, L. כְּצוֹצְרָה, cited above, § 44.

ג and ק: מְקָרְדִין to scrape, ʻEd. iii. 12, BH גרד; קִפֵּחַ very tall, B^e^k. vii. 6, BH גָּבֵהַ.

כ and ק: קִרְסֵם to cut, nibble, Pea ii. 7, BH כִּרְסֵם; קִפֵּל to double, fold, Šab. ii. 3, BH כפל.

For the mutation between כ and ח, cf. above, § 42.

3. The Dentals ד, ט, ת.

46. ד represents Gk. δ: דְּיָתֵיקֵי διαθήκη, MQ iii. 3; דְּרָקוֹן δράκων, 'AZ. iii. 3. Also sometimes τ: פְּרוֹזְדוֹר προστάς, Ab. iv. 16. Lat. *d*: דִּינָר *denarius*, M^e^n. xiii. 4; פּוּנְדָּה *funda*, B^e^r. ix. 5.

Jerome also renders ד by *d*, whether aspirate or soft (ד, דּ).

ט represents Gk. τ: טְפוּס τύπος, Dam. v. 3, 5; לִיטְרָה λίτρα, T^e^r. iv. 10; but also sometimes θ: אִסְטְנִיס ἀσθενής, B^e^r. ii. 6; אַבְטִינָס Εὔθυνος, Yo. i. 5. Rarely δ: קַפּוֹטְקִיָא (L. קפוד׳), Καππαδοκία, K^e^t. xiii. 10.

Lat. *t*: טַבְלָה *tabula*, אַסְקוּטְלָה *scutella*, MQ iii. 7. So Jerome renders ט by *t*.

ת represents the Gk. θ: תֵּיק θήκη, Šab. xvi. 1; תּוֹרְמוֹס θέρμος, Kil. i. 3; אַפּוֹתֵיק ἀποθήκη, 'AZ. ii. 7. Lat. *th*: קַלְתָּה *calathus*, Bik. iii. 8. So Jerome renders ת by *th*.

Mutation of Dentals.

47. ד and ט: דָּמוּעַ mixed, T^e^r. v. 6, and נטמע, K^e^t. 14 b; טְפוּס, Dam. v. 4, and דְּפוּס, in citation of Bab. Talmud, BM 56 a and elsewhere.

ד and ז: זלף to pour, drip, Pa. vi. 2, BH; דלף, שְׁדֶרָה spinal cord, Ḥul. iii. 2, L. שְׁיזָרָה.

ט and ת: טעה to err, B^e^r. ii. 3, BH תעה; perhaps טֶבֶל untithed, Dam. vii. 5, BH תֶּבֶל.[1] For mutation between ט, ס, צ, cf. below, § 51.

4. The Labials ב, פ.

48. ב, whether dageshed or raphe, represents Gk. β: בִּימוֹס or (L.) בּוֹמוֹס βωμός, 'AZ. iii. 7, Yo. viii. 6; בּוּלְמוֹס βούλιμος, קוּבְיָא

[1] Cf. Barth, *Etymol. Stud.*, p. 37.

κυβεία, San. iii. 3. Rarely through mutation also *π*: בַּרְדְּלֵס *πάρδαλις*, BQ i. 4 (some texts have פרד'); אַבְטוֹלְמוֹס Πτολεμαῖος, 'Er. iii. 4; and even *φ*: דּוּלְבְּקִי *δελφική*, 'AZ. v. 5 (in some texts more correctly דלפקי).

Further, ב represents *υ* in *ευ*: אַבְטִינָס Εὔθυνος, Yo. i. 5; לִבְקָן *λευκόν*, Bek. vii. 6; אָבִיתוֹס (L., other texts have ו: אַוְתִּיוֹס) *εὐθέως*, Nid. ii. 2. ב represents Lat. *b*: בָּסִילְקִי *basilica*, 'AZ. i. 7; טַבְלָה *tabula*, MQ iii. 7; לִבְלָר *libellarius*, Pea ii. 6; but also *v*: בִּיבָרִין *vivarium*, Šab. xiii. 5.

Jerome always transcribes ב by *b*, whether dageshed or raphe, never by *v*.

פ represents Gk. *π*: פּוּלְמוֹס *πόλεμος*, So. ix. 14; פַּרְצוּף *πρόσωπον*, Yeb. xvi. 3. The Gk. *φ*: פְּיָילִי *φιάλη*, So. ii. 2; אַפְרוֹדִיטֵי Ἀφροδίτη, 'AZ. iii. 4.

With ס the Gk. *ψ*: אַפְסוֹנְיָא *ὀψωνία*, San. ii. 4; פְּסַכְתֵּר *ψυκτήρ*, 'Er. x. 15; לַפְסָן *λαμψάνη*, Kil. i. 5.

The Lat. *p*: מַפָּה *mappa*, Ber. viii. 3; קַפַּנְדַּרְיָא (*via*) *compendiaria*. 'AZ. v. 4; נָפוּץ (L. נפוס) *napus*, Kil. i. 5.

Lat. *f*: פְּלָיְיטוֹן *foliatum*, Šab. vi. 2, viii. 2; אֲפוּנְדָּה *funda*, Ber. ix. 5. Perhaps also *b* in סַפְסָל *subsellium*, Šab. xxiii. 5.[1]

In LXX, פ is always transcribed by *φ*, never by *π*, except פסח, and foreign names. So Jerome transcribes it always by *ph*, never by *f*, or *p*. He expressly states that only פ in אַפַּדְנוֹ (Dan. xi. 45) equals Lat. *p*.

49. *Mutation between* ב *and* פ.

פקע to split, break, Ta'a. 15 b, BH בקע; עִפֵּשׁ to be mouldy, Pes. 7 a, BH עָבַשׁ; קִפֵּחַ, Bek. vii. 6, BH גִּבֵּחַ; אָבִיק outlet, Miq. vi. 10, perhaps BH אָפִיק; כַּבְכָּב arched, hollow vessel, Kel. ii. 3, from BH כָּפַף: הֶפְקֵר = הֶבְקֵר, in Pal. texts, ownerless property, Pea vi. 1.

For the mutation between ב and ו, cf. below, § 57.

[1] Jastrow, *Dictionary*, s. v. derives it from סֵפֶל.

5. The Sibilants ס, שׁ, שׂ, ז, צ.

50. MH has preserved the distinction between the three similar sibilants, ס, שׁ, שׂ. Thus שׂ is preserved in a considerable number of words: בִּשְׂמִים, בָּשָׂר, נָשָׂא, עָשָׂה, עֹשֶׂר, שָׂבֵעַ, שָׂדֶה, שָׂחָה (to swim), שָׂחַק, שִׂים, שֵׂכֶל, שָׂכָר, שְׂמֹאל, שָׂמַח, שָׂנֵא, שַׂק, שָׂרַף, &c. But many words that have שׂ in BH are regularly spelt in MH with ס, no doubt owing to a change of sound, due probably to Aram. influence, from שׂ to ס. Thus, the following which have שׂ in BH are spelt in MH with ס: אֵרַס, הִסִּיק, הִסְתַּכֵּל, חֶרֶס, סָב, סָבַר, סָדַר, סָחַט, סִיד, סַכִּין, סָפֵק, סָרַג, סֶרֶט, עֶרֶס, פָּרַס, &c., &c. Sometimes the texts waver: שָׂרָף—סָרָף, 'Or. i. 7; מְעוּשֶּׂה—מְעוּסֶּה, Giṭ. ix. 9.

Jerome, however, mentions only the distinction between ס (*samech*) and שׂ (*sin*). Perhaps his ear was not able to mark the finer distinction between the very similar sounds of שׂ and ס. He represents these sounds, as well as צ (*ṣade*) by *s*, owing, no doubt, to the poverty of the Latin alphabet in sibilants. Similarly, LXX transcribes these four sibilants by *σ*.

51. *Transcription from Greek and Latin.*

ס is very common for Gk. *σ*: סִיטוֹן *σιτώνης*, Dam. ii. 4; אִסְטָסִים *στάσις*, San. xii. 5; לִסְטִים *λῃστής*, Pes. iii. 7. With כ and ק for *ξ*, cf. above, § 44. With פ for *ψ*, cf. above, § 48.

So also for the Lat. *s*: אֶסְדָּה *esseda*, Ber. iv. 6; בָּסִילִיקֵי *basilica*, AZ. i. 7; קוּפְסָה *capsa*, Kel. xvi. 7.

ז represents Gk. *ζ*: זוֹם *ζωμός*, Pes. iii. 1; אוֹרֶז *ὄρυζα*, Pea viii. 3. But also *σ*: פְּרוֹזְבוֹל *προσβολή*, Šebi. x. 3, 4; פְּרוֹזְדוֹר *προστάς*, Ab. iv. 16;[1] אַטְלִיז *κατάλυσις*,[2] Tem. iii. 5. Also, perhaps, *ξ*: חֲוִינָה *ἀξίνη*, Kel. xiv. 2; כָּרוֹז *κήρυξ*, Šeq. v. 1.[3]

Jerome transcribes ז by *z*.

[1] Cf. Krauss, ii, p. 484.

[2] Also קַטְלִיזָא, 'AZ. 40 b.

[3] These are doubtful. כָּרוֹז may be a Semitic word; cf. the Lexicons.

צ represents sometimes Gk. σ: מַרְצוּף μάρσυπος, Šab. viii. 5; פַּרְצוּף πρόσωπον, Y^eb. xvi. 3; אֶצְטָדִין στάδιον, BQ iv. 4; אֶצְטְלִית στολή, Yo. vii. 1; כְּצוֹצְרָה ἐξώστρα (L. for גְּזוֹזְטְרָא in Bab. texts, cf. above, § 44), Mid. ii. 5. Also Lat. *s* in קַצְרָה *castra*, ʿAr. ix. 6; נָפוּץ (also נַפּוּס) *napus*, Kil. i. 5.

52. *Mutation of Sibilants.*

ס and שׂ: כָּבַשׁ to tread, press, and כִּבֵּס to tread, wash (BH); דָּרַס to tread, Syr. ܕܪܫ.[1]

ס and ז: מָזַג and מָסַךְ (cf. above, § 44).[2]

ס and ט: קִרְסֵם (§ 45) and קִרְטֵם to pluck, lop, Maʿa. iii. 3.

ס and צ: יִרְסֵם to crush, ʿUq. ii. 5, BH רצץ; צְלָעוֹת rocks, BH סֶלַע, Š^ebi. v. 4; סִיב fibre, ʿUq. iii. 3, and צִיב tassel, Ḥul. ix. 1.[3]

צ and ט: קוֹרֶט particle, drop, ʿAZ. ii. 6, BH. קָרַץ.

6. The Sonants ל, מ, נ, ר.

53. ל represents Gk. λ, Lat. *l*: לִסְטִים λῃστής, P^es. iii. 7; לִבְלָר *libellarius*, Pea ii. 6. By mutation, also ρ, *r*: אַסְכָּלָה ἐσχάρα, P^es. vii. 2; פַּלְהֶדְרִין πάρεδροι, Yo. i. 1; מַרְגָּלִית *margarita*, Ab. vi. 9; מַרְקוּלִים *Mercurius*, ʿAZ. iv. 1.

מ represents Gk. μ, Lat. *m*: מַרְצוּף μάρσυπος, Šab. viii. 5; מַפָּה *mappa*, B^er. viii. 3. מ is sometimes assimilated with the following consonant: לַפְּסָן λαμψάνη, Kil. i. 5; קַפַּנְדַּרְיָא (*via*) *compendiaria*, ʿAZ. v. 4.

נ represents Gk. ν, Lat. *n*: אַנְטִיגְנוֹס Ἀντίγονος, Ab. i. 3; נָפוּץ *napus*, Kil. i. 3. It is also found for μ, *m* before a labial: אַנְפּוֹרְיָא ἐμπορία (L. 'אמ), BM ii. 1; אַנְפִּלְיָא *impilia*, Y^eb. xii. 1.

1 Albrecht's suggestion (§ 4 e) that מִדְרָס may be an artificial form to distinguish it from מִדְרָשׁ Midrash, is altogether improbable. The verb דרס is extremely common in various connotations; cf. Kohut, iii, pp. 156–60.

2 Cf. the transcription of Gr. σ (= ס) by ז, above, § 51.

3 Cf. also the transcription of Gr. σ, Lat. *s* by צ, above, § 51.

ר. The evidence of Jewish tradition and the pointing of the MSS.[1] show that ר was pronounced as a guttural, as in BH, causing the same vowel changes as the regular gutturals. But it was also pronounced as a lingual, as is shown by its mutation with ל, as above, and below § 54.

It represents Gk. ρ, Lat. *r*: דְּרָקוֹן δράκων, ʻAZ. iii. 3; דִּינָר *denarius*, Ab. vi. 9.

Mutation of the Sonants.

54. ל and ר: הִשְׁתַּדֵּל to strive, Ab. ii. 5, Aram. אֶשְׁתַּדַּר, Dan. vi. 15; שַׁלְשֶׁלֶת chain, Kel. xiv. 3, BH שַׁרְשֶׁרֶת[2]; גַּלְעִינָה kernel, ʻUq. ii. 2, Tᵉr. xi. 5; נִתְאַרְמְלָה = נִתְאַלְמְלָה = נִתְאַלְמְנָה (L.) to be widowed, Kᵉt. ii. 1.

מ and נ: רֵיקָן empty, Pᵉs. v. 6, BH רֵיקָם; הֵן for הֵם; the plural ending ־ִין for ־ִים; the pronominal suffix for the 3rd masc. pl. ן for ם. (Cf. below, §§ 70, 281.)

7. Semi-vowels ו, י.

55. ו. While still retaining its semi-vocal character, ו appears to have been hardened into a real consonant. Hence, it is more frequent in MH as an initial letter than in BH. Thus, וִידּוּי confession, San. vi. 7; וַדַּאי certain, Yo. viii. 8; וָלָד child (BH), MŠ. iii. 9; וַעַד assembly, Ab. i. 4; וֶסֶת habit, Nid. i. 1; וָרִיד jugular vein, Ḥul. ii. 4; וָתִיק active, Bᵉr. 9 b. In verbs: וִיתֵּר to be plentiful, San. xi. 5, &c. (Cf. below, § 168.)

The consonantal character of ו is also shown by its mutation with soft ב (בֿ), cf. below, § 57.

In transcriptions the ו sometimes represents Lat. *v*: וִילוֹן *Velum*, Nᵉg. xi. 11. Perhaps also the Aeolic Digamma: וֶסֶת ἔθος, Nid. i. 1;

[1] e.g. עֲיָרָה, L., ʻAZ. v. 10.

[2] These may, however, belong to two different roots: שלל = שלה to draw, and שרר to be firm, hence שֵׁרוֹת rings, Isa. iii. 19; Šab. v. 1.

אַוֵּיר ἀήρ, Šab. xi. 3. ו is also found in the place of the Hiatus: אַסְטְוָה[1] στοά, P^es. i. 5.

Jerome renders ו by *u*.

56. י seems to have been pronounced very much like א (*spiritus lenis*). This explains its frequent mutation with א. However, it never transcribes a Greek or Latin initial vowel, for which א is used, cf. above, § 42. But י is regularly used to represent the first of the two vowels in the Hiatus: אַנְפּוֹרְיָא ἐμπορία, BM ii. 1; אַפְסוֹנְיָא ὀψωνία, San. ii. 4; קוּבְיָא κυβεία, iii. 3; פְּלְיָטוֹן *foliatum*, Šab. vi. 3; אוֹלְיָרִין *olearius*, Ṭoh. vii. 8; פֻּנְדְיוֹן *dupondius*, Pea viii. 7.

Jerome transcribes י by *i*.

57. When consonants, ו, י are often written twice, to prevent their being mistaken for vowel letters: וָורד rose, Š^ebi. vii. 6; נִתְכַּוֵּון to intend, T^er. iv. 4; פַּרְוָור outskirts, Ḥal. iv. 11; חַיָּיט tailor, Šab. i. 3; נְיָיר paper, viii. 2. So in Pal. texts: בַּפַּיי, Kel. xiv. 3; גּוֹבַיי, B^er. vi. 3; כְּדַיי worthy, i. 7, for בַּנַּאי, גּוֹבַאי, כְּדַאי, cf. above, § 38, foot-note.

Mutations.

58. ו and ב: נִוֵּל disfigure, So. i. 7, BH נָבֵל; עֲנִוָּה barley crop, Pea. vii. 7 (L. ענבה), i. 2, cf. BH עֵנָב[2]; לוּלָב *Lulab* = לִבְלֵב = לִוְלֵב to sprout; פַּרְוָור outskirts, BH פַּרְבָּר.[3]

י and א: מָבוֹי, BH מָבוֹא, entrance, alley, 'Er. i. 1; שְׁיָיר, BH שְׁאָר, remainder, Z^eb. v. 1; נוֹי beauty, 'AZ. iii. 4, for נוא, from נָאָה. Cf. also the textual variants: הוֹדָאָה and הוֹדָיָה thanksgiving, B^er. ix. 4; חֲצָאֵי from חֲצִי half, 'Ed. iii. 1; בְּלָאוֹת and בְּלָיוֹת old garments, Y^eb. ix. 3, from בְּלִי, &c. Cf. also the interchange between the third radical of the verbs ל"א and ל"ה.[4]

[1] So L. and some other texts. Others, again, especially Bab. texts, have אִצְטְבָה, אִסְטְבָה. Cf. Kohut, i, pp. 166 f. Also סְטָיו or סְטָיו, Suk. 51 b.

[2] Cf. the commentaries, especially Maimonides, ad. loc.

[3] Cf. אִסְטְבָה—אִסְטְוָה, above, § 55 note, and בִּיבָרִין—*vivarium*, above, § 48.

[4] However, this interchange between י and א, never occurs, as in Aram., at the beginning of a word; cf. Dalman, pp. 97–8.

8. The Letters ב, ג, ד, כ, פ, ת.

59. The BH distinction between the hard and the soft sounds of these letters (*dagesh* and *raphe*) existed also in MH. This is proved by many considerations. Thus, all the various Jewish systems of pronunciation have preserved this distinction. It is also supported by the transcriptions of Greek and Latin words, and by the sound mutations in MH.

Thus, ב represents β, *b* (= בּ), and also *υ*, *v* (= בֿ), § 47. It interchanges with ו (= בֿ), § 57.

ג interchanges with ק = גּ, § 44, and also with ח (= גֿ), § 42.

ד represents δ, *d*, and also τ, § 45. It interchanges with ט (= דּ), and also with ז (= דֿ), § 46.

כ represents κ, *c* (= כּ), and also χ, *ch* (= כֿ), § 43. It interchanges with ק (= כּ), and also with ח (= כֿ), §§ 44, 42.

פ represents π, *p* (= פּ), and also φ, *f* (= פֿ), § 47.

ת represents θ, *th* (= תֿ), § 45. It interchanges with ט (= תּ), § 46.

60. The difference in the *dagesh* and *raphe* sounds was not, however, so marked as in some of the modern Jewish pronunciations. This is proved by the dictum in a late Baraita (Bᵉr. 15 b), that in reading the Šᵉmaʿ (Singer, pp. 40 f.) a pause must be introduced between the enunciation of עֵשֶׂב and the following בְּשָׂדְךָ (Deut. xi. 5), between הַכָּנָף and פְּתִיל (Num. xv. 38), so as not to produce an assimilation of the final letters of one word with the initial letters of the following word (שֶׁיִּתֵּן רֶיוַח בֵּין הַדְּבֵקִים).

9. Other Consonantal Changes.

61. Transposition (*Metathesis*). זָקַר to fling (נִזְקָרִין), Yo. 38 b = זָרַק; עָלַב to insult, Yo. 23 a = לעב, j. So. 19 a, 2 Chron. xxxvi. 16 (Hiphʿil); מַלְגֵּז large fork, Šab. 92 b, t. ib. ix. 10[1] = מַזְלֵג; מַרְזֵב spout, BB iii. 8, from זָרַב = רָזַב (= זוּב) to flow[2]; עָמַץ to close the eyes, Šab.

[1] שְׁנַיִם אוֹחֲזִין בְּמַלְגֵּז וְלוֹנְזִין. So in the Mishna in Bab. Talmud, Šab. 122 b (xvii. 1).

[2] Cf. זְרִיבָה, a flowing, j. San. xi. 7. See Kohut, iii, p. 319, and *BDB.*, p. 279.

xxiii. 5 = עָצַם ; קִטְרֵג to accuse, j. Šab. 5 b, from קַטֵּיגוֹר (= κατήγορος), Ab. iv. 11. Perhaps also רָמַז to wink, Git. v. 7, רָזַם (Job xv. 12). Probably also הֲרֵי aspect, nature of a case, BQ i. 1 = אֲרֵי = רְאִי, BQ 4 a, &c.[1]

62. Rejection. (*a*) *Aphaeresis.* In addition to the rejection of initial weak consonants when without vowels in verbs פ״י, פ״נ, &c., as in BH (cf. below, §§ 165, 169; Ges.-K., § 19 h), MH shows aphaeresis also in a few other cases, viz. with the gutturals א, ח, ע, ה (as preformatives), and preformative מ:

גִּיס brother-in-law, San. iii. 4 = אֲגִיס, as in L. and j. ib. iii. 7; לִיעֶזֶר, לְעָזָר, in Pal. texts, for אֱלִיעֶזֶר, אֶלְעָזָר.

ח: פִּיר a pit, Ket. 79 b, Ned. 89 b = חֲפִיר; שִׁיפָה mat, Makš. v. 8 = חֲשִׁיפָה[2]; סְחוּס = חַסְחוּס cartilege, Bek. vi. 1 (cf. L.).

ע: שׁוּנִית cliff, Oh. xviii. 6 = עֲשׁוּנִית, Mekil. on Exod. xv. 5.[3]

ה: כָּרֵת cutting off = הִכָּרֵת (cf. below, § 115).

מ: מוּעָט small = מְמוּעָט; חוּתָּךְ cut off = מְחוּתָּךְ (cf. § 129).

Further, לִידָה birth, Ket. iv. 3 = יְלִידָה (cf. below, § 228). קִיחָה leather thong, Kel. xvi. 4; taking, Qid. 2 a = לְקִיחָה (cf. below, § 228).

63. (*b*) *Syncope.* MH shows the same cases of elision of a consonant in the middle of a word, as appear in BH (Ges.-K. § 19 k). In addition syncope takes place in a number of compounds, e. g. אִלְמָלֵא if not = לֹא + אִם + אִלּוּ, Ab. iii. 2; its equivalent in Pal. texts: אִילּוּלֵא = לוּלֵי + אִם; בְּרַבִּי (or בֵּרַבִּי ?) = רַבִּי + בֵּן, Pea ii. 4; כֵּיצַד how

[1] הֲרֵי cannot be a contraction of הַרְאִי (Levy i. 493 b), since it is in the construct state. Bacher's view (*Aelteste Terminologie*, pp. 46–8), that הֲרֵי is an interjection (= הֲרֵי) is improbable. הֲרֵי is synonymous with רְאִי. The two expressions are used in different types of texts with exactly the same significance.

[2] דוּת = חדות cistern, cited by Albrecht (§ 9 a), rests upon a scribal error. With two exceptions (t. Oh. xii. 6), it is always הדות (also in plur. הדותיות t. BB iii. 1), and should be הַהֲדוּת = הַחֲדוּת, as in Syr. and Arab.; cf. Kohut, iii. 32.

[3] Cf. the comment of Weiss, ad loc. (p. 46), and also Kohut, viii, p. 116 f.

=כְּאֵי+וָה+צַד, as often written in the Halakic Midrashim: כַּלֵּךְ get away = כַּלֵּה+וְלֵךְ, t. T^er. i. 1; San. 67 b (cf. Rashi, ad loc.); עַכְשָׁיו now, ʻAZ. i. 1, a compound of uncertain composition (cf. below, § 296); the elision of א in אֲנִי, when joined as an enclitic, especially to participles, e.g. הֲרֵינִי behold I = הֲרֵי + אֲנִי; חוֹשְׁשֵׁנִי I fear me, חוֹשֵׁשׁ+אֲנִי (cf. below, § 341, and foot-note).

Further examples of syncope of א are found in יְשֶׁבְאָב=יְשֵׁבָב, as in L. and BH, Ḥul. ii. 4, and in the popular זִיבָה = זְאֵבָה she wolf, j. Š^eq. v. 1.

64. (*c*) *Apocope.* The rejection of a final letter is found in אֵי not = אֵין, before words beginning with א; so כֵּי = כֵּן (cf. below, § 298); אִי = אִם if. Probably also הַלָּה that one = הַלָּז (cf. below, § 73). In proper names, יוֹסֵי (or Pal. יוֹסָה) = יוֹסֵף, Ab. i. 41; שַׁמַּאי = שְׁמַעְיָה, ib. i. 10.[1]

For elision of consonants in foreign words, cf. Krauss, LW i. §§ 214 ff.; Albrecht, § 9 b.

65. Augmentation. As in BH, an א is sometimes prefixed to a word: אֲגוּדָל thumb, Yo. ii. 1 = גּוּדָל (L., cf. גּוּדְלֵי רַגְלָיו, Šab. 151 b); אֲגַף wing, N^eg. xiv. 1 = גַּף (cf. BH); אַכְרוּב cabbage, ʻOr. iii. 7. ʻUq. ii. 7 (L., and elsewhere in Pal. texts) = כְּרוּב, T^er. x. 11.

The prosthetic א is especially frequent in the transcription of foreign words beginning with two or more consonants: אִסְטָסִים = στάσις, San. xii. 5; אַסְפְּלָנִית = σπληνίον, Šab. xix. 2; אַכְסַנְיָא = ξένος, Dam. iii. 1; אַסְקוּטְלָא *scutella*, MQ iii. 7. So also before one consonant: אִלְפָּס = λοπάς, Šab. iii. 5; אַפּוּנְדָּה = *funda*, ib. x. 3. Cf. Krauss, §§ 261 ff.; Albrecht, § 10.

Insertion of ר: חַרְטוֹם beak, Ṭoh. i. 2 = חוֹטָם nose, Kel. xxvi. 4 (cf. below, § 274), and in the formation of Quadriliterals, below § 107.

66. *Softening* of a sound, owing to dissimilation, is found in לוּלָב = לַבְלָב (cf. above, § 58); שְׁפוֹפֶרֶת tube, Šab. ii. 4 = שְׁפַרְפֶּרֶת (cf. below, § 245).

[1] Cf. BH, 1 Chr. ii. 28, &c. So יֵשׁוּ, Jesus, for יֵשׁוּעַ. Cf. J. Klausner, ישו הנוצרי, p. 237. These forms are, probably, caritatives.

PART II

MORPHOLOGY

I. THE PRONOUN

1. The Personal Pronoun.

67. (1) The 1st pers. sing. is אֲנִי. אָנֹכִי is found only in quotations from the Bible, or in direct allusions to Biblical passages.[1]

The disuse of אָנֹכִי dates already from BH times. Thus אנכי is not found in the later or popular BH books, like Canticles, Lamentations, Ḥaggai, Zachariah i–viii, Ezra, Esther, and Qohelet; and only once in Ezekiel, Daniel, Nehemiah, and Chronicles.[2] So also Aram. (with the exception of the Zinjirli dialect),[3] Arabic and Ethiopic have forms corresponding to אֲנִי only, while Assyrian, Moabite, and Phoenician use forms corresponding to אנכי only. In earlier Hebrew alone are the two forms found existing side by side, but אֲנִי, being the shorter of the two, gradually came to be employed more frequently, especially in colloquial speech, until the longer form disappeared entirely from common use.

68. The plural is always אָנוּ.[4] This form occurs, as is well

[1] e.g. San. vi. 2; Šab. 105 a.

[2] Cf. *BDB.*, p. 59 and reff.

[3] Cf. G. A. Cooke, *N. Sem. Inscr.*, Nos. 61, l. 1, אנך; 62, l. 19, אנכי; but 63, l. 20, אנה. For the origin and mutual relation of אני and אנכי cf. Stade, *Heb. Gr.*, p. 135, and Barth, *Pronominalbildung*, pp. 3–4.

[4] אֲנַחְנוּ occurs in the early portions of the Liturgy, cf. S. Singer, *The Authorized Daily Prayer Book*, pp. 4, 51, &c. So in Pᵉs. x. 5, but L. has אנו. אנחנו is also found exceptionally in an ordinary passage, Kᵉt. x. 2, but here also L. has אנו.

known, only once in BH, and then only in the Keṯib (Jer. xlii. 6). which is rather remarkable, since the Keṯib generally represents a more archaic type of language. אֲנוּ seems to be a popular formation from אֲנִי, on the analogy of the plural forms of the pronominal suffixes קְטָלַנִי, קְטָלָנוּ, or of מִמֶּנִּי, מִמֶּנּוּ; cf. also the verbal plurals קָטְלוּ, יִקְטְלוּ, &c. From the colloquial language the form crept into the Book of Jeremiah, but was struck out by the Massoretes as a vulgarism.

All other Semitic languages have forms corresponding to אֲנַחְנוּ. So especially the Aram. dialects, אנחנא, נחנא, אנחנן, and in the latest and most debased dialects אנן, with the syncope of the inaudible guttural.[1]

69. (2) In the 2nd pers. אַתָּה is used for the masc., and אַתְּ for the fem., as in BH. אַתְּ for the masc. is exceedingly rare in the earlier MH literature, and may always be due to scribal errors. It is, however, frequent in texts of a later date, particularly of Palestinian origin, and in the Haggadic Midrashim. This use must be considered an Aramaism (but sporadically also in BH).

The plural is אַתֶּם for the masc. Of the fem. plural, אַתֶּן, no example occurs in our literature. The form אַתֶּם is also found for the fem.: t. BB viii. 19: נִיזּוֹנְתֶּם אַתֶּם . . . נְשֵׂאתֶם אַתֶּם.

70. (3) The 3rd pers. has הוּא for the masc., and הִיא for the fem. The plur. is הֵם, הֵן respectively. הֵמָּה is found only in Biblical quotations (Ab. vi. 2).

The forms אַתֶּן for the 2nd masc. plur., and especially הֵן for the 3rd masc. plur., are also found, but they are merely due to a phonetic change common in MH (cf. above, § 54). They may, however, be also due to the influence of Aram., in which these pronouns end in ן.

[1] Barth (op. cit., p. 6 (e)), holds that אנן is formed from אנא by the addition of the plur. suff. ן, like אנו from אני.

71. *The Pronominal Suffixes.* The pronominal suffixes are in MH the same as in BH. The 3rd plur. masc. has, however, also here ן for ם. But often the reading is not certain, and varies from text to text. There are also examples of the masc. form used for the fem., e.g. אַחַת מִכֶּם, כּוּלְּכֶם, כּוּלָּם, Teṛ. viii. 11, 12; לָהֶם, Ḥal. i. 7.

2. The Demonstrative Pronoun.

72. (1) Singular זֶה masc., זוֹ fem., plur. אֵלּוּ.

The form זוֹ for זאת occurs in BH in Hos. vii. 16; in the cycle of North Israelitish stories in the Book of Kings (זֹה, 2 Ki. vi. 19), both of which exhibit a number of dialectal peculiarities; also, in Ezekiel (זֹה, xl. 45), in a late psalm (זוֹ, Ps. cxxxii. 12), and six times in Qohelet.

It is, therefore, very probable that the shorter form זֹה, or זוֹ, existed from early times as a dialectal form in the northern speech, from which it gradually spread to the south, and in the course of time supplanted the longer form זאת.

The plur. אֵלּוּ for BH אֵלֶּה occurs also in Sirach (אֵילּוּ, li. 24). The change of the second vowel may have been due to an unconscious desire to indicate more clearly the plural character of the word. The vowel chosen is the same as in אָנוּ, discussed above, § 67.

73. (2) BH has also preserved the demonstrative use of the pronoun of the 3rd pers., הוּא, הִיא, הֵם, הֵן; חֲמוֹרְךָ הוּא that ass of thine, opposed to חֲמוֹרְךָ זֶה, BB v. 2; so often הֲרֵי הוּא, הֲרֵי הִיא, הֲרֵי הֵם. More commonly with the article, as in BH הַהוּא, הַהִיא, הָהֵם.

74. (3) The stronger BH demonstrative הַלָּזֶה is found only in the shortened form הַלָּז (Judges vi. 20) for the masc., Ṭoh. vi. 5, 8. Fem. הַלֵּזוּ, Yeb. xiii. 7; t. ib. v. 4; xiii. 6.[1]

[1] But L. has הַלָּז. So in BH הַלָּז is also found for the fem., 2 Kings iv. 25.

This form הַלָּז is further shortened to הַלָּה by the apocope of ז.[1] It is only used substantivally, MŠ. iii. 2; San. viii 2, &c. In Y^e^b. iii. 5, 'Ed. iv. 9, הַלָּה stands also for the fem. וְהַלָּה תֵּצֵא מִשּׁוּם אֲחוֹת אִשָּׁה and that one goes forth[2] as a wife's sister.

The plur. of הַלָּז, הַלָּה is הַלָּלוּ, evidently a contraction of הַל + אֵלּוּ; מוּמִין הַלָּלוּ these defects, K^e^t. vii. 8, and frequently.

75. (4) The emphatic particle אֵת is also used as a demonstrative, either alone or with pronominal suffixes, e. g. אֶת שֶׁלִּפְנֵי הַמִּטָּה וְאֶת שֶׁלְּאַחַר הַמִּטָּה those before the bier and those behind the bier, B^e^r. iii. 1; אוֹתָהּ הַחַלָּה וְאוֹתוֹ הַסֵּדֶר that loaf and that order, M^e^n. ii. 2.

76. (5) *The Article.* In the form and use of the Article, MH agrees with BH. See further in the Syntax (§§ 373–78).

3. The Relative Pronoun.

77. The relative is in MH everywhere שֶׁ. אֲשֶׁר occurs only in quotations (Pe. ii. 2 from Isa. vii. 25; So. ix. 5 from Deut. xxi. 3, &c.), and in early liturgical language, which is conceived in an elevated and semi-Biblical strain; thus, in the Passover Haggadah, אֲשֶׁר גְּאָלָנוּ, P^e^s. x. 61; in the Evening Service, אֲשֶׁר בִּדְבָרוֹ (Singer, p. 96); and often in Benedictions, אֲשֶׁר קִדְּשָׁנוּ (ib. pp. 4, 134, 210, &c.); אֲשֶׁר נָתַן (pp. 5, 68); אֲשֶׁר יָצַר (pp. 4, 299); אֲשֶׁר בָּרָא (pp. 280, 299); and a few more. Elsewhere שֶׁ־ is used: שֶׁבְּכָל (p. 51), שֶׁיְּדַעְנוּ, שֶׁבָּרָאתָ (p. 239), and in Benedictions, B^e^r. vi. 3; vii. 3; ix. 1 ff.; Singer, pp. 5 f., 276, 290, 291, &c.

78. In BH the form occurs twice in the Song of Deborah (שַׁקַּמְתִּי), a North Israelitish production; three times in the story of Gideon, a North Israelitish hero; once in the North Israelitish

[1] Cf. above, § 64. Barth, however, holds that הַלָּה is the original form which was later strengthened by the addition of זה, op. cit., pp. 78, 105 f.

[2] i. e. הַחוּצָה, Deut. xxv. 5. L. has וְהַלָּז. So 'Ar. ix. 4 edd. have הַלָּה, but L. has הַלָּז.

section of the Book of Kings; exclusively, except in the late superscription, in the collection of popular songs known as Canticles, which probably originated in Northern Israel; sporadically in the later BH books, and very frequently in Qohelet (cf. Ges.-K., § 36). Now, whatever the relation of the two forms to each other,[1] there can be no doubt that שֶׁ is as old as אֲשֶׁר, if not older. Its confinement in the earlier books of the Bible to North Israelitish documents would prove that its use must have been common in the colloquial speech of Northern Palestine, under the influence, to some extent at least, of the Phoenician אש,[2] ש, the Assyrian *ša*, and, perhaps, also the Aram. זִי, די. The scarcity of its occurrence even in these documents must be explained by the assumption that it was regarded as a vulgarism which the literary language had to avoid. Its use gradually extended to Southern Palestine, and being the shorter and more pliable form, it must in the course of time have entirely supplanted the longer אֲשֶׁר in the language of the common people, and from this it descended directly to MH. But the literary prejudice against it seems to have remained even after BH had ceased to be a living speech. Hence its non-occurrence in Esther, its scarcity in Chronicles, and the anxiety to avoid it which is displayed by a studious imitator of the ancients like Sirach, and even by such an independent mind as the author of Qohelet.[3]

4. The Possessive Pronoun.

79. Possession is very frequently expressed in MH by the combination of the relative -שֶׁ with the preposition -לְ. In older texts this combination is still attached to the noun which it governs,

[1] Cf. Barth, op. cit., pp. 162–4; Bergsträsser, *ZAW.*, xix, pp. 41 ff.

[2] Cf. Schröder, *Phœniz. Sprache*, § 65 and foot-note.

[3] Note such awkward and inconsistent expressions as בְּשֶׁל אֲשֶׁר יַעֲמוֹל (= Aram. . . . בְּדִיל דִּי), viii. 17; מִבְּלִי אֲשֶׁר לֹא יִמְצָא, iii. 11, &c.

e. g. שֶׁלְּזְבָחִין, Z^eb. v. 1.[1] Gradually -שֶׁלְ was detached from the noun by the scribes, and now appears as an independent particle שֶׁל. So especially with pronominal suffixes שֶׁלִּי, שֶׁלְּךָ, &c., which have become regular possessive pronouns. Cf. Ab. v. 10; BM i. 5, &c. See further in the Syntax, §§ 406–9.

5. The Interrogative Pronoun.

80. (1) מִי, מָה, as in BH.

(2) By prefixing the interrogative particle אֵי to the demonstrative זֶה, זוֹ, a new interrogative pronoun has been formed, אֵיזֶה, fem. אֵיזוֹ which? This is often strengthened by the enclitic הוּא, הִיא, with which it is often written as one word, and the final א omitted: אֵיזֶהוּ, Z^eb. v. 1; אֵיזוֹהִי, Kel. xvii. 6. In the older texts, however, the three components are still kept separate: אֵי זֶה הוּא, אֵי זוֹ הִיא, cf. L., loc. cit.

Prepositions are attached to אֵי: בְּאֵיזֶה, בְּאֵיזוֹ, San. v. 1; מֵאֵיזֶה, Ab. vi. 9. Contrast BH אֵי מִזֶּה, 2 Sam. xv. 2, Jonah i. 8; אֵי לָזֹאת, Jer. v. 2.

81. The plural of אֵיזֶה, אֵיזוֹ is אֵי אֵלּוּ, which is found only once in MH literature, viz. Naz. 6 b (אֵי אֵלּוּ הֵן יָמִים . . .). Elsewhere it is contracted to אֵילוּ, spelt אֵלּוּ through the ignorance of the scribes, who confused it with the demonstr. plur. אֵלּוּ.[2] This confusion may account for the scarcity of this form in our literature. Perhaps the Rabbis, who had a passion for lucidity and precision, deliberately avoided it for fear of this confusion with the demonstr.

Exx.: אֵלּוּ מְצִיאוֹת שֶׁלּוֹ וְאֵלּוּ (ואילו L.) חַיָּיב לְהַכְרִיז Which things when found are his [the finder's], and which is he bound to proclaim?[3] BM ii. 1; וְרוֹאִים אֵלּוּ הָאֲבָנִים הָרְאוּיוֹת לְהִשְׁתַּבֵּר They

[1] Cf. Krauss, *MGWJ.*, li, p. 56.

[2] This confusion is found even in modern scholars, e. g. Albrecht, § 30 a.

[3] Cf. the parallel expressions: אֵיזֶהוּ נֶשֶׁךְ וְאֵיזֶהוּ תַּרְבִּית? אֵיזֶהוּ נֶשֶׁךְ . . ., ib. v. 1; אֵיזֶהוּ תָּם וְאֵיזֶהוּ מוּעָד? BQ ii. 4, &c. So, perhaps, also elsewhere,

consider which are the stones that are likely to have been broken, ib. x. 1; טָעָה וְאֵין יָדוּעַ אֵלּוּ שֶׁהָפְכוּ וְאֵלּוּ שֶׁקָּדְמוּ If he made a mistake and it is not known which had changed and which had advanced? t. Neg. ii. 7; בְּאֵלּוּ מַשְׁקִין אָמְרוּ In the case of which fluids have they said it? Makš. iii. 2;[1] בְּאֵילוּ נְדָרִים אָמְרוּ In the case of which vows have they said it? t. Ket. vii. 8 || Ket. 72 b; בְּאֵילוּ בְּנֵי מֵיעַיִם אָמְרוּ In the case of which intestines have they said it? t. Ḥul. iii. 15 || Ḥul. 56 b; בְּאֵילוּ פָּנִים בָּאִים לִפְנֵי הַמָּקוֹם With what face will they come before the Almighty? Pesiqta, § 25; עַל אֵלּוּ עֳמָרִים נֶחֱלְקוּ Over which sheaves did they dispute? t. Pe. iii. 2. So probably also עַל אֵלּוּ מוּמִים שׁוֹחֲטִין אֶת הַבְּכוֹר Over which blemishes may one slay the first-born animal? Bek. vi. 1; לְאֵילוּ נַאֲמִין Whom shall we believe? Pesiqta Rab., p. 138 b.

82. We can trace clearly in BH the development of this new interrogative. In אֵי זֶה בֵּית הָרֹאֶה, 1 Sam. ix. 18, the emphasis is on אֵי (= אַיֵּה), while זֶה serves merely as an enclitic particle to give directness to the question, and the proper answer to the question would be הִנֵּה, or פֹּה בֵּית הָרֹאֶה. Gradually, however, the emphasis was shifted from אֵי to זֶה, as in אֵי זֶה הַדֶּרֶךְ נַעֲלֶה, 2 Kings iii. 8, Which way shall we go up?, as is shown by the answer, דֶּרֶךְ מִדְבַּר אֱדוֹם, 2 Chron. xviii. 23. These two usages existed side by side, until, finally, the older usage disappeared, and אֵיזֶה ceased to be an interrogative of place, and became a pure interrogative pronoun or adjective. So in Qoh. ii. 3, and, especially, in xi. 6, where it stands before a verb, אֵי זֶה יִכְשַׁר, and is used exactly as in MH.[2]

e.g. Pea i. 1; BB. iii. 7. The interrogative style is exceedingly common in MH.

[1] Cf. the parallel expression: בְּאֵיזֶה מַקְדֵּחַ אָמְרוּ?, Oh. ii. 3, &c.

[2] See further the writer's remarks, *JQR.*, xx (1908), p. 661 f.

II. THE VERB

A. General Survey.

In all Semitic speech the verb forms the backbone of the language. A detailed study of the MH verb may, therefore, help us to a correct estimate of the character of the MH idiom, and of its relation to BH. In what follows we shall review the MH verb both from the lexical and the grammatical side.

1. Lexical.

83. Of the 1,350 verbs which are found in the Lexicon of BH MH has lost 250 verbs, and gained 300 new verbs. The majority of these lost verbs will be found on examination to consist of rare and poetical expressions which from an early date may have been confined to literature, or to certain dialects, and were rarely, or never, used in the normal language of every-day speech. A smaller, but still considerable number of verbs (over 50) consists of common and prosaic BH words which, for some reason, were lost in MH, and replaced by other equivalent verbs. A third group is of special interest: it consists of about 50 verbs which are common to both BH and Aram., but yet have not been preserved in MH, a fact which tells against the theory that MH is but an artificial conglomeration of BH and Aram.

In what follows will be found a classified list of BH verbs lost in MH.

(A) *BH Verbs not found in MH.*

84. (1) Rare or poetical expressions:[1] אזן weigh, אנק, אנש, אפף, בחל, בלג, בלק, בתק, גהה, גהר, גור stir up strife, דוץ, דכה,

[1] In this group have been entered verbs that cannot be included in any of the following groups. Groups (2), (4), (5), and (6) also contain numerous rare and poetical forms. The English equivalents have been given only where they are necessary for the identification of the verb. For the meaning of the other verbs in these lists, the reader is referred to the Dictionaries. For the purpose of this survey, Aram. verbs found in BH are regarded as BH verbs.

דלח, הדה, הדך, זבד, זור be loathsome, זור press down, זרב, זרם, חול be strong, חטם, חמץ be red, חמץ be ruthless, חמק, חנן be loathsome, חפף, חרשׁ engrave, חרת, טמה, יגב, יגה, ידד, יפח, יקשׁ, ירא shoot, ישׁם, כאה, כבר (Hiph'il), כסם, כשׁה, לאט, מאר, מלח tear away, מלל, מלץ, מרא flap, נאק, נאר, נבב, נהה, נון, נושׁ, נחץ, נסס be sick, נצא, נקע, נתם, נתע, סלא, סלה make light, סלה weigh, סעה, עדר, עול, עוף be dark, עור be exposed, עושׁ, עטף turn aside, עלל, עלם, ענד, ענה be occupied, עפל, ערג, ערף drip, עתם, פון, פושׁ spring about, פושׁ be scattered, פסס disappear, צעה, צפר, קומ, קושׁ, קיה, קשׁח, רגע disturb, רגע harden, רהה, רוד, רנה, רעל reel, רעף, רצד, רתם, שׁאה, שׂגל, שׁוע, שׁוק be abundant, שׁור travel, שׁור behold, שׁלה, שׁלו, שׁסה spoil, שׁסס, שׁעע be smeared, שׁקק, תאה, תזז.

85. (2) Verbs common to BH and Aram.: אזל, אלם, אלף, אתה, גיח, חוה, חזה, חלשׁ, חרג, טאטא, טלל, יאב, יהב, כפן, כתר (Pi'el), מגר, מוק, מרץ (= מרע), משׁה (= משׁא), נחת, נכא, נכל, סגד, עבט, עוק, עשׁת, עתר, פדע, פעל, פצה, פצח, פתה be wide, צום, צלח צלל (= טלל), קטל, קמל, רזה, רחם love, שׂבר hope, שׂגא, שׂגה (= סגי), שׂוה set, שׂוט, שׂחה, שׂיב (= סיב), תכן.

86. (3) Verbs frequent in BH: אבה, איב, האזין, אפס, התאפק, אצל, אשׁם, בגד, בוך, בתר, גור, גיל, גער, דפק, התל (תלל), חדל, חסה, חרב, חשׁף, טחוה, יגר, יהד, ינה, יצג, יקע, לוט, התמהמה, מוג, מחא, מעד, נגשׁ, נוט, נחה, נצב, סוג, סחב, סכל, סכר, עוז, עלז, ערב, העתיר, פצץ, פצר, קדד, רושׁ, רכשׁ, רמשׂ, רעה, שׁאנן, שׁגע, שׁית, שׁעה gaze, שׂרה.

(4) Denominative Verbs: אפד, גבל, לחם, מָהַר, נהר, נָכַר, נסס, נפשׁ, עלל, קרן.

87. (5) BH Verbs used in MH in cognate roots only: יעף = עיף, נפח—יפח; קוץ—יקץ; ירה—ירא; רקק—ירק; נכה—נכא; סוך, שׂוך—סוג (סִיָג); עפשׁ—עבשׁ; יעץ—עוץ; פקק—פוק; טען—צען; נקר—קור; רמז—רזם; רום—רמם; תלה—תלא; תקן—תכן.

88. (6) The following is a list, by no means exhaustive, of the equivalents used in MH for older BH verbs: יאב, חפץ, אבה,
בא—אתה; חזק—אמץ; למד—אלף; שנא—אָיַב; רצה—הואיל
גער, פחד; ירא—גור, יגר; חתך—בתק, בתר; גזל—שסה, חמס, בזז
—זרם; כעס—קצף, זעף, זעם; לגלג, לעג—תלל, התל; נזף—כהה
; כבד—טאטא; יבש—נתש, חרב; נהג—יבל; בטח—עוז, חסה; שטף
, יצג; התגייר—התיהד; נתן—יהב; התחיל—החל; שתק—החריש
—נגש; מרד—מרה; הוחלק—מעד; כסה—לאט, לוט; העמיד—נצב
, סגד; מסר—סִגֵּר, נִכֵּר; נפרע—נקם; נהג—נחה; בא אצל, קרב
, חכה; משכן—ערב, עבט; שוטה—סכל; גרר—סחב; השתחוה—קדד
; עשה—פעל; פגע—קרה, פגש; שמח—גיל, עלס, עלז; המתן—קוה
—משל, שוה; כחש—רזה; עני—דלל, ריש; הרג—קטל; התענה—צום
דין—פלל, שפט; דמה.

89. Of the 300 new verbs in MH, only a very small proportion are loan words from Aram. The majority are old Hebrew expressions which occur in BH either in cognate verbal roots, or in derivatives, usually substantives. A further large number of these new verbs are real denominatives which are consciously formed by MH from nouns found in BH. Of the residue which cannot be traced to BH sources, a very large proportion belong to the original stock of the old Hebrew vocabulary, which by mere accident have not been preserved in the scanty and fragmentary remains of BH literature. Some of these are found also in Aram. and in other Semitic languages, and are thus of a general Semitic character. Others are found in MH and in Aram. only, and are, probably, at least in most cases, as original in MH as in Aram. Others, again, are peculiar to MH, or may be also found in other Semitic languages, but not in Aram. The remainder (about thirty verbs) are direct borrowings from Aram., and a few more are derived from Greek.

It will, therefore, be seen that the Aram. influence on the lexical character of the MH verb is far less extensive than has been supposed. It may safely be said that the MH influence on the Aram. vocabulary was greater than that of Aram. on MH, particularly in the sphere of religion and the higher life.

We give in what follows a classified list of the new verbs in MH.[1]

(B) *MH Verbs not found in BH.*

90. (1) MH verbs, found in BH in a different form.

(*a*) In cognate roots: ינה—אנה ; יתר—ותר ; זחח—זוח ; זול—זלל ; חוש—חשש ; טחה—טוח ; נפש—פוש ; שוף—שפף ; שתה—שתת.

(*b*) With mutation of sound: בכר—בגר ; זבח—זבל[2]; חזם—גזם ; טבע—טמע ; מחה—מהה ; מלק—מלג ; ירד—מרד ; נבל—נִוֵּל ; נשל—נשר ; שׂים—סִיֵּם (?) ; שׂתר—סתר ; חוג—עוג ; עקב—עכב ; עשק—עסק ; עבש—עפש ; עקל—עקם ; פקח—פכח ; בקע—פקע ; פשר—פתר ; קצע—קטע ; קמץ—קמז ; קמט—קמע ; כפל—קפל ; גרד—קרד ; ריקם—ריקן ; נפח—תפח ; נתש—תשש.[3]

(*c*) By transposition of sound:[4] זרק—זקר ; חרג—חגר ; עלב—לעב ; עצם—עמץ.

91. (2) MH verbs found in BH in derivatives: אגד, אחה, בהק, בור, בשׂם, גבב, גבה (BH גֵּבִים, &c.), גבל knead (BH גַּבְלֻת), גבש, גדל twist (גְּדִילִים), גדשׁ, גמם (BH גם), גפף (BH גף), גנז, דרג, הבהב, זוז, זלג, חדק, חלד, חמר heap, חפף, חרר bore, חרר be free, חשׁר, יהר, ירק, כבל, כמן, כפת (? כפתור), כרך, מרא, מתן (? מתנים), נגב, נסר, נקד, סגל, סדר, סכה look, סרב, סרק (=שׂרק), עגל, עטן, ערב mix, ערם knead, פחת, פרז, פרך, צבע dye, צִיֵּן, צמם, צנן, צרך, קלח, קלט, קרשׁ, רהט, רטט, רתת, שׁגר, שׁחן, שׁחף, שׁפע.

[1] For further details about the derivation of these verbs, the reader is referred to Kohut's *Aruch* and to Jastrow's Dictionary.

[2] Of heathen sacrifices, probably an artificial change in a contemptuous sense as mere זֶבֶל dung. Cf. Kohut, iii, p. 265, and reff. to Tosaphot on 'AZ. 18 b

[3] Cf. further in the Phonology above, §§ 43, 45 ff.

[4] Cf. above, § 61.

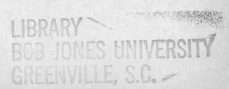

92. (3) Denominative Verbs.

(*a*) From BH nouns: אלמן, אפל, אשכן (from אשך), גבן (from גבינה), גפר, דגש, דרם face south, זפף (from זפת), זפת, חכה fish hook, חלב, חמר (from חמור), חסד, חפן, חרש (from חֶרֶשׂ), יבל (from יבלת), ימן (from ימין), כבר sift, כרכב, כרכם, כתף, נבל (from נְבֵלָה), נגב face south, נפה sift, סלת, סרם, עבב, עַיֵּין, ערם (ערשׂ), פגל, פחם, צבע (from אצבע), צדד (from צד), צייץ (from ציצית), צמת, צפן (from צפון), רוקן (Aramaized for ריקם), רעל (from רעלות), שמן (from שֶׁמֶן), שרב, שרבט, תִּוֵּךְ (from תוך) תחל (from תחלה), תלם, תמר (from תָּמָר), תרם (from תרומה), תרע (from תרועה), תשע be nine.

(*b*) From MH nouns: רבב, גרע (from גרעין), גשר, דמע, זבל, זרד, טבל (from טֶבֶל), מחה (from מומחה), מצע (from אמצע), משכן, עסס (from עיסה), רמץ, רתף (from מרתף), שבר (from שובר), שתף, תבל (from תבלין), תחם, תמד, תרמל.

(*c*) From Aram. nouns, only a few like סטר, סמא (=סמי), קטם. Perhaps also רוקן, רמץ, and a few more.

(*d*) From the Greek, cf. below, § 96.

93. (4) Old Hebrew verbs not found in Aram.: הדם (חדם), חבם, חבץ, חטט, חפת, טנן, כחח, כמש, לבלב, לקה, מחל, מסק, נונה, סנק, ספת, סתת, פזל, פחח, פחם, פשל, קמע, קרטם, קרטע, רהן, רתך, שגם, תחב, תסס, תרה, תרז, תרף.

94. (5) Old Hebrew verbs found also in Aram: אמר (or עמר), בחל, בלט, בלש, גהץ, גנח, דרס, חזר, חכר, כער, נכש, נתז, נעץ, נקז, סכם, סרח, פגם, פגן, פלה, פקר, צלב, צלף, קדר (or קדד), קִוֵּץ (Aram. כְּוֵּץ), קלח, קנח, קרצף, רסק, רשה, רתע, שדל, שמש.

95. (6) Old Hebrew verbs found also in other Semitic languages beside Aram.: גדם, גמר, גנה, גשר, הנה, זִוּג (?), זוף, זרז, חוץ, חכך, חלט, חשר, כדן, לתת, נזף, נזק, נחר, סגף, סנן, פהק, פסד, פרכס, פתק, קטם lop, קנב, קפח, רכן, רמז, שחל, שחם, שלק, שתף, תמם, תקל stumble.

96. (7) Verbs borrowed from Aram.: ארע, דבב, תהא, חצף, טוש, נגס, סטר, סַיֵם (?), סייע, סמא, פטם, פתך, קרע, קטם ashes, קלף, קנט, קנתר, קרקש (כרכש), קשט, רוקן (?), רמץ, רשל, שבש, שהה, שטה.

(8) Verbs borrowed from Greek:[1] לסטם λῃστής, ספג σπόγγος, פקס φυκόω, פרף πόρπη, קטרג κατηγορέω, קמר καμάριον, תרם θυρεός. The following are doubtful: זִוֵּג (from זוג) ζεῦγος, פקר (from אפיקורוס) Ἐπίκουρος, קלס καλῶς, קנס κῆνσος, טגן τήγανον.

97. (9) A few new formations are of an onomatopoetic character: כשכש or קשקש knock, פטפט chatter, babble, קעקע cackle, קרקר cackle, שכשך shake, knock. Perhaps also טפטף to drip, כסכס to chew, לגלג to mock.

98. A large number of verbs which MH has inherited from BH., have undergone certain changes in usage and meaning. Thus, many verbs which were common in BH have become rare in MH. Most of these belong to the elevated diction of BH literature. But a considerable number are quite ordinary prosaic expressions which for some reason or other went out of ordinary use in MH. Again, a number of verbs which were rare in BH have become very common in MH. Many of these will be found to belong also to the Aram. vocabulary. Finally, many verbs have developed in MH a new significance, sometimes analogous to their usage in Aram., sometimes of a technical or legal character Often this new significance is expressed by a new verbal stem not found in BH (cf. below, §§ 108 ff.). A small group of verbs is of special interest. These have preserved in MH their primary significance, while in BH they only occur in a derived and secondary sense.

(C) *BH Verbs with a different usage in MH*

99. (1) Verbs more common in BH than in MH: אטם, ארב, בהל, בחר, הגה, הדר, המה, המם, הרם, זכך, זעם, זעק (= צעק),

[1] Cf. Krauss, *Lehnwörter*, i, pp. 144–52. His etymologies, which are not always reliable, should be checked by Kohut and, especially, by Jastrow.

חבא, חמל, חמם, חנה, חפשׂ, חרד, חשה, טבח, יאל be foolish, יבל, יגע, יחל, יטב, יעל, כלא restrain, כלם, לאה, לכד, מוש, מחץ, מלט, מלל speak (Aram.), מסה, מסך (= מזג), מרה, נאץ, נבט, נגר, נגשׁ, נגשׂ, נדח, נהל, נהר, נוב, נוד, נוס, נזל, נטר (common in Aram.), נטש, נסע, נעם, נצר, נקם, נתח, נתש, סוף (common in Aram.), סור, סחר (common in Aram.), סלף, סער, ספה, עוד repeat, עוה, עִוֵּר, עזז, עזר, עטף be faint, עיף, עלץ, עצב be grieved, עצם be strong, ערץ, עתק, פאר, פסח, פעם, פער, פרה, פשע, צדה lie in wait, צדה lay waste, צהל, צות (common in Aram.), ציץ, עוק, צחק (= שׂחק), צפה look out, צפן, צרח, קוה wait for, קוץ, קלה be light, קצב, קרה, קשב, רגן, רגע be at rest, ריב, רמס, רנן, רעד, רעץ, רעש, שׂגב, שׂדד, שׂוט despise, שׂים, שׂישׂ, שחר be early, שׂטם, שׂכל, שלל, שעע take delight, תעב.

100. (2) Verbs more common in MH than in BH: אנס, בדה, בדק, בטל, בקר, גזר, גמר, געל, גרם, דחק, דין, דמע, זהם, זכה, זמן, זקק, חבב, חבל, חוב, חוש, חטף, חלט, חלף, חנך, חנף, חתך, טול, טמן, טען, טפל, טרד, טרח, יחשׂ (= יחס), כנס, כפה, כשר, לחש, מלך counsel, מרח, מתח, נאה, נאם (= נום), נדה, נטל, נתר, סכן, סלק, ספק sufficient,[1] פטר, פרח fly, פרט, פרשׂ (= פרס), צמק, צער, קבל, קפד, קרם, קרטם (= כרסם), רָוַח, שבח, שגח,[1] תקן.

101. (3) Verbs which show a change of meaning in MH: אבד, אבק, אות, אחז, אחר, אכל, אנס, אסר; בקר, ברך, ברר; גדל, גזר, גרם, גרר; דבק, דדה, דוח, דחה, דלג, דלה, דלל, דמה, דמע, דקק; הלך; זחל, זכה, זמם, זמן, זנב, זקק; חול, חזק, חוש, חטא, חלט, חלל, חלף, חנף, חנק, חצץ, חקה, חרט, חשב, חשך, חתך, חתם; טבל, טבע, טול, טען, טפח, טפל, טרד, טרף; ילד, יפה, יצא, יקר, ישב, ישן; כבד, כון, כנס, כפה, כפר, כרע, כשר; לבן, לוה, לקח; מאן, מול, מחה, מחק, מלך counsel, מנה, מצא, מרח; נבל, נשך, נתך, נתר; סבב, סבר, סכך, סמך, סעד, ספק, ספר; עבד, עבר, עלה, ענה, ענה, עצם, ערך, ערר; פוג, פטר, פלל, פנה, פסל, פקד, פרע, פשט; צחח, צלל, צער, צרף;

[1] Cf. Sirach xxxix. 16, 33; xlii. 17; xl. 29; l. 9.

קבל, קדח, קדם. קדש, קלל, קלס, קמץ, קנה, קפד, קפץ, קצה, קרסם, קשה; ראה, רבץ, רגל, רגש, רווח, רחם, רכס, רעם, רצה, רקד, רקם; שבח, שׂכר, שלל, שלש, שמד, שמן, שנה, שער, שפה, שקע; תנה, תקן.

102. (4) Verbs with the primary meaning in MH and a secondary meaning in BH.

כסף BH long, MH grow pale; מהל BH mix, MH circumcise; עין BH look with envy, MH look intently; סלד BH spring back, MH be scalded; סמר BH bristle up with fear, MH stud with nails; פלט BH escape, MH discharge, spit out; פצע BH bruise, MH split; פקח BH open the eye, MH open up; פרר BH frustrate, annul, MH break, crumble; פשׂק BH part, open wide, MH split, cut; צנע BH be modest, MH hide, retire; cf. also בצע, געל, דלק.

2. Grammatical

103. The differences between the BH verb and the MH verb are as marked on the grammatical side as on the lexical side. Many verbs in MH show a loss of verbal stems found in BH. Thus, the Qal has been lost in most verbs of an intransitive character, especially in the Babylonian dialect of MH. Of the Puʿal only the participle has been preserved as a living form. Formations that are rare in BH, like the Poʿel, Polʿel, and their derivative stems, have either disappeared entirely, or survived in only a few verbs. The common and regular stems have disappeared in those verbs in which their occurrence was rare in BH.

Against these losses, MH can, however, show some important gains. It has increased its quadriliteral formations, often, no doubt, under Aram. influence, either by reduplication, Piʿlel, Pilpel, &c., or by augmentation, Šafʿel, Pirʿel, &c. Further, MH has extended the use of Piʿel to ע״ו verbs, again often under Aram. influence. Finally, MH has applied the common and regular stems to many verbs in which these stems were lacking in BH.

104. In the field of syntax, MH has lost many constructions which imparted much beauty and distinction to BH, such as the use of the cohortative and jussive, and of the consecutive tenses; the manifold applications of the perfect and imperfect; the variety of constructions with the infinitive, &c. On the other hand, MH has developed and extended constructions which were rare or unknown in BH, e. g. the rise of a present tense in the participle; its use with the auxiliary verb הָיָה; the combination of two verbs to express continuous and progressive action (cf. below, §§ 364–5), and the periphrasis of the future with עָתִיד.

For these syntactical changes in MH the reader is referred to the Third Part of this work (§§ 306 ff.). On the Pu'al, cf. below, §§ 125–30. Here we append tables showing the changes which the verb has undergone in MH in regard to stem formation.

(A) *BH. Stems not found in MH.*

105. (1) Formations that are rare in BH.

Po'el in the following verbs: דמם, הגה, הלל, הרה, חנן, חקק, ידע, יעד, לשן, מדד, נדד, סבב, עלל.

Po'lel: בוש, חול, ליץ, מות, נזם, נזף, סור, צוד.

Po'lal: חול, עול, רום, רוע.

Pi'lel: צמת, נאה (נאוה).

Pe'al'al: חמר, יפה.

Tiph'el: רגל.

Hithpo'el: אנן, בלל, גלל, הלל, מדד, נאץ, נדד.

Hithpo'lel: בוש, גור, חול, מול, נום, עוד, עוף, רוע.

Hithpalpel: חול.

Hothpa'el: דשן, טמא, כבס, פקד.

106. (2) Regular stems of rare occurrence in BH in particular verbs:

Qal: אמן, ברה, דבר, דגל, חבב, חָוַר, חרך, ידה, מכך, מסס, נאץ, נוף, סמר, סער, עתק, צפה, קשב, קרס, רנן, שאר, שׂבע.

Niph'al: ברך, גרש, דגל, דוש, דכא, זחח, לבט, מטר, נגע, נכה, נסע, סער, עגן, פוג, פשע.

Pi'el: אחז, אסף, בעת, ברא, ברה, גרע, הרס, ידה, ידע, כתב, נגע, נכה, עתד, קהה, קפד, רתח.

Pu'al: אסף, אסר, גשם, דעך, הרג, הרה, זנה, חבל, חטב, חקה, ידע, יצר, כתת, נקר, עשק, רדף.

Hithpa'el: אמר, באש, גרד, דכא, חקה, מכר.

Hiph'il: אבל, אטם, אמר, גמא, גשם, חבר, חלם, חתם, כזב, כפש, כתת, מלט, נאץ, נפח, עדה, עצב, אמד, צעק, צרח, רדף, שבר.

Hoph'al: אחז, בקע, דבק, דוש, הפך, זון, טבע, יצר, כשל, כתת, מכך, נתק, עלה, צהב, רוה.

107. (3) Qal of the following intransitive verbs. This is usually expressed in MH by the corresponding adjective with היה, e.g. היה טמא, היה חולה, or in some cases by the Internal Hiph'il, האדים, הגדיל, הזקין; or by the Hithpa'el, התאבל, התגאה, הזדקן.

אבל, אדם, אור, ארך, דקק, זקן, חזק, חלה, חמם, טוב, טמא, יבש, יפה, כבד, מלא, מעט, מרר, נקה, עגה, עוּר, עזז, עמק, ענה (= עני), ערם, עשן, פרה, צמא, צער, קטן, קצר, קשה, רחב, רחק, רעב, שׂבע.

(B) *MH stems not found in BH.*

108. (1) *Quadriliterals.* These forms are found also in BH and in other Semitic languages.[1] MH has more of these forms than BH, but, unlike Aram., it has exercised a certain restraint in their formation.[2]

(*a*) By Reduplication.

1. Doubling the third radical (Pi'lel), ערבב, שׂרטט.
2. By repeating the whole root, only in verbs ע״ו and ע״ע.

ע״ו: בעבע (BH אבעבועות), נמנם, נענע, נפנף, ספסף.

ע״ע: בצבץ, דלדל, דקדק, הבהב (BH הבהבי), הרהר (הרר = הרת), כסכס, מקמק, משמש, עלעל, עמעם, פלפל, צחצח, רברב, רפרף.

[1] Cf. Ges.-K., § 56, i, p. 510 f.; pp. 515–20.

[2] Cf. Nöldeke, *Syr. Gr.*, § 180; Dillmann, *Ethiop. Gr.*[2], p. 251.

(*b*) By Augmentation.

1. The Causative stem Šaphʿel, cf. below, §§ 149, 150.
2. By inserting ר after the first radical: קרסם, קרצף. Cf. also קרזל (מקורזל rounded, t. Sab. xiii. 17); ר added at the end: קנתר (קנטר, Aram. loan-word). Further with מ at the end: פרסם from פרס = פרשׂ. With ס at the end: פרכס, פרנס. Cf. Jastrow, s. vv.

(*c*) Denominatives: אלמן, אשכן, כרכב, כרכם, שרבט. Cf. above, § 92.

109. (2) The Intensive stem (Piʿel, &c.) in verbs ע״ו, ע״י.
בֵּיֵּישׁ, בֵּיֵּיר, גֵּיֵּיד (גִּיד), גֵּיֵּיף, דֵּיֵּיר, טֵיֵּיב, טֵיֵּיל, טֵיֵּים (= טוּשׂ), סֵיֵּיג, סֵייד, סֵיֵּים (שׂוּם?), סֵיֵּיף (סוּף), פֵּיֵּיחַ (פִּיחַ), צֵיֵּיץ (צִיצִית), קֵיֵּים, קֵיֵּיץ (קוֹץ thorn), כִּוֵּון, קִוֵּוץ (קוֹץ thorn), רִוֵּוחַ.

110. (3) Application of the regular stems to verbs in which they were lacking in BH.

Qal: ארשׂ, בדל, זון, חוב, חתך, נקף, סבר (= שׂבר), עגן (partic. pass.), עדר, עקר, פשח, צהב, קדם, רפף, שׁבח.

Niphʿal: אנס, בדק, גמר, געל, דמה, דמע, דקק, זון, זמם, זקק, חסם, טען, טפל, כלל, כנס, כפה, לוש, מלק, מתח, נדר, נטל, נקף (go round), נשך, נתר, סבך, עקר, פטר, פסק, פצע, פרט, פשח, צבה, צלה, קמץ, שכב, שדף, שחק, שׂכר, שלה.

Piʿel: אבק, אהב, אנס, ארח, בזה, גמר, גרף, דור, דמע, זון, חמץ, חתך, חתם, טבל, טול, טרף, יתר, כון, לבן, לוה, מעך, מתח, מתק, נסף, סוף, סכך, ספק, עדר, עשן, עשה, פסל, פסע, פצע, פתח, פרר, פרשׂ, פרשׁ, צבה, צמק, צנע, קמץ, רבע, רגש, רדד, רכס, רקם, שאר, שלה, שמד, שער, שקע, שרט, שתק.

Puʿal (only participle): אהב, אחר, בזה, בצר, דלל, דמה, דמע, זון, זמם, חלט, טפל, ישן, יתר, כון, כנס, סוף, סכך, סלק, עשן, פרט, קום, רמה, שאר, שבח, שמד, שקע.

Hithpaʿel (Nithpaʿel): אבק, אהב, אכל (עכל), ארח, ארשׂ (ארס), בצר, בקר, געל, דור, דלל, זמם, זמן, זקק, חוב, חסם, טפל, טרף, יסף, ישן, יתר, כון, כנס, כשר, לבן, מעך, מתך, נבל, נהג, נסה, סבך,

סוף, סלק, ספק, עטף, עצם, עקר, עשן, פלג, פסק, פצע, פקח, פרש, פרשׁ, פתה, צוה, צמק, צער, צרע, צרף, קבל, קטן, קרר, רגש, רעם, רפף, שדף, שלח, שמד, שמן, שער, שקע, שתק.

Hiph'il: אהב, בקר (פקר), זול, זקק, חלט, חמם, חמץ, טען, טרף, כנס, לוה, לקק, נגח, נדר, נהג, נסח, נצץ, נקע, נשך, סבר (שׂבר), ספד, עשה, פוג, פלג, פסע (פשׂע), פצע, פרש, צהב, צלל, קדח, קטן, קמץ, קרא, קרם, רגל, רגש, רווח, רכס, שבח, שחט, שׂכר, שלש, תנה,

Hoph'al: בדל (participle), זול, זקק, חמם, נדר, נקף (knock off), נקף (go round), נתר, סבך, סגר, פרש, צנע, קבל, קדם, קדש, קרר, שחר (be black), שלש, תאם.

B. The Stems.

1. The Simple Stem.

111. (1) The *Qal.* The Qal is identical, both in form and meaning, with the Qal in BH. The form *Qaṭel* is exhibited in the intransitive verbs: בָּטֵל, Ab. v. 16; כָּשֵׁר, Ḥul. ii. 10; עָמֵל, Ab. ii. 14; קָרֵב, Pᵉs. ix. 61, &c. *Qaṭol* is found only in the common verb יָכוֹל. These, however, occur only as participles.

112. The *Participle* coincides almost completely with the partic. in BH. The fem. sing. ends in ת, e.g. גּוֹזֶלֶת robbing; נוֹשֶׁרֶת dropping (of leaves), 'AZ. iii. 8; טוֹחֶנֶת grinding, Giṭ. v. 9; תּוֹבַעַת claiming, ib. iv. 8. In verbs ע"ו, ל"ה, and frequently also in ל"א, it ends in ה: בָּאָה coming, Yᵉb. xv. 10; בּוֹשָׁה ashamed, Dam. iii. 6; רוֹצָה desirous, ib.; חוֹתָה poking, Ṭoh. vii. 9; יוֹצְאָה going forth, Šab. v. 1; but also יוֹצֵאת, Kil. iv. 6; נוֹשֵׂאת וְנוֹתֶנֶת taking and giving, i. e. trading, Šᵉbu. vii. 8.

113. The Partic. of intransitive verbs, being treated as an adjective, forms the fem. with ה: טְמֵאָה unclean, Nid. iii. 1; בְּטֵלָה ceases, Ab. ii. 2; קְרֵיבָה comes near, Pᵉs. ix. 6, &c.

The Passive Partic., which always expresses in MH a state or condition, is also treated almost like an adjective, and the fem.

sing. always ends in ה, גְּרוּשָׁה divorced, Y^eb. vii. 1; נְשׂוּאָה married, ib. i. 2; שְׁרוּיָה dwelling, Ab. iii. 2.

114. In this frequent use of the older termination ת for the fem. sing., MH has remained faithful to the BH tradition, in which this termination is far more common than the younger termination ה (cf. Ges.-K., § 94 d). In Aram., on the other hand, the fem. partic. always ends in אָ.

115. (2) Niph'al. The Niph'al also agrees in form and in meaning with the Niph'al in BH.

In the Infinitive the preformative ה is usually elided after the ל. In most texts the short *ĭ* of the ל is then written *plene* with י, in order, presumably, to differentiate it from the inf. Qal. Thus, לִיבָּטֵל = לְהִבָּטֵל to cease, Yeb. vi. 6; לֵיהָרֵג = לְהֵהָרֵג to be slain, 'Ar. i. 3; לֵיהָנוֹת to enjoy, Ket. vii. 1; לִיטָּהֵר to be purified, Kel. iii. 1; לִיטַּמֵּא to be defiled, Mei. iv. 6; לִיכָּנֵס to enter, BB iii. 6; לִיסָּקֵל to be stoned, San. vi. 6.

The full form is, however, also common, especially in weak verbs: לְהִבָּרְאוֹת to be created; לְהִפָּרַע to be paid, Ab. v. 1; לְהִוָּדַע to be known, ib. iv. 22; לְהִנָּטֵל to be taken, Šebi. iii. 9; לְהִסָּקֵל to he stoned, BQ iv. 8; לְהִשָּׁעֵן to lean, So. ix. 15.

Often the texts waver, thus: לִיגָּזֵז, L. לְהִגָּזֵז to be shorn, BQ ix. 1; לִיגָּלַע, L. לְהִגָּלַע to break open, Nid. viii. 3; לִינָּשֵׂא, L. לְהִנָּשֵׂא to be married, Yeb. ii. 10; לִיפָּרַע [היפרע] BM iv. 2; לְהִקָּרֵא, L. לִיקָּרוֹת to be called, 'Ed. v. 6; לִישָּׁבַע, L. לְהִשָּׁבַע to swear, BM iii. 1.

116. In one case, the frequently occurring technical expression הִכָּרֵת (derived from Num. xv. 31, &c.), the preformative ה is dropped even when not preceded by ל: כָּרֵת, e.g. Pes. iii. 5, &c. Often, however, particularly when preceded by ב, and especially in Palestinian texts, the full form הִכָּרֵת is found: Ḥal. i. 2; Pes. ix. 1; Keri. ii. 6, &c.

117. This elision of the ה is merely an extension to the Inf. when preceded by a preposition, of the phonetic principle followed in the formation of the Imperfect. Cf. also the elision of the article after a preposition, and other cases of the elision of the ה in Ges.-K., § 23 k. It is found in the Inf. Niph. in isolated cases also in BH (Ges.-K., § 51 l., 53 q.), and may have been quite common in the colloquial language.

118. The fem. Partic. always ends in ת, even in verbs ע"ו, ל"א, and ל"ה (cf. above, § 112), e.g. נִגְנֶזֶת to be hidden, So. iii. 3; נִמְכֶּרֶת to be sold, Ket. iii. 7; נִזּוֹנֶת, to be fed, Ket. xii. 2; נִקְרֵאת to be read, Meg. i. 1; נֶהֱנֵית to enjoy, Ned. vii. 9.

Signification of the Niphʿal.

119. (i) Reflexive: נֶחְלְקוּ they divided themselves—disagreed, ʿEr. i. 2; נִטְמָן hiding himself, ʿAr. ix. 4; תִּכָּנֵס to gather oneself, to enter, Ned. x. 4; נִמְנוּ to count oneself, Šab. i. 4; נִפְטָרִין to depart,[1] Ab. i. 8; נִישְּׂאוּ to marry oneself, Ket. vii. 10.

In a few cases it is found in a tolerative sense: נִגְנַב to allow oneself to be stolen from, t. BQ vii. 8; נִשְׁאַל to allow oneself to be consulted, t. Dam. ii. 24; הִשָּׁמְעִי to consent,[2] San. 82 a, Sifre, Num. xxv. 1.

120. (ii) Middle: נֶהֱנֶה to enjoy, Ab. iv. 5;[3] נִזְכַּר to recollect, Ber. iii. 5; נִמְלָךְ to change one's mind, Dam. iii. 2; נִפְרַע to obtain payment, Ab. iii. 16; נִשְׁאַל to consult, MQ iii. 1; נִשְׂכַּר to make profit, Šebi. ix. 10; נִפְסַד to incur loss, Pes. 50 b; נַעֲנֶה to answer Šab. 33 b.

121. (iii) Passive to Qal: נֶאֱכָלִין to be eaten, Ber. i. 1; נִגְמַר to be finished, Pea iv. 8; נִשְׁכַּב to be lain with, San. 54 b.[4]

As passive to Piʿel: נִדְמְעוּ to be mixed with tithe, Ter. v. 6

[1] Cf. 1 Sam. xix. 10 in Qal.

[2] To sexual intercourse, by the woman. Perhaps, however, שמע in this sense is equivalent to the Aram. שמע = שמשׁ to serve, and the Niphʿal would, therefore, be passive to Piʿel שִׁימֵּשׁ, sc. הַמִּטָּה

[3] So Sirach xxx. 19, &c.

[4] Of illicit intercourse, cf. שכב את in BH. See *BDB.*, s.v., p. 1012 (3).

(cf. ib. 5). To Hiph'il: נִגְעַל to be cleansed by boiling, j. T^{e}r. xi. 5 (cf. 'AZ. v. 12).

As passive to an intransitive verb: חֵרֵשׁ רוֹמֵז וְנִרְמָז . . . קוֹפֵץ וְנִקְפָּץ A deaf mute makes signs (with his hand or head), and signs are made to him . . ., makes signs with his mouth, and signs are made to him,[1] Giṭ. v. 7.

Denominative verbs in the Simple Stem are but few. Examples are: חוֹלֵב Šab. 95 a; לְיַחֲלֵב to milk, ib. 53 b; חָפַן to take a handful (from חפנים), MŠ. ii. 5; כּוֹבְרִין to sift (—כברה), Šab. xx. 3; סוֹפֵג to absorb (—ספוג = σπόγγος). T^{e}m. i. 1; נִפְסַח to be lame, j. B^{e}r. i. 5.

2. The Intensive Stem.

122. (1) *Pi'el.* The Pi'el is identical with the BH Pi'el, except that it is often spelt with י after the short *ḥireq*. This is merely an orthographical device to prevent its confusion with the Qal, and has no grammatical significance whatever.[2]

The fem. of the Partic. sing. ends in ת, as מְבַשֶּׁלֶת cooking, מְכַבֶּסֶת washing, K^{e}t. v. 2, except in verbs ל"א, ל"ה, in which it has ה: מְטַמְּאָה defiling, Ḥul. i. 1; מְדַדָּה causing to hop, Šab. xviii. 2.

Signification of the Pi'el.

123. (i) Intensive or iterative: תְּהַלֵּךְ to walk,[3] 'Er. x. 2; זִינְּתָה to commit fornication (repeatedly), San. vii. 5; מְחַמַּדְתָּן she covets them, Mak. iii. 5; מְחַתְּכוֹ he cuts it up[4]; מְעַבְּדוֹ he tans it, Šab. vii. 2; מְנַשֶּׁבֶת blows, M^{e}n. x. 4; מְתַלְּשִׁין plucking violently, Yo. vi. 4.

[1] The Niph'al is used here loosely, in order to preserve the personal construction with the subject which is characteristic of MH style. With these uses of the Niph'al in MH, cf. BH, Ges.-K., § 51 c–g.

[2] Similarly the Pu'al is spelt with ו after the short u, see below, §§ 126, 129, and above, § 39. So regularly in Aram. Stein's suggestion (*Das Verbum*, p. 31) that this spelling signifies a lengthening of the vowel consequent upon the dissolution of the doubling, cannot be entertained at all.

[3] Contrast Qal הוֹלֵךְ to go, Y^{e}b. vii. 5.

[4] Contrast Qal חוֹתֵךְ to cut, 'Er. x. 13.

124. (ii) Causative: טִיהַרְתֶּם ye have declared to be clean, 'Ed. i. 14; יִפּוּהָ they beautified her, Nᵉd. ix. 10; מִיעֵט diminish; רִיבָּה increase, BQ viii. 4; סִילֵּק to put aside, 'AZ. iii. 7; עִיבְּרָהּ he caused her to be pregnant, Yᵉb. vii. 5; לְשַׁכַּח to cause to forget, 'Er. vii. 9; מְשַׁתְּקִין they silence, San. v. 2; חֵירְשׁוֹ he caused him to be deaf, BQ 86 a.

125. (iii) Denominative: מְחַכִּין to angle (— חַכָּה), BQ 81 a; לְכַתֵּף to carry on the shoulder, Šab. 5 b; מְסַלֶּת (— סֹלֶת), Tᵉr. xi. 5. Some of these have a privative force: מְדַשֵּׁן to remove ashes, Yo. ii. 3; מְזָרְדִין to nip off shoots; מִיבַּלִין to remove wens (= יַבֶּלֶת); מְסַקְּלִין remove stones; מְפָרְקִין remove faded leaves, Šᵉbi. ii. 2, 3; מְזַנְּבִין to trim, ib. iv. 6; לְקַוֵּץ to remove thorns, MQ 6 a; מְתַלֵּע to remove vermin, j. Šab. vii. 2.[1]

126. (2) *Pu'al.* Of the Pu'al only the Partic. is common. Of the other parts of the stem only the following examples have been preserved: אוּרַע it happened, t. Šᵉbu. 1, 2; חוּיַּבְנוּ we were made liable, Mak. 3 a; יְחוּלַּל to be rendered common, Qid. 77 a; יְחוּנְּנוּ to find favour,[2] So. ix. 15; חוּתַּךְ (so pointed in L.) to be cut up, Ḥul. iv. 1; יוּפִּי to be made fair, good,[3] Pea vi. 6; לוּקַּט be gathered, ib. v. 1; יְנוּגְּבוּ they will be dried up,[4] Makš. v. 3; נוּטַּל to be taken away,[5] Kel. iii. 2; תְּעוּבַּר צוּרָתוֹ let its form be made to pass away,[6] Pᵉs. vii. 9; תּוּרְמָה to be tithed, t. Ma'a. ii. 2.

[1] Cf. with BH, Ges.-K., § 52 f–h.

[2] In elevated style. The whole passage is a later addition to the Mishna, not found in the *Editio Princeps*. The form may, however, be Po'al. L. has יוחננו, Hoph'al.

[3] The reading is uncertain. L. has יופי; other texts have יפי, ייפה, יפה. The form יפה is given in all texts in the same phrase in Kᵉt. viii. 4, where it is also parallel to הורע. Cf. also Krauss, *ZDMG.*, lxvii. 732.

[4] So in most texts. In L. the whole passage is missing.

[5] Some texts, including L., reads ניטל.

[6] This is a common technical expression in connexion with sacrifices. Cf. the active עִיבֵּר צוּרָה, Bᵉr. 40 b, and the noun עִיבּוּר צוּרָה, Pᵉs. 82 b. The reading of the Pu'al is not, however, quite certain. T. has תעבר, תעיבר, Pᵉs. vi. 6, &c.

Further, as an imitation of BH: וַיְבוּקַּשׁ הַדָּבָר Qid. 66 a.[1] The following are doubtful: קֻדְּשׁוּ to be sanctified, parallel to נִטְמְאוּ, M^e^n. xii. 1, but probably read Qal, קָדְשׁוּ;[2] פוּתֵּיתִי I have been enticed, Gen. R., § 71.

127. The finite parts of the Pu'al have been replaced by the Hithpa'el (Nithpa'el), which latter has greatly extended its usage as a passive, in the same way as the old passive of Qal was already in BH replaced by its corresponding reflexive, Niph'al. The Partic. alone has been preserved in the Pu'al as a living form, but only in an adjectival sense to express a state or condition.[3] Thus, the Partic. Pu'al bears the same relation to Pi'el as the passive partic. *Qaṭul* bears to the Qal (cf. above, § 112).

128. In the formation of the fem. sing. of the Partic., the same rule is observed as in the Pi'el. The short vowel *ŭ* is regularly followed by ו, to prevent confusion with the Partic. Pi'el.

129. The following are examples of the Partic.: מְאוּכָּלוֹת consumed, Tam. i. 4; מְבוּצֶּרֶת fortified (of an eruption surrounded by sound flesh), N^e^g. i. 3; מְגוּלֶּה uncovered, open, Šab. xix. 1; מְזוּיָּן armed, BQ 57 b; מְחוּלָּל made common, Dam. v. 1; מְכוּוֶּנֶת direct, Mak. ii. 5; מְיוּפָּה beautified, j. Giṭ. ii. 1; מְנוּדֶּה excommunicated, N^e^d.

[1] An imitation of BH derived from Esther ii. 23. This *Baraita*, so different from the ordinary oral *Baraita*, seems to be an extract from a historical chronicle. It exhibits a number of other imitations, such as the use of the consecutive tenses (cf. below, § 156), and poetical expressions. Cf. also above, § 16.

[2] In some texts קפלה and הבהבה, Šab. 33, 3, are also pointed as Pu'al: קֻפְּלָה, הֻבְהֲבָה. יבוקר, 'Ed. iv. 5 in L. is an error for יובקר, as in Pea vi. 1 in L.

[3] Cf. MŠ. v. 11, where מְחוּבָּר joined to the soil, is parallel to תָּלוּשׁ plucked from the soil, and both these participles are parallel to יָשָׁן, חָדָשׁ. So. ib. 6 מִתְבַּעֲרִים has the force of a present participle, 'may be cleared away', whereas מְבוּעָר, represents a past participle, expressing a condition, almost like an adjective, 'cleared away'. Cf. also the adjectival use of מְזוּמָּן appointed, as contrasted with the verb נִזְדַּמְּנוּ, Ab. d^e^RN. ii. 3.

i. 1; מְעוֹרֶבֶת mixed, Šab. xvi. 3; מְקוּיָּם confirmed, BM 7 a; מְרוּבַּעַת squared, Kil. v. 5; מְתוּלַּעַת wormy, BB vi. 2; מְתוּקָּן prepared,[1] Ab. iii. 16; מְתוּשָּׁעִים divided into nine, j. Šebi. i. 4.

130. In a few cases the preformative מ has been dropped: חוּתָּךְ = מְחוּתָּךְ cut up, 'Uq. iii. 2; מוּעָטִין = מְמוּעָטִין (as in L.) few, Ber. vii. 3; Dam. v. 5, &c.; עוּבָּרוֹת = מְעוּבָּרוֹת pregnant women, Par. iii. 2 (L. has עברות, so Yo. x. 5). So probably תּוֹעָב = מְתוֹעָב abominable, 'Er. 68 b. Cf. above, § 62. So sometimes also in BH, Ges.-K., § 52 s.

131. The disappearance of the finite parts of the Pu'al, and their replacement by the originally reflexive Nithpa'el, is evidently due to the decay of the inflexional power of the language. It was no longer capable of expressing the modification of the stem idea by internal change alone without the aid of external additions to the stem. The partic. with its firm preformative has been preserved, and even extended to newly acquired verbs. But the imperfect, with its continually changing preformatives, and, especially, the perfect which has no preformatives at all, were no longer able to maintain themselves. This decaying tendency was already strong in BH, in which the finite parts of the Pu'al are very scarce, as compared with other stems.[2] The same tendency was at work in the disappearance of the old passive of the Qal,[3] and its replacement by the reflexive Niph'al.

The same phenomenon appears in all the other Semitic languages. In Assyrian the reflexive stems were gradually supplanting the passives. In Ethiopic, Modern Arabic, and Aramaic the passive forms have disappeared, and been replaced by the corresponding

[1] L. has Hoph'al, מוּתקן. So wherever this verb occurs in the passive, e.g. Para iii. 3, &c.

[2] The finite parts of the Pu'al are not found at all in Joshua, 1 Samuel, Micah, Jonah, Habakkuk, Chronicles, Nehemiah, and Daniel, and only once or twice in Judges, 2 Samuel, Amos, Lamentations, Canticles, and Ecclesiastes.

[3] Cf. Ges.-K., § 52 e, s. 53 u, and the reff. to Böttcher and Barth.

reflexives.[1] MH, however, did not go so far, since it has preserved remnants of the Puʿal, and in addition has retained the Hophʿal as an active and living stem in all its parts.

132. (3) *Hithpaʿel—Nithpaʿel.* The reflexive of the intensive stem in MH is, with a few exceptions, Nithpaʿel instead of the BH Hithpaʿel. These two formations are identical both in form and in meaning, except that in the perfect the one has ה as the preformative, the other נ. There can be no doubt that they are really one and the same stem. The preformative —הִ was in the course of time changed in popular speech into —נִ, on the analogy of Niphʿal. In the popular mind ה became associated with the causative idea, through the influence of Hiphʿil, Hophʿal, and —נִ with the reflexive idea, through the influence of Niphʿal. This change extended only to the perfect. For in the imperfect there is no room for either of these preformatives, and in the infinitive and imperative Niphʿal itself has —ה, hence also Hithpaʿel-Nithpaʿel has retained —ה (e.g. לְהִתְגַּדֵּל to magnify one-self, Ab. iv. 5; לְהִתְקַיֵּם to exist, v. 7; הִסְתַּכֵּל consider, iii. 1, &c.). In the participle the preformative —מְ has maintained itself, in spite of the Niphʿal partic. נקטל, through its firmly established nominal force. Besides, it would be unreasonable to expect that an analogy-formation of this kind should be worked out to its full logical extreme.

133. The preformative —הִ survives only in a few cases: וְהִשְׁתַּחֲוָה and he bowed down, Bik. iii. 6 (probably a reminiscence of וְהִשְׁתַּחֲוִיתָ Deut. xxvi. 10); הִתְפַּלַּלְתָּ thou hast prayed, Taʿa. iii. 8; in the legal phrase הִתְקַבַּלְתָּ thou hast received; הִתְקַבַּלְתִּי, Keṭ. ix. 8;[2]

[1] Cf. Delitzsch, *Assyr. Gr.*, § 115; Dillmann, *Ethiop. Gr.*, § 80; Spitta, *Gram. d. Arab. Vulg. Dialect von Aeg.*, § 90 a (4); the various Aram. Grammars.

[2] Four times. L. has twice נתקבלתי. So in v. 1 L. has ניתקבלתי for edd. התקב׳. Contrast also t. Keṭ. ix. 4 with xi. 1.

הִתְנַדֵּב he 'donated', M^e^n. xii. 3 (L נתנדב); הִתְעַנִּינוּ we fasted, 'Er. 41 a; הִשְׁתַּעְבַּדְתֶּם ye were enslaved, Šab. 88 b; הִתְכַּעַרְתִּי I made myself ugly, Gen. R., § 17 הִתְמַלֵּאתִי, הִתְמַלְּאוּ ib., § 33.[1]

The Nithpa'el agrees with the BH Hithpa'el both as regards its meaning and its formation (cf. Ges.-K., § 54).

134. *Formation.* The preformative syllable is, as stated above, —נִתְ in the perfect, in the other parts it is exactly like Hithpa'el in BH. The fem. sing. of the participle follows the rules given above (§§ 112, 122).

The phonetic rules regulating the preformative are the same as in BH. (i) When the first radical is a sibilant ז, ס, צ, שׁ, the ת is transposed after the sibilant. In the case of the ז, the ת is changed into ד, as in Aram. (cf. Dan. ii. 9), and of צ, into ט. Exx.: הִזְדַּיֵּיף to be forged, Giṭ. ii. 4; מִזְדַּוְּגִין to join themselves together, San. v. 5; נִסְתַּחֲפָה to be swept away, K^e^t. i. 6; מִצְטָרְפִין to be joined, Naz. vi. 1; מִצְטַעֵר to be grieved, San. vi. 5; נִשְׁתַּיֵּיר to be left over, Y^e^b. viii. 2.

135. (ii) When the first radical is ד, ט, or ת, the preformative ת is assimilated to the first radical. The short *ĭ* of the preformative syllable is then often written with י, as in Pi'el: נִדַּיְּירָה to be manured by cattle; נִטַּיְּיבָה to be improved, Š^e^bi. iv. 2; מִיטַּהֲרִים to be purified, Yo. viii. 9;[2] נִיטַּמֵּאת to become unclean, Ḥag. iii. 2; הִתַּלֵּשׁ to be plucked out, Š^e^bi. vi. 3; מִיתַּרְגֵּם to be translated, M^e^g. iv. 1.

Assimilation of the ת is sometimes found also with other consonants, מִנַּתְּזִין to squirt off, BQ ii. 1; so, perhaps, מִקַּדְּשִׁין to become holy, 'Or. iii. 3.

[1] The forms נִכַּפֵּר, Deut. xxi. 8, and נִוַּסְּרוּ, Ezek. xxiii. 48, are also usually explained as Nithpa'els. Cf., however, Eitan, *JQR*. (N. S.), xii, p. 25, who holds that these two forms are survivals of a stem *Nippa'el*, reflexive of Pi'el corresponding to Niph'al in the Simple Stem.

[2] But also מִתְטַמֵּא, Naz. iv. 3. Cf. especially, Kel. ii. 1.

Signification of Nithpaʿel. The Nithpaʿel bears the same relation to the Piʿel as the Niphʿal to the Qal.

136. (i) It is primarily Reflexive: מִתְאַבֵּק to cover one self with dust, Ab. i. 4; תִּתְוַדַּע to make oneself known, ib. i. 10; מִתְחַכֵּךְ to rub oneself, BQ iv. 6; לְהִתְכַּסּוֹת to cover oneself, Nᵉd. vii. 3; נִסְתַּפֵּג to dry oneself, Yo. vii. 3; תִּתְלַבֵּשׁ ... תִּתְעַטֵּף ... תִּתְכַּסֶּה ... תִּתְאַזֵּר clothe, wrap, cover, gird thyself, Bᵉr. 16 b. It is sometimes strengthened by the addition of a reflexive pronoun: הֵן מִתְעַצְּמִין מֵאֲלֵיהֶן they shut of themselves, Šab. 151 b.

137. (ii) Internally reflexive, or in a middle sense: תִּתְיָרֵא to fear, So. vii. 8; נִתְכַּוַּנְתִּי I intended, Mᵉn. xiii. 4; מִתְנַדְּבִין to 'donate', Zᵉb. x. 8 (cf. Ezra iii. 5; 1 Chron. xxix. 17); תִּתְיָאֵשׁ to despair, Ab. i. 7; הִסְתַּכֵּל to consider, ib. iii. 1; הִשְׁתַּדֵּל to strive, ib. ii. 5. Further, the performance of an act in which the subject is interested, which thus assumes a purely active significance: הִתְקַבֵּל to receive (for oneself), Kᵉt. ix. 8.

138. (iii) Inchoative, to describe the entry into a new state or condition, especially of the body or mind: נִתְאַרְמְלָה (= נִתְאַלְמְנָה, cf. above, § 54) she became a widow, Yᵉb. xiii. 4; נִתְגַּיְּירוּ they became proselytes, Kᵉt. iii. 1; נִתְחָרֵשׁ to become deaf-mute, Yᵉb. xiv. 1; נִסְתַּמֵּא to become blind, ʿAr. 17 b; נִתְפַּקֵּחַ to regain one's hearing; נִשְׁתַּפָּה to regain one's sanity, BQ iv. 4; נִשְׁתַּטָּה to become mad, Giṭ. ii. 6; נִשְׁתַּתֵּק to become dumb, ib. vii. 1.

139. (iv) Reciprocal: נִתְעָרְבוּ they become mixed up one with the other, Yᵉb. xi. 5; נִצְטָרְפוּ they joined one another, ʿOr. ii. 11; נִשְׁתַּתְּפוּ they joined each other in partnership, Dam. vi. 8. Often, however, the reciprocal idea is strengthened by the addition of reciprocal pronouns: נִתְעָרְבוּ זֶה בָּזֶה Pᵉs. iii. 5; נִתְעַצְּמוּ זֶה בָּזֶה they quarrelled, t. BM i. 16; מִתְרַצִּים זֶה לָזֶה they become reconciled to each other, Nᵉd. v. 6; נִתְקַבְּלוּ ... זֶה מִזֶּה MŠ. v. 9 they received ... from each other.

140. (v) Finally, the Nithpaʻel is extensively used in a passive sense, serving as a substitute for the Puʻal (§ 127); נִתְבַּשְּׁלוּ to be boiled, Ned. vi. 6; נִזְדַּבְּלָה to be manured, ʻAZ 49 a; מִתְחַלֵּל to be profaned, Ab. i. 11; יִתְמַעֵךְ to be pressed, Men. x. 4; נִתְנַסֵּה to be tried, Ab. v. 3; נִתְפַּצְּעוּ to be cracked, ʻOr. iii. 8; נִתְפַּתְּתָה to be seduced, Ket. iv. 1; נִתְקַוְּוצָה to be cleared of thorns (privative) Šebi. iv. 2; מִתְקַדֶּשֶׁת to be betrothed, Qid. ii. 1,[1] corresponding to the Piʻel active: בשל, זבל, חלל, מעך, נסה, פצע, פתה, קווץ (cf. MQ 6 a), קדש.

This passive use of a reflexive stem is common to all Semitic languages in their later stages, cf. above, § 131. In BH it is comparatively rare in the Hithpaʻel, cf. Mic. vi. 16; Prov. xxxi. 30; Qoh. viii. 10, and the cases cited in the Note to § 133. See Ges.-K., § 54 g.

141. (4) *Poʻel, Poʻal, and Hithpoʻel.* These stems, already rare in BH, have practically disappeared in MH (cf. above, § 105). Poʻel is found in a few ע״ע verbs, cf. below, § 191. In the strong verb it is found only in the forms מְשׁוֹעֲרִים gate-keepers, by analogy from the parallel מְשׁוֹרְרִים singers, ʻAr. 11 b,[2] and רוֹקֵן to empty, Lev. R. 24, a secondary form of רִיקֵן San. 60 b. This is a denominative of רֵיקָן, BH רֵיקָם; cf. above, § 54. Of the Poʻal no trace is to be found in MH. The Hithpoʻel is found as Nithpoʻel in a few ע״ע verbs, cf. below, § 191, and in the form נִתְרוֹקְנָה she was made empty, Ned. x. 2.

3. The Causative Stem.

(1) *Hiphʻil.* The Hiphʻil is identical with the Hiphʻil in BH, both in form and in meaning.

142. The preformative א, instead of ה, is found in some texts in אוֹנִיתַנִי thou hast cheated me (= הוֹנִיתַנִי, as in L, cf. Exod.

[1] Of a woman. The corresponding reflexive is קִדְּשָׁה אֶת עַצְמָהּ, Qid. iv. 9

[2] But the verb is in the Piʻel: שִׁיעֵר, ib.

xxii. 20, &c.), BM iv. 4, no doubt on the analogy of the cognate verbal noun אוֹנָאָה, ib. (L הוֹנָאָה). For BH cf. Ges.-K., § 53 k, p.

143. In the Infinitive the ה is elided in לָרְבּוֹת (= לְהַרְבּוֹת) to increase; לַשְׁהוֹת (= לְהַשְׁהוֹת) to cause delay, ʿEr. x. 15; לָדִיחַ (= לְהָדִיחַ) to rinse, j. ʿAZ. iii. 5.[1] Cf. above on Niphʿal, § 119, and for BH Ges.-K., § 53 q. Elsewhere the ה is preserved: לְהַבְעִית to frighten, Yo. v. 1; לְהַחְמִיר to be strict; לְהָקֵל to be lenient, Kil. ii. 2; לְהַכְנִים to bring in, Kᵉt. vi. 3; לְהַצְנִיעַ to hide, Dam. iii. 3, &c.

144. The fem. sing. of the Partic. follows the rule given above, § 112: מַשְׁכַּחַת causing to forget, Ab. ii. 2; מַתְרַעַת blowing the horn (denom. of תרועה, cf. above, § 92), Taʿa. iii. 3, 4; but מְטִיבָה doing good, San. vii. 10; מְנִיקָה nursing, Kᵉt. v. 5; מְרֵעָה doing evil, San. vii. 10.

The shortened Hiphʿil (Jussive) is rare: תַּשְׁכֵּן mayest thou cause to dwell, Bᵉr. 16 b; אַל תַּאֲמֵן do not believe, Ab. ii. 4 (L most texts have תַּאֲמִין); אל תַּחֲזֵק טוֹבָה ib. ii. 8 (L).

145. *Signification.* (i) Usually Causative: לְהַבְטִיל to cause to cease, Suk. v. 5; מַקְרִיא to make to read, to read to, Bik. iii. 7; הִשִּׁיךְ to cause to bite, San. ix. 1; הִקְדִּיחָה to cause to burn, BQ ix. 4, &c.

146. (ii) Inchoative, or Internally Causative, describing the entry into a state or condition. This usage is even more frequent in MH than in BH (cf. Ges.-K., § 53 e). Exx.: יַבְרִיא to become healthy, Šab. xix. 5; הִבְרִיקָה to become bright (euphemistically—blind), BM vi. 2; תַּגְדִּיל to grow up, come of age, Kᵉt. vi. 6; הֶעֱשִׁיר . . . הֶעֱנִי to grow rich, poor, ib.; יַעֲנוּ they will become poor, Mᵉʿil. 17 a; מַחְכִּים to grow wise, Ab. ii. 5; יַאֲדִימוּ ,הִבְאִישׁוּ ,יַבְחִילוּ to become ripe, ill-smelling, red, Maʿa. 1, 2; הֶחֱמִיץ ,הִרְקִיבוּ ,הִזְקִינוּ

[1] לשטיח, cited by Stein (p. 10 b) and by Albrecht (§ 101 b) is a noun, for a spread, or mat, cf. Bertinoro to Ḥul. ix. 3.

to become old, rotten, sour, BQ ix. 2; הִשְׁחִירוּ, הִקְצִירוּ to become black, short, Neg. i. 5; הִלְבִּינוּ, הֶאֱרִיכוּ to become white, long, ib. 6.

Examples of Denominative verbs in Hiph'il are הִתְחִילוּ (—תְּחִלָּה) to begin, Šab. 1, 2; הַצְבִּיעוּ (—אצבע) to put up the finger, Yo. ii. 2; הִנְגִּיב to face south (—נגב), 'Er. 53 b; יַדְרִים, יַצְפִּין to face south, north, BB 53 b, &c.

147. (2) *Hoph'al.* The Hoph'al is extremely common. It differs in no respect from the BH Hoph'al, except that it takes the vowel *ŭ* after the preformative, always written *plene* with ו: —הוּ, —מוּ,[1] &c., even in strong verbs, instead of the usual BH *hŏ*. This form of the vowel is found occasionally in BH in strong verbs (Ges.-K., § 53 s), and regularly in most of the weak verbs, viz. ע״ע, פ״נ, פ״ו, ע״ו, and ל״א. As *ŭ* is also the regular vowel of the Pu'al it must have become in the popular mind the only characteristic vowel of the passive stems, resulting in the total suppression of the vowel *ŏ*.

148. Examples of Hoph'al: הוּחְזְקוּ to be made strong, confirmed, Yeb. xii. 6; הוּסְבַּךְ to become intertwined, Pe. vii. 3; מוּסְגָּר to be shut up, Neg. i. 7; מוּצְנָע to be hidden, Ter. viii. 8; מוּקְדָּמִים early, Šebi. x. 5; הוּשְׁחֲרוּ to be made black, Ḥag. 22 b; הוּשְׁלַשׁ to be deposited with a third party, Ket. vi. 7; הוּרַע to become bad, Pe. vi. 6; הוּזְלוּ to become cheap; הוּקְרוּ to become dear, BM v. 8; מוּדָּר to be forbidden by vow; מוּפְרָשׁ to be separated, Ned. i. 1; מוּדְרָמוֹת facing south, Men. 85 a: תּוּדַח to be rinsed, Makš. iv. 3; יוּרַע to be made bad, BB x. 5; יוּצַּן to be made cold; יוּתַּץ to be destroyed, 'AZ iii. 9, &c.

149. (3) *Saph'el.* This old stem is found in the verb סֵרֵב[2]

[1] This traditional pronunciation as *ŭ* is proved to be correct by the invariable spelling with ו. So also in BH even in strong verbs, according to the Babylonian punctuation, cf. Kahle, *Masoreten d. Ostens*, p. 193.

[2] Also in Sirach iv. 25 a; xli. 2, and, probably, also in the BH noun סָרָבִים.

(contracted from סְרְהֵב), to rebel, refuse; מְסָרְבִין Nᵉd. viii. 7; Bᵉr. 4 a, &c., and in סִרְגֵל to draw lines; מְסַרְגְּלִין j. Mᵉg. i. 9; Sopherim i. 1.

150. (4) *Šaph'el.* The causative stem Šaph'el is found in the following verbs: שִׁחְרֵר to liberate, manumit; שִׁעְבֵּד to enslave, subject; שִׁכְלֵל to furnish, decorate; שִׁלְהֵב to be aflame; שִׁעְמֵם to be dim, dull; and שִׁרְבֵּב to be much, great.

Examples. Active: שִׁחְרְרוֹ Yᵉb. xi. 5; Passive Participle: מְשׁוּחְרָר Giṭ. iv. 4; מְשׁוּחְרֶרֶת Yᵉb. vi. 5; מְשׁוּחְרָרִים MŠ. v. 14; Ništaph'el, in a passive sense; נִשְׁתַּחְרֵר BQ viii. 4; נִשְׁתַּחְרְרָה Yᵉb. ii. 8; נִשְׁתַּחְרְרוּ ib. xi. 2; אֶשְׁתַּחְרֵר, תִּשְׁתַּחְרְרִי Qid. iii. 5.

Active: מְשַׁעְבְּדִין RH iii. 8; Passive: מְשׁוּעְבָּדִים mortgaged, Kᵉt. ix. 7, 8; Ništaph'el: יִשְׁתַּעְבֵּד Giṭ. iv. 4.

שִׁכְלְלָן he furnished them, San. 38 a; מְשׁוּכְלָל Sifra (Weiss) 88 c; מְשׁוּלְהָב Qoh. R. i. 5; מְשׁוּלְהָבִין Mᵉkil. (Weiss) 79; מְשׁוּעֲמֶמֶת BM 80 a; נִשְׁתַּעְמְמוּ Num. R. x. 8; שִׁרְבַּבְתָּ Bᵉr. 54 b; נִשְׁתַּרְבְּבָה she became prolonged, So. 53 a.[1]

These formations are found in all Semitic languages, including BH.[2] Nevertheless, these verbs may, perhaps, be loan-words in MH from Aram.

C. The Tenses.

The inflexion of the verb in MH follows generally the verbal inflexion in BH. The following few variations may be noted.

151. (1) The second masc. sing. of the perfect is sometimes spelt with ה at the end, especially in Palestinian texts: קִיַּימְתָּה

[1] In the partic. מְהַלְקְטִין to cause birds to pick up corn from the hand, we have a secondary Hiph'il of לקט with the retention of the preformative ה, formed on the model of Šaph'el, as distinguished from the regular Hiph'il— מַלְקִיטִין to cause birds to pick up corn from the ground, t. Šab. xviii. 4; cf. Šab. 155 b.

[2] Cf. Ges.-K., § 55 c. Also the nouns enumerated below, § 262.

thou hast fulfilled, Suk. ii. 9 (L); נָתַתָּה, עָבַרְתָּה, but also עברת Z^eb. viii. 11 (L); הִקַּלְתָּה Sifra (Weiss) 15 b; הֶחֱמַרְתָּה ib. 48 d, &c.

152. (2) The second masc. plur. of the perfect often ends in תֶּן, instead of תֶּם, e.g. עֲשִׂיתֶן Mid. ii. 2 (but עֲשִׂיתֶם in Ab. ii. 3). This is a common phonetic change, which may, however, have been assisted by Aram. influence.[1]

153. (3) In the Imperfect the form תִּקְטֹלְנָה (second and third fem. plur.) has entirely disappeared from MH.[2] Both genders use יִקְטְלוּ and תִּקְטְלוּ, just as in the perfect they both use קָטְלוּ, and sometimes in MH, קְטַלְתֶּן, e.g. הַנְּשׂוּאוֹת יִתְאָרְסוּ וְהָאֲרוּסוֹת יִנָּשְׂאוּ women who had been married may become betrothed, and women who had been betrothed may be married, Y^eb. iv. 10; הַבָּנוֹת יִזּוֹנוּ the daughters must be fed, K^et. iv. 6; xiii. 3.

So also in the Imperative the form קִטְלוּ is used also for the fem., e.g. וְאָמַר לְאִמּוֹ וּלְאִשְׁתּוֹ רַחֲצוּהָ . . . וְרִקְדוּ he said to his mother and to his wife: bathe her . . . and dance before her, Ab. d^eRN. xli. 13.

In this MH has merely developed to the full a tendency already strong in BH.[3] Modern Arabic has gone further in this respect than MH, and has given up all the fem. plural forms, both in the perfect and the imperfect.[4] Aram., on the other hand, has carefully preserved the distinction of gender in all its dialects.[5]

154. (4) The imperfect and imperative Qal is spelt *plene* with ו, יִקְטוֹל, קְטוֹל. The plur. is יִקְטְלוּ, קִטְלוּ, except in pause where they

[1] Cf. above, § 70, and *JQR.*, xx. 680 f.

[2] The few cases found are all imitations from BH. Thus: כִּלְיוֹתֶיךָ תַּעֲלוֹזְנָה מֵישָׁרִים, B^er. 17 a, from Prov. xxiii. 16; תִּכְהֶינָה עֵינָיו, Pea viii. 9 (L; editions have עֵינָיו כֵּהוֹת, from 1 Sam. iii. 2), from Gen. xxvii. 1; וְתֶחֱזֶינָה עֵינֵינוּ (Singer, p. 51), from Isa. xxxiii. 17; Ps. xvii. 2.

[3] Cf. Gen. xxx. 39; Lev. xxvi. 33 b; Judges xxi. 21 a; Cant. ii. 7; iii. 5; v. 8; vi. 9; viii. 4—ten examples of MH usage against three examples of the older BH usage, viz. iv. 11 and iii. 11 (imperatives).

[4] Cf. Spitta-Bey, op. cit., § 90 a (1).

[5] Mandaic forms the only exception, cf. Nöldeke, *Mand. Gr.*, § 162.

are יִקְטוֹלוּ. Exx.: יַחֲלוֹקוּ they shall divide,[1] BM i. 1, 2; יִטְבּוֹלוּ they will bathe, Ṭoh. x. 3; אַל תִּכְתּוֹבוּ do not write, Giṭ. vii. 1 (L); יִמְתּוֹקוּ they will become sweet, ʽUq. iii. 4; יִפְלוֹטוּ they shall spit out, Tᵉr. viii. 2; יִשְׁטוֹפוּ they will overflow, Miq. i. 5; יִתְרוֹמוּ they will tithe, Tᵉr. i. 1. Cf. also the pointing in L: יִגָּנֵזוּ they shall be hidden, San. x. 9.

Imper.: כְּתוֹבוּ write ye! חֲתוֹמוּ seal ye! Giṭ. vi. 7; vii. 2; שְׁתוֹקוּ be ye silent! Šᵉbi. viii. 9, 10; תֵּינוּ give ye! t. Giṭ. vi. 8.

155. (5) The lengthened forms of the imperfect and imperative (cohortative) are not found in MH. The shortened form of the imperfect (jussive) is found only occasionally; cf. for the Hiphʽil above, § 144, and for ל״ה verbs below, §§ 205, 212.

156. (6) The Consecutive Tenses have practically disappeared from MH. In the few cases where they occur, they are conscious imitations of BH. Thus הִשָּׁבַע לִי וַיִּשָּׁבַע לוֹ Mᵉkil. (Weiss), 66, from Gen. xxv. 33. Five examples occur, besides more than a dozen simple tenses, in that remarkable *Baraita* in Qid. 66 a, which must be a fragment of some historical work written in a mixed style of BH and MH (cf. above, §§ 16, 126 n.). They are וַיֹּאמֶר (three times), וַיְבוּקַּשׁ הַדָּבָר (Esther ii. 23); וַיִּבָּדְלוּ they were separated (Ezra x. 16; Neh. ix. 2); וַתּוּצַץ הָרָעָה and the evil sprouted forth; וַיֵּהָרְגוּ and they were slain. They are found occasionally in the older, but not the oldest, parts of the liturgy: וַתִּתֶּן (Singer, op. cit., pp. 228, 230, &c.); וַתְּלַמְּדֵם (p. 39); וַתַּבְדֵּל, וַתְּלַמְּדֵנוּ (pp. 46, 227, 240, six times beside one perfect with simple *waw*); וַתִּפְקְדֵהוּ (p. 250); וַתַּשְׁמִיעֵם (p. 252); וַתַּכִּירֵהוּ, וַתְּלַמְּדֵנוּ (p. 267); וַיְבַלְּעוּהָ, וַיִּירָשׁוּהָ, וַיָּטִילוּ, וַיַּהַרְגוּ[2] (p. 49): וַיְכַסּוּ (p. 43) is a quotation from Psalms cvi. 11.

[1] The occurrence of this form not in pause is due to scribal error. Thus, in Kᵉt. viii. 6; BM. viii. 8, read יַחַלְקוּ, as in L. So Ab. iii. 16. L has יַחַלְקוּ, but edd. יַחֲלוֹקוּ may also be right.

[2] Cf. j. Taʽa. 11. 2.

157. As is well known, numerous passages are found even in the oldest portions of the Bible, in which the simple tenses are used in place of the usual consecutive tenses. This becomes more frequent from the time of Jeremiah onward, until in Qohelet the relation between the consecutive and simple tenses is reversed, i. e. the use of the simple tense becomes regular, while that of the consecutive sense becomes exceptional. The explanation of this phenomenon as due to Aram. influence is inapplicable to the numerous cases in the earlier books of the Bible.[1] Probably this irregularity in the use of the simple for the consecutive tense arose at an early time within the Hebrew language itself, and independently of outside influence. It may even be doubted whether the consecutive construction ever attained in popular speech that dominating position which it occupies in the literary dialect. It may be plausibly assumed that the more convenient construction with the simple tenses had survived in the every-day speech side by side with the more difficult construction by means of the consecutive tenses.[2]

Similarly in Phoenician, which also possesses the consecutive tenses, the simple tenses are used very often where BH would employ the consecutive tenses. Thus: ושמע . . . וּפָעַל (Cooke, *N. Sem. Inscriptions*, No. 3, l. 8); ופעלת אנך וְיִקְדַּשְׁתִּ (No. 29, l. 13); בן וּפָעַל (No. 33, l. 3), פעל וְחִדֵּשׁ (No. 38, l. 1); and the common phrase יתן ויטנא (No. 13, l. 2, &c.), both of which verbs are perfects.

The contact with Aram. naturally strengthened the simpler construction, until eventually the consecutive construction disappeared from the living speech, and survived only in literature, largely by the force of the literary tradition, as in the later books of the Bible, in Sirach, and other literary productions of the MH period.

[1] Cf. Driver, *Hebrew Tenses*, § 133.

[2] Cf. also H. Bauer, *Die Tempora im Semitischen*, p. 37 f.

D. Weak Verbs.

(1) Guttural Verbs.

158. In the absence of a trustworthy system of punctuation in MH texts, it is not possible to determine whether the Guttural verbs have suffered any change in MH, as compared with BH. It may, however, be safely assumed that these verbs obey the same phonetic rules in MH as in BH. (Cf. above, §§ 36, 40.)

Examples of Guttural Verbs.

159. Guttural in the First Radical. Qal: לַחֲזוֹם to trim, Dam. ii. 2; יַעֲלֶה to go up, Ber. i. 1; עֲמוֹד stand up, Yo. i. 7. Niph'al: נֶעֱגָל to be round, j. 'AZ 41 b: נַעֲנוּ they answered, Qid. 40 b; לְהֵחָיוֹת to be revived, Ab. iv. 22. Hiph'il: הֶחֱשִׁיךְ he remained till darkness, Šab. xxiv. 1; יַעֲצִים to shut (eyes), Qid. 32 b; מַחְכִּיר to farm, BM 104 b.

160. Guttural in Second Radical. Qal: צָהֲבוּ to be bright, Men. 18 a; סוֹחֲטִין to squeeze, Šab. xxii. 1. Pi'el: אֵחַרְתִּי to delay, Pes. ix. 9; עֵירָה (L points עֵירֵה) to empty, 'AZ. v. 7 (L 10); מְאָרֵחַ to entertain, Ber. 63 b; יְשָׁרֵשׁ to uproot, Šebi. iv. 4. Pu'al: מְכוֹעָר ugly, Ket. 105 a. Nithpa'el: נִסְתַּחֲפָה to sweep away, Ket. i. 6; יִתְאָרְסוּ to be betrothed, Yeb. iv. 10.

161. Guttural in Third Radical. Qal: נוֹבֵעַ bubbling up, BB x. 8; רוֹוֵחַת spread wide, t. San. vii. 1; לָקוּחַ bought, MŠ. iii. 11. Niph'al: נִיטַּעַת to plant; נִזְרַעַת to sow, Oh. xviii. 5. Pi'el: מְפַצֵּעַ to split, Šab. 145 a; מְקוּפַּחַת cut, fragmentary, Oh. xvi. 1. Hiph'il: הַגְבַּהּ lift up, Yo. iv. 1; מַתְרַעַת to blow trumpet, Ta'a. iii. 3; Hoph'al: מוּצַּעַת spread out, 'Ar. vi. 3.

162. The verb שׁאר to leave, hardens the א into י in the Pi'el and Nithpa'el: שִׁיֵּיר Pea iii. 2, 3; יְשַׁיֵּיר Kil. ii. 3; מְשַׁיֵּיר Pes. i. 3; נִשְׁתַּיְּירוּ Kil. vi. 6. Contrast Partic. Pu'al: מְשׁוֹאָר Pea iii. 3; Zeb. viii. 12.

(2) Verbs פ״א.

163. These verbs follow generally their BH models. Thus, Qal: יֶאֱרַע to happen, Yo. i. 1; יֹאכַל Pes. x. 1; אוֹכַל Ned. i. 3; אוֹמַר I shall eat, say, Šebi. viii. 9; תֹּאפֶה (but L תופה) to bake, Pes. iii. 3; לֶאֱגוֹד to bind, Šebi. viii. 3; לֶאֱכוֹל Ber. i. 1. The Palestinian texts, however, often have לוֹכַל = לֹאכַל ('Er. iii. 1, &c.) on the analogy of the imperfect יֹאכַל, &c. So, usually, in all texts לוֹמַר = לֹאמַר Šab. ii. 6; Ab. v. 1, &c., on the analogy of יֹאמַר.

Niph'al: נֶאֱנְסָה she was violated, Ket. i. 10; נֶאֱנַסְתִּי ib. 6; נֶאֱמֶנֶת ib. 7; נֶאֱגַד, יֵאָגֵד Ma'a. i. 5; תֵּאָכֵל Be. i. 1. Pi'el: אִיהֵל to make a tent, Me'il. 17 a; אֵירְעוּ Ta'a. iv. 6; אֵחַרְתִּי to delay, Pes. ix. 9; יְאַבֵּד to destroy, 'AZ iv. 7. Pu'al: מְאוּחָר delayed, Pes. 6 b. Hiph'il: הֶאֱהִיל Oh. iii. 1; מַאֲפִיל to make dark, Šab. 86 a; מַאֲחִיזִין to cause to take hold, kindle, Šab. i. 11. Some texts (L, &c.) have מַחִיזִין, with א elided. Similarly מוּגִירוֹת = מָאגִירוֹת = מַאֲגִירוֹת t. Dam. i. 10, from אגר to store. Hoph'al: יוּאֲחַר j. Yo. iii. 4.

164. Note. The verb הפך forms the imperfect Qal on the analogy of the פ״א verbs. Thus, יוֹפַךְ = יֹאפַךְ = יֶהֱפֹךְ; אוֹפַךְ = אאפך = אֶהֱפֹךְ Kil. ii. 3, 4; Ter. ix. 3. The ה in this verb seems to have been weakened into א. Cf. R. Jonah, *Riqmah*, p. א.

(3) Verbs פ״י.

165. MH has preserved the distinction between the three classes of verbs as in BH. (i) Original פ״ו; (ii) Original פ״י; (iii) With י assimilated to a following צ.

Qal. (i) תֵּדְעוּ Šebu. iv. 9; תֵּצֵא Yeb. iii. 5; צֵא Pes. iv. 2; but also יִישַׁן Šab. 25; אִישַׁן Šebu. iii. 5. (ii) יִיבַשׁ Šebi. iii. 1; יִינַק to suck, So. 12 b; יִירַשׁ to inherit, BB viii. 5; תִּירָשֵׁנִי ib.; יִישַׁר to be straight, strong, Ber. 42 a. (iii) לִצּוֹק to pour, Šab. xvii. 5.

The Infinitive is formed on the analogy of the imperfect. Thus: לֵידַע Ab. iv. 22; לֵילֵד Yeb. iii. 10; לֵירֵד 'Er. iv. 2; לִישַׁן BB ii. 3;

לִינַע j. Ber. ix. 5 ; לִינַק Pes. 112 a ; cf. the imperfects יֵרֵד, יֵלֵד, יֵדַע, יִישַׁן, יִינַע, יִינַק.[1] Exceptions are : לָצֵאת Šeq. iii. 2, and לִירָאָה Ber. 16 b (a liturgical phrase), which are formed as in BH.[2]

Niph'al : נוֹלָד Ab. ii. 9 ; נוֹתָר Ker. iii. 4 ; נוֹצַרְתָּ Ab. ii. 8 ; לְהִוָּדַע ib. iv. 22[3] ; לִיוָּדַע Šebu. 9 b ; יִוָּדַע ib. i. 4 ; יִוָּלֵד Bek. v. 3. (iii) נִצּוֹק Makš. v. 9.

166. Pi'el, Pu'al retain the י, as in BH : יִחֵסוֹ to give a pedigree, San. 82 b ; יִיפִּיתָה to make fair, good, j. BB viii. 1 ; מְיַיסֵּר to chasten San. 39 a ; מְיַיתֵּם to make orphaned, Pes. 49 a ; יְיַבֵּם to marry a brother's widow, Yeb. xv. 10 ; יְיַחֲדֶנּוּ to set apart, Ṭoh. viii. 6 ; לְיַגְּעָהּ to weary her, So. ii. 1 ; לְיַישְׁנָן to make old, BB 91 b ; מְיוּגָּעִין Ket. 8 b ; מְיוּחֶדֶת BQ i. 2 ; מְיוּפָּה j. Giṭ. ii. 1 ; מְיוּשָּׁן Ned. ix. 8.

Nithpa'el. (i) תִּתְוַדַּע Ab. i. 10 ; הִתְוַדֵּה (imperat.) ; לְהִתְוַדּוֹת to confess, San. vi. 2, but also מִתְיַשֶּׁבֶת Kin. iii. 6 ; נִתְיַישְּׁבָה Ber. 31 a. So the forms נתוספו 'Er. vii. 7 ; יתוספו Pes. 87 b ; מתוספת to be added, Šab. 152 a ; מתוקדת to be burnt, Lev. R. 7 ; נתותרו to be left over, Pes. 159 b ; Yo. 46 a, traditionally pronounced like the Aram. Ittaph'al : נִתּוֹסְפוּ, מִתּוֹסֶפֶת, מִתּוֹקֶדֶת, נִתּוֹתְרוּ.[4] (ii) נִתְיַחֵד Giṭ. vii ; נִתְיַבְּמוּ Yeb. i. 4 ; נִתְיַפְּתָה Ta'a. 23 b ; נִתְיַפֵּיתָ Gen. R. 59 ; תִּתְיָאֵשׁ to despair, Ab. i. 7 ; תִּתְיַיפִּי Ta'a. 23 b ; יִתְיַחֵד Qid. iv. 12 ; מִתְיַבְּמוֹת Yeb. 3. 1 ; לְהִתְיָהֵר to be haughty, BB 10 b.

167. Hiph'il : (i) הוֹאִיל Kil. v. 1 ; הוֹדִיעַ Ab. iv. 22 ; הוֹתִירָה

[1] Albrecht's suggestion (§ 106 e) that these and similar infinitives (לֵאמַר, לִיתֵּן, &c.) are a combination of the imperf. with the preposition (= לְיֵרֵד, לְיִתֵּן, לְיֹאמַר) is against the spirit of the language.

[2] לידתה Ket. iv. 3, cited by Albrecht (§ 111 b), is not an infin., but a verbal noun : לֵידָתָהּ = יְלִידָתָהּ ; cf. below, § 228, and above, § 62.

[3] The preformative ה may have been preserved here because of the assonance with the preceding לְהוֹדִיעַ ; cf. above, § 115.

[4] This traditional pronunciation seems to be more correct than that of the simple Nithpa'el : נִתְוַתְּרוּ, מִתְוַקֶּדֶת, מִתְוַסֶּפֶת, נִתְוַסְּפוּ. In this latter the ו, as a consonant, would have been written twice ; cf. above, § 57. Cf. also the Targum : אִתּוֹקַד, Lev. x. 16 ; 2 Sam. xxiii. 7.

Ter. v. 9; אוֹנְתַנִי (cf. above, § 142); הוֹקִירוּ to become dear, BM v. 9; הוֹתַרְתֶּם ib. vii. 2; יוֹצִיא, מוֹצִיא Ket. viii. 4; הוֹשַׁע save! Ber. iv. 4; הוֹדוּ to agree, Pes. iv. 9; מוֹרִיקוֹת to become yellow, So. iii. 4; לְהוֹדִיעַ Ab. iv. 22.

(ii) יֵישִׁירוּ Ber. 17 a (from Prov. iv. 25); מֵטִיבָה San. vii. 10; מֵנִיק Bek. 7 b; מֵנִיקָה Ket. v. 5; מֵינֶקֶת Ket. 60 a; לְהֵנִיק Pes. 112 a; לְהֵיטִיב[1] Yo. iii. 4.

(iii) הִצִּית BQ 22 b; יַצִּית[2] to kindle, Yo. vi. 7; מַצִּיעִין to spread, Šab. xviii. 3; מַצִּיק Ker. 5 b.

Hoph'al: הוּקְרוּ BB. v. 8; מוּבָל to be led, Ṭoh. vii. 5; מוּסָף to be added, Šebu. i. 6: מוּטָב San. vii. 10; מוּצַּעַת 'Ar. vi. 3; מוּצֶּתֶת Num. R. 12.

168. The two verbs יעד, יתר (original פ"ו), have formed in MH secondary roots ועד, ותר. Exx. Pi'el: וִיעֵד Lam. R. ii. 13; לְהִתְוַעֵד, נִתְוַעֲדוּ Num. R. 14. Qal: וָתְרוּ j. Suk. v. 5; Cant. R. i. 6. Pi'el: מְוַותֵּר San. xi. 5. Nithpa'el: יִתְוַותְּרוּ BQ 50 a. These may, perhaps, be loan-words from Aram.

The verb הלך forms the imperfect Qal and the whole of the Hiph'il from ילך, as in BH. Exx. Qal: יֵלֵךְ Ket. xiii. 7; תֵּלֵךְ ib. vii. 4; תֵּלְכִי Ned. vii. 9; אֵלֵךְ, נֵלֵךְ 'Er. iii. 5, Inf. לֵילֵךְ ib. iv. 10; BQ i. 1, but also לָלֶכֶת[3] Nid. iv. 2; לְכִי Ket. xii. 3; San. vii. 10, Hiph'il: הוֹלַכְתֶּם Šebu. vii. 6; מוֹלִיךְ Ket. xii. 1; מוֹלִיכִין 'Er. vi. 7; הוֹלֵךְ (imperat.) Giṭ. vi. 1; יוֹלִיךְ 'AZ iii. 9; לְהוֹלִיכוֹ Pea vi. 3. The Intensive stem is formed throughout from הלך.

(4) Verbs פ"נ.

169. These verbs conform generally to the BH פ'נ verbs. The נ is regularly assimilated to the following consonant whenever

[1] Some of these forms may be derived from the cognate ע"ו roots: טוב, נוק; cf. below, § 185.

[2] L and other texts have יצת = יַצַּת, Qal.

[3] The form להלוך in edd. is an error for לְהַלֵּךְ, Pi'el, as always in L, and also in edd. BQ ii. 1, &c.

preceded by a preformative with a vowel, or it is dropped altogether where it would have to begin a word with a *sh*ᵉ*wa* as in the imperative Qal.

(i) Qal. Imperfect: יִגּוֹב, תִּגּוֹב to dry up, ʻAZ v. 3; יִגּוֹם to bite off, ʻUq. ii. 6; יִגַּע to touch, BM ii. 3; תִּטּוֹל, תִּטְּלִי to take up, Yᵉb. xv. 3; אֶטּוֹל Pe. vi. 11; אֶטַּע to plant, Kil. i. 8; יִקּוֹב to bore, Šab. ii. 4; יִקָּבֶנָּה ib. xxii. 3; יִתֵּן to give, ib. iii. 5; יִתְּנֶנָּה ib. ii. 4; יִדּוֹר to vow, Naz. viii. 1; אֶתֵּן Tᵉr. x. 6; תִּשֹּׁךְ Šab. xvi. 7; יִטְּלוּ Kᵉt. x. 2. The vowel *ō* is sometimes retained on the analogy of ע"ע verbs (— תִּסּוֹבִּי, יִסּוֹבּוּ) in the second fem. sing. and in the plural: תִּדּוֹרִי Nᵉd. x. 7; יִשּׁוֹכוּ to bite in, adhere, Ḥal. ii. 4.

Imperative: דּוֹר San. iii. 5; טוֹל Yo. vi. 4; טְלִי Giṭ. 78 a; טְלוּ Maʻa. ii. 1; but also טוֹלוּ Meʻil. vi. 1 (L טְלוּ); תֵּן Giṭ. vi. 1; תְּנוּ ib. i. 6; תֵּינוּ in pause, t. Giṭ. vi. 8; שָׂא lift, Taʻa. iv. 8.

The Infinitive is formed from the Imperfect: לִידּוֹר Nᵉd. iii. 1 (BH לִנְדּוֹר Num. vi. 2); לִיגּוֹף to strike; לִישּׁוֹךְ BQ i. 4; לִיטּוֹל Ab. v. 8; לִיזּוֹר to become a Nazirite, Nᵉd. 3 b; לִיתּוֹר to loosen, j. Bik. i. 8. So לִישָּׂא to marry, Yᵉb. i. 4; לִיתֵּן Šab. i. 8, except in the standing expression לָשֵׂאת וְלָתֵת ʻAZ i. 1; ii. 3, &c. (literally: to take and give, i.e. to buy, to deal), where the old forms have been preserved for their assonance.[5]

These infinitives may, perhaps, be older than the BH forms with the termination ת. Cf. לְתִתֵּן 1 Kings vi. 19, which may be a *forma mixta* of a colloquial לִתֵּן and the literary לָתֵת. So, perhaps, תתן ib. xvii. 14 (Kᵉtib), is a *forma mixta* of תֵּן (לִתֵּן) and תֵּת.

170. When the second radical is a guttural, the נ is preserved: יִנְעוֹל to put on a shoe, Para viii. 2; תִּנְעוֹל Yo. viii. 1; לִנְעוֹל Šab. xiii. 16; לִנְהוֹג Ab. vi. 3. So also sometimes in other cases: תִּנְזוֹר Naz. 17 a; נְצוֹר guard, Bᵉr. 17 a (liturgical); לִנּוֹטְעָה Kil. ii. 4 (cf. לִנְטוֹעַ Jer. i. 10).

[1] Cf. the writer's remarks, *JQR.*, xx, p. 686, footnote 3.

171. (ii) Niph'al. Perfect: נִיקַּב, נִיקְּבָה Ḥul. iii. 1: נִיקְּרוּ to be bored, j. Ter. viii. 5; נִשֵּׂאת Ket. iv. 4; נִישְּׂאוּ ib. v. 2; נִשֵּׂאתֶם t. BB viii. 9 (fem.!) Imperfect: תִּנָּשֵׂא Yeb. ii. 9; יִנָּקְדוּ to be spotted, Ma'a. i. 3; יִנָּתְנוּ Ket. ix. 2. Infinitive: לְהִנָּטֵל Para v. 9; לִינָּשֵׂא Yeb. ii. 10; לִזּוֹק to be injured, Pes. 8 b (cf. לִידּוֹן below, § 177). Participle: נִידָּב to be donated; נִידָּר Meg. i. 10; נִידָּרִים 'Ar. i. 1; נִיטַּעַת Oh. xviii. 3; נִשֵּׂאת Ket. i. 1; נִישְּׂאוֹת t. BB xviii. 19; נִתָּז to squirt, Ḥul. vi. 6; נִיתָּזִין[1] Makš. v. 2; נִיתָּנִין Zeb. viii. 9. Some show ō in the second syllable instead of ā: נִיזּוֹקִין Pes. 8 b; נִסּוֹק to be kindled, Kel. v. 6; נִיסּוֹקֶת j. Ber. ix. 4; נִיצּוֹל to deliver, Šab. 32 a; נִצּוֹלֶת, נִצּוֹלִין Para xi. 1; נִשּׁוֹל to slip off, Lev. R. 37; נִיתּוֹרִין j. Bik. i. 8; נִיתּוֹשׁ to pluck out, Gen. R. 56.

נ is retained in verbs with second radical ע: נִנְעֲלוּ to be locked, Pes. v. 5; נִנְעֶלֶת 'Ed. v. 6; נִנְעָר to be shaken, BB 74 b.

The Intensive Stem is regular.

172. (iii) Hiph'il: הִגִּיעוּ to reach, Bik. iii. 3; הִדִּירוּ Ned. iii. 3; הִדַּרְתָּהּ Ned. 23 a; הִדַּרְתִּי Šab. 127 b; הִזִּיק BQ i. 2; הִיטֵּתִי to incline, Ber. i. 3; הִסִּיקוּהָ to kindle, Šab. iii. 1; הִכִּישָׁהּ to strike, BM 30 b; הִשִּׂיא Ket. vi. 6; הִתַּרְתֶּם to permit, Yeb. xv. 3; but also with נ retained: הִנְהִיג to lead, Kil. viii. 2, 3; הִנְעִילוֹ Qid. 22 b; הִנְגִּיב to face south (denom. from נגב), 'Er. 53 b. Imperfect: יַגִּיחוּהוּ BQ iv. 4; יַסִּיחַ to move, Šab. 82 b; יַסִּיק Kel. v. 1; תַּתִּירוּ Yeb. xv. 3; but also יַנְקִידוּ j. Ma'a. i. 3. Infinitive: לְהַזִּיק BQ i. 1; לְהַסִּיעוֹ to move, Kel. v. 7; לְהַקִּישׁ to compare, BM ii. 5; לְהַשִּׂיאוֹ Qid. 29 a.

Participle: מַדִּיר, מַדֶּרֶת So. iii. 8; מַטִּיל Yo. iii. 2; מַקִּיף to strike, Bek. vii. 6, but also מַנְקִיף So. 22 b; מַשִּׁיר to drop, Šab. 67 a; מַשֶּׁרֶת Naz. vi. 3; מַשִּׁילִין to cause to drop, Be. v. 1.

173. (iv) Hoph'al. Perf.: הוּכַּר Qid. iii. 5; הוּזַּק, הוּזְּקוּ BQ iii. 2; הוּסַּק Kel. v. 4; הוּקְּשָׁה to be compared, Ker. 3 a. Imperf.: יוּדַּח San. x. 4; יוּתַּז Ḥul. 27 b; יוּתַּךְ Me'il. ii. 3; יוּתַּץ 'AZ iii. 2.

[1] L has Qal in both passages: נותזים, נותזן.

Partic.: מוּגָּה corrected, Pes. 112 a; מוּדָּר Ned. iv. 1; מוּזֶּה Pa. xii. 8; מוּכֵּה Ket. vii. 11; מוּכַּת ib. i. 3; מוּטִּין Kel. x. 1; מוּטָּה Oh. ix. 9; מוּקֶּפֶת surrounded, Suk. i. 10; מוּקָּפוֹת Meg. i. 2.

174. The verb לקח forms the imperfect Qal on the analogy of the פ״נ verbs, as in BH: יִקַּח Yo. vi. 1; יִקְחוּ.

The Niph'al is regular, but some later texts show assimilation: נִיקַּח 'Er. iii. 1 (L נלקח); נִקְחֵית, נִקְחִין Men. 42 b.

(5) Verbs ע״ו, ע״י.

175. In this class of verbs, MH follows faithfully the model of BH, but has carried certain forms to a fuller development, especially in the Intensive Stem. The ע״י forms, like בין, דין, דיש, זין, לין, &c. differ very little from the ע״ו forms, and the two classes may be treated together.

176. (i) *The Simple Stem.*

Qal. MH has preserved the distinction between transitive verbs which have the vowel *ā* in the perfect, and intransitive verbs which have *ē* or *ō* in the perfect.

Exx. Transitive: גָּפָם he corked them, MŠ iii. 12; זָן to feed, Ber. 58 b (Singer, p. 319); סָג to fence, Ab. deRN. i. 7; עָג to draw a circle, Ta'a. iii. 8; חָס to pity, Neg. ii. 5; with the older fem. termination ת: שָׁבָת to return, Lev. R. 23; חַבְתִּי to be guilty, BQ i. 2; חָסוּ j. Ket. iv. 14; דָּשׁ ע״י to thresh, Ber. 58 a; זָזָה to move, Ket. ii. 9; זָזוּ 'Er. iv. 1; נָרָה to harrow, 'Ar. ix. 1; שַׂמְתָּ to put, Ber. 28 b; דַּנְתֶּם to judge, San. vi. 6; דַּנְתִּי Sifre Num. xix. 2.

Intransitive: מֵתוּ, מֵתָה, מֵת to die, Yeb. i. 2; מַתִּי Giṭ. vii. 3; בּוֹשָׁה to be ashamed, Qid. 81 b; בּוֹשְׁתִּי t. Oh. v. 11; בּוֹשׁוּ So. ix. 15; בָּא to come, Naz. iii. 6; בָּאָה Yeb. xv. 6; with termination ת: בָּאָת Ned. ix. 5; בָּאתָה Yeb. xv. 1 (L בָּאָת); בָּאתֶם, בָּאנוּ Ber. 63 a.

Imperf.: יָדוּךְ to pound, j. Be. ix. 9; אָזוּן, יָזוּן to feed, Ket. xii. 1; יָזוּעַ to sweat, Ṭoh. ix. 1; יָחוּץ to form a partition; תָּחוּץ Zeb. 19 a; יָחוּצוּ Makš. iii. 8; תָּזוּחַ to move, be elated (with דַּעַת as subject)

Keṭ. 67 b; תָּפוּג to grow cold, weak, Yo. iii. 5 (L and other texts תָּפִיג); יְשׁוּפֶנּוּ to rub, Kel. xiv. 5; יְשׁוּפֵם ib. xvi. 1; יָזוּנוּ Mid. iv. 5; נָשׁוּט to go to and fro, Ber. 18 a; אָדוּן BQ ii. 10 (L אָדִין); תָּמוּת Tem. iv. 2; תָּחוּבוּ Ab. i. 11; יָבֹא Naz. iii. 6; תָּבוֹאוּ Šebu. iv. 5.

Infin.: לָדוּכָהּ Be. 14 a; לְזוּנָהּ Ket. xii. 3; לָזוּז ib. 1; לָחוּץ 'Er. iii. 1; לָמוּל to circumcise, Šab. xix. 4; לָסוּךְ to anoint, Dam. iii. 1; לָשׁוּחַ to bend, Ab. iii. 21. Imperat.: לִין 'Er. 52 a; בּוֹאִי Ber. 18 b; בּוֹאוּ Yo. ii. 4.

Partic.: זָן, זָנִין, זָנָה Ket. xii. 1; חָב BQ i. 1; חָבִין 'Er. vii. 11; חָלוֹת dance, L (ed. חוּלוֹת), Ta'a. iv. 8; לָשׁ to knead, Šab. vii. 2; לָשׁוֹת Pes. iii. 9; צָד to catch, Šab. vii. 3; צָדִין Be. iii. 1; דָּשׁ Šab. vii. 2; דָּן, דָּנִין San. ii. 1; מֵת Yeb. xvi. 6; גֵּר proselyte, Yad. iv. 4; עֵר awake, BQ ii. 5; בָּא BQ iii. 5 (*ā* because of א), but בּוֹר; בּוֹרָה to be waste, BM 101 a; בּוֹשׁ Ma'a. iii. 5; בּוֹשָׁה Dam. iii. 6; בּוֹשִׁין Ket. viii. 1; חוֹצָה Miq. x. 3; נוֹחַ easy, Men. x. 3; נוֹחִין Gen. R. 11.

Passive: טוּחַ to plaster, Mid. iv. 1; טוּחוֹת Nid. 24 a; לוּשָׁה j. So. ix. 14; מוּלִים Pes. v. 3; סוּכוֹת j. Bik. i. 3; שׁוּמָה to value, t. BQ x. 1; נִירָה t. BM ix. 29; נִיר, נִירוֹת 'Er. 17 b.

177. *Niph'al.* Perfect: The preformative נ is pointed with *ḥireq* (— נִי), evidently on the analogy of the strong verb. Exx. נִידּוֹנוּ RH 12 a; נִיטּוֹחַ Ab. deRN. xxiv. 5; נִלּוֹשָׁה Ḥal. ii. 2; נִיפּוֹחוּ Gen. R. 13; נִיצּוֹד Šab. 106 b; נִצּוֹדוּ Be. iii. 2; נִיזּוֹנְתֶּם (fem.) t. BB viii. 19.

Imperf.: יֵאוֹר to be light, j. Ber. i. 1; יֵיאוֹרוּ Yo. viii. 5; יֵאוֹתוּ to enjoy, Ber. viii. 6; יִדּוֹן Oh. vi. 3, 7; San. viii. 8, 9 (L ed. נִידּוֹן Partic.); יִזּוֹנוּ Ket. xiii. 3; תִּלּוֹשׁ Ter. v. 2, 3; יִלּוֹשׁוּ ib. 1; יִמּוֹל, יִמּוֹלוּ Šab. xix. 5; יִצּוֹדוּ ib. i. 6; תֵּירוֹם to be lifted, Ter. v. 2; יִשּׁוֹף to rub, t. BM xi. 8.

Infin.: לִידּוֹן Giṭ. iii. 4; Ab. iv. 29; לִידּוֹחַ Miq.

Partic.: נֵיאוֹתִין Šab. iii. 6; נֵיאוֹתוֹת Yo. 11 a; נִידּוֹן, נִידּוֹנִין RH i. 2; נִידּוֹנֶת RH 16 a; נִידּוֹכִין Bez. i. 7; נִיזּוֹן Giṭ. xii. 6; נִיזּוֹנֶת, נִיזּוֹנוֹת Ket. xii. 2; נִיסּוֹטִין to move, t. Zab. iv. 6; נֵעוֹר Ab. iii. 4;

נֵעוֹרִין Ber. 61 b. But with *ā* in the preformative: נָדוֹן BQ ii. 5; Ya. iv. 3, &c. (cf. 2 Sam. xix. 10); נָלוֹז to twist, Kil. ix. 8; נָמוֹךְ to be low, ib. iv. 7; נְמוֹשׁוֹת to feel (aged persons who grope their way), Pea viii. 1.[1]

178. (ii) *The Intensive Stem.* In the formation of this stem MH has further developed the two methods already found in BH, viz. (a) Hardening of the vowel into the cognate consonants (ו or י) on the analogy of the strong verb, and (b) Reduplication.

(*a*) Hardening the vowel into a consonant.

(*α*) Into ו. Pi'el: כִּיוֵּן to make firm, direct, Ber. ii. 1; כִּוְּונוּ MQ ii. 3; יְכַוֵּן ib.; יְכַוְּונוּ Ber. v. 1; לְכַוֵּין Kil. v. 1; לְקַוֵּיץ to remove thorns, MQ 5 a; מְזַוֵּג BM 90 b; מְתַוְּוכוֹת to halve (from תּוֹךְ), j. Br. i. 1. Pu'al: מְכֻוָּן Ṭoh. iii. 2; מְכֻוֶּנֶת Kel. xxviii. 7; מְכֻוָּנוֹת Makš. ii. 5; מְתֻוֶּכֶת j. Ber. i. 1. Nithpa'el: נִתְכַּוֵּן BQ iv. 6; נִתְכַּוַּנְתִּי, נִתְכַּוְּונוּ ib. viii. 1; מִזְדַּוְּוגִין to join together, San. v. 5; נִתְקַוְּוצָה Šebi. iv. 2.[2]

179. (*β*) Into י. *Pi'el.* Perf.: בִּיֵּישׁ to shame, BQ iii. 10; טִיֵּיל to walk, Suk. 28 b; כִּיְּירוּ to decorate; סִיְּידוּ to plaster, 'AZ iii. 7; טִיְּיבָה to improve, j. Šebi. iv. 2; זִיַּפְתָּ, זִיַּפְתֶּם to forge, j. So. vii. 3; קִיַּמְתָּ to confirm, fulfil, BQ iii. 9; קִיְּימוּ 'Ed. i. 3; חִיְּיבוּ to declare guilty, Šab. xii. 3; חִיַּבְתֶּם Exod. R. 32; תְּסַיֵּיעַ to accompany, assist, Šab. 104 a; גַּיְּרֵנִי (imperat.) ib. 31 a; לְסַיֵּיף to destroy, Gen. R. 100; לְפַיְּיסוֹ to appease, Ber. 28 b; מְבַיֵּישׁ BQ viii. 1; מְחַיֵּיב Šab. x. 6; מְחַיְּיבִין Dam. i. 3; מְעַיֵּין to look, Ber. 55 a; מְדַיְּירִין to cause cattle to dwell on a field, to manure, Šebi. iii. 1; מְדַיֶּינֶת, מְדַיְּינִין Qoh. R. ii. 8.

Pu'al: מְגוּיָּד cut up (from גִּיד artery), Yeb. xvi. 3; מְזוּיָּף Giṭ. x. 6; מְצוּיָּן marked, t. Šeq. i. 5; מְקוּיָּים BM 7 a; מְקוּיָּמִין Neg.

[1] Another reading has מְשׁוֹשׁוֹת; cf. the comment of R. Simson, *ad loc.*

[2] The verb נוול, So. i. 6; Naz. iv. 5, &c., cited by Albrecht (§ 114 b) does not belong here. It is a MH modification of the BH verb נבל; cf. above, § 58.

v. 3; מְצוּיָּיצוֹת with fringes, Šab. 25 b: מְצוּיָּירוֹת painted, Kel. xxviii. 4.

Nithpa'el: נִדַּייר to be manured, Šebi. iv. 2; נִטַּייְבָה to be improved, ib.; נִתְפַּיֵּים Ber. 33 a; נִסְתַּיְּיפוּ j. Dam. i. 1; יִתְקַיֵּים Giṭ. i. 3; נִתְגַּיַּירְתִּי Yeb. 47 a; אֶתְגַּיֵּיר, תִּתְגַּיְּירִי Qid. iii. 7; לְהִזְדַּיֵּיף Giṭ. ii. 4; לְהִתְגַּיֵּיר Yeb. 47 a; מִתְבַּיֵּישׁ BQ viii. 1; מִתְחַיֵּיב Ab. iii. 4; מִתְקַיֶּימֶת ib. iii. 9.

180. Of this formation BH shows only one example with ו (עִוְּדוּנִי Ps. cxix. 61) and two examples with י: חִיֵּב (Dan. i. 10; cf. Sirach xi. 21), and קִיֵּם Esther ix. 31, &c.; cf. Sirach xlii. 23, and Ges.-K., § 72 m). The formation is generally considered to have been borrowed by late BH from Aram. But it is found also in other Semitic languages, e.g. Arabic. That earlier Hebrew possessed this power of converting the vocalic middle radical into a hard consonant, is shown by the cognate nouns אָוֶן, מָוֶת, תָּוֶךְ, דַּיִשׁ, חַיִל, צַיִד, &c., and by uncontracted verbs like רָוַח, עָוַד, עִוֵּת, קִוָּה, צִוָּה, which have hardened the middle *waw*, owing to the presence in the root of another weak letter. It is, therefore, quite probable that this formation for the intensive stem was developed within Hebrew itself on the analogy of the strong verb. It may even be assumed that the formation existed in the spoken language long before it appeared in literature, and that MH received it from the spoken language of BH times.[1]

181. (*b*) Reduplication. (*a*) Doubling of the second radical, Po'lel, and Nithpo'lel. These forms are rarer in MH than in BH Only the following examples are found in MH:

Po'lel: יְעוֹרֵר to awake, MQ i. 5; לְכוֹנֵן Ex. R. 15; לְרוֹמֵם to exalt, Pes. x. 5 (liturgical passage); מְכוֹנֵן to wheel round (denom. of מֵכַנִי μηχανή, Yo. iii. 10. L has, perhaps, correctly מְכוּנַן, Pol'al); Makš. iv. 1; מְעוֹפֶפֶת to fly, Ḥul. xii. 3; מְעוֹרְרִים MŠ v. 15; מְפוֹצֶצֶת

[1] Cf. Koenig, *Lehrgebäude*, i, p. 452 f.

to shatter, Lev. R. 27; מְקוֹנֶנֶת to lament, Ket. iv. 4; מְקוֹנְנוֹת MQ iii. 9; מְרוֹמַמְתּוֹ Ab. vi. 2; מְשׁוֹרְרִים singers, 'Ar. 11 b.

Nithpo'lel: נִתְמוֹטְטוּ to totter, Ber. 32 b; יִתְעוֹרְרוּ Lev. R. vii. 9; הִתְנוֹפְפִי (imperat.), to wave, 'AZ 24 b; לְהִתְבּוֹנֵן BQ 27 b; מִשְׁתּוֹקֶקֶת to long, Yeb. 62 b; Ab. deRN. i. 7; מִתְמוֹטְטִין BM 71 a (cf. Sirach xxxii. 2); מִתְפּוֹצֵץ Qid. 30 b.

182. (*β*) Doubling of the whole root. This is more frequent in MH than in BH; cf. above, § 108.

Pilpel: וִעְוְעוּ, וִעְוַעְתּוּ to shake, 'Or. i. 3; לִגְלֵג to mock, Šab. 30 b; נִעְנְעוּ to shake, Suk. iii. 9; נִעְנַעְתִּי Yeb. 121 a; יְנַעְנְעֶנּוּ Šab. xx. 5; יְקַעְקַע to tattoo, Mak. iii. 6; יְשַׁלְשְׁלוּ to let down by chain, Šebi. iv. 10; מְטַלְטֵל to move, 'Er. x. 4; מְטַלְטֶלֶת BB iv. 3; מְלַגְלֵג Ber. 39 a; מְנַפְנֶפֶת Oh. viii. 5; מְשַׁלְשְׁלִים, שִׁלְשְׁלוּ BQ 82 b.

Pulpal. Participle only: מְחוּלְחֶלֶת shaken, Kel. x. 3; מְשׁוּלְשֶׁלֶת ib. viii. 1; מְנוּנָרוֹת (= מְנוּרְנָרוֹת), well harrowed, Men. 85 a: מְטוּשְׁטָשׁוֹת rubbed off, Meg. 18 b; מְנוּנָעִין Be. 25 a.

Hithpalpel: נִזְדַעְזְעָה to be shaken, BQ 82 b; נִתְנַמְנְמוּ to slumber, Pes. x. 8; תִּטַּמְטֵם (= תִּתְטַמְ׳), to be kneaded through, Ḥal. iii. 1; לְהִתְנַמְנֵם Yo. i. 7; לִיטַּלְטֵל Kel. xv. 1; מִטַּלְטְלִין Šab, iii. 6; מִתְחַלְחְלִים Miq. iv. 3.

(iii) *The Causative Stem.*

183. *Hiph'il*: הֵמִיר to change, Temu. i. 1; הֵרִיחָה to smell, Yo. viii. 4; הֱקִיצָתוּ to awaken, Num. R. 10; הֲבַנְתָּה to understand, Šab. 31 a; הֵנַחְתָּ to give rest, ib. 152 b; הֵעַדְתָּ to testify, Yeb. vii. 3 (L הֶעִידוֹתָה); הֵעַדְתִּי Yeb. 99 b; הֵעַדְנוּ Mak. 3 a; הֵמַכְתִּי to lower, t. Naz. iv. 7; הֵצַצְתִּי to gaze, Ḥul. 47 b; הֵרַחְתִּי Yo. 39 b; הֵשַׁבְתָּה to reply, Sifra (Weiss), 113 a; הֱשַׁבְתַּנִי Pes. 69 a.

For the omission of the separating vowel before the afformative in BH, cf. Ges.-K., § 72 k.

Imperf.: יָזִיזֵם. יְזִיזֶנּוּ to move, Be. iii. 5; יְמִירֶנּוּ Tem. i. 1; נְעִידְךָ Šebu. iii. 8; תְּעִידוּנִי ib. iv. 5; יָפִיחַ to blow, Šab. 49 a; יְשִׁיבֶנּוּ Ber. v. 1; יָבִיאוּ Naz. iv. 6. Imperat.: הָבֵא Pes. vi. 2; הָפֵג to cool,

Yo. i. 7; הֶעִידוּנִי Šᵉbu. iii. 8; הָרִיעוּ Ta'a. ii. 10. Infin.: לְהָמִיר Tᵉm. i. 1; לַהֲמִיתוֹ San. 53 a; לְהָסִיט Zab. iii. 3.

Partic.: מֵבִין Ḥag. ii. 1; מֵסִיט Zab. v. 1; מְטִיבָה San. vii. 10; מְזִיזִין Ab. iii. 17; מְמִירִין Tᵉm. i. 1.

184. *Hoph'al*: הוּחֲלָה to occur, Bᵉr. 31 a; הוּרְמָה to be lifted, Ḥal. ii. 8; יוּנַף to be waived, Mid. iii. 4; תּוּדַח to be rinsed, Makš. iv. 3; תּוּצַץ to sprout forth, Qid. 66 a; מוּכָן prepared, Be. i. 1; מוּמָר Tᵉm. i. 1; מוּרָם Zᵉb. v. 6; מוּמָתִין San. vi. 2.[1]

185. Note 1. As in BH, so in MH some ע"ו roots are found also in פ"י forms. Thus, טוב to be good = יטב; נוק to suck = ינק; קוץ to awake = יקץ. So also in ע"ע forms: דוך to crush = דכך; זוח to move = זחח: זול to be cheap = זלל; חוץ to separate = חצץ; מוש to feel = משש.

186. Note 2. The verb נוח forms also a causative by assimilation, as in BH, in the sense 'to lay down', e.g. הִנִּיחַ BB ix. i; מַנְּחָה Bᵉr. viii. 4; הַנַּחְנוּהוּ So. ix. 6; מוּנַּח BM iii. 4; מוּנַּחַת Qid. 66 a.

187. Note 3. The verb נום (BH נאם) to speak, shows some strange forms, probably of an artificial character. Thus נוֹמִי he spoke, Zᵉb. iv. 5; נוֹמָת, נוֹמְיָת she spoke, Yᵉb. xvi. 7; נוֹמֵיתִי I spoke, ib.; נוֹמֵינוּ (L נוֹמֵנוּ) we spoke, Giṭ. vi. 7; but also נָם, נַמְתִּי t. Naz. iv. 7; נָאַמְתִּי Sifre Num. xix. 2; נָאַם, ibid. xxviii. 2.

(6) Verbs ע"ע.

188. The tendency, already strong in BH, to make these verbs approximate to the standard of the strong triliteral type is carried still further in MH. Biliteral forms are the regular type

[1] In the curious expression אהיה אובין, 'AZ iii. 5 (L) the form אובין seems to be treated as a participle Qal, and should be pointed אוֹבֵין. It is probably a scribal expansion of אָבִין = אוֹבִין. הוֹבִירָהּ, BM. ix. 3, is an Aramaism for הבירהּ, from בּוּר to be fallow, due to the influence of the following Aram. form אוֹבִיר. L has the correct reading הבירה in BM. In 'Ar. ix. 1 L is defective.

only in the causative stem and, to a smaller extent, in the Imperf. Qal and Niph'al. In the other parts of the Qal and the Niph'al triliteral forms predominate. In the Intensive Stem they are used exclusively.

Aram., on the other hand, has preserved and accentuated more strongly than any other Semitic language the natural affinity of the ע"ע verbs with the ע"ו verbs. The biliteral forms of the ע'ע predominate in Aram.

189. (i) *The Simple Stem.*

Qal. Perfect. Triliteral: חֲצָצוֹ to divide, Oh. xv. 4; מָדַד to measure, 'AZ v. 7; פָּקַק to stop, Miq. iii. 2; רָקַק to spit, BQ viii. 6; שָׁגַג to err, Šab. 95 a; רְקָקָה Y^eb. xii. 3; קָצַצְתָּ to cut, BQ 91 b; חָקַקְתִּי to enact a law, Yo. 67 b; טָנְנוּ to become moist, Makš. iii. 4; עָמְמוּ to become dim, t. Šab. iii. 2; צָלְלוּ to clarify, t. Nid. iii. 11; חֲגַגְתֶּם to offer the Festival sacrifice, P^es. 70 b.

Biliteral: חַג Ḥag. i. 9; כַּח to cough, 'Er. 99 a; רַק Ḥag. 9 a; רַבּוּ to be many, Šab. i. 7.

Imperfect: יִקְצְצֶנּוּ to cut, BQ 91 b; יִשְׁגּוֹג Šab. 69 a; יִשְׁלוֹל to baste, j. MQ iii. 5. But usually biliteral: יָבוֹר to choose, Ab. ii. 1; תָּבוֹר Giṭ. v. 9; אָבוֹר Ma'a. ii. 6; יָגוֹד to cut, Pa. ii. 2; אָגוֹד BB 13 a; יָחוֹף to cleanse the head, Naz. vi. 3; יָמוֹד B^er. 30 b; יָקוֹץ BQ x. 2. So Imperat.: גוֹד BB 13 a; כּוֹף to bend, B^er. 60 b; קוֹצוּ Ab. d^eRN. xxxix. 1; but also מְדוֹד Yo. 39 a.

Infinit.: לִגְזוֹז to shear, Ḥul. 138 a; לִגְרוֹר to drag, Kel. v. 7; לַחֲצוֹץ Be. iv. 6; לְלוֹתְתָן to mix, t. Makš. iii. 7; לְמוֹלְלָן to hem, MQ 26 a; לִקְצוֹץ Miq. x. 5; לְקוֹצְצוֹ (L לְקוֹצוֹ) Š^ebi. iv. 10. Biliteral: לָבוֹז to spoil, Pe. iv. 1, 2; לָחוֹף to rub, Naz. 59 a; לָמוֹד MŠ v. 9; לָפוֹק Kel. xxviii. 2; לָקוֹץ 'AZ i. 8.

Participles, only triliteral: בּוֹרֵר San. iii. 1; זוֹמֵם, זוֹמֶמֶת, זוֹמְמִין, to give false evidence, Mak. i. 1, 2, 3, &c.;[1] מוֹרְדִין 'Er. v. 4; רוֹפֶפֶת

[1] From Deut. xix. 19.

to shake, t. Ḥul. ii. 12; שׁוֹתֵת to flow gently, Oh. iii. 5; גָּמוּם to level, Ḥul. 59 a; רָעוּעַ, רְעוּעָה to break, Kel. iii. 5; צְפוּפִין to press, Ab. v. 5.

190. *Niph'al.* Perf.: נִגְמַם Šebi. i. 8; נִגְמְמוּ Bek. vi. 4; נִזְקַק to bind, Naz. ix. 4; נִקְצַץ BM ix. 2; נִכְפְּפָה 'Ar. 19 a; נִבְזְזָה Bik. i. 8; נִכְלְלוּ to complete, include, j. So. vii. 4. Biliteral: נִימוֹק to decay, Nid. iii. 4; נִימַקּוּ Bik. i. 8 (L נימוקו).

Imperf.: יִקָּצֵץ 'AZ i. 8; תִּקָּצֵץ Nid. ii. 1; יִקָּצְצוּ Ned. iii. 5; but biliteral forms are more common: יֵחַם to be hot, Be. ii. 5; יֵחַמּוּ Šab. iii. 5; יִמַּסּוּ to melt; יִצַּנּוּ to be cold, Šab. xxii. 4; יִצַּלּוּ to clarify, ib. xx. 2.

With *ŏ*, instead of *ă*, on the analogy of the ע"ו verbs: יִגּוֹלּוּ to roll, Ber. 7 a; יֵחוֹלּוּ to be common, Šebi. i. 8; יֵחוֹמּוּ Šab. 41 b;[1] יִמּוֹקּוּ (L יִמַּקּוּ) Ta'a. iii. 8.

Infin.: לְהִבָּלֵל to mix, Men. xi. 4; לִיגָּזֵז BQ ix. 1; לְהִמָּדֵד Dam. ii. 5; but also לֵחַם Kel. xiv. i.

Partic.: נִבְלָלִין Men. xii. 4; נִגְרָר 'Er. x. 11; נִגְרֶרֶת, נִגְרָרִין Be. ii. 10; נִזְקָקִין Šab. 12 b; נִמְדָּדִין 'Ar. vii. 1; נִקְצָצוֹת Ned. iii. 5, but also Biliteral: נֵרוֹק to spit, Miq. vii. 1; נִימוֹק Ber. 61 b; נִימוֹקִין RH iii. 8.

191. (ii) *The Intensive Stem.*

(a) *Po'el, Po'al, Nithpo'el*: These forms are still more rare in MH than in BH. The following are the only exx. found: מְחוֹטֵט, מִתְחוֹטֶטֶת to dig, cut, Meg. 12 a; מְסוֹלֶלֶת to coddle, San. 69 b; מְסוֹלְלוֹת Yeb. 76 a; לְקוֹצֵץ Miq. x. 4; יְסוֹבְבוּ So. ix. 15; חוֹנַנְתָּנוּ Singer, pp. 46, 280. An example of Po'al may be יְחוֹנְנוּ So. ix. 15, but this is more probably a Pu'al: יְחוּנְנוּ, cf. above, § 126; נִתְרוֹעֲעָה Kel. iii. 4; iv. 2 (L נתרעעה); מִתְרוֹסֵס to crush, Ḥul. 77 a; מִשְׁתּוֹמֵם to be desolate, Qid. 66 a.

192. (b) *Pi'el*: בֵּרֵר 'Er. iv. 5; גֵּרְרָה Pes. i. 2; סִיכֵּךְ to cover,

[1] For יְזוֹמּוּ אֶת עַצְמָן, L reads correctly יָזֹמּוּ, Mak. i. 4.

Suk. i. 4; מֵרֵרוּ to embitter, Pes. x. 5; קִינְנוּ to make a nest, Ḥul. xii. 1; יְרַפֵּס ʻUq. ii. 6; יְקַצֵּץ ʻAZ i. 8; אֲצַנֵּן, אֲקָרֵר to make cold, Pes. 118 a; לְבָרֵר San. 23 b; לְחַמֵּם j. Ned. iv. 2; לְפָרֵר to crumble, Pes. 10 b; לְחַמְמָהּ, לְצַנְנָהּ Šab. 53 a; מְנַפֵּף to caress, San. vii. 6; מְלַקֵּק to lick, San. 68 a; מְפָרֵר Pes. ii. 1; מְצַדֵּד to move to the side, Yo. 55 a; מְגָרֶרֶת t. Šab. vi. 1; מְסַנֶּנֶת to sift, Kel. ii. 5; מְסַבְּבִין ib. i. 7. Biliteral only: מְחַמִּין Yo. iii. 5 (unless this is Hiphʻil: מְחִמִּין), and perhaps also מַלֶּקֶת = מְלַקֶּקֶת Pa. ix. 3 (L מלקה).

193. *Puʻal*: מְזוּמָּם San. vi. 2; מְזוּפָּפִין pitched, BM 40 b; מְחוּדָּד sharpened, Qid. 30 a; מְסוּבֶּבֶת BB 25 b; מְסוּכֶּכֶת Suk. 8 b; מְצוּדָּדִים BB 99 a; מְצוּנֶּנֶת Ḥul. iii. 5; מְרוּדָּד, מְרוּדָּדִין beaten, Miq. vii. 7. Biliteral only, מְסוּבִּין reclining round the table, San. ii. 1, 3, &c.[1]

194. *Hithpaʻel-Nithpaʻel*: הִתְפַּלַּלְתָּ, הִתְפַּלֵּל Taʻa. iii. 8; נִתְאָרְרוּ to curse, t. So. xv. 2; נִצְטַנֵּן Šab. 129 a; נִתְקַלְּלָה to curse, ʻEr. 18 a, b; מִתְחַכֵּךְ BQ iv. 6; מִתְחַלֵּל Ab. i. 11; מִתְחַמֵּם ib. ii. 10.

(c) Reduplicated Forms.

195. *Pilpel*: דִּקְדֵּק to be thin, exact, Ber. ii. 3; הִרְהַרְתִּי to reflect, Ḥul. 37 b; פִּלְפְּלוּ to search, t. BB vii. 6; קִלְקְלָה to damage, corrupt, Yeb. x. 2; קִלְקְלוּ Ber. ix. 5; יְחַרְחַר to bore, ʻUq. iii. 11; תְּכַשְׁכֵּשׁ to shake, Ḥul. ii. 6; יְצַחְצְחָן to polish BM 84 a; יְקַלְקְלוּ Ḥul. i. 1; לְחַטְטֵט j. ʻOr. iii. 2; לְכַסְכֵּס to chew, Nid. ix. 7; לְמַשְׁמֵשׁ to feel, BM 21 b; מְהַרְהֵר Ber. iii. 4; מְכַלְכֵּל to maintain, Naz. i. 1; מְסַלְסֵל to wave the hair, ib.; מְסַכְסֶכֶת to intertwine, t. BQ vi. 22; מְקַלְקֶלֶת Ned. xi. 11; מְמַשְׁמְשִׁין BQ ii. 4.

Pulpal: מְגוּלְגָּלוֹת Pes. 7 a; מְגוּלְגָּלִין ʻAZ ii. 7; מְדוּלְדָּל to hang down, Ker. iii. 8; מְדוּלְדָּלִין Ḥul. ix. 7; מְצוּחְצָחוֹת Lev. R. 1.

Nithpalpel: נִתְגַּלְגֵּל Šab. xi. 3; נִתְגַּלְגְּלָה Šebu. vii. 8; נִידַּלְדְּלוּ to be impoverished, So. ix. 15; יִתְמַקְמֵק Taʻa. 25 b; יִתְקַלְקְלוּ Men. xi. 1; מִתְקַלְקֵל Dam. iii. 6; מִתְפַּרְפֶּרֶת t. Makš. iii. 8.

(iii) *The Causative Stem.* Biliteral; triliteral forms are very rare.

[1] The sing. is always מֵסֵב, in Hiphʻil; cf. below, § 196.

196. *Hiph'il*: הֵפֵר Ned. x. 1; הֵקֵל to make light, be lenient, MŠ iii. 2; הֵחֵלּוּ[1] to begin, Tam. ii. 2, 3; vi. 1; הֵסַבּוּ Ber. vi. 6; הֵזִימּוּם to convict of false evidence, San. xii. 5; הֵרֵעוֹתִי Qid. iv. 14. Without separating vowel (cf. BH הֲחִלֹּתָ Jud. xvi. 10; Ges.-K., § 67 dd, and above, § 183): הֵמַסְתָּ Deut. R. 2; הֵעַזְתָּ to strengthen, Ber. 62 b; הֵעַזְתִּי BB 131 a; הֵיקַלְתָּ Yeb. 88 a. Triliteral: הֶזְקַקְתּוּנִי Suk. 28 a.

Imperf.: יָחֵם Be. ii. 5; יָסֵב Pes. x. 1; יָפֵר Ned. x. 5; יָצֵן j. Hor. ii. 5; יָקֵל Ber. ix. 5; נָקֵל MŠ iii. 2; תָּנֵץ to shine, Meg. ii. 4; יָנֵצּוּ Šebi. iv. 2; יָזִימּוּ Mak. i. 7; יָרִיצּוּ to crush, t. Oh. xviii. end.

Inf.: לְהָחֵם Šab. 40 a; לְהָטֵן to moisten, Makš. iii. 5; לְהָפֵר Ned. x. 3; לְהָקֵל 'Er. iv. 9; לְהָקֵר Makš. iv. 2.

Imperat.: הָחֵל j. Ber. v. 2; Singer, p. 46.

Part.: מֵדֵל to thin grapes, Pe. iii. 3; מֵיחֵל, מְחִלִּין to defile, Ber. 32 a; Dam. vii. 4; מֵחֵם t. Šab. iii. 7; מְחִמִּין[2] Yo. iii. 5; מֵטֵן (so correctly L for edd. מטנן), מְטִנִּין Makš. iii. 5; מֵצֵן j. Hor. ii. 5; מֵיצֵר RH ii. 9; מֵיקֵל, מְקִילִּין Šab. 129 a; מֵסֵב to recline, San. ii. 1, 3; מֵסֵךְ Šab. vii. 2; מֵפֵר, מְפִירִין Ned. x. 1, 2; מְרֵיעָה to do evil, San. vii. 10; מְמַקְּתוֹ to cause decay, Ket. vii. 11; מֵצֶמֶת to restrain (צמם), Cant. R. iv. 1; מֵתֶשֶׁת to weaken (תשש) San. 26 a.

197. *Hoph'al*: הוּזְלוּ BB v. 8; הוּזְמוּ[3] San. x. 8; הוּזְמְנוּ Mak. 3 a (without the separating vowel); הוּחַמָּה BM vi. 3; הוּחַמּוּ Šab. iii. 4; הוּמַק San. 92 b; הוּסַבָּה BB 112 a; הוּרַע Pea vi. 6. Triliteral: הוּגְלְלוּ Ta'a. 21 b; הוּזְקַק BB 170 a; הוּזְקְקוּ Men. 45 b; יוּצַן 'AZ iii. 9; יוּרַע BB x. 6.

מוּדָק j. So. ii. 2; מוּזָרוֹת smashed, San. 82 b; מוּפָר, מוּפָרִין Ned. viii. 7. Triliteral: מוּבְלֶלֶת j. Šeq. vi. 1 end; מוּכְלָל Yo. 54 b.

[1] Elsewhere always the denominative of תְּחִלָּה = הִתְחִיל; cf. § 92. So ib. vi. 3.

[2] The traditional pronunciation is מְחַמִּין = מְחַמְמִין, plur. of מְחַמֵּם; cf. § 192; j. Šab. ix. 3.

[3] This is the traditional pronunciation, and not הוּזַלּוּ, הוּזַמּוּ. Cf. BH הֻמַּכּוּ, Job xxiv. 24; Ges.-K., § 67 v.

(7) Verbs ל״א.

198. The inflection of these verbs follows on BH lines. The interchange of forms between these verbs and verbs ל״ה, already frequent in BH (Ges.-K., § 75 m, n, ff.), becomes more frequent in MH. Sometimes we find forms combining both ל״א and ל״ה types. Nevertheless, the distinction between these two classes has been clearly preserved in MH. Many of the ל״ה forms in ל״א verbs may be ascribed to the negligence and the Aramaizing tendencies of the scribes, as is proved by comparing different texts. MH also shows more frequently than BH the older termination ת for the third fem. sing. in Qal, Niph'al, and Nithpa'el (cf. Ges.-K., § 74 g).

199. *Qal.* Perfect: יָצָא Yo. v. 3; מָצָא BM ii. 1. The fem. wavers between יָצְאָה, יָצָאת (so usually in L and other Palestinian texts), יָצָאתָה and יָצְתָה; cf. Šab. vi. 1, 3; xi. 6; Pᵉs. v. 7; Yᵉb. xvi. 1; Ṭoh. iii. 1. So קָרְאָה and קָרָאתָה Yᵉb. xii. 3, in various texts. חָטָאתִי Yo. iii. 8, but also קָרִיתִי ib. i. 6; מָצְאוּ Yᵉb. xvi. 6; מָצָאנוּ ib. xvi. 7, but also מָצִינוּ Bᵉr. vii. 3; Kil. iii. 7; קָרִינוּ Bᵉr. i. 1, especially in later texts. Imperf., as in BH.

Infin.: לִקְרוֹת Bᵉr. i. 1, but also לִקְרָאוֹת MŠ v. 9 (L), as Judges viii. 1.

Imperat.: קְרָא Yo. i. 6; שְׂנָא Ab. i. 10.

Partic.: קוֹרֵא Yo. i. 6; קוֹרִין ib.; Bᵉr. i. 1 (cf. Psalm xcix. 6); יוֹצֵא Šab. v. 2; יוֹצְאָה ib. v. 4; but also יוֹצֵאת Kil. iv. 6; נוֹשֵׂאת Šᵉbu. vii. 8; יוֹצְאִין, יוֹצְאוֹת Šab. v. 4; נוֹשְׂאִין MQ i. 7; נְשׂוּי married, Yᵉb. iii. 7 (L has the mixed form נְשׂאוּי, cf. Psalm xxxii. 1); קְרוּי Tᵉr. iii. 7; סְמוּיָה blind, hidden, Qid. 24 b.

200. *Niph'al*: נִטְמָא Pᵉs. i. 6; נִטְמֵאת Tᵉr. viii. 2; So. vi. 2; נִשֵּׂאת to be married, Yᵉb. vii. 2 (also spelt נִיסֵּת ib. vii. 3, 6, and often in L and the Talmud); נִסְמֵית to be blind, Zᵉb. vii. 5; נִטְמֵאתָ Tᵉr. viii. 2; נִטְמֵאנוּ Pᵉs. 78 b; נִמְצֵינוּ.

The imperf. as in BH.

Infin.: לִינָּשֵׂא Y^eb. ii. 10; לְהִיקָּרֵא ʿEd. v. 6 (L לִיקָּרוֹת); and the mixed form לְהִבָּרְאוֹת Ab. iv. 1.

Partic.: נִשֵּׂאת, or נִיסֵּת K^et. i. 1; נִקְרֵאת M^eg. i. 1; נִקְרָאִין, also נִקְרִין Giṭ. ix. 5.

201. *Piʿel*: מִילֵּא, אֲמַלֵּא Pa. vii. 4; אֲטַמְאָה, יְטַמְאֶנָּה T^er. viii. 11; יְטַמְאוּ, נְטַמְאָה ib. 12; יְמַלְאֶנָּה Šab. ii. 4; סִימֵּא BQ viii. 1; מַלֵּא (imperat.) Be. iii. 8; מְמַלֵּא Pa. vii. 5; מְמַלְּאִין ib. 11 (L מְמַלִּין and so often, ʿEr. viii. 7, &c.); מְקָרֵא to read to, Suk. iii. 10; מְקָרִין ib.; Bik. iii. 6 (L also מְקָרְאִים, beside מְקָרִין); מְקַפֵּא to congeal, Maʿa. i. 7; מְחַבְּאִין = מְחַבִּין to hide, Šab. 25 b.

The Infin. has mixed forms: לְמַלְאוֹת K^et. i. 10; לְרַפְּאוֹתוֹ to heal, BQ viii. 1. So in BH, cf. Ges.-K., § 74 h.

Puʿal: מְדוּכָּאִין to crush, K^et. 8 b; מְקוֹרָאִין Num. R. 13.

202. *Nithpaʿel*: נִסְתַּמֵּא ʿAr. 17 b; נִתְמַלֵּאת P^es. v. 5; לִיטַּמֵּא Yo. 38 b; מִיטַּמֵּא ʿUq. i. 1; מִיטַּמְּאָה Naz. iv. 3; מִיטַּמְּאִין (also מִתְטַמְּאִין) Kel. ii. 1; מִתְחַטֵּא Taʿa. iii. 8; מִתְרַפְּאִין, also מִתְרַפִּין ʿAZ ii. 2.

203. *Hiphʿil*: הִשִּׂיאוּ to move, ʿAZ ii. 5; יַבְרִיא to become healthy, Šab. xix. 5; יַקְפִּיאֶנָּה to ladle off, T^er. iv. 11; מַמְצִיא Ḥag. 5 a, but מַמְרִין to fatten, (BH מריא) Šab. xxiv. 3.

Hophʿal: מוּפְלָא distinguished, Hor. i. 4.

(8) Verbs ל״ה.

204. These verbs also conform to the BH rules. As in BH (Ges.-K., § 75 rr), ל״ה verbs sometimes assume ל״א forms. This happens usually in the third sing. and plur. of the perf. Qal when they have pronominal suffixes attached to them, and further, in the third fem. sing. perf. Niphʿal, and in the fem. sing. of the Partic. Niphʿal. The older termination ָת for the third fem. sing. of the perf. Qal is regularly found in Palestinian, and sometimes also in other texts. Cf. the ל״א verbs above, § 199, and Ges.-K., § 75 m.

205. *Qal.* Perfect: זָכָה to acquire, BM i. 3; שָׁהָה to tarry, Šebu. ii. 3; גָּבְתָה (L גבת) to collect, Ket. iv. 1; זָכְתָה (L זכת) BM i. 4; כָּבְתָה to extinguish, Šab. 21 a, but כָּבַת j. Yo. ii. 3; כָּהֲתָה to dim, Qid. 24 b; עָלְתָה (L עָלַת) to go up, Zeb. ix. 1; פָּשְׂתָה (L פשת) to increase, Neg. iv. 9; שָׁפְתָה (L שפת) to be quiet, Nid. iv. 4; שָׁתָת to drink, Pa. ix. 5; שָׁרַת to be loose, Qoh. R. vii. 2; צָבַת to swell, j. BQ vii. 1.

The original third radical י reappears in the third sing. and plur. of the perfect with suffixes: טְלָיָיהּ to patch, Kel. xxiv. 17; פְּדָיָין to redeem, Pea iv. 8. Often, however, this י is changed into א, especially in Babylonian texts: עֲשָׂאָהּ Suk. i. 1; עֲשָׂאֲךָ Ter. viii. 1; כְּוָואוֹ to burn, BQ viii. 1; אֲפָאָהּ (L אפייה) to bake, MŠ ii. 3; cf. below, § 216, and above, §§ 56, 58.

זָכִיתִי Ber. i. 5; לָוִיתָ to borrow, BB 6 a; בָּדוּ to invent, Ned. 10 a; נָשִׁינוּ to forget, ib. 50 b; צָלוּ to roast, Pes. v. 9.

Imperf.: יִלָּקֶה to be smitten, BM iii. 12; יִרְעֶה to feed, Yo. vi. 1. Jussive: אַל תַּעַשׂ do not make, Ab. i. 8; ii. 12.

Infin.: לְחִתּוֹת to take fire, Šab. viii. 7 (BH); לִרְדּוֹת to chastise, Yo. 40 b.

Imperat.: צְלֵה Pes. vii. 2; שְׁנֵה to repeat, Nid. 5 b; לְוִי to borrow, Be. 15 b.

Partic. Active: הוֹגֶה to utter, San. x (xi.) 1; זוֹכֶה ʻEd. ii. 9; חוֹתָה Yo. iv. 4; טוֹוָה to spin, Ket. vii. 6; דּוֹחִין to push off, Oh. vii. 6; חוֹפִין to cover, Ḥul. iii. 7; פּוֹדִין to redeem, Giṭ. iv. 6; שׁוֹרִין to soak, Šab. i. 5.

206. A few participles are found in an adjectival form with *ā* in the first syllable: זָכֶה ʻEd. ii. 10 (L; elsewhere always זוֹכֶה), זָכִין in the dictum: זָכִין לְאָדָם שֶׁלֹּא בְּפָנָיו וְאֵין חָבִין לְאָדָם אֶלָּא בְּפָנָיו — one can confer an advantage upon a person in his absence, but one cannot confer a disadvantage upon a person, except in his presence, 'Er. vii. 11; Giṭ. i. 6. The form זָכִין may perhaps be due to assonance with חָבִין. So זָכִין Yo. ii. 3; זָכוֹת Giṭ. vi. 2, in L, for זוֹכִין, זוֹכוֹת in other texts. Further, כָּבָה, fem. כָּבָה to be extinguished, Šab. 151 b; כָּלָה to come to an end, Tᵉr. vi. 7; כָּלִין San. 17 a; פָּרֶה וְרָבֶה fruitful and multiplying (a standing expression, derived from Gen. i. 28); פָּרִין וְרָבִין Šab. 107 b; Ab. dᵉRN. xxxvii. 2, 3.

Partic. Passive: טָווּי Kil. ix. 8; צָפוּי to see, Ab. iii. 15; רָאוּי fit, Nid. vi. 4; כְּרוּיָה to dig, Kel. iii. 5; שְׁבוּיִים to capture, Šᵉq. ii. 5; שְׁרוּיָה to dwell, Ab. iii. 2.

207. *Niph'al.* The third fem. sing. of the perfect is identical in form with the fem. sing. of the Participle. They usually both end in ־ֵית, or ־ת in L, as in the ל״א verbs (§ 200).

Perfect: נֶהֱנֵית to enjoy, BQ ii. 2; נִפְדֵּית Kᵉt. iii. 2; נִשְׁבֵּית ib. ii. 5; נַעֲשֵׂית 'Er. v. 6; Šab. xi. 6 (L נעשתה); נִמְנֵיתָ, נִמְנִינוּ to count, Pᵉs. ix. 10; נִפְנֵיתִי to have leisure, Ab. dᵉRN. xxv. 3; נִשְׁבֵּיתִי Kᵉt. ii. 5; נַעֲנֵתִי to be humble, Bᵉr. 28 a; נַעֲנָה Zᵉb. 57 a; נַעֲנוּ to answer, Qid. 40 b; נִימְחוּ to wipe out, dissolve, Ṭoh. iii. 1; נִשְׁרוּ to soak, Šab. xxii. 4.

Imperf.: יִדָּחֶה Mᵉg. 5 b; תִּפָּנֶה, אֶפָּנֶה Ab. ii. 4; יִפָּדוּ Tᵉr. v. 1; תִּצָּלֶה Šab. iii. 3; written *plene* יִצּוֹלוּ ib. i. 10; so יִשּׁוֹרוּ ib. i. 5.

Partic.: נִדְחֶה Mᵉg. 5 b; נִפְדֶּה MŠ iii. 10; נִתְלֶה, נִתְלֵית (L נִתְלֵת), נִתְלִין to hang, San. vi. 4; נִכְסֶה, נִכְסִין to cover, ib. ii. 1; נִבְנֵית to build, ib. x. 6; נַעֲשֵׂית Pa. iii. 7; נִקְנֵית to acquire, Qid. i. 1; נִכְווֹת Kᵉt. 5 b.

Infin.: לִיגָּבוֹת BM 59 a; לֵיהָנוֹת Kᵉt. vii. 1; לֵיעָשׂוֹת 'Ed. v. 6; לִיפָּנוֹת to ease oneself, Šab. 82 a.

The Intensive Stem is regular, as in BH.

208. *Pi'el*: זִיכָּה BB viii. 6; זִינְּתָה to commit fornication, San. vii. 2; לִיבָּה to kindle a flame; לִיבְּתָה BQ vi. 4; עִירָה to pour out, Yo. v. 4; דִּימּוּ to imagine, ib. iii. 2; פִּתִּיתִי to seduce, Kᵉt. iii. 9. יְרַצֶּה to make acceptable, Yo. viii. 9; יְחַפֵּהוּ to cover, Šᵉbi. iv. 5,

נַפֵּה (imperat.) to sift, M^e^n. 85 a; לְיַיפּוֹת to make fair, good, BB vii. 2; לְעָרוֹת MŠ iii. 10; מְדַדָּה, מְדַדִּין to cause to hop, Šab. xviii. 2; מְכַסָּה K^e^t. vi. 5; מְעָרֶה MŠ iii. 13; מְקָרֶה to cover a ceiling, Suk. i. 8.

209. *Pu'al*: יוּפִּי to be made good, Pea vi. 6 (cf. above, § 126).

Partic.: מְהוּהָא, L מְהוּהָה worn out (מהה = מחה), cf. L נימהו = נימחו Ṭoh. iii. 1) Kel. xxiv. 17; מְנוּדֶּה excommunicated, MQ iii. 1; מְנוּפֶּה, מְנוּפָּה sifted, M^e^n. vi. 7; מְעוּבֶּה thickened, Suk. ii. 2; מְעוּשֶּׂה forced, Giṭ. ix. 8; מְרוּבֶּה, מְרוּבִּים, מְרוּבּוֹת many, Ḥag. i. 5.

210. *Nithpa'el*: נִזְדַּבֶּה San. 30 a; נִתְנַסֶּה, נִתְנַסּוּ to be tried, Ab. v. 3; נִתְגַּלְּתָה to uncover, Suk. iv. 10; נִתְלַבְּתָה Šab. 37 a; נִתְפַּתְּתָה K^e^t. iv. 1; but also נִשְׁתַּטֵּית she is become insane, Y^e^b. xiv. 1; נִצְטַוּוּ, נִצְטַוִּינוּ to command, Qid. 38 a, b; נִשְׁתַּהוּ to be delayed, RH iv. 4; הִתְעַנִּינוּ to afflict, 'Er. 41 a; יִתְנָאֶה to become beautiful, RH. 26 a; יִתְעַלֶּה to be elevated, Šab. 33 b; תִּתְיַיפִּי Ta'a. 23 b; יִתְקַשּׁוּ to be hardened, t. Nid. vi. 4; לְהִתְכַּסּוֹת B^e^r. iii. 4; מִתְכַּסָּה K^e^t. v. 8; מִתְכַּסִּין Ta'a. i. 1; מִתְעַנָּה ib. iii. 3, 4.

The Causative Stem is exactly as in BH.

211. *Hiph'il*: הִלְוָה to lend, BM v. 1; הִתְנָה to stipulate, K^e^t. ix. 1; הִתְרוּ to warn, Mak. i. 12; הִרְצֵתִי to discourse, t. Nid. vi. 6; תַּרְשֵׁנִי to permit, Ḥag. 14 b.

Imperat.: הַעֲלֵם, הַעַל MŠ iii. 1; הַשְׁנֵינִי teach me, Lam. R. i. 6.

Infin.: לְהַקְווֹת to collect water, t. Š^e^q. i. 2; with elision of the ה (cf. above, § 143); לַמְחוֹת to object, BM x. 6 = לְהַמְחוֹת; לַשְׁהוֹת = לְהַשְׁהוֹת 'Er. x. 5.

Partic.: מַמְחֶה to wipe, cleanse, BB v. 10; מַמְחָה, מַמְחִין j. P^e^s. viii. 5; מַשְׁקִין to give to drink, 'Ed. v. 6; מַשְׁהִין Nid. 31 a; מַתְעֶה to lead astray, San. 55 a.

Note.—The denominative Hiph'il of עני poor, preserves the י in the sing.: הֶעֱנִי 'Ar. iv. 2; יַעֲנִי Š^e^q. iii. 2; N^e^d. ix. 4, but plur.: הֶעֱנוּ B^e^r. 33 a; יַעֲנוּ M^e^'il. 17 a.

Hoph'al: הוּמְנָה t. P^e^s. vii. 2; הוּקְשָׁה Num. R. 16; הוּרְצָה Yo.

7 a; הוּרְאוּ j. MQ iii. 5; הוּשְׁווּ to be like, Šab. 15 a; הוּרְשֵׁיתָ Ḥag. 13 a (from Sirach).

Partic.: מוּמְחֶה expert, Bek. iv. 4; מוּפְנֶה free, Yeb. iii. 5; מוּטְעָין in error, RH 25 a; מוּטֶה bent, Kel. iv. 3; מוּטִין ib. x. 1; מוּטָה Oh. ix. 11; מוּטוֹת ib. xv. 3.

212. Note.—The verb היה has in the imperf. Qal the following shortened forms: יְהֵא Yo. i. 3; תְּהֵא, אֱהֵא Naz. iii. 6.[1] יְהוּ Kil. iv. 5 (L often יהוא, cf. Qoh. xi. 3). The Imperat. is formed from הוה: הֱוֵי Ab. i. 4 (cf. BH Gen. xxvii. 29; Isa. xvi. 4); plur.: הֱווּ ib. ii. 3. The partic. is always הוֹוֶה Šab. vi. 6, 10; 'Er. i. 10, as already in BH: Qoh. ii. 22; Neh. vi. 6. Examples of the Pi'el, causing to be, are found in the partic. only: מְהַוָּה Ket. 40 b, but also מְהַיֶּיה Qid. 58 a and parallels.

The rest of the verb is regular, and even for the forms given above, the regular forms are also found.

Note also the jussive forms יְהִי, תְּהִי Ab. iii. 10, &c.

(9) Verbs with Pronominal Suffixes.

213. The object of a verb can be expressed in MH, as in BH, by a suffix. The phonetic rules governing the modification of the verb when it assumes a pronominal suffix, are the same in MH as in BH. The following points may be noted:

The third sing. imperf. usually inserts the so-called *nun energicum* before the suffix of the third sing. masc. and fem. (cf. Ges.-K., § 58 i).

In ל"ה verbs the original י reappears before the suffix in the third sing. and plur. of the perfect Qal, or is softened into א (cf. § 205).

These suffixes are used in MH somewhat less frequently than in BH, their place being taken by את. The most common suffixes

[1] These forms also occur sometimes in Aram.; cf. Dalman, § 73 (p. 354); Nöldeke, *Syr. Gr.*, § 183 (8), but they are more common in MH.

are those of the third person sing. and plur. The suffixes of the first person are also fairly common, especially in the sing. The suffix of the second person sing. is much rarer, and that of the second person plur. is exceedingly rare, just as in BH.

Examples of Verbs with Suffixes.

(1) Suffix of the First person.

214. Sing.: מְצָאַנִי to find, Y^e^b. xvi. 7; נְשָׁכַנִי to bite, ib. 6; עֲקָצַתְנִי to sting, Ab. d^e^RN. i. 7; נְשָׂאתַנִי to marry, K^e^t. ii. 1; קִדַּשְׁתַּנִי to betroth, Qid. iii. 3; דַּנְתּוּנִי to judge; חֲשַׁדְתּוּנִי to suspect, Šab. 117 b; תְּשַׁמְּשֵׁנִי to serve, Giṭ. vii. 7; יִירָשֵׁנִי, תִּירָשֵׁנִי BB viii. 6; תּוֹצִיאֵנִי to bring forth, B^e^r. 60 a; גַּיְּרֵנִי to make a proselyte, Šab. 31 a.

Plur.: גְּאָלָנוּ to redeem; הִגִּיעָנוּ, יַגִּיעֵנוּ to cause to reach, P^e^s. x. 5; לִמַּדְתָּנוּ to teach, B^e^r. ii. 8; יְלַמְּדֵנוּ P^e^s. 48 b; תַּעֲמִידֵנִי to place; תַּצִּילֵנִי to deliver, B^e^r. 17 a; רַחֲקֵנוּ to remove; דַּשְּׁנֵנוּ to fatten, ib. 29 a.

(2) Suffix of the Second person.

215. Sing.: מְכָרְךָ to sell; נְתָנְךָ to give, T^e^r. viii. 1; הִגִּיעַתְךָ ʿAr. viii. 1. ל"ה verbs: עֲשָׂאֲךָ to make, T^e^r. viii. 1; הִנָּאֲךָ to give pleasure, ʿAZ 16 b; נְשָׂאתִיךָ K^e^t. ii. 1; גֵּרְשֵׁךְ to divorce, T^e^r. viii. 1; קִידַּשְׁתִּיךָ Qid. iii. 1; יְבָרְכוּךָ to bless, M^e^g. iv. 10; יְקָרְבוּךָ to bring near; יְרַחֲקוּךָ ʿEd. v. 9; אַרְאֲךָ to show, Qid. iii. 2; נַעַשְׂךָ ʿEd. v. 6.

Plur.: The following are the only exx. found: לַהֲקִימְכֶם to raise; לְהַחֲיוֹתְכֶם to revive, B^e^r. 58 b; cf. Singer, p. 319. (Contrast with four times אֶתְכֶם in the following finite verbs.)

(3) Suffix of the Third Person.

216. Sing. Masc. Perfect: שְׁכָחוֹ to forget, Pea vii. 7; סִיְּדוֹ to plaster; כִּיְּרוֹ to decorate, ʿAZ iii. 7; הִשִּׂיאוֹ to move, ib. ii. 8; הִכָּהוּ to strike, Pea iv. 8; הֶרְאָהוּ Kil. vi. 4; כְּוָואוֹ to burn, BQ viii. 1; צְלָאוֹ to roast, P^e^s. v. 9; סִיעֲרַתּוּ to carry off by storm, Kil. v. 7; גְּנָבַתּוּ

to steal; הִכַּתּוּ N^{e}d. iii. 2; טְוָאַתּוּ to spin, Z^{e}b. 79 b; נְתַתּוֹ, נְתַתִּיו Š^{e}bu. vii. 7; הֲבֵאתִיו to bring, MŠ v. 12; שְׁכָחוּהוּ Pea vii. 7; רָאוּהוּ to see, RH iii. 1; הוֹלִיכוּהוּ to lead; הֶחֱזִירוּהוּ to return; נְתָנוּהוּ ʽEr. iv. 1; פִּטְרְנוּהוּ to dismiss; רְאִינוּהוּ, הִנַּחְנוּהוּ to leave, So. ix. 6.

Imperfect: יְשִׁיבֶנּוּ to answer, B^{e}r. v. 1; יְכַסֶּנּוּ to cover, Šab. iv. 2; יַנִּיחֶנּוּ P^{e}s. i. 3; יַסְפִּידֶנּוּ to lament, MQ i. 5; אֲלַקְּטֶנּוּ to gather, Kil. v. 6, but also תִּתְּנֵהוּ, תְּנֵהוּ Š^{e}bu. vi. 2; יְחַפֵּהוּ to cover, Š^{e}bi. iv. 5 (L יְחַפֶּה).

Infin.: לְפַיְּיסוֹ to appease, B^{e}r. 28 b; לְיָירְשׁוֹ BB viii. 5; לִיתְּנוֹ Š^{e}bu. vi. 1.

Partic.: מְלַבְּנוֹ to whiten, wash; מְנַפְּצוֹ to beat; צוֹבְעוֹ to dye; שׁוֹחֲטוֹ to slay; מַפְשִׁיטוֹ to skin, Šab. vii. 2, 3; מַטֵּהוּ to bend, Be. i. 4; חוֹצֵהוּ to divide, M^{e}n. iv. 7; עוֹקַרְתּוֹ to uproot; הוֹפַכְתּוֹ to overthrow, Ab. iii. 17; מַאֲכִילָתוֹ to give to eat; מְשַׁמַּשְׁתּוֹ K^{e}t, vii. 6; מְנִיקַתּוֹ to suckle, Giṭ. vii. 6.

Sing. Fem. Perfect: דְּרָשָׁהּ to expound, B^{e}r. i. 8; קְרָאָהּ to read, M^{e}g. ii. 1, 2; אֵירְשָׁהּ to betroth; גֵּירְשָׁהּ K^{e}t. iv. 3; אֲפָאָהּ to bake, MŠ ii. 3 (L אֲפָיָיהּ); עֲשָׂאָהּ Suk. i. 1, 2; שְׁפָיָיהּ to rub, ʽAZ iii. 10; טְלָיָיהּ to patch, Kel. xxiv. 7; פְּדָאתָהּ (L פדיתה) to redeem, Ḥal. iii. 3; הִקְדִּישַׁתָּהּ to sanctify, ib.; הִכַּתָּה Kel. vii. 11; עֲקָצַתָּה to sting, Ab. d^{e}RN. i. 7; פְּדִיתִיהָ, גֵּרַשְׁתִּיהָ, קִדַּשְׁתִּיהָ Qid. iii. 8; הֶאֱדִימוּהָ to be red; הִלְבִּינוּהָ Oh. xvii. 4; מִלְּאוּהָ to fill; נִקַּבְנוּהָ to bore; הִנַּחְנוּהָ Šab. 29 b.

Imperf.: יִתְּנֶנָּה Šab. ii. 4; יַפְקִיעֶנָּה to break, ib. iii. 3; יַקְפִּיאֶנָּה to congeal, T^{e}r. iv. 11; יְגַלֶּנָּה, יְכַסֶּנָּה, יַנִּיחֶנָּה ib. viii. 8.

Infin.: לְנָוטְעָהּ to plant, Kil. ii. 4; לְדוּכָהּ to pound, Be. 14 a; לְנָאוֹתָהּ to beautify, Suk. 10 a.

Partic.: מַנִּיחֶנָּה B^{e}r. viii. 3; מַשִּׂיאָהּ Be. iii. 7; מַשְׁבִּיעָהּ K^{e}t. ix. 4; כּוֹפָהּ to force, ib. v. 5; מְטַהַרְתָּהּ Ḥul. iv. 4.

Plur.: רִיסְּקָן to crush, Šab. xxii. 1; שִׁינָּן to change, P^{e}s. v. 6; וְעִנְעֲתָן to move, Š^{e}bi. iii. 7; פְּדָאָן Pea iv. 8 (L פדיין); נְתָנָתַם Kin. iii. 6; הוֹלַכְתָּם, הִשְׁלַכְתָּם to throw; נְתַתִּים Š^{e}bu. vii. 6; הֱזִימוּם to convict of false evidence, Mak. i. 5; יְזָרְעֵם to sow, Kil. ii. 10; יְזִיזֵם to move, Be. iii. 5; יְשׁוּפֵם Kel. xvi. 1; יִטְּלֵם to take, Dam. iv. 4; הַעֲלוּם to bring up, Suk. ii. 5; לְלָוּתְתָן to mix, t. Makš. iii. 2; Pes. 36 a; לְמוֹלְלָן to hem, MQ 26 a.

זוֹרְעָם Kil. ii. 9; מְהַנָּן to benefit; מַפְסִידָן to cause loss, Yad. iv. 3; מְבַשְּׂרָתָן to bring good tidings, So. ix. 6; מְסַעֲיִיעְתָּן to assist, Ab. ii. 2.

III. THE NOUN

1. General Survey.

217. As in the other parts of speech, so also in the treatment of the noun MH has followed faithfully the traditions of BH. This is true of the formation of the noun and also of its inflexion. With regard to the formation of the noun, MH has retained the original forms of those BH nouns which it still uses. Further, all its new nouns are formed on the basis of the old BH ground-forms.

Noteworthy features in the MH noun formation are: (*a*) the wide development of the verbal nouns to replace the old BH infinitive construct, viz. the forms קְטִילָה for the Simple Stem (§ 228); קִיטּוּל and קַטָּלָה for the Intensive Stem (§§ 237, 241); הַקְטֵל and הַקְטָלָה for the Causative Stem (§§ 251–2); (*b*) the more frequent use of Reduplication (§§ 244–8); (*c*) of the *nomen agentis* (קַטּוֹל (§ 235); (*d*) of the use of the suffixes ָן, וֹן—, and ָנִי— (§§ 267–8, 270); (*e*) and the various forms of the Diminutive (§ 276). But all these forms are based on BH ground-forms, and have parallels in the BH vocabulary.

218. As regards the lexical character of the MH noun, the results of our review of the MH verb (§§ 83 ff.) apply also to the MH noun, except that the noun has borrowed more freely than the verb from Aram., from Greek, and, to a less degree, from Latin. The nouns which are most common in MH are also found in BH. A number of BH nouns have disappeared in MH, especially nouns of a poetical character or of rare occurrence in BH, though common in Aram. (e.g. בְּעִיר, גֶּרֶם, &c.). The new MH nouns are usually formed from BH roots, or from old Hebrew roots not found in BH. Many of these MH nouns occur also in Aram., just as many old BH nouns occur in Aram. But the majority of such nouns are native in MH.

219. Even Aram. loan-words usually receive a Hebraic form, like רֶמֶץ, זָרָז, &c. This has also happened in the case of a number of Gk. and Latin nouns, e.g. אִצְטְלִית στολή, Yo. vii. 1; קִילוּרִית κολλύριον, Šab. viii. 1; מַרְגָּלִית μαργαρίτης, Ab. vi. 9; בַּלָּן βαλανεύς, Šᵉbi. viii. 5; קָרוֹן *carrus*, ʻAZ v. 4; אַכְסַנְיָא ξένος, Dam. iii. 1, &c.[1]

MH also follows BH in the other grammatical changes of the noun, viz. in the formation of the feminine (§§ 277 ff.); the plural (§§ 281 ff.); the dual (more frequent in MH than in BH, § 293); the construct state (§ 380), and the use of the noun with pronominal suffixes.

For the forms of nouns derived from Greek and Latin cf. Albrecht, § 82.

2. Formation of Nouns.

(1) *Nouns derived from the Simple Stem.*

(i) Ground-form *Qaṭl*, *Qiṭl*, *Quṭl*.

220. (*a*) *Qaṭl.* Strong Verb. Concrete: דֶּקֶל date-tree, Pea iv. 1; זֶבֶל manure, BM v. 7; דֶּקֶר mattock, j. Be. i. 2; כֶּבֶשׁ preserves, Tᵉr. ii. 6; לֶבֶד felt, Kil. ix. 8; סֶדֶק slit, Pᵉs. iii. 2; קֶרֶץ partition, Kel. viii. 6; רֶמֶץ hot ashes, Nᵉg. ix. 1. With guttural in second or third radical: בַּעַץ tin, Kel. xxx. 3; נַחַר jetty, Oh. viii. 2; שַׁחַת fodder, Pea ii. 1; נֶקַע cleft, Kil. v. 4; קֶלַח stalk, Pea iii. 3; שֶׁבַח improvement, MŠ ii. 1.

[1] Cf. Krauss, i, §§ 326 ff.; Albrecht, § 82 g–h.

Abstract: חֶנֶק strangulation, San. vii. 1; פֶּרֶךְ cracking, ʿOr. vii. 7; וַעַד assembly, Ab. i. 4; צַעַר pain, BQ viii. 1; קֶבַע permanence, Yo. vi. 3; שֶׁבַח praise, ib. iii. 9, 10.

ע״י, ע״ו: גַּיִס troop, Pes. iii. 7; סַיִף sword, Šab. vi. 4; נוֹי beauty, ʿAZ iii. 4.

ע״ע: חַף pivot of door, Šab. viii. 6; סַם spice, Giṭ. ii. 3; גַּס gross, Ab. iv. 7.

ל״ה: גְּמִי reed-grass, Šab. viii. 2; טְנִי basket, Kel. xii. 3; לְחִי cheek, board, ʿEr. i. 2.

Fem.: חַרְבָּה knife, Šebi. viii. 7; צַחֲנָה offensive matter, Ter. x. 1; גַּפָּה stone fence, Pea iv. 2; אַשְׁפָּה dung-hill, BM ii. 3; שַׁעֲוָה wax, Šab. ii. 1; שַׁקְיָא irrigation, Ter. x. 11 (L has the masc. form: שְׁקִי).

221. (*b*) *Qiṭl.* אֵבֶר limb, Šab. viii. 1; חֵלֶשׁ lot, ib. xxiii. 2; סֵדֶר order, Yo. i. 3; סֵבֶר countenance, Ab. i. 15; עֵסֶק business, ib. iv. 10; עֵקֶל bale for pressing, Maʿa. i. 7; דִּיר shed, ʿEr. iv. 1; צִיר hinge, ib. xi. 2; כִּיחַ[1] phlegm; נִיעַ mucus BQ 3 b; נִיץ spark, BQ vi. 6; ל״ה: רְעִי excrements, Kel. xvii. 2.

Fem.: אִכְפַּת pressure, BM iii. 7 (with older fem. termination ־ַת = אִכְפָּה j. So. v. 2; Sirach xlvi. 5, 16); צִנְעָה privacy, Pes. i. 3; שִׁכְחָה forgetfulness, Pea iv. 6. ל״ה: גְּנוּת disgrace, Pes. x. 4; רְשׁוּת permission, ib. iii. 7.

222. (*c*) *Quṭl.* The vowel *u* is represented by ו. בּוֹרֶךְ knee, Kel. xxii. 2; דּוֹפֶן side, Ker. i. 5; חוֹמֶשׁ fifth part, Yo. vii. 1; סוֹרֶג lattice work, Mid. ii. 3; עוֹקֶץ point, Tam. iii. 1; רוֹטֶב broth, Pes. vii. 2; אוֹנֶס force, Kil. vii. 2; גּוֹדֶל full age; קוֹטֶן minority, Ket. ii. 11; כּוֹשֶׁר fitness, Yeb. viii. 4; צוֹרֶךְ need, Ab. ii. 3; מוֹהַל (or מוֹחַל) secretion, Ṭoh. ix. 2; פּוֹתַח opening, Kel. xi. 3; רוֹבַע quarter, Oh. ii. 1; דּוֹחַק need, Ab. ii. 3; כּוֹרַח force, ib. iv. 22.

ע״ו: דּוּר rim, Kel. xvi. 3; כּוּךְ sepulchre, MQ i. 6; כּוֹי a kind of

[1] From כחח, by assonance with ניע, with which it is always combined.

antelope, Bik. ii. 8; בּוֹר uncultivated, Ab. ii. 5; נוֹחַ pleasing, ib. 10; ע"ע: רוֹק spittle, Yeb. xii. 6; זוֹל cheapness, MŠ iv. 1; קוֹל lightness, Ḥal. iv. 7; ל"ה: קוֹשִׁי hardness, Nid. iv. 6; שׁוֹפִי ease, ib.; יוֹפִי[1] beauty, Suk. iv. 5.

Fem.: זוֹהֲמָה filth, Ter. x. 1; חוּלְדָּה mole, Kel. xv. 6; עָרְלָה forbidden fruit of a tree under four years old (cf. Lev. xix. 23), ʿOr. i. 1.

ע"ו: חוֹבָה duty, San. iv. 1; עוּקָה cavity, Maʿa. i. 7.

ע"ע: גּוּמָּה, hole, Ḥul. ii. 9; קוּפָּה basket, Kel. viii. 2.

ל"ה: חוּלְיָה limb, looseness, Kel. v. 10.

223. To this ground-form belong also nouns in which the characteristic vowel has been moved forward to the second radical: *Qaṭl*, דְּבַשׁ honey, Ter. xi. 3; גְּמַר completion, Šab. xxii. 2; צְבַת tongs, Ab. v. 6; ל"ה: הֲבַאי (L הווי) vanity, Ned. iii. 1; חֲשַׁאי modesty, privacy, Šeq. v. 6; כְּדַאי worthy, Nid. 9 b; פְּנַאי leisure, ʿAZ v. 6; תְּנַאי condition, Qid. iii. 4.

Qiṭl: בְּאֵר well, ʿEr. x. 14; זְאֵב wolf, BQ i. 4. Fem.: כְּרֵישָׁה leek, Šab. viii. 5.[2] Cf. Ges.-K., § 84 a e.

Some texts point in this fashion many nouns which properly belong to the regular *Qaṭl* type, like קְבַע, פְּלַג half, Ber. iv. 1, &c. The extension of this form by the scribes is no doubt due to the influence of Aram., in which this is the regular form for the *Qaṭl* (cf. Nöldeke, *Syr. Gr.*, §§ 93–4). So, sometimes, in BH: גְּבַר beside גֶּבֶר; חֲדַר and חֶדֶר, &c. Cf. Stade, § 191 c.

(ii) Ground-form *Qaṭal*, *Qaṭil*, *Qaṭul*.

224. (*a*) *Qaṭal*: אָבָק dust, Šab. iii. 3; בָּקָר kine, San. iii. 2; זָרֵז girdle, Kel. xxiii. 2; כָּרָךְ city, Ber. ix. 4; נָגָר bolt, Zab. iv. 3; רָקָב rottenness, Naz. vii. 2.

[1] This full form is the only one found in MH, even when not in pause.

[2] כְּרֵיסָה belly, cited by Albrecht, § 41, does not belong here. It is כְּרֵיסָהּ, from כָּרֵם = כֶּרֶשׂ; cf. כְּרֵיסוֹ his belly, Šab. 151 b.

ע״ע: חָלָל defiled priest, Qid. iv. 6 (from Lev. xx. 7); מָלָל hem, Kel. xxviii. 7; פְּקָק stopper, Šab. xvii. 7.

ל״ה: טָלֶה lamb, Tam. iii. 3; יָפֶה worth, BQ viii. 1; נָאֶה beautiful, Ab. iii. 7; שָׁוֶה worth, BQ iv. 1; עָנָיו humble, Ber. 6 b.

Fem.: הֲלָכָה rule, Šab. i. 4; חֲזָקָה possession, usucaption, BB iii. 1; חֲזָרָה return, Yeb. xiii. 6; סְבָכָה net work, hairdress, Neg. xi. 11; עֲדָשָׁה lentil, Šab. x. 5; צְוָחָה cry, Ber. ix. 3; חֲטֶרֶת hump, Ḥul. ix. 2; מְלֶחֶת saltiness, Oh. iii. 7; צְלֶקֶת scar, Neg. ix. 2;[1]

ע״ו: נָפָה sieve, Šab. viii. 2; זְוָעָה earthquake, Ber. ix. 2.

ע״ע: גְּבָבָה rakings, Šab. iii. 1; חֲרָרָה cake, ib. i. 10; סְכָכָה covering, overhanging boughs, Naz. vii. 3; קְטָטָה strife, Yeb. xv. 1; שְׂרָרָה dominion, Mak. ii. 8.

ל״ה: הֲנָאָה enjoyment, benefit, 'AZ ii. 3; לְוָיָה escort, So. ix. 6; רְאָיָה proof, Šab. viii. 7.

225. (*b*) *Qaṭil*: גָּדֵר stone fence, Pea ii. 3; חָבֵר associate, Dam. ii. 3; כָּרֵס belly, j. San. iii. 9; כָּתֵף shoulder, Šebi. iii. 9; סָפֵק doubt, Yo. viii. 6; בָּטֵל nought, Ket. ix. 1; טָפֵל subordinate, Ber. vi. 7; כָּשֵׁר proper, legal, Šab. vii. 3.

Fem.: אֲבֵדָה lost property, BM ii. 7; גְּזֵלָה robbed property, Yeb. xv. 7; בְּרֵיכָה pond; פְּסֵיקָה pool, MQ 4 a; עֲרֵבָה kneading trough, Pes. iii. 2; קְדֵרָה pot, 'Or. ii. 15; דְּלֵקָה conflagration, Šab. xvi. 1; חֲשֵׁכָה darkness, ib. i. 3; עֲבֵרָה transgression, Yo. viii. 8.

226. (*c*) *Qaṭul*. The vowel *ŭ* = *ŏ* is represented by ו, וֹ.

רָטוֹב birdtrap, Kel. xxiii. 5; חָשׁוֹךְ dark, Bek. vii. 8; יָרוֹק yellow, 'Ed. v. 6; מָתוֹק sweet, 'Er. 18 b; עָגוֹל round, Nid. viii. 4; עָמוֹק deep, t. Neg. i. 5.

(iii) Ground-form *Qaṭâl*, *Qaṭîl*, *Qaṭûl*.

227. (*a*) *Qaṭâl*, with *â* obscured into *ô*. Concretes are rare: מָרוֹר bitter herbs, Pes. ii. 6. Usually abstract nouns and adjectives

[1] רְכָבָה, Šebi. ii. 6, cited by Albrecht, § 42, is an error. The text has הַרְכָּבָה grafting, a verbal noun; cf. below, § 252.

derived from BH, e.g. כָּבוֹד honour, Ab. ii. 10; שָׁלוֹם peace, ib. i. 12; גָּדוֹל great, ib. vi. 5; קָדוֹשׁ holy, ib. v. 4; טָהוֹר pure, Kel. xii. 2.

228. (*b*) *Qaṭîl*: אָרִיחַ lath, ʿEr. i. 3; אָרִיג web, Šab. xiii. 1; בָּזִיךְ dish, Yo. ii. 5; חָרִיץ trench, Kil. v. 3; יָרִיד a fair, ʿAZ 13 a; אָסִיף gathering; זָמִיר pruning; חָרִישׁ ploughing, Sifra 105 b, c, d; מָסִיק olive gathering, Ḥal. iii. 9; זָהִיר careful, Ab. i. 9; חָבִיב beloved, ib. ii. 10; צָרִיךְ necessary, Šab. ii. 7; רָגִיל accustomed, Yo. i. 3; ל״ה: בָּקִי experienced, San. vii. 2; נָקִי clean, t. Ṭoh. iii. 8.

The Fem. form *Qᵉṭîlā* is exceedingly common in MH as a *nomen actionis* for the *Qal*, taking the place of the old BH construct infinitive. The form is also found in BH with the same significance, both in early and in late texts. Thus, שְׁרִיקוֹת Jud. v. 16; אֲכִילָה 1 Kings xix. 8; שְׁגִיאוֹת Psa. xix. 13; שְׁחִיטָה 2 Chron. xxx. 7; יְגִיעָה Qoh. xii. 12; perhaps also פְּצִירָה filing, 1 Sam. xiii. 21. In ע״ו: קִימָה Lam. iii. 63, and in a derived concrete sense: מְלִילָה Deut. xxiii. 26; בִּיאָה entry, Ezek. viii. 5. It is also found in Sirach: גְּוִיעָה xxxviii. 16; שְׁעִיָּה ib. 25; שְׁקִידָה ib. 26. The form is used in Ethiopic in exactly the same way as in MH, cf. Dillmann, *Eth. Gr.*, § 124; Barth, *Nominalbildung*, p. 137. In Aram., however, it occurs only occasionally in Jewish dialects,[1] in which it is most probably borrowed from MH. The fact that in earlier BH it occurs only in the Song of Deborah and in the story of Elijah may, perhaps, tend to show that it was originally a Northern dialectal form, which was received into the literary language only after it had established itself in the spoken language. From the latter it may have descended into MH.

Concrete nouns in this form are comparatively few in MH, as compared with the extremely numerous examples of abstract nouns of a verbal nature. This seems to show that the concrete

[1] Cf. Dalman, p. 158, 5 and foot-note.

significance is only secondary, and that it was derived from the original abstract meaning; cf. בִּיאָה, in BH, cited above.

Exx. of concrete nouns: חֲתִיכָה piece, Ḥul. vii. 5; כְּרִיכָה bundle, BM ii. 1; מְלִילָה parched ear of corn, Ma'a. iv. 5; מְשִׁיחָה cord, Kil. ix. 9; סְרִידָה bag, Kel. viii. 3; עֲנִיבָה loop, Pes. 11 a; פְּתִילָה wick, Šab. ii. 1; קִיתָה = לְקִיתָה handle, Kel. xvi. 4.

ע"ע: חֲגִיגָה festival sacrifice, Ḥag. i. 2; חֲצִיצָה intervening object, BQ 82 a; כְּפִיפָה basket, So. ii. 1. ל"ה: נְבִיָּה leaf, 'AZ iii. 8; רְטִיָּה plaster, 'Er. x. 13.

Abstracts (*nomina actionis*) can be formed at will from every verb. Exx.: אֲכִילָה eating, MŠ i. 7; בְּדִיקָה searching, Pes. i. 1; גְּמִיאָה quaffing, Šab. viii. 1; דְּרִיסָה treading, Šebi. v. 2; דְּרִישָׁה inquiry; חֲקִירָה investigation, San. iv. 1, 5; סְמִיכָה laying on of hands; קְמִיצָה taking of a handful; מְלִיקָה pinching bird's head, Qid. i. 8; רְחִיצָה washing, Yo. iii. 1; שְׁחִיטָה slaying, ib. i. 7; קְרִיאָה reading, Ber. i. 1; קִיחָה (= לְקִיחָה) taking, Sifra 45 c; Qid. 2 a; יְצִיאָה going out, Šab. i. 1; לֵידָה = יְלִידָה birth, Ket. iv. 3.

ע"ו: בִּיאָה coming, Pes. ix. 4; טִיחָה daubing, Neg. xii. 6; לִישָׁה kneading, Men. v. 2; מִיתָה death, Yo. viii. 8; סִיכָה anointing, Šab. ix. 4 (L יסיכה: so elsewhere, e.g. Yo. viii. 1).

ע"ע: בְּלִילָה mingling, Men. vi. 3; חֲפִיפָה cleansing the head, MŠ ii. 3; פְּתִיתָה crumbling, Men. vi. 4; רְקִיקָה spitting, Ber. ix. 5.

ל"ה: אֲפִיָּה baking, Men. v. 2; דְּחִיָּה pushing, Yo. vi. 6; כְּרִיָּה digging, BQ v. 6; עֲלִיָּה going up, Šeq. viii. 2; צְלִיָּה roasting, Pes. vi. 1; רְבִיָּה increasing; פְּרִיָּה fruitfulness, Yeb. vi. 7; שְׁתִיָּה drinking, Yo. viii. 1.

A number of nouns add the abstract suffix וּת— (cf. below, § 272) to strengthen the abstract significance, e.g. אֲרִיסוּת tenancy, Pea v. 5; גְּמִילוּת doing, ib. i. 1; פְּרִישׁוּת separation, Ab. iii. 13; שְׁתִיקוּת silence, Giṭ. iv. 8, &c.

229. (*c*) *Qaṭûl*. To this form belong the Passive Participles *Qal*, and verbal adjectives like חָמוּר weighty, strict, Kel. i. 4;

עָרוּם subtle, So. iii. 41; פָּחוּת[1] less, Yo. ii. 5. Further, nouns: בָּחוּר young man, Ta'a. iv. 8; חָלוּק smooth, shirt, Šab. x. 3; חָרוּב carob tree, Šebi. vii. 5; חָתוּל cat, BQ 18 b.

Fem.: בְּתוּלָה virgin, Ket. i. 1; חֲבוּרָה company, Ber. vii. 51; חֲלוּדָה rust, Kel. xiii. 5; סְעוּדָה meal, Ber. vi. 6; שְׁמוּעָה report, Ber. ix. 2.

To this class may, perhaps, be reckoned also fem. nouns with sharpening of the third radical: כְּהוּנָּה priesthood, Ab. vi. 5; כְּתוּבָּה writ, marriage settlement, Qid. ii. 5; קְדוּשָּׁה holiness, RH iv. 5 cf. Barth, op. cit., § 95.

(iv) Ground-form *Qᵉṭál, Qᵉṭíl, Qᵉṭúl.*

230. (*a*) *Qᵉṭál.* אֱלָל offal, Ḥul. ix. 1; חֲטָם nose ring, Šab. v. 1; כְּתָב writing, Ket. ii. 3; סְיָג hedge, Ab. i. 2; סְיָח young ass, BB v. 3; פְּרָס reward, Ab. i. 4; שְׂרָף resin, 'Or. i. 7; שְׁאָר, שְׁיָר remainder, So. vii. 7; סְתָם undefined, 'AZ i. 5; פְּגָם blemish, Me'il. v. 1; שְׁטָר document, Šebi. x. 1. ע״ע: כְּלָל general rule, Ber. vi. 2.

With *á* obscured into *ó*: בְּכוֹר first-born, Zeb. v. 8; חֲמוֹר ass, Bek. i. 2; חֲסוֹם muzzle, Kel. xvi. 7; טְחוֹל milt, Ḥul. iii. 2. ע״ע: צְרוֹר knot, Kel. xxvi. 4; צְנוֹן radish, Kil. i. 5.

Fem.: יְרוֹקָה sea-weed, Šab. ii. 1; עֲבוֹדָה service, Kil. vi. 1; שְׂעוֹרָה barley corn, 'Ed. vi. 3. Segolate forms[2]: כְּתוֹבֶת tattooing, Mak. iii. 6; נְחוֹשֶׁת copper, Kel. viii. 3; נְסוֹרֶת chips, Šab. iv. 1; שְׁחוֹלֶת metal shavings, Kel. xi. 3.

231. (*b*) *Qᵉṭíl.* בְּדִיד spade, Kel. xxix. 7; גְּזִיר log, Yo. ii. 5; גְּרִיד dry season, BM v. 10; גְּרִיס pounded grain, Kel. xvii. 12; חֲזִיר swine, Ḥul. ix. 2; טְפִיחַ pitcher, Šab. xvii. 6; מְלִיחַ pickled food, Ned. ii. 4; סְנִיף attachment, Men. xi. 6; פְּקִיעַ wick, Šeq. v. 1;

[1] Some texts point פַּחוּת; cf. Krauss, *MGWJ.*, li, p. 57.

[2] Cf. Stade, § 208 c; Ges.-K., § 84 A n.

קְמִיעַ amulet, Kel. xxiii. 1; שְׁבִיל path, Pea ii. 1; שְׁלִיל embryo, Ḥul. vii. 1; פְּנִים[1] interior, Šab. i. 1.

232. (*c*) *Qᵉṭûl*: גְּבוּל border, Šᵉq. vii. 3; כְּבוּל hair net, Šab. vi. 1; צְלוּב gallows, Šab. vi. 10; תְּחוּב shoot, t. Šᵉbi. i. 9; תְּחוּם boundary, 'Er. iii. 4; מְלוּג usufruct, Yᵉb. vii. 1; פְּטוּר discharge, Giṭ. ix. 3; פְּסוּל disqualification, Yo. i. 1; שְׁבוּת resting, Pᵉs. vi. 2.

(v) Ground-form *Qáṭāl, Qáṭil, Qáṭūl.*

233. (*a*) *Qáṭāl,* the *á* obscured to *ó*: חוֹטָם nose, Bᵉk. vi. 4; חוֹתָל wrapper, Kel. xvi. 11; חוֹתָם seal, Šab. viii. 5; שׁוֹבָךְ dovecot, ib. xxiv. 3; שׁוֹפָר trumpet, RH iii. 3.

234. (*b*) *Qáṭīl.* To this form belongs the Active Participle *Qal* of transitive verbs. Also a number of nouns of participial origin, e.g. סוֹחֵר merchant, Šᵉq. vii. 2; פּוֹשֵׁר lukewarm water, Šab. xx. 3; צוֹנֵן cold water, ib. iii. 4; קוֹזֵז (= קוֹצֵץ) clods, MŠ v. 1.

Fem.: חוֹצֶלֶת mat, 'Ed. iii. 4; יוֹתֶרֶת lobe; כּוֹתֶבֶת date, Yo. viii. 2.

235. (*c*) *Qáṭūl.* To this class belong the following *nomina agentis* with *ū* modified to *ó*: טָחוֹן miller, Dam. iii. 5; BQ 99 b; BB 93 b; לָעוֹז (so L), לָעוֹזוֹת speaker of foreign tongue, Mᵉg. ii. 1; סָרוֹק woolcomber, Kel. xxvi. 5; סָרוֹקוֹת ib. xii. 2: the following occur in the plural only: דָּרוֹכוֹת wine pressers, Tᵉr. iii. 4; חָכוֹרוֹת tenants, Bik. i. 2; גָּרוֹסוֹת grist makers, Mᵉn. x. 4; דָּשׁוֹשׁוֹת groat makers (דישׁ = דשׁשׁ) MQ ii. 5; מָסוֹרוֹת informers, 'AZ 26 b; מָשׁוֹחוֹת measurers, surveyors, 'Er. iv. 11; לָקוֹטוֹת gatherers, BM 72 b; t. BM vi. 1; מָשׁוֹשׁוֹת j. Pea viii. 1 (cf. § 177, note); לָקוֹחוֹת purchasers, Kᵉt. viii. 1: the sing., however, is always לוֹקֵחַ. This form may, perhaps, be due to a deliberate change of spelling by the scribes, who mistook the form לָקוֹחַ for the participle passive לָקוּחַ. To the ignorance of the scribes are also due the forms טוֹחֵן, סוֹרֵק, and לוֹעֵז, in some texts.

The form *Qáṭūl* is also found in the following names of instru-

[1] This is the traditional pronunciation; cf. BH. 1 Kings vi. 29.

ments: דָּקוֹר a borer, Kel. xiv. 3; מָחוֹק an instrument for levelling a measure of grain, ib. xvii. 6; שָׁחוֹר a razor, ib. xiii. 1; סָמוֹכוֹת supporters, artificial legs, Šab. vi. 8; רָחוֹשׁ reptile-shaped ornament, t. ʿAZ v. 2. Perhaps also אָרוֹס timbrel, Kel. xv. 6 (L, but So. ix. 14: אירוס, also in L).

The form is very common in Aram. (קָטוֹלָא ܩܛܘܿܠܐ), but it also occurs in BH nearly as often as in MH, viz. אָמוֹן, בָּחוֹן, חָמוֹץ, יָקוֹשׁ, עָשׁוֹק, רָזוֹן; perhaps also צָרוֹף a refiner, Jer. vi. 29; the fem. בָּגוֹדָה, perhaps also שָׁדוֹדָה (Psa. cxxxvii. 9, for שְׁדוּדָה), and as *nomen instrumenti*: תָּקוֹעַ (Ezek. vii. 4).

236. (vi) Ground-form *Qûṭāl*: גּוּדָל thumb, Nid. viii. 1; with prosthetic א: אֲגוּדָל Yo. ii. 1; כּוּפָּח small oven, Šab. iii. 2; שׁוּעָל fox, Šab. vi. 10.

(2) *Nouns derived from the Intensive Stem.*

(i) Ground-form *Qăṭṭal, Qăṭṭil, Qăṭṭul.*

237. (*a*) *Qaṭṭāl, Qaṭṭâl*: chiefly *nomina opificum*, describing the occupation or profession of the substantive: אַנָּס robber, Kil. vii. 6; בַּהָם cattle-driver, j. Pes. i. 1; בַּקָּר cowherd, j. Be. v. 3; גַּמָּל camel-driver, Qid. iv. 13; חַמָּר ass-driver; סַפָּן sailor; סַפָּר barber, ib.; גַּנָּב thief, BM iii. 1; כַּתָּף porter, Kel. xii. 2; נַגָּר carpenter, t. BQ vi. 25; פַּטָּם poulterer, ʿEr. x. 9; צַמָּר wool dealer, ib.; קַדָּר potter, BQ iii. 4.

With ר in the second radical: הָרָג murderer; חָרָם confiscator, Nᵉd, iii. 4; גָּרָד weaver, Kil. ix. 10.

ע״ו, ע״י: רַוָּוק bachelor, Qid. iv. 13; בַּיָּר well sinker, Šᵉbi. viii. 5; דַּיָּין judge, Pea viii. 9; חַיָּט tailor, Šab. i. 3; טַיָּל man of leisure, Kᵉt. v. 7.

ל״ה, with ַ in the second radical for ָ, in Aram. fashion: בַּנַּאי builder, Kel. xiv. 3; גַּבַּאי collector, Dam. iii. 1. Adjectives: דַּמַּאי suspect, Dam. i. 1; וַדַּאי certain, ib. iv. 4; זַכַּאי innocent,

Ab. i. 8; חַשָּׁאי silent, modest, Š^{e}q. v. 6; לַוִּי accompanying, N^{e}g. xiv. 6; רַשַּׁאי permitted, Šab. xxiii. 3.

Fem. Concrete: יַבָּשָׁה dry land, Giṭ. 56 b; עַכָּבָה rim, ʻAZ v. 1; and with ת at the end: בַּלֶּשֶׁת[1] reconnoitring troop, t. Be. ii. 6; גַּמֶּלֶת caravan of camels; חַמֶּרֶת caravan of asses, San. x. 5; יַבֶּלֶת wart, ʻEr. x. 3; כַּבֶּשֶׁת pressed vegetables, t. Š^{e}bi. iv. 16; כַּוֶּרֶת beehive, Š^{e}bi. viii. 10; קָרַחַת bald, empty space, Kil. iv. 1.

Abstracts, including *nomina actionis*, chiefly with ָה: בַּטָּלָה idleness, Ab. iii. 4; הַוָּיָה being, M^{e}kil. (Weiss), 85; Qid. 5 a; יַבָּבָה cry, RH iv. 9; כַּוָּנָה intention, ʻEr. iv. 4; כַּפָּרָה atonement, N^{e}g. ii. 1; סַכָּנָה danger, B^{e}r. iv. 4; עַכָּבָה or עַקָּבָה detention, ʻAZ v. 7; קַבָּלָה reception, Z^{e}b. i. 6. Cf. BH בַּקָּרָה, בַּקָּשָׁה, נֶאָצָה, &c.; see Ges.-K., § 84, B e.

The form is comparatively rare in MH, as in BH, and cannot like the other verbal nouns *Qiṭṭûl* (§ 241) and *Q^{e}ṭîlā* (§ 228) be formed at will.

238. (*b*) *Qaṭṭil, Qaṭṭîl*: the infinitive of Piʻel; יַקִּיר notable, Yo. vi. 4; כַּשִּׁיל axe, BQ x. 10; סַכִּין knife, ib. iv. 9; פַּצִּים board, Šab. viii. 5; צַדִּיק righteous, Ab. i. 2.

239. (*c*) *Qaṭṭūl, Qaṭṭûl*: חַדּוּד point, Kel. ii. 9; חַנּוּן gracious, Šab. 133 b; טַבּוּר navel, Šab. xviii. 3; כַּדּוּר ball, Kel. x. 4; עַמּוּד pillar, B^{e}r. i. 2; שַׁפּוּד spit, ʻAZ v. 12.

Fem.: חַבּוּרָה wound, BQ viii. 1; בַּצּוֹרֶת drought, Ab. v. 8; מַסּוֹרֶת tradition, ib. iii. 13.

(ii) Ground-form *Qiṭṭal, Qiṭṭil, Qiṭṭul, Qiṭṭôl*.

240. (*a*) *Qiṭṭāl, Qiṭṭâl*: אִכָּר husbandman, ʻArak. vi. 3; עִיקָּר root, principal, B^{e}r. vi. 7.

(*b*) *Qiṭṭīl, Qiṭṭîl*: דִּיבֵּר speech, M^{e}kil. 5; fem.: דִּבְּרוֹת BQ 54 b; כִּסֵּא chair, Tam. i. 1; רִבִּית usury RH i. 8; עִדִּית choice land, Giṭ. v. 1. The form is further used, as in BH, to express a

[1] Some texts have בולשת, a participial form, § 234.

physical defect: אִלֵּם dumb, T^e^r. i. 6; גִּבֵּן hunchback, B^e^k. vii. 2; גִּדֵּם with hands cut off; חִגֵּר lame; חֵרֵשׁ deaf, San. viii. 4; עִקֵּל with crooked feet; צִמֵּם with large ears; צִמֵּעַ with small ears, B^e^k. vii. 4, 6; קִפֵּחַ lanky, ib.;[1] קִטֵּעַ crippled, Šab. vi. 8; and by analogy: פִּיקֵּחַ hearing, Y^e^b. xiv. 1.

241. (*c*) *Qiṭṭûl.* This form is widely used as a verbal noun for Piʿel, and can be formed at will from any verb. It has primarily an abstract significance, but is also found in concretes in a derived sense.

Exx.: אִיסּוּר prohibition, ʿAZ ii. 3; בִּיטּוּל idling, interruption, Šab. xvi. 1; גִּדּוּל growth, B^e^r. vi. 3; דִּיבּוּק joining together, Ab. vi. 5; הִילּוּךְ walking, Yo. ii. 3; חִיבּוּר joining, Kil. ix. 10; יִבּוּם levirate marriage, Y^e^b. i. 1; כִּבּוּד honouring, Pea i. 1; לִימּוּד learning, Ab. vi. 5; נִסּוּךְ libation, Suk. iv. 9; סִידּוּק cleaving, P^e^s. iii. 5; זֵירוּד trimming, Š^e^bi. ii. 3; טֵירוּף confusion, B^e^r. v. 4; פֵּירוּשׁ explanation, ʿAZ i. 5; צִיהוּב gilding, Ḥul. i. 5.

עִוּוּת perverting Ab. v. 8; קִיּוּם confirming, Giṭ. ii. 5; שִׁיּוּר (cf. above, § 162) remainder, K^e^r. ii. 5; תֵּיחוּחַ crushing, Oh. xviii. 9.

בִּיטּוּי vain talk, Š^e^bu. iii. 9; וִידּוּי confession, San. ii. 6; מִלּוּי filling, Dam. vi. 5; עִינּוּי afflicting, Ab. v. 8; רִפּוּי healing, BQ viii. 1.

Concrete: גִּידּוּלִים products, B^e^r. 40 b; חִילּוּף exchange, relay, B^e^r. iii. 1; טִינּוּף filth, B^e^k. iii. 1; יִשּׁוּב civilized world, Qid. i. 10; לִמּוּדִים boards, MQ ii. 2; חִיסּוּם steel edge, Kel. xiii. 4; עִגּוּל round cake, BM ii. 1; עֵירוּב *ʿerub*, ʿEr. iii. 2; צִבּוּר heap, BM ii. 2; שֵׁיעוּר measure, Pea i. 1.

פֵּירוּר crumb, Šab. xxiv. 3; חִיפּוּי wrapping, Kel. xvi. 8; כִּסּוּי cover, Šab. xvii. 8; קִיפּוּי froth, T^e^r. iv. 11.

Fem.: בִּכּוּרָה early fig, T^e^r. iv. 6.

The form is found in a number of technical terms in the plural

[1] So יִיתֵּר one with superfluous fingers or toes, ib., in L, for יָתֵר in edd.

only: אֵירוּסִין betrothal, Yᵉb. vi. 4; נִישּׂוּאִין matrimony Kᵉt. i. 4; קִידּוּשִׁין betrothal; גֵּירוּשִׁין divorce, Yᵉb. iii. 8; בֵּירוּרִין arbitration; מֵיאוּנִין annulment of minority marriage, BM i. 8; זֵירוּזִין urgings (of vows), Nᵉd. iii. 1; also יִסּוּרִין suffering, Bᵉr. 5 a.

The form is found in BH both as abstract and concrete, in the sing. and in the plural: חִבּוּק, שִׁלּוּם, צִפּוּי, שִׁקּוּץ, לִמּוּד, גִּדּוּפִים, מִלֻּאִים, &c. Cf. Ges.-K., § 84 B i; Stade, § 228. So in Sirach: חִמּוּד xiv. 14; יִסּוּר xl. 29; לִמּוּד xli. 28; נִסּוּי xxxii. 1; xliv. 20.

242. (*d*) *Qiṭṭol*, *Qiṭṭôl*: גִּבּוֹר mighty, Ab. iv. i; גִּיחוֹר crimson red, Bᵉk. vii. 6; יִלּוֹד born, Ab. iv. 21; נִיפּוֹל young birds fallen out of their nest, BB ii. 6; נִיצוֹץ spark, t. Yo. ii. 3; צִנּוֹר pipe, Miq. iv. 1; קִיפּוֹף long-tailed ape, Bᵉk. 8 a; שִׁכּוֹר drunkard, Bᵉk. vii. 6.

Fem.: בִּקּוֹרֶת inquiry, Kᵉt. xi. 5; טִינּוֹפֶת filth, BB vi. 2; קִיבּוֹלֶת contract labour, t. MQ ii. 5; קִיבּוֹרֶת biceps, Mᵉn. 37 a, b; שִׁיבּוֹלֶת ear of corn, Pea v. 2.

243. (iii) Ground-form *Quṭṭal*: שׁוּתָּף partner, Pᵉs. viii. 1 (cf. Sirach xl. 24); אוּמָּן artisan, ʽAV v. 7; עוּבָּר embryo, Ḥul. iv. 1.

(3) *Nouns formed by Reduplication.*

244. (i) Reduplication of the Third radical. These have the vowel *ŭ* in the second syllable, and are mostly of a diminutive significance.

Exx.: גַּבְלוּל lump of dough, j. Ḥal. iii. 1; דַּבְלוּל excrescence, t. Kel. BM vii. 11; קַמְצוּץ compressed, bent up, j. So. ix. 1; סְמַרְטוּט (Saphʽel of מרט to pluck, cf. above, § 149), lappet, Šab. xi. 2, and perhaps also זַאטוּט or זַעֲטוּט (= זַטוּט from זוט) young man, Mᵉg. 9 a.[1]

[1] Kohut, iii. 283 f., holds that זַעֲטוּטֵי is an error for נַאטוּטֵי = νεώτατοι. The noun is also found in the Arabic dialect of Iraq, cf. Brockelmann, *Grundriss*, i, § 172 a.

The other examples are all fem.:

עַרְבּוּבְיָה mixture, confusion, Kil. v. 1; קַרְוָיָה (from קרה) hollow pumpkin, Pa. v. 3. With the termination ־ִית: אַדְמוּמִית redness, Ḥul. 87 b; לַבְנוּנִית whiteness, Neg. iv. 4; שַׁחֲרוּרִית blackness, ugliness, Ta'a. 23 b; מַשְׁכּוּכִית leading ram, BQ 52 b; רַקְבּוּבִית rottenness, Yo. 38 b; שַׁמְנוּנִית oily substance, Be. 28 a.

Diminutives: גַּבְשׁוּשִׁית a hillock, heap, Šab. 23 b; גּוּמָמִית little hole, t. Miq. iii. 4; גַּנּוּנִית little garden, BB 68 a, b; דְּגוּגִית a light fisher-boat (contracted to דּוּגִית), BB 78 b; זַרְבּוּבִית little pipe, Lev. R. 5; Num. R. 10; עַפְרוּרִית little dust, BB 93 b; שְׁלוּלִית pool, Oh. xvi. 5; תְּלוּלִית hillock, ib. 7.

Cf. BH נַעֲצוּץ, נַאֲפוּפִים, שַׁעֲרוּרִיָּה, &c., Stade, § 231.

A BH parallel to the diminutive significance of reduplicated form is to be found in שְׁחַרְחֹרֶת Cant. i. 6, which can only mean blackish, dark. Perhaps also יְרַקְרַק, אֲדַמְדָּם[1] Lev. xiii. 42, 43; אֲסַפְסוּף rabble, Num. xi. 4, and פִּרְחָח low brood, Job xxx. 12 (cf. פִּרְחֵי כְהוּנָּה young priests, Yo. i. 7; Tam. i. 1), are to be regarded as diminutives, the last two nouns with a contemptuous significance.

245. (ii) Reduplication of Second and Third radicals.

אֲדַמְדָּם red; יְרַקְרַק yellow, Neg. iii. 8; חֲוַרְוָר spotted, white, Bek. vi. 3; סְגַלְגָּלָה round, Šab. 31 a; שְׁרַפְרַף camp stool, Kel. xxiii. 2; שְׁרַקְרַק gier eagle, Ḥul. 63 a.

With *ō* in the second syllable, cf. BH שְׁחַרְחֹרֶת, פְּתַלְתֹּל, &c. (Ges.-K., § 84 B n); חֲלַגְלוֹג purslane, Šebi. ix. 1; חֲלַחְלוֹחַ a species of peas, t. Pea i. 7; יְרַקְרוֹקֶת yellowish, Meg. 13 a; צְמַרְמוֹרוֹת feverish flushes, Nid. ix. 8.

Diminutives: בְּצַלְצִיל dwarf onion, Kil. i. 3; פְּרוֹטְרוֹט units, details, t. MŠ ii. 11. So the caritative form: יְפֵיפִין very beautiful,

[1] Cf. Ibn Ezra, *ad loc.*, and on Cant., l. c. In Neg. xi. 4; Sifra, xiii. 49, however, these terms are explained as intensives. Cf. also Brockelmann, ib., i, § 172.

Ned. 20 b; יְפֵיפִיָּה Pes. 6 b; יְפֵיפִיּוֹת Meg. 15 a; Ta'a. 31 a, cf. Jerem. xlvi. 20. For the diminutive character of the vowel *é* = *ai*, cf. § 273.

If the third radical is ל or ר it is sometimes omitted: מְטוֹטֶלֶת (= מְטַלְטֶלֶת) plummet, Kel. xii. 8; Šab. v. 3; שְׁפוֹפֶרֶת (= שְׁפַרְפֶּרֶת), tube, ib. ii. 4. So עֲנְקוּקְלוֹת for עֲנַקְלְקָלוֹת (from ענקל = ענק), undeveloped grapes, ʽOr. i. 8.

246. (iii) Reduplication of the whole Stem,[1] in ע"ו and ע"ע roots.

(*a*) Ground-form *Qaṭqaṭ*, *Qaṭqiṭ*, *Qaṭquṭ*: גַּלְגַּל wheel, Mid. v. 4; גַּרְגַּר berry, Šebi. iii. 7; כַּבְכָּב lid, Kel. ii. 3; קַנְקָן cylindrical vessel, Ab. iv. 20.

Fem.: קַלְקָלָה disgrace, Ab. iv. 18; קַרְקָרָה bottom of vessel, Kel. ii. 2; צַפְצָפָה a species of willow, Suk. iii. 3; כַּלְכָּלָה basket, Pea vii. 3; גַּרְגֶּרֶת windpipe, Ḥul iii. 1; פַּרְפֶּרֶת hash, Ber. vi. 5; שַׁבְשֶׁבֶת paste, Šab. viii. 4; שַׁלְשֶׁלֶת chain, BQ vii. 7.

Qaṭqiṭ. The Infinitives of Pilpel: טַלְטֵל, קַלְקֵל, &c., cf. §§ 182, 195.

Qaṭquṭ: דַּרְדּוּר, cask on wheels, Kel. xv. 1; חַסְחוּס cartilage, Bek. vi. 1; חַרְחוּר coulter, Kel. xiii. 3; פַּטְפּוּט peg, Šab. viii. 4.

Fem.: גְּנוֹגֶנֶת parasol, Kel. xvi. 7 (L); גְּרוֹגֶרֶת dry fig, Šab. vii. 4; קְנוֹקְנוֹת (from קנה) branch sinews, Ḥul. 92 a, b.

247. (*b*) Ground-form *Qiṭqaṭ*, *Qiṭqiṭ*, *Qiṭquṭ*.

Qiṭqaṭ: כִּכָּר (= כִּרְכָּר) loaf, Pea viii. 7; פִּשְׁפָּשׁ wicket, Mid. i. 7; לִשְׁלֶשֶׁת secretion, Šab. xxi. 2.

Qiṭqiṭ: פִּלְפֵּל pepper (diminutive of פול) TY i. 5; פִּשְׁפֵּשׁ bug, Ter. viii. 2.

Qiṭquṭ: This form is very common as a verbal noun of Pilpel, corresponding to *Qiṭṭul* for the Intensive Stem (§ 241), and also in a secondary sense as a concrete: כִּלְכּוּל growth of hair, Šab. viii. 4; לִפְלוּף glutinous substance, Miq. ix. 4; מִלְמוּל crumbs, ib. ix. 2; קִלְקוּל disorder, MQ 12; בִּעְבּוּעַ swelling, Miq. x. 4; דִּקְדּוּק subtle

[1] Here may also be mentioned the form לֵילֵי, construct of לַיְלָה night, Suk. 48 a, and often, for BH לֵיל; cf. BDB s. v. and reff.

thinking, Ab. vi. 5; הִרְהוּר meditating, Naz. ix. 4; טִלְטוּל moving, Šab. 43 b; לִכְלוּךְ moistening, Miq. ix. 4; נִדְנוּד shaking, t. Yᵉb. iv. 8.

248. (*c*) Ground-form *Quṭquṭ*: טוּמְטוּם of unknown sex, Ḥag. i. 1; קָדְקֹד skull, Nᵉg. x. 10; גֻּלְגֹּלֶת skull, Ab. ii. 6.

(4) *Nouns formed by means of Prefixes.*

249. (i) With Prefix א: אַבּוּב flute, Kel. ii. 3; אֲגוּדָל thumb, Yo. ii. 1; אֲגַף door-step, Nᵉd. vii. 5; אַרְכּוּבָה knee, Kil. vii. 1; אַשְׁבּוֹרֶן pond, Oh. iii. 3; אַשְׁפּוֹת[1] dung-hill, Kel. xxvii. 11; אֶגְרוֹף fist, ib. xvii. 12; אֶמְצַע middle, Šab. ix. 2; אֶפְרוֹחַ chicken, Ḥul. xii. 3; אָפוּן bean, Pea iii. 3; also אָפוּל t. Tᵉr. x. 15; אַסְקוּפָּה threshold, Šab. x. 2.

In the following verbal nouns the א is a phonetic modification of ה (cf. the next section and above, § 43); אַבְעָיָה search, Pea iv. 5; אַגָּדָה Agadah, Nᵉd. iv. 3; אַזְהָרָה warning, Pᵉs. iii. 1; אוֹנָאָה wrong, BM iv. 3.

250. (ii) Prefix ה. These are all verbal nouns with an abstract significance formed from the Hiph'il. They fall into two classes: (*a*) masculines in the form *Haqṭel*, confined chiefly to strong verbs, and (*b*) feminines in the form *Haqṭala*, for all classes of verbs. Some of the *Haqṭel* forms have assumed a secondary concrete significance.

251. (*a*) *Haqṭel*. This is practically the old Infinitive Hiph'il

[1] From שׁפת, as is shown by the plur. אַשְׁפַּתּוֹת, Šᵉbi. i. 1–3; So. 42 b, &c. The form אַשְׁפּוֹת is for אַשְׁפָּת with *ā* obscured to *ō*. אַשְׁפָּת, which seems to have survived in popular speech, was reduced to אַשְׁפָּה by the elision of the final ת, on the analogy of the fem. termination. So Kᵉt. vii. 5; BM. v. 7; BB. v. 3; Mᵉ'il. iii. 6. L and other texts have, however, אַשְׁפּוֹת. In BM. ii. 3 also L reads אַשְׁפָּה. So often in the Talmud: Šab. 15 a (contrast with 'Ed. i. 3); Pᵉs. 8 b, &c. The Palestinian Talmud has often אִישְׁפָּה: j. Sab. ii. 3; j. Kᵉt. i. 10. Cf. also *JQR.*, xx, p. 715.

fossilized into a noun. The traditional, and no doubt correct, pronunciation of the prefix with *e* for *a*, seems to have arisen through assimilation to the *ē* in the second syllable.[1]

Exx.: הֶבְעֵר burning, BQ i. 1; הֶבְקֵר or הֶפְקֵר (cf. above, § 49), ownerless property, Pea vi. 1; הֶפְסֵד loss, Ab. v. 4; הֶפְשֵׁט flaying, Yo. ii. 7; הֶקְדֵּשׁ consecrated property, Tᵉr. i. 5; הֶרְגֵּל habit, Šab. i. 5; הֶסְגֵּר shutting up, Mᵉg. i. 7.

פ״נ: הֶיכֵּר recognition, ʿEr. 11 b; הֶיסֵּט shaking, Ṭoh. xi. 1; הֶיקֵּף circumference, Kel. xvii. 8; הֶיקֵּשׁ comparison, Zᵉb. 50 a; הֶנֵף waving, Suk. iii. 12.

When followed by a genitive, the prefix preserves, if tradition can be trusted, the old BH vowel. Thus: הַכְשֵׁר כָּל נִזְקוֹ rendering fit (= responsibility for) all its damage, BQ i. 1; הַעֲלֵם שֶׁרֶץ unconsciousness of the reptile, Šᵉbu. iii. 4; הַעֲרֵב שֶׁמֶשׁ setting of the sun, Ḥal. i. 9; הַשֵּׂג יָד reaching of the hand, ʿAr. iv. 1 (cf. Lev. xxvii. 8); הָשֵׁב אֲבֵדָה restoring lost property, BM vii. 4; הָנֵץ הַחַמָּה the rising of the sun, Bᵉr. i. 2.

This substantival use of the Infin. Hiphʿil is found also in BH, e.g. הַפְצַר 1 Sam. xv. 23; הַשְׁמֵד Isa. xiv. 23; הַמְשֵׁל Job xxv. 2; הוֹכֵחַ ib. vi. 25; cf. Stade, § 245.

252. (*b*) *Haqṭala*: הַבְדָּלָה separation, Ḥul. i. 7; הַבְעָרָה kindling, Šab. ii. 6; הַגְבָּהָה lifting, Qid. i. 4; הַטְמָנָה hiding, Šab. 39 a; הַכְנָסָה bringing in, ib. 2 a; הַפְסָקָה interruption, Taʿa. 4 b; הַקְטָרָה burning incense, Qid. i. 8; הַרְכָּבָה grafting, Šᵉbi. ii. 6; הַרְקָדָה sifting, Pᵉs. 11 a.

ל״ה: הַשְׁקָיָה giving to drink, Mᵉg. ii. 7; הַזָּיָה or הַזָּאָה sprinkling, Qid. i. 8.

פ״נ: הַגָּשָׁה bringing near, ib.

ע״ו: הֲבָאָה bringing, Pea i. 1; הֲדָחָה rinsing, Šab. xxii. 2; הֲטָבָה

[1] For a similar change in BH, cf. Ges.-K., § 27 p; Stade, § 81; also Sznejder, p. 231.

doing good, Š^e^bu. iii. 5; הַנָּחָה laying down, K^e^l. viii. 8; הֲרָעָה doing ill, Š^e^bu. iii. 5.

פ״י: הוֹדָאָה confessing, ib. vi. 1; הוֹצָאָה bringing out, Šab. 2 b; הוֹרָדָה bringing down, Mid. iv. 1.

For the change of ה to א cf. above, § 249.

This form which is identical with the Aram. infin. Aph'el (Haph'el) is probably older than the ordinary infin. with *ē* (= *ī*) in the second syllable.[1] In BH it is found already in Isaiah: הַכָּרָה iii. 9; הֲנָפָה xxx. 28. Further, with א in אַזְכָּרָה Lev. ii. 2, &c.; besides הֲנָחָה Esther ii. 18; הַצָּלָה ib. iv. 14. In Sirach: הַשָּׂגָה xxxv. 10; הוֹדָאָה li. 17; הַצְנֵעַ xvi. 25; xxxii. 3; cf. Micah vi. 8.

253. (*c*) With the prefix הִ is found the reflexive verbal noun הִשְׁתַּחֲוָאָה bowing down, Š^e^bu. ii. 3; .הִשְׁתַּחֲוָיוֹת Š^e^q. vi. 1; Tam. vii. 3, formed on the analogy of בְּהִשְׁתַּחֲוָיָתִי 2 Kings v. 18. Cf. Stade, § 254.

254. (iii) Prefix י. In a few nouns, consisting, chiefly, of names of animals and plants; cf. BH יַחְמוּר, יוֹנָה, &c. Stade, § 259, Barth, p. 226 f.

Exx.: יַבְחוּשׁ a kind of gnat, Nid. iii. 2; יַתּוּשׁ gnat, t. Šab. xii. 4; יַרְבּוּז strawberry-blight, Š^e^bi. ix. 1; יִחוּר branch, Kil. i. 8; further, יְצוּל handle of a plough, Kel. xxi. 2; יַתּוּכִין tongs, ib. xii. 3.

255. (iv) Prefix מ. As in BH, מ is extensively used for the formation of nouns of the following classes: (1) subjective nouns, including the Participles of the derived active stems of Verbs; also a number of *nomina actionis*, e.g. מַגָּע, מִדְרָשׁ, מִמְכָּר; (2) objective nouns, including the Participles of the derived passive stems of Verbs; also a number of concrete nouns, representing the result of an action, e.g. מַאֲפֶה, מַעֲשֶׂה, מוֹתָר; (3) names of instruments and tools, e.g. מָדוֹךְ, מַכְבֵּשׁ, מַנְעָל; (4) nouns of a local significance, e.g. מָבוֹי, מַחְצָב, מֶרְחָץ.

[1] Cf. Barth, *Nominalbildung*, pp. 73, 90.

256. (*a*) Ground-form *Maqṭal, Maqṭil, Maqṭul.*

Maqṭal: מַאֲכָל food, Šab. 10 a; מַחְצָב quarry, Šebi. iii. 5; מַנְעָל shoe, Šab. viii. 2; מַעְצָד adze, BQ x. 10. With *ă* changed to *ĕ*: מֶרְחָץ bath, Šab. i. 2; cf. Stade, § 270; also Ges.-K., § 85 h.

פ״נ: מַגָּע touch, Ḥul. iv. 4; מַדָּף instrument for driving away, Kel. xvi. 7; מַסָּר saw, Šab. xvii. 4; מַשָּׂא or מַשּׂוֹי burden, Šebi. iii. 6; מַתָּן gift, Ab. ii. 1.

פ״י: מוֹתָר remnant, Kil. v. 4; מֵיחָם heating-pan, Šab. iii. 3 (from יחם = חמם); מֵיטָב best, BQ i. 1.

ע״ו: מָאוֹר light-hole, Šab. xxiv. 5; מָבוֹי (= מָבוֹא) entrance, 'Er. i. 1; מָדוֹךְ pestle, Be. i. 7; מָזוֹן food, 'Er. iii. 1; מָחוֹל circle, Kil. iv. 2; מָקוֹף the eye of a coulter, Kel. xiii. 3.

ע״ע: מַמָּשׁ palpable, real, San. v. 4; מַגָּפַיִם greaves, Kel. xi. 8.

ל״ה: מַאֲפֶה baked, 'Er. vii. 10; מַקְלֶה roasting-place, Ta'a. iii. 1; מַקְפֶּה mess of grist, Šab. xvii. 5.

Fem.: מַחֲשָׁבָה thought, Ber. 61 a; מַטְהֶרֶת gutter, Miq. vi. 11; מַקְלָעָה braid, Yo. vi. 7; מַרְדַּעַת pack-saddle, Šab. v. 2; מַרְפֶּסֶת veranda, Ma'a. iii. 6.

מַכָּה wound, So. iii. 4; מַתָּנָה gift, Zeb. v. 1.

מְגוּפָה stopper, Šab. xxii. 3; מְדוֹכָה mortar, Kel. xxiii. 2; מְצוּדָה net, ib. xxi. 3; מְדִינָה district, RH iv. 3; מְחִיצָה partition, Kil. iv. 4; מְעִיסָה flour paste, Ḥal. i. 6.

Maqṭil: מַטְבֵּעַ coin, Šab. vi. 7; מַכְבֵּשׁ press, ib. xx. 5; מַלְבֵּן frame, Neg. xiii. 3; מַלְקֵט (or מַלְקֶטֶת L) pincher, Mak. iii. 5; מַסְמֵר nail, Kel. xii. 5; מַסְרֵק comb, ib. xiii. 8; מַעְבֵּר pitchfork (or מַעְדֵּר) ib. 7; מַעְטֵן vat, BM v. 7; מַפְתֵּחַ key, Kel. xiv. 8; מַרְפֵּק elbow, 'Ar. v. 1; מַרְצֵעַ awl, Qid. 21 b; מַרְתֵּף store-room, Pes. i. 1; מַשְׁבֵּר travailing chair, Kel. xxiii. 4; מַתְבֵּן store of straw, 'Er. vii. 5.

Fem.: מַגְרֵפָה shovel, Tam. ii. 1; מַזְחֵלָה gutter, BB iii. 6; מַשְׁפֵּלָה wicker-basket, Šebi. iii. 2; מְאֵירָה curse, Suk. iii. 10; מַגֵּפָה wound, Makš. vi. 8.

Maqṭul, only fem. nouns. The *ū* is changed to *ō* and usually spelt with ו: מַאֲכוֹלֶת louse, Šab. 12 a; מַחֲרוֹזֶת string, BM ii. 1; מַחֲלֹקֶת controversy, Ab. v. 20; מַסְפּוֹרֶת scissors, Šab. 48 b; מַפּוֹלֶת fall, Pes. ii. 3.

257. (*b*) Ground-form *Miqṭal, Miqṭil, Miqṭul.*

Miqṭal: מִדְבָּר wilderness, Ber. ix. 2; מִדְרָס treading, Kel. xxiv. 1; מִזְרָן mattress, ib. xix. 3; מִמְכָּר selling, Meg. iii. 2; מִנְהָג custom, BM vii. 1; מִשְׁתֶּה feast, Ber. i. 1; מִקַּח taking, Ab. iv. 22.

Fem.: מִדְלָעוֹת, מִקְשָׁאוֹת fields of pumpkins, of cucumbers, Šebi. ii. 1; מִזְוָדָה travelling-bag, Kel. xx. 1; מִכְוָה burn, Neg. ix. 1; מִלְוֶה loan, 'AZ iv. 10; מִקְלֶה burning, Ta'a. ii. 1; מִשְׁנָה repetition, study, Ab. iii. 7; מִחִלָּה cavity, t. Yeb. xiv. 6; מִסִבָּה winding staircase, Tam. i. 1; מִעִיסָּה flour paste, Ḥal. i. 6.

Miqṭil: מִזְבֵּחַ altar, Zeb. v. 1.

Miqṭul, only fem.: מִכְמוֹרֶת net, Kel. xxiii. 5; מִשְׁקוֹלֶת plummet, ib. xxix. 3.

258. (*c*) Ground-form *Muqṭal*: Participle Hoph'al; further, מוּגְמָר perfume, Ber. vi. 6; מוּקְצֶה store of fruit, Ma'a. i. 5; מוּרְסָה blister, 'Ed. ii. 5.

259. (*d*) Ground-form *Maqṭâl-Maqṭôl, Maqṭîl, Maqṭûl.*

Maqṭâl. The long *â* is obscured to *ô*: מַכְחוֹל eye-painter, Kel. xiii. 8; מַלְקוֹט bag, ib. xvi. 7.

Maqṭîl: Participle of Hiph'il; further, fem. nouns: מַעֲזִיבָה plaster of ceiling, BM x. 1; מַטְלִית patch, lining, Šab. xxiv. 5; מַרְאִית sight, appearance, ib. xix. 6.

Maqṭûl: מַפּוּחַ bellows, t. Be. iii. 15.

260. (*e*) Ground-form *Maqaṭṭel*: Participle Pi'el; further some fem. nouns of a participial origin: מְסַנֶּנֶת sieve, Kel. xiv. 8; מְשַׁמֶּרֶת strainer, Ab. v. 15.

261. (v) Prefix נ: Participle Niph'al; further the following nouns: נִבְרֶכֶת pool, MQ i. 6; נִבְרֶשֶׁת lamp, Yo. iii. 10; נִדְבָּךְ stone wall, Ber. ii. 4; נַחְשׁוֹל storm, Yo. 38 a; נַחְתּוֹם baker, Dam. ii. 4;

נִצְפָּה caper berry, ib. i. 1; נְמוֹשׁוֹת aged (groping), Pea viii. 1; cf. § 177, נִיצוֹק uninterrupted flow, Ṭoh. viii. 9.

262. (vi) Prefix ס, שׁ: Verbal nouns formed from Saph'el and Šaph'el: סִרְגּוּל drawing lines, Gen. R 25; שִׁחְרוּר manumission, Giṭ. i. 4; שִׁעְבּוּד subjection, Ber. 9 b; שִׁעֲמוּם idiocy, Ket. v. 5; further, סְגַלְגַּל round, Šab. 31 a; סְמַרְטוּט lappet, Šab. xix. 2; סָרָק empty (of a tree that bears no fruit), Kil. vi. 5.

263. (vii) Prefix ת, chiefly in abstracts.

(*a*) Ground-form *Taqṭal, Taqṭil.*

Taqṭal, mostly BH nouns: תַּאֲוָה desire, Ab. iv. 21; תּוֹדָה thank-offering, Zeb. v. 6; תּוֹרָה law, Ab. i. 1; תַּרְבָּץ court, front, Ḥul. 43 b; תַּרְוָד spoon, Kel. xvii. 12.

Taqṭil, only fem.: תּוֹסֶפֶת addition, Bik. iii. 10; תְּחִיָּה resurrection, San. x. 1; תְּפִלָּה prayer, Ber. iv. 1.

264. (*b*) Ground-form *Tiqṭal, Tiqṭul.*

Tiqṭal: תִּגְלַחַת shaving, 'AZ i. 3; תִּקְרָה rafter, BM x. 2.

Tiqṭul, only fem.: תִּכְבּוֹסֶת washing, MQ 15 a; תִּסְפּוֹרֶת hair cutting, Sab. 9 b; תַּרְעוֹמֶת complaint, BM vi. 1; תִּקְרוֹבֶת gift, t. BB iv. 14; תִּשְׁחוֹרֶת youth, AB iii. 2.

265. (*c*) Ground-form *Taqṭîl, Taqṭûl.*

Taqṭîl: תַּבְשִׁיל cooked food, Šab. iii. 1; תַּכְרִיךְ bundle, BM i. 8; תַּכְשִׁיט ornament, MQ 9 b; תַּלְמִיד disciple, Ab. iv. 12; תַּמְצִית juice, Zeb. viii. 7; תַּעֲנִית fast, Ta'a. i. 4; תַּשְׁמִישׁ use, service, Yo. viii. 1.

Taqṭûl: תַּחֲרוּת strife, Ber. 17 a; תַּלְמוּד study, Pea i. 1; תַּמְחוּי dish, ib. viii. 7; תַּנְחוּמִין consolation, Ber. ii. 7; תַּרְבּוּת rearing, Nid. x. 8; תַּשְׁלוּם payment, BQ i. 1; תַּפּוּחַ apple tree, Kil. i. 4; תְּבוּסָה weltering, Oh. ii. 2; תְּמוּרָה exchange, Tem. i. 1; תְּנוּפָה waving, Qid. i. 8; תְּרוּעָה blowing, RH iv. 9; תְּשׁוּבָה repentance, Ab. iv. 11; תַּעֲרוּבוֹת exchange, Yeb. xi. 3.

(5) *Nouns formed by means of Suffixes.*

266. (i) Suffix ל[1]: אֶשְׁכּוֹל cluster, Mid. iii. 8; גִּבְעוֹל calyx, Pa. xii. 2; קַרְסוֹל ankle, Oh. i. 8; רִבְצָל small bag, Kel. xx. 1.

267. (ii) Suffix ָן, וֹן. This suffix is used to form abstract nouns and abjectives. Nouns of a concrete sense with this suffix are mostly of an originally adjectival character (cf. Stade, § 292; Barth, p. 316 f.).

(*a*) Suffix ָן.

Ground-form *Qaṭlan*: אַרְכָן prolonger; קַצְרָן shortener, Ber. 34 a; בַּיְשָׁן shamefaced, Ab. ii. 5; גַּמְלָן (also גַּמְלוֹן) camel-like, large, Kil. iii. 2; וַתְּרָן indulgent, BQ 50 a; קַרְחָן bald, Bek. 43 b; מַקְבָן mallet-shaped, Bek. vii. 1; סַרְבָן stubborn (L סוּרְבָן) Ber. v. 2; עַקְרַבָן scorpion-like, 'Er. ii. 6; קַפְּדָן quick-tempered, Ab. ii. 5; גַּזְלָן robber, 'Or. i. 2; דַּרְשָׁן lecturer, So. ix. 15; רַצְחָן murderer, ib. 9; חַזָּן overseer, Šab. i. 3; סַדָּן block, Kil. i. 8; קַבְּלָן contractor, Šebi. iii. 9 (L קוּבְּלָן); רַצְעָן saddler, Pea iv. 6.

Qiṭlan: לִפְתָּן turnip-shaped, Bek. vii. 1; צִיקָן avaricious, Pes. vii. 8; רֵיקָן empty, Yo. v. 4 (L רֵיקָם, so Ta'a. ii. 2); עִנְיָן subject, t. Meg. iv. 3; פִּשְׁתָּן flax, Šab. iv. 11; תִּלְתָּן fenugreek, Kil. ii. 5.

Quṭlan: מוּרְסָן bran, Ḥal. ii. 6; קָרְבָּן sacrifice, Ned. i. 4; some *Qaṭlan* forms are in certain texts given as *Quṭlan*, e.g. סוּרְבָן, קוּבְלָן, in L, cf. above.

Cf. also the adverbial ending ָן (= ָם) in כָּאן, לְהַלָּן, מַעְלָן, מַטָּן, § 295.

268. (*b*) Suffix וֹן.

Adjectives: אַחֲרוֹן last, BQ iv. 1; חִיצוֹן external, Zeb. v. 1; עֶלְיוֹנָה uppermost, BM iv. 2; תַּחְתּוֹן lower, San. viii. 1; תִּיכוֹן middle, Ber. 3 b; כִּילוֹן wedge-shaped, Bek. vii. 1; קֵיצוֹן of summer, Šebi.

[1] These are probably diminutive forms, cf. Prätorius, *ZDMG.*, lvii, p. 530 ff. Brockelmann, ib., p. 402.

v. 4; also adjectival nouns: אֶבְיוֹן needy, BM 111 b; אַלְמוֹן widower, Ket. 7 a; אַיְלוֹנִית barren woman, Yeb. i. 1.

Abstract: חֶסְרוֹן loss, t. Ta'a. i. 2; חֶשְׁבּוֹן reckoning, BB 9 b; סִירְחוֹן stench, Pes. 35 a; פִּדְיוֹן ransom, Bek. i. 6; כִּבְשׁוֹן secret, Ḥag. 13 a.

With sharpening of the second radical: גֵּרָעוֹן diminution, 'Ar. ix. 7; הֶשָּׁבוֹן restoration (from השב), BM 58 b; זִכָּרוֹן remembrance, RH iv. 6; חִיסָּכוֹן saving, Men. 86 b; נִסָּיוֹן trial, Ab. v. 3; נִצָּחוֹן victory, So. viii. 1; עִשָּׂרוֹן one-tenth, Men. xiii. 1; פִּקָּדוֹן deposit, Šebu. v. 1; פֵּרָקוֹן redemption, Ket. iv. 4; פִּשָּׁיוֹן spreading, Neg. i. 3; רֵאָיוֹן appearance, Pea i. 1.

Concretes with this ending are found only in a few denominatives with a diminutive significance: זֵרְעוֹנִים seeds, Kil. iii. 2 (only plur., cf. Dan. i. 16); צִמְחוֹנִים green buds, MŠ ii. 3 (only plur.); חֲבִיוֹנוֹת little jars (from חָבִית), Kel. ii. 2; כִּידוֹן, כִּיקוֹן little javelin, ib. xi. 8; קָנוֹן little reed-basket, Be. i. 8.

Cf. BH אִישׁוֹן, שַׂהֲרוֹנִים (Stade, § 296 c; Ges.-K., § 86 g; Barth, p. 348 f.). The form is as scarce in MH as in BH. In Aram., on the other hand, it is extremely common, and can be formed at will from any noun, cf. Nöldeke, *Syr. Gr.*, § 131.

269. (iii) Suffix ַי, usually spelt ַאי, or ַיי (in Palestinian texts), to distinguish it from the vowel letter ִי. It is only found in a few nouns: אַחֲרַי responsible, Dam. iii. 5 (cf. Prov. xxviii. 23); בַּרְקַאי (or בּוּרְקַי) morning star, Yo. iii. 1; גּוֹבַאי a kind of locust, Ber. vi. 3; and לִפְנַי within, Zeb. 52 a (cf. 1 Kings vi. 17; Stade, § 301; Ges.-K., § 86 i).

270. (iv) Suffix ִי. To this formation belong denominative adjectives describing origin.

Of names of peoples: אֱדוֹמִי Edomite, Pes. iii. 1; אִיטַלְקִי Italian, Šebi. i. 3; אֲרַמִּי Aramaean, Pes. x. 4; יִשְׂרְאֵלִי Israelite, Qid. iv. 1 (but more often without suffix; יִשְׂרָאֵל 'AZ iv. 9, 12). Of names of places: גְּלִילִי Galilean, Pes. vii. 1; דְּרוֹמִי southern, Šeq. vi. 3;

יְרוּשַׁלְמִית Jerusalemite; מִדְבָּרִית belonging to the wilderness, Men. vii. 1; בֵּישָׁנִי of Beth Shean; and with נ inserted: חֵיפָנִי of Haifa, Meg. 24 b; so טִבְרָנִית Tiberian, j. Šeq. iii. 2;[1] כּוּפְרִי rural, wild, Kil. i. 6.

Of numbers, Ordinals: שְׁלִישִׁי, רְבִיעִי Yo. ii. r. 4; שְׁלָשִׁית; רְבָעִי three, four years old, Pa. i. 1 (cf. below, § 398).

Of other nouns: אֱלוּלִיִּים born in the month of Elul, Bek. ix. 5; אֶמְצָעִית middle, Kil. v. 2; אֶצְבָּעִי smallest, dwarf, Bek. 48 b; בֵּיתִיּוֹת domestic, Be. v. 7; יְחִידִי alone, Ab. iii. 4; עוֹלָמִית ever, Yeb. iii. 9; פְּנִימִי inner, Tam. i. 4; צוֹאִי filthy, Ḥul. xi. 2; פִּשְׁתָּנִי flax dealer, j. Yeb. xiii. 1; שֻׁלְחָנִי money changer, BM ii. 4.

Sometimes the suffix ִי— is combined with ָן—, וֹן—: חֶנְוָנִי shopkeeper, Ned. iv. 7; טוּבְעָנִי flooded; יוּבְשָׁנִי rainless, dry, Ta'a. 10 a; קַרְתָּנִי villager, Dam. vi. 4; רְהִיטָנִי clipper, Mak. iii. 5; רֵיחָנִי aromatic, Nid. 52 a; בֵּינוֹנִי middle, Ter. iv. 3; עִירוֹנִי urban, 'Ed. ii. 5; פְּלוֹנִי So-and-So, Giṭ. vi. 3; גַּדְגְּדָנִיּוֹת a species of berry, Ber. 57 b.

271. (v) Suffix ִית—, Fem. and chiefly denominative: גִּגִּית tub, Šab. xxiv. 5; זִבּוּרִית poorest soil, Giṭ. v. 1; זַרְעִית family, San. iv. 5; חָבִית cask, Šab. xvi. 3; חַרְסִית pottery, MŠ v. 1; טַלִּית shawl, Me'il. vi. 4; יַבְלִית pulp, Kel. iii. 6; כָּפְנִית date berry, 'Or. i. 9; עִדִּית best soil, Šebi. v. 4; עַרְבִית evening, Ber. i. 1; שַׁחֲרִית morning, ib. 2; שַׁחֲצִית insolence, j. Šeq. iv. 4.

With Diminutive force: גְּדוּדִית a little band,[2] Sifra 110 c; ruined partition wall, 'Er. v. 1; כַּדִּידִית little pitcher, t. Men. ix. 10; קִטְנִית pulse, Pea i. 4. Perhaps also: דוּגִית a light fisher-boat, BB 78 b; סְנוּנִית a swallow, Šab. 77 b; עֲסָסִית pounded wheat or peas, t. Be. i. 23.

[1] Cf. BH. שֵׁלָנִי from שֵׁלָה, &c. Ges.-K., § 85 v.

[2] So Raši to Lev. xxvi. 31. But *Rabad* to the Sifra, l.c., explains our word as 'foundation', and this is adopted by Levy, s.v.

Cf. also the reduplicated forms with this suffix enumerated above, § 244.[1]

272. (vi) Suffix וּת—, chiefly used in forming abstracts from concrete nouns: אוּמָּנוּת handicraft, Qid. iv. 14; אֲנִינוּת grief, MŠ v. 12; אֲרִיסוּת tenancy; חֲכִירוּת tenure, Bik. i. 11; גְּנוּת disgrace, Pes. x. 4; זְכוּת merit, So. iii. 4; חֵרוּת freedom, Pes. x. 5; טָעוּת error, Ned. ix. 10; יַלְדוּת childishness, So. i. 4; מַלְכוּת kingdom, Ab. iii. 5; מְשִׁיחוּת office of anointed priest, Ho. iii. 1; נְקִיּוּת cleanliness, So. ix. 15; עֲנִיּוּת poverty; עֲשִׁירוּת riches, Qid. iv. 14; קַלּוּת lightness, Ab. iii. 13; רְשׁוּת permission, ib. 15; רָשׁוּת authority, ib. i. 10; שָׁהוּת while, RH 30 b; תַּרְפּוּת obscenity, 'AZ. ii. 3.

Also in *nomina actionis*: גְּמִילוּת doing, Ab. i. 2; פְּרִישׁוּת separation, abstinence, So. ix. 15; שְׁפִיכוּת shedding, 'AZ. ii. 1; cf. above, § 228.

This suffix is sometimes combined with another suffix: אַחֲרָיוּת responsibility, BM ii. 7; פּוּרְעָנוּת, punishment, Ab. ii. 7; רַבָּנוּת authority, ib. 10; קַבְּלָנוּת contract, BM x. 4 (cf. also Dalman, p. 182).

(6) *Formation by Sound-insertion.*

273. (i) Insertion of a Vowel Sound to form Diminutives. The original Ground-form was *Quṭail* (cf. Barth, *Nominalbildung*, pp. 312 ff.; Brockelmann, *Grundriss*, i. § 137), but in MH the diphthong *ai* was contracted to *ê* and *î*. The first vowel *u* was also contracted in most cases to Shewa. We thus get the forms *Quṭêl*, *Qeṭêl*, and *Qeṭîl*.

Quṭêl. The only examples are the feminines בּוּדֵידָה[2] a little oil press, Šebi. viii. 6 and שׁוּמֵירָה[3] a watchman's hut, 'Er. ii. 5.

[1] Several BH nouns ending in ִית— may also, perhaps, be regarded as diminutive forms, e.g. צְלֹחִית, 2 Kings ii. 20, as compared with צַלַּחַת (ib. xxi. 13, and, especially, 2 Chron. xxxv. 13), מְנַקִּית, Exod. xxv. 29, שְׁאֵרִית.

[2] This is the reading of the best texts, including L. Other texts have בְּדִידָה, like the Qetîl forms below.

[3] So N., M., and editions. In BB iv. 8 editions have שׁוּמֵירָה, but N.

Qeṭél: חֲרֵיר[1] eyelet of a needle, Kel. xiii. 3; סְלֵיל shuttle, Neg. xi. 9. Cf. BH וְעֵיר. Perhaps also פְּלֵיטָה, שְׁאֵרִית, and אֱלִיל, a contemptuous diminutive of אַל, or אַל naught.[2] Also Aram. וְלִיל, וְלִילָא Targum Prov. xiv. 6; xii. 9; xxvii. 7.

Qeṭíl, all feminine: חֲפִיסָה a small bag, BM. i. 8 (cf. t. ib. i. 14); כְּנִימָה vermin, Makš. vi. 1; כְּפִיפָה or קְפִיפָה (L)[3] basket, Ter. ix. 3; עֲרִיסָה cradle, Kel. xvi. 1 (contrast with BH עֶרֶשׂ. A full-sized bed is always מִטָּה in MH); סְלִילָה a little basket, 'AZ ii. 7 (L and N. Other texts have סְלוּלָה). So in proper names: חֲנִינָה (or חֲנִינָא) from חֲנַנְיָה; עֲקִיבָה (עֲקִיבָא)—עֲקַבְיָה.

That the formation is original in MH, and not borrowed from Aram. (Barth, loc. cit.), is shown by its comparative frequency in MH as compared with its scarcity in Aram.

274. (ii) Insertion of a Consonantal Sound.

ר: גַּרְדּוֹם stump, t. Pa. xii. 2; חַרְגּוֹל a kind of locust, Šab. vi. 10; חַרְטוֹם beak, Ṭoh. i. 2; קַרְטוֹב a small measure, Miq. iii. 2; קַרְפֵּף enclosure, 'Er. ii. 3.

נ: תַּרְנְגוֹל cock, fem. תַּרְנְגוֹלֶת Pes. iv. 7 (from רגל, רנן, if not a foreign word).

(7) *Formation of Nouns from Biblical Expressions.*

275. Certain Biblical expressions have given rise to new nouns of a technical nature. Thus, בְּרֵאשִׁית creation (Gen. i. 1); Ber.

שׁוּמֵרָה; t. ib. iii. 4, שׁוּמֵירָה. In Kil. v. 3, M. and edd. have שומירה, N. שומרה. L has in all these passages שומרה. Cf. Maimonides and other commentaries, *ad loc.*

[1] מַחַט שֶׁנִּיטַּל חֲרֵירָהּ a needle, the eyelet of which has been removed שֶׁל סַקָּיִין שֶׁנִּיטַּל חֲרֵירָהּ a needle of sack-makers, the eyelet of which, &c. Cf. Syr. ܚܪܘܪܐ.

[2] Cf. Sirach xi. 3: אֱלִיל בָּעוֹף דְּבוֹרָה.

[3] From כפף. L and other texts have more correctly קפיפה, diminutive of קוּפָּה. So elsewhere, e.g. So. ii. 1; Kel. xxvi. 1. Cf. Wright, *Comp. Gr.*, p. 167; Kohut, iv. 298.

ix. 2; אַכִּין וְרַקִּין, the particles אַךְ and רַק RH 17b; אֵתִין the particle אֵת BQ 41 b; לָאוִין prohibitionists (לאו = לא) Y^{e}b. 10 b; עוֹדִין (L, edd. עודיין) extras, plur. of עוֹד M^{e}n. vii. 2; T^{e}r. iv. 7; אוֹיִים plur. of אוֹ or א Š^{e}bu. 33 b; ‘עֲשֵׂה’ (מִצְוַת) command of affirmation; ‘לֹא תַעֲשֶׂה’ (מִצְוַת) command of prohibition, Qid. i. 7; ‘שֶׁהוּא בְּלֹא יָבֹא’ who is included in the command: ‘He shall not enter’ (Deut. xxiii. 3); Y^{e}b. iv. 13; מִשּׁוּם ‘לֹא תִתֵּן’ because of the command ‘Thou shalt not give’ (Lev. xxv. 37), BM v. 11; ‘אוֹתוֹ וְאֶת בְּנוֹ’ נוֹהֵג the command ‘It and its young’ (Lev. xxii. 28) is in force, &c., Ḥul. v. 1.

(8) *Diminutives.*[1]

276. We may summarize here the various methods employed by MH to express the diminutive. Most of these forms have already been given above.

(i) Reduplication.

- (*a*) Ground-form *Qaṭlul*, especially with the termination ־ִית, § 244.
- (*b*) Ground-form *Qṭaḷṭul*, § 245.

(ii) By means of Suffixes.

- (*a*) Suffix ־ִוֹן, § 268.
- (*b*) Suffix ־ִית, § 271.

(iii) Insertion of Vowel-Sound (*Quṭail*).

- (*a*) Ground-form *Quṭel*, § 273.
- (*b*) Ground-form *Q^{e}ṭel*, § 273.
- (*c*) Ground-form *Q^{e}ṭil*, § 273.

(iv) By periphrasis with בֵּן: בְּנֵי בְּצָלִים young onions, t. ʿUq. ii. 8; בֶּן גָּמָל young camel, Ḥul. 59 a; בֶּן חָרִיץ small ditch, BB vii. 4; בֶּן נֵץ young hawk, M^{e}kil. (Weiss) 40; בֶּן פַּטִּישׁ small hammer, Kel. xxix. 7. Perhaps also בַּת קוֹל the *Bath Qol*, Y^{e}b. xvi. 6. Cf. BH בֶּן בָּקָר; בְּנֵי יוֹנָה, &c.

[1] For a full treatment of diminutive forms in BH and MH cf. M. H. Segal, הַזְּעֵירוּת בְּעִבְרִית in מדעי היהדות, vol. i (Jerusalem, 1926), pp. 139–54.

3. Formation of the Feminine.

277. In the formation of the Feminine, MH follows faithfully the rules of BH, except that it uses more frequently the older and more expressive termination ת—. But the termination ָה is still the more common of the two.

(i) ָה is found in nouns like יְבָמָה a brother's childless widow, Y^eb. ii. 3; חֲלָלָה illegitimate issue of a priest, Qid. iv. 6; לְוִיָּה a Levite woman, Qid. iii. 5; נְתִינָה female descendant of the Gibeonites, Y^eb. ii. 4; גְּדִיָּיה she-kid, M^en. xiii. 7; חֲמוֹרָה she-ass, t. Kil. v. 4; רְחֵלָה ewe, Ḥul. xi. 2.

Further, concrete nouns: גּוּמָּה hole, Ḥul. ii. 9; מְגוּפָה stopper, Šab. xxii. 3; מְחִיצָה party-wall, Kil. iv. 4. Abstracts: חֲזָקָה usucaption; קְטָטָה strife; שְׂרָרָה dominion (§ 224); חוֹבָה duty, Naz. ii. 8; קוֹרָה cooling, Ab. iv. 17.

Verbal nouns: אֲכִילָה, זְרִיעָה, שְׁתִיָּה (§ 228); בַּטָּלָה, סַכָּנָה (§ 237); הַבְדָּלָה, הֲבָאָה, הוֹצָאָה (§ 252).

Usually in Adjectives: טְהוֹרָה pure, K^et. ii. 5; צְרִיכָה necessary, Y^eb. v. 2; עֲנִיָּה poor; עֲשִׁירָה rich, Qid. iii. 5; פַּסָּה stout, big; דַּקָּה thin, small, ib. i. 4.

Participles: Exclusively in Participle active Qal of Intransitive verbs of the form *Qaṭel*, and Participle passive Qal (§ 113). Predominantly in Partic. of ע״ו (except the Intensive Stem and Hoph'al (§§ 178 ff.); ל״ה verbs, and often in ל״א (§ 112).

On the Aramaizing spelling of ָא for ָה cf. above, § 38 footnote.

278. (ii) ֶת, ַת (after a guttural): גִּיּוֹרֶת woman proselyte, Y^eb. vi. 5; כֹּהֶנֶת female descendant of the priests, ib. xvi. 7; מַמְזֶרֶת bastardess, ib. ii. 4; חֵרֶשֶׁת mute; פִּיקַּחַת with full senses, ib. xiii. 8; אִלֶּמֶת dumb; גִּדֶּמֶת without arm, Ḥul. 79 a; קֵרַחַת bald, BB 132 a; גַּרְגֶּרֶת windpipe, Ḥul. iii. 1; עוֹלֶלֶת small bunch, Pea vii. 4; פַּרְפֶּרֶת dessert, Ab. iii. 18.

Participles: cf. §§ 111, 118, 122, 144.

279. (iii) Termination ־ִית, in nouns and adjectives: חָבִית, עֲדִית, שַׁחֲרִית (§ 271); אֲרָמִית Pes. 112 b; מִדְבָּרִית, צוֹרִית Tyrian, Ma'a. iii. 5; אֶמְצָעִית, עוֹלָמִית, פּוּנְדְּקִית inn-keeper, Yeb. xvi. 7; חַבְלָנִית destructive, Mak. i. 10; חֶנְוָנִית shop-keeper, Ket. ix. 4; יוֹצְאָנִית gadding about, Gen. R. 45; בֵּינוֹנִית Kel. xvii. 9 (§ 270).

280. (iv) Termination ־וּת, only in abstracts: מַלְקוּת scourging, Mak. i. 3; עַבְדוּת slavery, Pes. 116 b; גְּנוּת, זְכוּת (§ 272).

4. The Formation of the Plural.

(1) *Masculine Nouns.*

281. The plur. termination of masc. nouns is in MH almost as often ־ִין as ־ִים. The termination ־ִין is not an Aramaism. *-in* is probably the more original of the two terminations, since *-n* is common to nearly all Semitic languages. It is the only one found on the Meša' stone, though Phoenician uses only *-im*. In BH the form *-in* is found frequently,[1] and as early as the Song of Deborah (מִדִּין Judges v. 10). It must have been more common still in the spoken language. Its frequent occurrence in MH can, therefore, be explained as a purely Hebraic phenomenon. However, in very many cases it is due to the Aramaizing proclivities of the copyists, as is proved by comparing different texts.

282. The following peculiarities may be noted about the plur. of masc. nouns in MH.

Nouns of the Ground-form קוֹטֶל (*Quṭl*) retain in many texts, especially those of Babylonian origin, the vowel letter ו also in the plur. Thus, אוֹנֶס compulsion, אוֹנָסִים Ned. iii. 1; חוֹמֶשׁ one-fifth, חוֹמָשִׁים Ter. vi. 4; יוֹחֶס pedigree, יוֹחָסִין Qid. iv. 1. This may be merely an orthographic peculiarity, and the first letter should be pronounced with a short vowel *ŏ* (ֳ), as usually in L. But it

[1] Cf. Stade, § 323 a, where twenty-five examples are enumerated.

is also possible that the traditional pronunciation of the first vowel as long (ō- וֹ) is correct. The full spelling with וֹ would, therefore, represent a dialectal variation. Cf. in BH אֹהָלִים, אוֹרְחוֹתֶיךָ, &c.; Ges.-K., § 93 r.[1]

The plur. of נֶזֶק damage, is נְזִיקִין BQ i. 1, as if from נָזִיק; cf. BH פֶּסֶל—פְּסִילִים.

The plur. of שׁוֹר is שְׁוָרִים, construct, שְׁוָרֵי Men. xiii. 9; of שׁוּק market, שְׁוָקִים Šab. 33 b; לוּחַ, לְוָחִים BM 117 a, לְוָחֵי Šab. xiv. 4. Cf. Ges.-K., § 93 w.

Some nouns from ע״ע roots, show the reduplicated form in the plur., on the analogy of the tri-radicals: צַד side, צְדָדִים Šab. xx. 4, צְדָדֵי BQ ii. 2 (so L correctly for צִידֵּי in editions); טַל dew, טְלָלִים[2] Ḥag. 12 b; שֵׁן cliff, שְׁנָנִים Oh. viii. 2. סַם also inserts נ before the termination, סַמְמָנִים[3] spices, Ker. 6 a.

גַּרְדִּי weaver, Dam. i. 4, has the plur. גַּרְדִּיִּים ʿEd. i. 3, on the analogy of עֲנִיִּים.

Nouns with suffix ־ַי (־ַאי, cf. §§ 38, 237) reproduce the vowel letter א in the plur.: זַכַּאי innocent, זַכָּאִים Ab. i. 8; רַשַּׁאי permitted, רַשָּׁאִים ib. iv. 8. So בָּקִי expert, San. vii. 2, בְּקִיאִין Yo. viii. 5. L and other Pal. texts often have ־ִיִּין, זַכִּיִּין, &c. So בְּקִיִּין, וַדָּיִין Ker. vi. 4.

Similarly, the ל״ה noun חֲצִי half, BQ iv. 9 = plur. constr. חֲצָאֵי ʿEd. iii. 1, חֲצָאִין Qid. 20b, but also חֲצָיִין Ker. 5 a; Sifra 108b; חֲצָיֵי Oh. viii. 6 (L. חֲצָאֵי). Cf. BH Ges.-K., § 93 x.

The plur. of שֶׂה lamb is שֵׂיִין Bek. 11 a; cf. BH שֵׂיו Deut. xxii. 1. Forms ending in a vowel insert י (or א in Babylonian texts) between the final vowel and the plur. termination: מַשֶּׁהוּ (= מַה

[1] So also with pronominal suffix; cf. above, § 39 and foot-note.

[2] Cf. BH הֲרָרִים, so Ḥag. i. 8; Ges.-K., § 93 aa. Contrast Aram. טַלִּין j. Targ. Gen. xxvii. 28, &c.

[3] Other forms are: סַמָּנִים BQ 101 a; סַמָּנִיּוֹת Šab. xii. 3, editions, or סַמְּיוֹנוֹת L and N.

+שֶׁהוּא) something, מַשֶׁהוּיִין ʿEv. 87 a; אוֹ or, אוֹיִים, אוֹיֵי, j. Šebu. iv. 5; אוֹאִין Šebu. 33 b (cf. § 275).

שְׁאָר remainder, has plur. constr. שְׁיָרֵי Ab. i. 2. The plur. is שירים (L) spelt in editions שיריים, as dual and so pronounced traditionally: שִׁירַיִים. Cf. also the verbal form, § 162, and below, § 293.

A few nouns of the form *Qaṭîl* take in the plur. the form *Qaṭûl*: מָלִיחַ salty food, מְלוּחִין; צְלִי roasted food, צְלוּיִין Ned. vi. 3; שָׁלִיחַ messenger, Giṭ. iv. 1, שְׁלוּחִין RH i. 3, שְׁלוּחֵי Yo. i. 5. So with suffixes: שְׁלוּחוֹ, שְׁלוּחָהּ Qid. ii. 1; שְׁלוּחֵנוּ Yo. i. 5. L. has also שְׁלוּחַ for constr. sing., Giṭ. iii. 6, but absolute: שְׁלִיחַ.

(2) *Feminine Nouns.*

283. (i) Feminine nouns ending in the sing. in ־ָה, or ־ֶת, ־ַת, form the plur. in ־וֹת, e.g. שׁוּרָה vow, שׁוּרוֹת Pea vi. 3; תִּינוֹקֶת little girl, תִּינוֹקוֹת Yo. viii. 4.

Some segolate nouns ending in ת retain the ת in the plur.: דֶּלֶת door, דְּלָתוֹת Tam. iv. 1; חֵמֶת leather bottle, חֲמָתוֹת Kel. xxvi. 4; לֶפֶת turnip, לְפָתוֹת San. 19 b; כֶּסֶת bolster, כְּסָתוֹת Kil. ix. 2; סוֹלֶת fine flour, סְלָתוֹת Šeq. iv. 3; שׁוֹקֶת trough, שְׁקָתוֹת Pa. v. 8. Cf. for BH Ges.-K., 95 f.

The plur. of אַשְׁפָּה, אַשְׁפָּת dunghill, is אַשְׁפַּתּוֹת Šebi. i. 1, cf. above, § 249 note.

The plur. of עֶרְוָה incest, is עֲרָיוֹת Yeb. i. 2, as if from עֶרְיָה. This last form is actually found in L., Hag. i. 10, and in K.,[1] ʿEd. i. 12. Cf. also Bek. vi. 5—genitals of animal; further, Habak. iii. 9.

284. (ii) Nouns ending in ־ִית form the plur. in ־ִיּוֹת:[2] בֵּינוֹנִית

[1] Cf. Krauss, *MGWJ.*, li, p. 325, note 1.

[2] The י in these forms, and also in the plur. of the nouns in the next section, serves to remove the *hiatus* between the final vowel of the sing. (־ִי without the fem. termination ת—) and the vowel at the beginning of the plur. termination וֹת— ; cf. מַשֶׁהוּיִין § 282, and the plur. of the nouns in § 286.

middle, בֵּינוֹנִיּוֹת Kel. xvii. 10; חָבִית jar, חֲבִיּוֹת Ned. viii. 7; טַלִּית cloak, טַלִּיּוֹת Zab. iv. 5 (but also טַלִּיתוֹת in later texts, e. g. Num. R. 18); רְבִיעִית quart, רְבִיעִיּוֹת Pes. 112 a; תַּעֲנִית fast, תַּעֲנִיּוֹת Ta'a. ii. 1; חַכְמָנִיּוֹת, דַּרְשָׁנִיּוֹת, צַדְקָנִיּוֹת BB 119 b.

The plur. of בְּרִית covenant, is בְּרִיתוֹת Ned. iii. 2 (בְּרִיּוֹת is plur. of בְּרִיָּה = בְּרִיאָה creature, San. iv. 5); so טַלִּיתוֹת above. Cf. חֲנִיתוֹת Ges.-K., § 87 k.

285. (iii) Nouns ending in the sing. in וּת— form the plur. in ־וּיוֹת: חָנוּת shop, חֲנוּיוֹת 'AZ i. 4; רְשׁוּת premises, רְשׁוּיוֹת t. Šab. i. 1; Hag. 15 a.

Some nouns in וּת— take the termination ־ִיּוֹת; אוּמָּנוּת handicraft, אוּמָּנִיּוֹת Bik. iii. 3; זְכוּת merit, זְכִיּוֹת Yo. 86 b. So אוֹת letter of the alphabet, אוֹתִיּוֹת Šab. viii. 3 (אוֹתוֹת is plur. of אוֹת sign, Kil. ix. 10).

So also a few other nouns: בְּקַעַת log of wood, בְּקָעִיּוֹת Ḥul. 37 b; Sifre 99 d; פְּקַעַת skein, פְּקָעִיּוֹת Kel. xvii. 2; כְּנֶסֶת (בֵּית) Synagogue, כְּנֵסִיּוֹת (בָּתֵּי)[1] Ab. iii. 10; פָּרָשָׁה section; פָּרָשִׁיּוֹת sections of Scripture (פָּרָשׁוֹת sections of the spine, Ḥul. 45 b).

(3) *Foreign Nouns.*

286. The plur. of nouns borrowed from Gk. and Lat. is formed, like that of native nouns, by attaching the plur. termination ־ִים, ־וֹת, to the sing. in its MH form,[2] thus: טְפוּס (דְּפוּס = τύπος), טְפוּסִים (דְּפוּסִים) Da. v. 3, 4; סִיטוֹן (= σιτώνης), סִיטוֹנוֹת ib. ii. 4; אֶפִּיקוֹרוֹס (= Epicurus), אֶפִּיקוֹרוֹסִים, אֶפִּיקוֹרְסִים Ber. ix. 5; אִסָּר (assarius), אִסָּרוֹת Pea viii. 1; הֶדְיוֹט (= ἰδιώτης), הֶדְיוֹטוֹת San. x. 2.

[1] This gave rise to the sing. כְּנֵסִיָּה, Ab. iv. 11. L has כְּנִיסָה.

[2] Cf. Krauss, *Lehnwörter*, i, §§ 315–25; Albrecht, § 84 k, l. לִיסְטִים, Pea ii. 7, plur. of לִסְטִים (= λῃστής: לסטים אחד, Yeb. 25 b) forms an exception, cf. Kohut, v, p 46 a. Usually the sing. is also written לסטים. Further: אֶסְקָרִיטִים = ἐσχαρίτης, Ḥal. i. 4.

In the case of fem. nouns ending in the sing. in the vowel *ā* (=אָ—, הָ—), א, or usually in Palest. texts, י, is inserted between the final vowel of the sing. *ā*, and the vowel *ô* (= וֹת—) of the plur. termination, in order to obviate the meeting of two vowels. Thus: טַבְלָה (טַבְלָא = tabula), טַבְלָאוֹת Pes. 57 a; דְּיָיטָה, דְּיוֹטָא (= δίαιτα), דְּיוֹטָאוֹת, דְּיָיטָיוֹת (L), ʿEr. viii. 11; גְּזוּזְטְרָא (= ἐξώστρα), גְּזוּזְטְרָאוֹת ib. 9 (L כצוצרה, כצוצריות, cf. §§ 44, 51); גִּימַטְרִיָא (= γεωμετρία) גִּימַטְרִיָאוֹת Ab. iii. 18. Some foreign nouns have become fully naturalized in the language, and form their plur. regularly, e.g. דּוּגְמָא (= δεῖγμα), דּוּגְמוֹת BQ 119 b.

This form of the fem. plur. termination for foreign nouns, —ָאוֹת, —ָיוֹת, is also used for Gk. nouns ending in the sing. in —ִי (= η): דְּיָיתִיקִי (= διαθήκη), דְּיָיתִיקָאוֹת, אַפּוֹתִיקִי (= ὑποθήκη), אַפּוֹתִיקָאוֹת BM 19 a; so: קַטַבְלָאוֹת, plur. of καταβολή, Šeq. iii. 4. Further, גְּלוּסְקִין (= κόλλιξ), Da. vi. 12; also: גְּלוּסְקָא Pes. 6 b, plur.: גְּלוּסְקָאוֹת Ket. 111 b; סַנְהֶדְרִין (=συνέδριον; also: סַנְהֶדְרִי), plur.: סַנְהֶדְרָיוֹת San. i. 5 (L. סנהדראות; so Cant. R. iii. 7).

287. This plur. termination, —ָאוֹת, —ָיוֹת became very common through the influx of Gk. and Lat. nouns into the language, especially in later MH. As a result this termination is also found sometimes in native nouns, thus: מִקְוֶה a ritual bath, מִקְוָאוֹת Šeq. i. 1 (but L has מִקְווֹת; so Miq. i. 1, &c.); מֶרְחָץ a bathing establishment, מֶרְחֲצָאוֹת (מֶרְחֲצִיּוֹת) Taʿa. i. 6; מִשְׁתֶּה a feast, מִשְׁתָּאוֹת Nid. 16 b; פַּרְפֶּרֶת dessert, פַּרְפְּרָאוֹת (beside גימטריאות!) Ab. iii. 18, but also: פַּרְפְּרוֹתָיו Šab. 148 b; שַׁלְשֶׁלֶת chain, שַׁלְשְׁלָאוֹת ʿEr. 58 a; also the Aram. noun בֵּירָאוֹת (ביריות) cisterns, ʿEr. ii. 1.

The plur. of אֵם mother, is אִמָּהוֹת Qid. iv. 4; Pea iii. 4 (cf. BH אֲמָהוֹת maids; also Dalman, p. 199), but also: אִמּוֹת אִימּוֹתֵיהֶם t. BB vii. 9. Of אָחוֹת sister, אֲחָיוֹת Yeb. ii. 6, as in BH.

288. As in BH, numerous masc. nouns form the plur. by וֹת—, e.g. חוֹתָם seal, חוֹתָמוֹת Šeq. v. 1; חֵן favour, חֵנּוֹת So. 47 a; כְּלָל

general rule, כְּלָלוֹת ʿEr. 25 a; מִדְבָּר wilderness, מִדְבָּרוֹת Ḥul. ii. 8; מִקְרָא verse, מִקְרָאוֹת Ber. 32 a; נְיָיר paper, נְיָירוֹת Pa. x. 6; תִּינוֹק male infant; תִּינוֹקוֹת (שְׁנֵי) Šab. xix. 4; especially nouns with the suffix ָן, וֹן: אִילָן tree, אִילָנוֹת Šebi. i. 2; זָדוֹן act of presumption, זְדוֹנוֹת BM 33 b; סִילוֹן pipe, סִילוֹנוֹת Kel. ii. 3; עִנְיָן subject, עִנְיָינוֹת Šab. 61 b; צְנוֹן horse-radish, צְנוֹנוֹת Šab. ii. 2; קָרְבָּן sacrifice, קָרְבָּנוֹת Zeb. xiv. 10. Further, *nomina agentis* of the form *Qaṭôl* (§ 235): דָּרוֹכוֹת, לָקוֹחוֹת, &c.

So also a number of nouns from ע״ו roots; גַּיִס troop, גְּיָסוֹת Yeb. xvi. 7; חַיִל army, חֲיָילוֹת Sifra 89 d, but also חֲיָילִים Mekil. 63; עִיר city, עֲיָירוֹת Meg. i. 1, but also עָרִים ʿEr. v. 1; פַּיִס lot, פְּיָסוֹת Yo. ii. 3. Similarly, מַיִם water, מֵימוֹת j. So. ii. 2; יַיִן wine, יֵינוֹת Šeq. iv. 4.

ל״ה nouns: קָלִיא parched corn; קְלָיוֹת BM iv. 12; בְּלִי (or, perhaps, בְּלָי) בְּלָאוֹת, (L בליות; cf. בְּלוֹאֵי and בְּלוֹיֵ Jer. xxxviii. 11, 12); but the construct is בְּלָאֵי Suk. v. 3, בְּלוֹיֵי Kel. xxvii. 5.

The same difference between the plur. absolute and construct is found also in other nouns; thus: שְׁטַר document, שְׁטָרוֹת, שִׁטְרֵי, BM ii. 5; וָלָד child, וְלָדוֹת, וַלְדֵי, in the phrase וַלְדֵי וְלָדוֹת Bek. ii. 4; פְּרִי fruit, פֵּירוֹת, פֵּירֵי, in the phrase פֵּירֵי פֵירוֹת Ket. ix. 1; אִילָנוֹת trees, Šebi. i. 2; אִילָנֵי So. viii. 2, 3; כַּת group, כִּתּוֹת Pes. v. 5; כִּתֵּי Naz. iii. 7.

Verbal nouns of the Ground-form *Haqṭel* (§ 251), being really fossilized infinitives, have no plur. of their own. They use the plur. of the corresponding verbal noun *Haqṭala*, e.g. הֶעֱלֵם concealed act, plur. הַעֲלָמוֹת Šab. xii. 4, 6; הֶקְדֵּשׁ sanctified property, Ter. i. 5; הַקְדָּשׁוֹת San. i. 3, &c. So the infinitival noun כָּרֵת (§ 116) is in the plur. כְּרִיתוֹת, from the verbal noun כְּרִיתָה (§ 228), Ker. i. 1.

289. Conversely, many fem. nouns take the masc. termination in the plur. Thus, חִטָּה wheat, חִטִּים; שְׂעוֹרָה barley, שְׂעוֹרִים; כּוּסֶּמֶת spelt, כּוּסְמִין Šebu. iii. 3; דְּלַעַת pumpkin, דִּלּוּעִין Kil. iii. 7;

כְּרֵישָׁה leek, Makš. i. 5, כְּרֵישִׁין Kil. i. 2; קִישׁוּת cucumber, קִישׁוּאִין Kil. xx. 4, 6; פַּגָּה fig, t. Šebi. i. 1, פַּגִּים Šebi. iv. 7; further, אַרְנֶבֶת hare, אַרְנָבִים Šab. 27 a; יוֹנָה pigeon, יוֹנִים San. iii. 3; נְמָלָה ant, נְמָלִים Pea iv. 1; בֵּיצָה egg, בֵּיצִים Ḥul. xii. 3. Further, גְּדִילָה, גְּדִילִים (Deut. xxii. 12), Sifre Num. xv. 38; נִימָה chord, נִימִים Šeq. viii. 5. Cf. Ges.-K., § 87 q.

290. Some nouns show both plurals: פְּרֵידָה pair of pigeons, פְּרֵידִים Kin. iii. 6 in L; Sifra 8 d; פְּרֵידוֹת Kin. ib. (in editions); BQ 38 b; רְחֵלִים and רְחֵלוֹת ewes, Ḥul. xi. 1, 2 (in L; cf. Ḥul. 137 b (above, § 3)); מַסְמְרוֹת BB 7 b, and מַסְמְרִים Gen. R. 68, nails, מְשָׁלִים So. 9 a, and מְשָׁלוֹת Ab. deRN. i. 4; San. 38 b, parables.[1]

Sometimes there is a variation in meaning between the two plurals: יָמִים days, Yo. i. 1, and יָמוֹת collective: season (only in constr.). Ber. i. 5; Šeq. viii. 1; Ṭoh. vi. 7; שָׁנִים years, Ab. v. 21, and שָׁנוֹת collective: age, only with suffix, Ber. 58 b; עֲצָמִים single bones, and עֲצָמוֹת collective, 'Ed. i. 7; קְבָרִים graves, Ta'a. 25 b, and קְבָרוֹת collective, burial-place, Naz. ix. 3.[2] With a derived significance in the secondary plur.: עֲדָשִׁים lentils, Kil. xi. 8, and עֲדָשׁוֹת lentil measures, Neg. vi. 1; שְׂפָתַיִם lips, Ket. 61 b (also שפתות San. 90 b, with suffix only), and שְׂפָיוֹת rims, Kel. iv. 4; רַבִּים many, 'AZ i. 7, and רַבּוֹת teachers (only with suffix), 'Er. v. 3; תְּמָרִים date palms, Bik. i. 5, and תְּמָרוֹת young branches of other trees, Ma'a. iv. 6, &c.; שִׁינַּיִם teeth and שְׁנָנִים teeth of rock, cliffs, Oh. viii. 2; תְּפִלָּה, תְּפִלּוֹת prayer, Ber. iii. 1, and תְּפִלָּה, תְּפִלִּין phylacteries, Men. iv, 1; iii. 7; אֱלוֹהוֹת gods; אֱלֹהִים God; 'AZ iv. 7; יָדַיִם hands; יָדוֹת handles, Yo. iii. 2.

291. In the lists given above, the reader will have observed several nouns with plur. in MH which in BH are only found in the sing., e.g. בְּרִית, יַיִן, סוֹלֶת, &c. To these may be added many

[1] But prob. read ממשלות; cf. Lewin, אגרת ר׳ שרירא, p. iii (נספחים).

[2] For the original collective sense of the fem. termination, cf. Stade, § 322 c.

more examples: אֵבֶר, אֲבָרִים limbs, parts of the body, Yo. vi. 6; דֶּשֶׁא, דְּשָׁאִים herbs, Ber. vi. 1; זְוָעָה, זְוָעוֹת earthquakes, ib. ix. 2; זֶרַע, זְרָעִים plants, Šab. 95 b; 31 a; חול, חוּלִּין common things, Ḥul. v. 1; יָרָק, יְרָקוֹת vegetables, Ber. vi. 1; כֶּסֶף, כְּסָפִים money, BM 42 a; מָזוֹן, מְזוֹנוֹת maintenance, Sebi. iv. 1; קֶמַח, קְמָחוֹת various kinds of flour, Men. viii. 7; רֶמֶשׂ, רְמָשִׂים creeping things; שֶׁקֶץ, שְׁקָצִים reptiles, Šebu. iii. 4; רַעַם, רְעָמִים thunders, Ber. ix. 2; שֶׂה, שֵׂיִין sheep, Bek. 11 a; שֶׁלֶג, שְׁלָגִים snow, Pes. 94 b; שֶׁמֶן, שְׁמָנִים oils, Suk. iv. 4; תָּמִיד, תְּמִידִים the daily offerings, sacrifices (Num. xxviii. 3), Šeq. iv. 1.

292. Conversely, many nouns which in BH appear only in the plur., are found in MH also in the sing. In addition to those given in the above lists (e.g. בֵּיצָה, חָנוּת, סַם, &c.) may be mentioned: אַלְמוּג red sandal wood, Kil. xiii. 6; בָּצָל onion, Šebi. i. 10; זָוִית corner, Šab. xii. 4; סְגָן chief of priests, Pes. i. 6; כִּירָה hearth, Šab. iii. 1 (BH כִּירַיִם); שִׁקְמָה sycamore, Kil. i. 8, &c.

5. The Dual.

293. The Dual, which has practically disappeared from Aram., is quite common in MH. Not only has MH retained the old BH duals like עֵינַיִם, רַגְלַיִם, שׁוֹקַיִם, כִּכָּרַיִם, כִּפְלַיִם, מָאתַיִם, &c., but it has also preserved the absolute form of the dual of nouns which in BH occur only in the construct or with suffixes, e.g. גַּבַּיִם back, Kel. xxv. 5; עַפְעַפַּיִם eyelids, Šab. 109 a; קִרְבַּיִם intestines, Tam. iv. 2; קַרְסוּלַּיִם ankles, Ḥul. iii. 7; שׁוּלַיִם skirts, Kel. xv. 1. The following are new formations: אֲחוֹרַיִם back, Kel. xxv. 1; אֶצְבָּעַיִם two fingers, Oh. iii. 1; בֵּינְתַיִים between, BM x. 6; גַּפַּיִים wings. Ḥul. iii. 4;[1] דִּירַיִים shed, t. Ned. i. 3; זְרָתַיִם two spans, t. Men. ix. 3; Ta'a. 5 a; חֲנִיכַיִים gums, Ḥul. 103 b; טַלְפַּיִם hooves, Ḥul. ix. 1; טִפְחַיִים two

[1] i.e. the limbs on which the plumage, כְּנָפַיִם, grows. Hence the Mishnah says: נִשְׁתַּבְּרוּ גַּפֶּיהָ, but נִמְרְטוּ כְּנָפֶיהָ, ib.

handbreadths, BB i. 1; כּוֹרַיִם two *kors*, Kel. xv. 1; מְגַפַּיִם greaves, ib. xi. 8; מַחֲלָצַיִם windlass, MQ. i. 10; (בֵּית) הַמַּטְבְּחַיִם slaughter-house, Ab. v. 5; מַסְפָּרַיִם scissors, Kel. xvi. 8; קַבַּיִם two *qabs*, 'Ed. i. 2; רִבְעָתַיִם two-fourths, Kᵉr. i. 7; שִׁירַיִם[1] remainder, 'Er. ii. 6.

IV. PARTICLES

1. Adverbs.

294. MH has lost a considerable number of BH adverbs. Some of these have been replaced by MH formations, or by borrowings from Aram. Others, mostly of a poetical nature, have found no exact substitutes in MH.

The following is a list of BH adverbs not found in MH. The words in brackets represent their MH substitutes.

אוּלַי (שֶׁמָּא); אָז, אֲזַי (בְּשָׁעָה זוֹ); אַיֵּה, אֵיפֹה (אֵיכָן, הֵיכָן); אוּלָם, אַךְ, רַק (אֶלָּא); אָכֵן (common in Aram. in a different sense), אָמְנָם (אֱמֶת); אֶפֶס, בַּל, בְּלִי, בִּלְתִּי, בִּלְעֲדֵי (לֹא, אֵין &c.); הֲלוֹם, הֵנָּה (כָּאן); טֶרֶם (לִפְנֵי שֶׁ־, קוֹדֶם שֶׁ); עֵקֶב, תָּמִיד (תָּדִיר; תָּמִיד only of the daily sacrifice, § 291); further, יוֹמָם (בַּיּוֹם, בְּכָל יוֹם); פִּתְאֹם, רֵיקָם (רֵיקָן), only as adjective, Ta'a. ii. 2.

אֵיכָה, אֵיכָכָה, and כָּכָה are used in shortened forms: אֵיךְ, or with the demonstrative particle הֵי—: הֵיאַךְ, or הֵאֵיךְ, and כָּךְ. So הָלְאָה (also in Aram.) is represented by לְהַלָּן;[2] כֹּה by כָּן, כָּאן; מֵאַיִן is shortened to מִנַּיִן.

Other new forms peculiar to MH are: בֵּינְתַיִם, כְּדֵי, כֵּיוָן, כַּיּוֹצֵא בְּ־, כֵּיצַד, כְּלוּם (§ 437); כְּלוֹמַר, לְמַפְרֵעַ, עֲדַיִן (BH עֲדֶן; Aram. אֲדַיִן),[3] עַכְשָׁו, עַכְשָׁיו (probably = עַד + כְּשֶׁהוּא).

[1] This is the traditional pronunciation and the usual spelling. L, however, has always שירים. Also the construct is pronounced שְׁיָרֵי, as if from שְׁיָרִים; cf. above, § 58. שיריים silk, σηρικόν, should be pointed שִׁירָיִים, L שִׁירָאִין.

[2] Or, perhaps, לְהָלָן, viz. ָן + הָל + לְ, cf. § 267, and לְשָׁם for BH שָׁמָּה, § 295.

[3] Krauss's view (*ZDMG.*, 1913, p. 737) that עֲדַיִן is composed of עד + אַיִן

Borrowings from Aram. are: תָּדִיר, (עַל אֲתַר) לְאַלְתַּר, אֶשְׁתַּקָּד; probably also עֲרַאי, כְּגוֹן (= כְּעֵין), and perhaps also תֵּכֶף, לָאו.[1] So also שׁוּב is an Aramaism = תּוּב.

(1) *Adverbs of Place.*

295. אֵיכָן (אֵי + כָן), commonly הֵיכָן, especially in Babyl. texts, where? Šab. i. 3; Šeq. vi. 1. So in Aram. (cf. Barth, *Pronominalbildung*, p. 81), but very probably indigenous in MH.

With prepositions: לְהֵיכָן whither? Šab. xvi. 1; מֵהֵיכָן whence? Yo. v. 5; עַד הֵיכָן until where? Pes. x. 6.

אֵילָךְ, or הֵילָךְ, הֵלָךְ, only in phrase הֵילָךְ . . . הֵילָךְ, hither and thither, Pes. vii. 13; Zab. iii. 2; or הֵילָךְ וְהֵילָךְ Mak. iii. 12.

אַיִן where? only with prepos.: לְאַיִן whither? Ter. iv. 11; Ab. iii. 1 (many texts have לְאָן); מֵאַיִן whence? Ab. ib.; וּמֵאַיִן וּלְאַיִן Ḥag. 15 a; more often מִנַּיִן: Ber. v. 3; Yo. vi. 8; especially when introducing quotations from Scripture: Šab. ix. 1 ff., &c.

בֵּינְתַּיִם, בֵּינְתַּיִם, בֵּינְתַּיִים (especially in L.) between, BM x. 6. Cf. BH בֵּנַיִם 1 Sam. xvii. 4; בֵּינוֹת Ezek. x. 2; perhaps there was a form בֵּינוֹתַיִם Gen. xxvi. 28. So בֵּינַיִים וּבֵינְתַּיִים in the very centre, Gen. R. 4.

הַלָּן there, j. Ket. 28 d; Giṭ. 46 d; usually with לְ: לְהַלָּן beyond, Dam. i. 3. So. vii. 5.

חוּץ outside, with prepositions: בַּחוּץ Zeb. vii. 5; מִבַּחוּץ from outside, ʿEr. vii. 9; לְחוּץ outside, after verb of motion, Zeb. viii. 12; מִן הַמּוֹדִיעִית וּלְחוּץ from Modin and outside beyond, as opposed to מִן הַמּוֹדִיעִית וְלִפְנִים Ḥag. iii. 5.

is improbable. Perhaps the Aram. form אֲדַיִן is more original, and is to be equated with the BH אָז. On עַכְשָׁו cf. Dalman, p. 212, foot-note.

[1] From לָא + הוּא, cf. Dalman, § 46. This particle is, however, much more common in MH than in Aram. The traditional pointing לָאו is incorrect, as is shown by the cognate form עַכְשָׁו, עַכְשָׁיו; cf. also BH יַחְדָּו, יַחְדָּיו. Some Palest. texts also write לִיו for לָאו above § 39.

כָּאן, כָּן in Pal. texts, here, there (BH כֹּה = כֹּא): כָּאן וְכָאן here and there, ʽEr. x. 11; לְכָאן, after a verb of motion, ʽEr. 40 b; מִכָּאן . . . מִכָּאן on the one side, on the other side, Kil. vi. 6; מִכָּאן וְעַד כָּאן from here to there, Be. iv. 7.

מָה: כַּמָּה how far? Ber. iii. 5.

מַטָּה, or מַטָּן in Palest. texts and also occasionally in others, especially in passages connected with the Temple and its ritual, Mid. i. 5, &c. This adverbial termination ן ָ is a modification of the BH ם ָ, cf. Ges.-K., § 100 g, h, and above, § 267.

Always with prepositions: לְמַטָּה below, Ḥag. ii. 1; מִלְּמַטָּה from below, ʽEr. viii. 6; מִלְּמַטָּן Šab. 98 b.

מַעְלָה, מַעֲלָן, לְמַעְלָה, מִלְּמַעְלָה above, used exactly as מַטָּה cf. the passages cited above.

מַפְרֵעַ, only with לְ: לְמַפְרֵעַ backwards, Ber. ii. 3.

שָׁם there; after verbs of motion: לְשָׁם (= BH שָׁמָּה, which is not found in MH) RH ii. 5; Šab. xvi. 4, &c.

(2) *Adverbs of Time.*

296. אָחוֹר only with prepos. לְ: לְאָחוֹר backwards, Ḥag. ii. 1.

אֵילָךְ, הֵילָךְ further, onwards; מִכָּאן וְאֵילָךְ Ber. i. 2; מֵעֶזְרָא וְאֵילָךְ Pa. iii. 5.

אֵימָתַי, אֶמְתַּי (L) when, Pea iii. 5; אֵימָתַי שֶׁתִּרְצֶה whenever thou wishest, BM v. 3; מֵאֵימָתַי from when, Ber. i. 1; עַד אֵימָתַי till when, ib. viii. 7.

אֶשְׁתָּקַד last year, Šeq. vi. 5 (Aram. compound: שַׁתָּא קַדְמָיָא; cf. אֶשְׁתָּדָא this year, j. MŠ 35 b).

אֲתַר place (Aram.), with עַל: עַל אֲתַר on the spot, forthwith, in Pal. texts; contracted in Babyl. texts to לְאַלְתַּר Giṭ. iii. 3; viii. 8.

בֵּינְתַּיִים between, meanwhile; Ṭoh. v. 3, 4.

הַלָּן, only with לְ: לְהַלָּן further, beyond; מֵחֲצוֹת הַיּוֹם וּלְהַלָּן from noon and further, Men. x. 5.

יָד, with the preposition מִן: מִיָּד at once, BB i. 5; opposed to עַל יָד gradually, Pa. vii. 7; אֵין מְחַיְּיבִין אוֹתוֹ לִמְכּוֹר מִיָּד אֶלָּא מוֹכֵר עַל יָד עַל יָד they do not compel him to sell at once, but he may sell very gradually, BQ 80 a. (So perhaps BH, Prov. vi. 5; cf. מִן יָד j. Targ. Gen. i. 3, &c.; BH עַל יָד by degrees, Prov. xiii. 11.)

(כָּן) כָּאן only with מִן: מִכָּאן from now; מִכָּאן וּלְהַבָּא from now and in the future, Kel. vii. 1; לְאַחַר מִכָּאן afterwards, Qid. ii. 6.

כְּבָר already, Yad. iv. 4; וּכְבָר a formula introducing a report of an event in confirmation of a previous statement, j. Ket. v. 4.

כָּךְ, only with אַחַר: אַחַר כָּךְ afterwards, Ber. viii. 6; לְאַחַר כָּךְ BM viii. 1.

מָה: עַד כַּמָּה how long? Bek. iv. 1.

מָחָר usually לְמָחָר to-morrow, 'Er. iii. 9. So וּלְמָחָרָת San. v. 5.

אֶמֶשׁ yesterday; אֶמֶשׁ הֲרָגוֹ he slew him yesterday, San. 40 b; מֵאֶמֶשׁ, opposed to מֵהַיּוֹם Be. i. 6 (BH אֶתְמוֹל, which is common in Aram., is never used in MH).

מַפְרֵעַ: לְמַפְרֵעַ before, backwards, Miq. ii. 2.

עוֹד yet, again, Yo. vi. 1; with suff.: עוֹדֵהוּ Bik. iii. 6; עוֹדָהּ Ket. vii. 8; עוֹדְךָ Šab. 151 b; עוֹדָן ib. 43 b; מִבְּעוֹד while yet, Šab. i. 5.

עֲדַיִן yet, Ned. xi. 10 (L אֲדַיִין, as in Aram., Dan. ii. 15).

עוֹלָם with prepos.: לְעוֹלָם always, Ter. ii. 4; with negative: never, MQ 26 b; so מֵעוֹלָם, with negative: never, Mak. i. 10; עוֹלָמִית for ever, Yeb. iii. 7; with negative: never, Šab. xxiii. 4.

עַכְשָׁו, עַכְשָׁיו now, 'AZ i. 1; מֵעַכְשָׁו from now, Giṭ. vii. 3.

עֲרַאי, עֲרַיי in Palest. texts, irregular, improvised, Ḥal. iii. 1 (opposed to קֶבַע fixed, Suk. 2 a).

פַּעַם: פַּעַם אַחַת once upon a time, 'Er. iv. 2, פְּעָמִים sometimes, BB v. 2.

שׁוּב again (Aram. תּוּב), Yeb. xvi. 4, especially common in later literature.

תָּדִיר continually, always, BB iii. 1.

תֵּכֶף immediately, only once in Mishna: Men. ix. 8, but frequent in later literature, e.g. Ber. 42 a, &c. Cf. the verb, Kil. ix. 10.

297. Other adverbial expressions of time are: בָּרִאשׁוֹנָה at the beginning, formerly, Šebi. iv. 1; תְּחִילָּה first, So. i. 7, כַּתְּחִלָּה (in Babyl. texts always לְכַתְּחִלָּה) as at the beginning, Šab. vi. 5, primarily, מִתְּחִלָּה 'AZ iii. 7, בַּתְּחִלָּה Yeb. v. 6; בָּאֶמְצַע in the middle; בַּסּוֹף in the end, ib.; מִיָּמַי Zeb. xii. 4, מִיָּמֶיךָ Suk. ii. 7, מִימֵיהֶם Pes. i. 6, with לֹא, never; cf. BH 1 Kings i. 6, &c.

(3) *Adverbs of Manner.*

298. אֵין not; אֵין אַתָּה בָא thou comest not, Ab. iv. 1; אֵין אַתֶּם 'Er. v. 9; אֵין אֲנוּ Šebu. iv. 2 ff. Suffixes are attached in some persons without the so-called *nun epentheticum*, as in BH (Ges.-K., § 100 o, p), thus: 1 sing. אֵינִי Ber. ii. 5; 3 sing. masc. אֵינוֹ; fem. אֵינָהּ So. vi. 3; 3 plur. אֵינָן ib. viii. 3.

Before words beginning with א, אֵין is sometimes shortened to אֵי: אֵי אַתָּה אִם BM v. 3. So always before אֶפְשַׁר: אֵי אֶפְשַׁר impossible, Šebu. iii. 8, &c.; and אֶפְשִׁי: אֵי אֶפְשִׁי I do not want, Naz. iv. 5.

אַל not, Ab. i. 3, &c.

בַּל = לֹא in quotations of Biblical prohibitions: Pes. iii. 1 (cf. below, § 472).

לְבַד alone, only with suffix: לְבַדָּהּ So. 8 a; or with בְּ: בִּלְבַד, after a negative, Ber. i. 1; or אֶלָּא Dam. iii. 5 (§ 507).

הֵיאַךְ how? BH; אֵיךְ RH ii. 8, &c.

הֵן yes, Giṭ. vii. 1.

וַדַּאי, וַדַּיי certainly (from ודה to confess, agree), Ker. v. 2; וַדַּאי מָעַלְתִּי I have certainly used sacred property; opposed to סָפֵק doubt: סָפֵק אָכַל perhaps he has eaten, ib. iv. 1.

חֲלִילָה round about, over again, Suk. v. 6; Pes. 48 b.

יָכוֹל one might assume, possibly, Ab. iii. 8; כִּבְיָכוֹל as if one could say (of an anthropomorphic expression applied to the Deity), San. vi. 5. (Cf. Kohut, iv. 130–2.)

כְּ־, כְּמוֹ, כְּמוֹת (with the collective termination ־וֹת, as in BH סביבות, בינות, &c.) like, followed by the relative שֶׁ־ MŠ v. 2, &c.

With suff.: כְּמוֹתִי BM 59 b; כְּמוֹתְךָ Ned. 4 b; כְּמוֹתוֹ Ber. v. 5; כְּמוֹתָהּ Qid. iii. 2; כְּמוֹתָן Suk. i. 8.

כְּ־ as prefix: כְּאֶחָד together, t. Neg. i. 1; Ber. vii. 1 (in edd.); כְּאַחַת Pea i. 4; Ber. ib. (L, of masc.).

כְּגוֹן like the colour of—like, as, for instance, Šebi. viii. 1; cf. כְּעֵין.

כְּדֵי[1] as much as, Šab. viii. 1.

כְּדֶרֶךְ as Kil. vii. 6; כְּדַרְכּוֹ as his manner, as usual, Ma'a. iii. 10.

כַּיּוֹצֵא בְ־ like, similarly; כַּיּוֹצֵא בוֹ[2] Pea iv. 8; כַּיּוֹצֵא בָהֶן Šebi. viii. 2; כַּיּוֹצֵא בְאֵילּוּ Mak. i. 7; כַּיּוֹצֵא בַדָּבָר Sifra (Weiss) 4 a.

כֵּיצַד (כְּ + אֵי + צַד, in Halakic Midrashim כְּאֵיזְצַד, also בְּאֵיזֶה צַד) how? Ber. vi. 1, &c.

כְּלוֹמַר as if to say, San. vi. 4, 6; very common in later MH in sense of 'that is to say', 'namely'.

כַּמָּה how? Kil. ii. 3; בְּכַמָּה for how much? BM iv. 10; כַּמָּה נָאִים how beautiful, Šab. 33 b; עַל אַחַת כַּמָּה וְכַמָּה how much more and more? Mak. i. 7 (in arguments from minor to major).

כְּמִין like the kind of, like, Suk. ii. 2.

כְּנֶגֶד against, Dam. i. 2.

כִּיוָּן straight, immediately, Tam. iii. 6; Pes. 37 a, 54 a.

כָּךְ so, Ber. vii. 3; בְּכָךְ at this, in this, Dam. i. 4; בֵּין כָּךְ וּבֵין כָּךְ

[1] Cf., however, Barth, *Etymolog. Stud.*, p. 39, who holds that the כ is a radical which suffered aphaeresis in BH.

[2] Cf. Sirach xxxviii. 17. It is also found in Aram., no doubt, as an adaptation from MH., כְּנָפֵיק בֵּיהּ j. Targ. Gen. ii. 18, 20; Deut. xiv. 18. The origin of the expression is obscure. Perhaps we may derive it from the use of יצא ב— in such a phrase as יָצָא שְׂכָרוֹ בְּהֶפְסֵדוֹ, &c., Ab. v. 11. 12, viz. to annul, and hence—to balance, to be equal, like.

whether so or so, Ḥal. i. 8; לְכָךְ for this, Ab. ii. 8; לְכָךְ וּלְכָךְ Ṭoh. vi. 6, 7; עַל כָּךְ for this purpose, 'Ed. viii. 3.

כֵּן so, Bᵉr. 11 b; וְכֵן likewise, Pea vi. 9; כָּל שֶׁכֵּן everything agrees that it is so—how much more so? (in arguments from the minor to the major).

Before אֶלָּא, כֵּן is contracted to כֵּי in the phrase לֹא כֵי אֶלָּא it is not so but, Yᵉb. viii. 3; BQ iii. 11.[1]

לֹא not, no.

לָאו not, no, particularly in alternatives after אִם, when the verb is omitted, Bᵉr. iii. 2, 5, &c. (§§ 466, 489).

מָה how? Bᵉr. 10, 2, with preposition: לָמָּה why? 'AZ ii. 7; מִפְּנֵי מָה wherefore? Šab. xvi. 1; בִּשְׁבִיל מָה for which cause, purpose?

299. Other adverbial expressions of manner are: בְּיִיחוּד privately, San. vii. 8; with certainty, Šᵉq. vi. 2; בַּעֲלִיל clearly, distinctly,[2] RH i. 5; בְּטוֹבָה with thanks, i.e. with owner's permission; שֶׁלֹּא בְטוֹבָה without thanks, against owner's will, Šᵉbi. iv. 2; with, without gratuity, 'AZ iv. 3; שֶׁלֹּא בְטוֹבָתוֹ against his will, San. vii. 2; בְּפֵירוּשׁ distinctly, 'Or. i. 7.

כָּל עִיקָּר 'all the root'—altogether, in a negation, Be. iii. 6; כָּל צוֹרֶךְ all the need—completely, with suff.: כָּל צָרְכָּן, כָּל צָרְכָּהּ Kil. vii. 7.

עַל כֹּרַח perforce, Ab. iv. 22; in later MH with -בְּ: בְּעַל כָּרְחָהּ against her will, So. 19 a, &c.

לוֹכְסָן (λοξόν) across, in a hypotenuse line: שְׁתֵּי שׁוּרוֹת לוֹכְסָן two rows in a cross line, Dam. vii. 8; Kel. xviii. 5.

[1] Others, following Geiger, *Lehrbuch*, p. 24, point כִּי, and regard the expression as an imitation of the BH לֹא כִּי (1 Sam. viii. 19, &c.; cf. *BDB*., p. 475 a), which was misinterpreted by the Rabbis. But such an artificial explanation is most improbable. לא כי only occurs before א, and is, therefore, parallel to אֵי from אֵין before א, as above.

[2] Cf. RH 21 b from Ps. xii. 7; further, Šab. 133 b; Mᵉn. 64 a; Gen. R. 23; cf. also Barth, *Etymol. Stud.*, p. 65.

סֵירוּגִין ('chequer work'), alternately; קְרָאָהּ סֵירוּגִין he read it in alternate verses, Meg. ii. 2; BQ 37 a.

סְתָם ('stopping up'), undefined, unspecified, Dam. iii. 1.

כְּלָל general statement; לֹא הָיוּ מִתְעַנִּין כְּלָל they did not fast at all, Ta'a. ii. 6.

בְּבַת אַחַת in one *bat* (name of measure, Isa. v. 10)—in one stroke, at once, Ḥul. ii. 3.

2. Prepositions.

300. MH prepositions are all of Heb. origin. They include (*a*) BH prepositions preserved in their old significance; (*b*) BH nouns or other forms turned by MH into prepositions, e.g. חֵמָה wrath: מֵחֲמַת through the fury of, the energy, or activity of—through, by; קוֹדֵם לְ־ preceding, before; so עוֹבֵר לְ־; עַל גַּב upon the back of, upon; עַל מְנָת on the portion of, for the advantage of, for the sake of, on condition, in order that; so שֵׁם name, subject, and its various combinations.

The following BH prepositions have been lost in MH: אֵת (= עִם), בִּגְלַל, בַּעֲבוּר, בְּעַד, מוּל, לְמַעַן and פֶּן (Aram. פּוֹן).

301. אָחוֹר the back, is used as a prepos. in the dual אֲחוֹרַיִים (§ 293), in the sense of 'behind', corresponding to פָּנִים (below).

אֲחוֹרֵי שְׁתֵּיהֶן behind both, Mid. v. 4; אֲחוֹרֵי רַבּוֹ behind his master, opposed to כְּנֶגֶד רַבּוֹ Yo. 37 a. With prefixes לְ־, מִ־: לַאֲחוֹרָיו behind him, Kil. v. 7; לַאֲחוֹרֵיהֶן behind them, ib. 9; מֵאֲחוֹרֵי הַגָּדֵר behind the wall, San. vii. 10; מֵאֲחוֹרָיו Giṭ. viii. 2; מֵאֲחוֹרֵיהֶם So. viii. 6.

אַחַר, אַחֲרֵי with suffixes. Of time, after: אַחַר חֲצוֹת after midnight, Pes. x. 8; אַחֲרָיו שֶׁל מֹשֶׁה after Moses, So. v. 4; אַחֲרֵיהֶן after them, Ber. vi. 8. With prefix: לְאַחַר זְמַן after the time, afterwards, 'AZ i. 1; לְאַחַר חֲצוֹת after midnight, Zeb. ix. 6; לְאַחֲרֵיהֶם after them, 'AZ i. 2; מִלְּאַחֲרֶיהָ after it, opposed to מִלְּפָנֶיהָ before it, 'Er. iii. 6.

Of place, behind; usually with prefix לְ: לְאַחַר הַחַמָּה behind the sun, RH ii. 6; שֶׁלְּאַחַר הַקּוֹצְרִים that which is behind the reapers (L שֶׁאַחַר) Pea iv. 11; לְאַחֲרָיו, לְאַחֲרֵיהֶם behind him, them, opposed to; לְפָנָיו, לִפְנֵיהֶם before him, them, ib. vi. 4; כִּלְאַחַר יָדוֹ behind, with the back of, his hand (L לְאַחַר), Šab. x. 3.

אֶל rare: אֶל תַּחַת הַמּוֹתָר into the space under the remainder (L omits אל), Kil. vi. 3, 4; מִיּוֹם אֶל יוֹם from day to day, Nᵉd. viii. 1 (so L, probably a reminiscence of Num. xxx. 15).[1] With suff. in the plur., as in BH, only in a few exx.: בָּא אֵלַי Naz. 4 b; חָזַר אֵלָיו it returned to it, Pᵉs. vii. 2 (some texts have עָלָיו); לְהַקִּישׁ אֵלֶיהָ to compare to it, BM ii. 6; וִידַבְּרוּ אֵלָיו they shall speak to him, Mak. ii. 5. Frequently with prefix מֵ־ and the suff. of the 3rd person in a reflexive sense: מֵאֵלָיו of itself, 'Or. i. 2; בָּאוּ מֵאֲלֵיהֶן they came by themselves, BM vii. 9; לֹא מֵאֵלַי אֲנִי אוֹמֵר I do not say it from my own authority, Yo. 5 b.

אֵצֶל by the side of, at, to (after verbs of motion—BH אל): בָּאִין זֶה אֵצֶל זֶה they come one to the other, Šᵉq. v. 4; מַנִּיחַ טַלִּיתוֹ אֶצְלוֹ he leaves his cloak with him, Šab. xxiii. 1.

בְּ in, as prefix and also with suff. (בִּי, בָּךְ, בִּיךְ, as in Aram., Nid. 58 b, &c.), as in BH. Also in combination with nouns to give them a prepositional character, e.g. בִּשְׁבִיל, בְּצַד, בִּפְנֵי, בִּלְבַד, בְּתוֹךְ, בִּשְׁעַת, בְּשֶׁל, &c.

בֵּין between; also with suffixes: בֵּינִי, &c. Correlatives ('between . . . and') are expressed by בֵּין . . . לְ־: בֵּין יוֹם טוֹב לְשַׁבָּת between a festival and the Sabbath, Mᵉg. i. 5 ff.; Yo. iii. 5, &c. Also: בֵּין . . . וּלְ־: בֵּין הָאוּלָם וְלַמִּזְבֵּחַ Yo. iii. 8 (a standing expression, Ḥal. i. 9; from Joel ii. 17); בֵּינוֹ לְבֵין הָעָם between him and the people, ib. 4, 6; בֵּינוֹ לְבֵין עַצְמוֹ Bik. i. 4; בֵּינָם לְבֵין עַצְמָם Ḥul. vi. 2, between him and himself, and themselves—privately; so בֵּינוֹ לְבֵינוֹ

[1] Other scriptural phrases with אֶל are: Yo. v. 6; So. vii. 2, 5; viii. 1; Mak. iii. 2 (L על); Zᵉb. xiv. 1; Pa. xi. 4, 5 (L לְ).

privately, ʽAZ ii. 2; בֵּינוֹ לְבֵינָהּ Y°b. xii. 5. Also as noun: עַל בֵּין הַבַּדִּים on the space between the staves, Z°b. v. 1.

חוּץ, followed by לְ־, outside: חוּץ לִתְחוּם outside the boundary, ʽEr. v. 7; also with ה local, but without any special significance: חוּצָה לָהּ outside it, ib. 6; חוּצָה לוֹ Š°bi. i. 2; especially in the expression חוּצָה לָאָרֶץ outside the Land (of Israel), as opposed to הָאָרֶץ T°r. i. 5; Ḥal. ii. 1, 2, &c. So בְּחוּצָה לָאָרֶץ Dam. ii. 1.

Followed by מִן except: חוּץ מִן הַפְּתִילָה except the wick, Šab. ii. 5; חוּץ מִזּוֹ בִּלְבַד except this alone, Yo. iii. 3.

כְּ, combines with some nouns to form prepositions: כְּנֶגֶד over against; כְּנֶגֶד הַיְסוֹד in front of the foundation, P°s. v. 6; זוֹ כְּנֶגֶד זוֹ one facing the other, Šab. xi. 2; תַּלְמוּד תּוֹרָה כְּנֶגֶד כֻּלָּם the study of the Torah against (= compares, outweighs) them all, Pea i. 1; כְּנֶגְדּוֹ, כְּנֶגְדָּן against (corresponding to) it, them, Š°bi. viii. 8.

כְּדֵי sufficient for: כְּדֵי מְזִיגַת הַכּוֹס sufficient for mixing a cup, Sab. viii, 1 ff.

כְּלַפֵּי (כְּ+לְאַפֵּי, cf. לְאַפֵּי 1 Sam. xxv. 23) towards: כְּלַפֵּי הָעָם facing the people; כְּלַפֵּי הָעֵץ facing the gallows, San. vi. 4; כְּלַפֵּי צָפוֹן towards north, Tam. ii. 5.

לְ־ to, as prefix and with suffixes (לִי, לָךְ fem. לִיךְ Giṭ. iv. 8, &c.), as in BH. Also prefixed to prepositional nouns: לְבֵין, לְאַחַר. לְמַטָּה מִן: לְמַטָּה מִירוּשָׁלַיִם below Jerusalem, Suk. iv. 5; לְמַעְלָה מִן: זֶה לְמַעְלָה מִזֶּה one above the other, ʽEr. i. 9; viii. 8; לְעוּמָּתָן towards them (rare), Š°q. vi. 3.

לִידֵי to the hands of, to (after verb בָּא): אֵין אַתָּה בָא לִידֵי עֲבֵרָה thou wilt not come to transgression, Ab. ii. 1; לִידֵי סַכָּנָה to danger, Yo. ii. 2.

לְעִנְיַן to the subject of, in respect to: לְעִנְיַן דְּבָרָיו in respect to his words, Ya. iv. 3.

לְפִי to the mouth of—according to: לְפִי הָאוֹרְחִין according to the guests, Šab. xx. 2; לְפִי רוֹב הַמַּעֲשֶׂה according to the abundance of the works, Ab. iii. 15; לְפִי חִיבָּתָן because of the love entertained for them, Ya. iv. 6.

לִפְנֵי before; מִלִּפְנֵי from before; also with suffixes: לְפָנַי, לְפָנֶיךָ, &c., as in BH.

לְשֵׁם to the name of—for the sake of, for the purpose of: לְשֵׁם שָׁמַיִם for the sake of Heaven, Ab. v. 16; לְשֵׁם עֲבוֹדָה זָרָה for the purpose of idolatry, ‘AZ. iii. 7.

מִן from, used separately or as prefix; also with suffixes: מִמֶּנִּי, מִמְּךָ, &c., as in BH. Often the demonstrative particle הֵי (= BH הֵא) is prefixed instead of מִ־ when it has the pronominal suffix: הֵימְךָ from thee, Nᵉd. 5 a; הֵימֶנּוּ from him, Šᵉbi. x. 9; Giṭ. viii. 9; הֵימֶנָּה from her, Pea iv. 3; vii. 8; Kᵉt. 27 b. The texts often waver between these and the older forms: מִמֶּנָּה, מִמֶּנּוּ.

Also in the sense of ‘in the power of’: לֹא הֵימְךָ לוֹמַר it is not in thy power to say, Num. R. 4; especially with כָּל־: כָּל הֵימְךָ לוֹמַר Gen. R. 15; לֹא הַכֹּל מִן הָרִאשׁוֹן לְאַבֵּד זְכוּתוֹ שֶׁל שֵׁנִי L.; edd. with anticipation of the genitive (cf. § 389); . . . לֹא כָל הֵימֶנּוּ מִן הָרִאשׁוֹן the first has no power to destroy the right of the second, Giṭ. viii. 8; לֹא הַכֹּל הֵימֶנּוּ L.; לֹא כָל הֵימֶנּוּ edd., he has no power, BQ x. 3; cf. Aram.: לָאו כָּל כְּמִינָךְ Sᵉbu. 41 a; אִיהוּ כָּל כְּמִינֵיהּ? BB 154 b.

With לְ־ as correlative: מִכְּנֶגֶד הַחוֹמָה וְלִפְנִים; מִכְּנֶגֶד הַחוֹמָה וְלַחוּץ from the front of the wall and towards within, towards without, MŠ. iii. 7, 8.

Prefixed to prepositional nouns:

מֵחֲמַת because of: מֵחֲמַת הַמַּכָּה because of the wound, BQ viii. 1; מֵחֲמַת חוֹלִי in consequence of the sickness, Giṭ. vii. 3.

מֵעֵין of the colour, appearance, character of: מֵעֵין שְׁמוֹנָה עֶשְׂרֵה an abstract of the eighteen benedictions, Bᵉr. iv. 3 (cf. Bᵉr. 29 a); הָרָעָה מֵעֵין הַטּוֹבָה evil of the nature of good; הַטּוֹבָה מֵעֵין הָרָעָה good of the nature of evil, ib. ix. 3; מֵעֵין מְלָאכָה אַחַת of the nature of, similar to one work, Šab. vii. 1.

מִשֵּׁם in the name of (also often מִשּׁוּם, cf. § 37): מִשֵּׁם ר׳ יִשְׁמָעֵאל in the name of Rabbi Ishmael, Kil. iii. 7; because of: אֲסוּרִין מִשּׁוּם גִּלּוּי forbidden because of uncovering, Teṛ. viii. 4; נוֹהֵג בּוֹ מִשּׁוּם אֱלוֹהַּ he behaves to it as to a god, ʿAZ iii. 4.[1] Cf. also on אֶל, above, and תּוֹךְ, below.

עַד to, as far as; עַד חֲצוֹת up to midnight, Ber. i. 1; עַד בֵּית סָאתַיִם as far as a space of two *seahs*, ʿEr. ii. 3. עַד is not found with pronominal suffixes.

עַל upon; also with suffixes: עָלַי, עָלֶיךָ, as in BH; cf. also below, § 363.

In combination with nouns:

עַל גַּב upon the back of, upon: הַנּוֹתֵן עַל גַּבָּן who puts upon them, Šab. xi. 2; טָמֵא עַל גַּב עַם הָאָרֶץ unclean upon, because of, the ʿAm ha-Areṣ, ʿEd. i. 14; עַל גַּב רוּקָהּ because of her spittle, Miq. viii. 5. More frequently with the constr. dual (§ 293): עַל גַּבֵּי הַמִּטָּה upon the bed, Suk. ii. 8; עַל גַּבֵּי רַגְלָיו upon his feet, ib. iv. 9; Kil. ii. 11; עַל גַּבָּיו upon it, BM x. 4.

עַל יַד by the hand of, through: עַל יָדִי through me, Ber. iv. 2; עַל יָדוֹ through him, on his behalf, Šebi. vii. 3. More frequently with the constr. dual: עַל יְדֵי יְחֶזְקֵאל by Ezekiel, Tam. iii. 7; עַל יְדֵי עוֹרָהּ together with its skin, MŠ. i. 6; iii. 11.

עַל מְנָת on condition; עַל מְנָת כֵּן on this condition, Dam. vi. 3; Ab. i. 3.

עַל פִּי through: עַל פִּי עֵדִים through witnesses, Šab. xix. 1.

עַל שֵׁם for the name, purpose, of—because of: עַל שֵׁם סוֹפוֹ because of his end, San. viii. 5, 6.

עִם with; also with suffixes: עִמִּי, עִמְּךָ, &c. (BH עִמָּדִי is not found in MH).

[1] Literally: from the name, category of; cf. אֵינוֹ מִן הַשֵּׁם, it is not of this name—it does not belong to this category, Ker. iii. 4; so לֹא מִן הַשֵּׁם הוּא, Šebu. 3 b; מִשֵּׁם אֶחָד, מִשְּׁנֵי שֵׁמוֹת, of one category, of two categories, Kin. i. 3, 4.

Of time: עִם הַשֶּׁמֶשׁ with the sun—while the sun still shines, Šab. i. 8; עִם חֲשֵׁכָה while it is getting dark, ib. ii. 7; עִם יְצִיאַת נֶפֶשׁ while, before, the soul goes forth, ib. xxiii. 5.

קוֹדֵם preceding, before (properly a participle), followed by the accusative, or by לְ־ (indirect object, cf. § 351). The texts waver.

קוֹדֵם הַבָּצִיר before the vintage (L לַבָּצִיר) Pea vii. 7; קוֹדֵם לָעֲצֶרֶת (or עֲצֶרֶת), before Pentecost, Ḥal. iv. 10; קוֹדֵם אֶת חֲבֵירוֹ precedes its fellow; קוֹדְמִין לְמוּסָפִין precede the additional sacrifices, Zeb. x. 1 ff. Similarly:

עוֹבֵר לְ־: עוֹבֵר לַעֲשִׂיָּיתָן before doing them, Pes. 7 b.

תּוֹךְ within; תּוֹךְ זְמָן within the time, opposed to לִפְנֵי זְמָן before the time, Nid. 45 b, but usually with another preposition prefixed.

בְּתוֹךְ in, at: בְּתוֹךְ הַבַּיִת in the house, Suk. i. 2; בְּתוֹךְ חֵיקוֹ within his bosom, Šab. x. 3; ii. 7; לְתוֹךְ into: יִתֵּן לְתוֹכוֹ מַיִם he will put into it water, Ber. vii. 5; מָדַד לְתוֹךְ צְלוֹחִיתוֹ he measured into his flask, 'AZ v. 7; מִתּוֹךְ from: נָטַל מִתּוֹכָהּ he took from it, Šab. i. 1; מִתּוֹךְ שֶׁלּוֹ from his own, Šebi. iii. 6.

תַּחַת under, as in BH: תַּחְתֶּיהָ under it, Kil. vi. 9; תַּחַת הַמִּטָּה under the bed, Suk. ii. 1; יוֹצֵא מִתַּחַת יָדוֹ comes forth from under his hand, BB 173 a.

3. Conjunctions.

302. Of the old BH conjunctions and conjunctive expressions, MH has lost the following (the words in brackets give the MH substitutes):

אֲשֶׁר (שֶׁ־); כִּי (שֶׁ־)[1]; גַּם (אַף־); לוּ (אִלּוּ Qoh. vi. 6; Est. vii. 4); מִפְּנֵי) יַעַן אֲשֶׁר); (עַד שֶׁ־; קוֹדֵם שֶׁ־) טֶרֶם; (פּוֹן .Aram) פֶּן (שֶׁמָּא;

[1] כִּי is common in MH only with וְ as an interrogative particle, וְכִי §§ 303, 462. כִּי alone is preserved only in elevated diction, under the influence of BH, e.g. in the liturgy (cf. Singer, pp. 46, 47, &c.), or in a poetical passage like אוֹי נָא לָהּ . . . כִּי אָבְדָה כְּלִי חֶמְדָּתָהּ woe to her . . . for she has lost her precious jewel, MQ 25 b.

שֶׁ־, &c.); לְמַעַן אֲשֶׁר (כְּדֵי שֶׁ־, &c.); עֵקֶב אֲשֶׁר (מִפְּנֵי שֶׁ־, &c.; cf. on Adverbs, § 294).

Of Aram. origin is אֶלָּא (also אִילָּא = לָא + אִן—אִם לֹא), and perhaps also the form כֵּיוָן שֶׁ־, which is common in Aram.

The conjunction שֶׁמָּא (= שֶׁלָּמָּה, שַׁלָּמָּה Cant. i. 7; Aram. דִּילְמָא), was adopted by Aram. from MH. But Aram. influenced its spelling in MH with final א for ה: שֶׁמָּה.

MH shows some other interesting new formations, such as the use of the verbal form הוֹאִיל וְ;[1] the compounds אִלְמָלֵא or אִלְמָלֵי (אִלּוּ + אִם + לֹא), or the Palestinian equivalent אִילוּלֵי, אִילוּלֵא (אִלּוּ + לֹא); אֲפִילוּ (אַף + אִלּוּ); לְפִיכָךְ; the adaption of a number of other expressions to conjunctive use: וּבִלְבַד, בִּשְׁבִיל, בִּזְמַן, אַף עַל פִּי, כְּשֵׁם, מִשֵּׁם, מִתּוֹךְ, עַל מְנָת, עַל תְּנַאי, &c., all followed by שֶׁ־. MH has also greatly extended and developed the uses of the BH conjunctions שֶׁ־, אֲבָל, אִלּוּ, and וְכִי.

303. We give here a list of the conjunctions and conjunctive expressions. For examples of their usage and their various constructions, the reader is referred to the respective sections in the Syntax.

Co-ordinating: וְ and; אַף also, moreover, indeed.

Adversative, restrictive, and exceptive: אֲבָל; אֶלָּא but, except; בֶּאֱמֶת of a truth, however.

Disjunctive: אוֹ or; בֵּין . . . בֵּין whether . . . or.

Conditional: אִם, אִלּוּ, אִלְמָלֵא (אִלְמָלֵי), אִילוּלֵא (אִילוּלֵי) if.

Concessive: אַף, אֲפִילוּ even; אַף עַל פִּי (שֶׁ) although; אַף עַל פִּי כֵן nevertheless.

Interrogative: הֲ, וַהֲלֹא, וְכִי, כְּלוּם; שֶׁמָּא perhaps?

Comparative: כְּ like; כָּךְ so; כְּאִילּוּ as if.

Consecutive: לְפִיכָךְ therefore.

[1] The verb הוֹאִיל is not found otherwise in MH. It is always followed by וְ as in BH: Joshua vii. 7; 2 Sam. vii. 29. Cf. Bacher, *Aelteste Terminologie*, p. 37.

שֶׁ־ (שֶׁאֵין, שֶׁלֹּא). Its primary function, like BH אֲשֶׁר and כִּי, is to introduce a subordinate clause. Hence like אֲשֶׁר, כִּי, it assumes different meanings in accordance with the character of the clause it introduces, viz. a causal, concessive, conditional, or final meaning.

Like BH אֲשֶׁר, שֶׁ combines with prepositional and adverbial expressions to form the following new conjunctions.

Temporal: כְּשֶׁ־, לִכְשֶׁ־ as; מִשֶּׁ־ after, opposed to עַד שֶׁ־ before; אַחַר שֶׁ־. לְאַחַר שֶׁ־, after; קוֹדֶם שֶׁ־ before; אֵימָתַי שֶׁ־ when, whenever; כֵּיוָן שֶׁ־ as soon as; בִּזְמַן שֶׁ־, בְּשָׁעָה שֶׁ־ when; כָּל זְמַן שֶׁ־: כָּל שָׁעָה שֶׁ־ all the time that; מִשָּׁעָה שֶׁ־ from the time that; עַד כְּדֵי שֶׁ־ until.

Comparative: כְּמוֹ שֶׁ־; כְּמוֹת שֶׁ־; כְּשֵׁם שֶׁ־; כְּדֶרֶךְ שֶׁ־; כְּעִנְיָן שֶׁ־ as.

Causal: בִּשְׁבִיל שֶׁ־; לְפִי שֶׁ־; מֵאַחַר שֶׁ־; מִפְּנֵי שֶׁ־; מִשּׁוּם שֶׁ־; מִתּוֹךְ שֶׁ־; עַל שֶׁ־; עַל שֵׁם שֶׁ־ because.

Final: כְּדֵי שֶׁ־; עַל מְנָת שֶׁ־; עַל תְּנַאי שֶׁ־ in order that.

Restrictive: וּבִלְבַד שֶׁ־ only that.

4. Interjections.

304. (1) Pure Interjections.

אוֹי לוֹ woe! Y^e^b. iii. 5 (edd.); xiii. 7 (L); B^e^r. 28 a, &c.

אִי לוֹ woe! Y^e^b. xiii. 7; iii. 5 (L); ʿEd, iv. 8 (L has אִילוֹ in one word, as Qoh. iv. 10; cf. x. 16); אִי שָׁמַיִם Oh, heavens! RH 19 a.

הוֹי: הוֹי אִישׁ טוֹב וְנֶאֱמָן alas! a good and faithful man, B^e^r. 16 b.

אַלְלַי woe! Ab. d^e^RN. xxv 3.

אָנָּא pray, Yo. iii. 8 (only liturgical). So נָא in a poetical passage MQ 25 b, and in the liturgy.

הָא, הֵא behold, Mak. iii. 17; הֵילָךְ (L הֵא לָךְ) behold, take thee, Maʿa. ii. 5, 6.

הֲרֵי behold, B^e^r. vii. 5; הֲרֵינִי behold I!

וְהַלְוַאי would that! M^e^g. 14 a; or וּלְוַאי B^e^r. 28 b (prob. Aram.).

The following BH pure interjections have been lost in MH: אֲבוֹי, אָח, אַחֲלֵי (all rare); אֲהָהּ, לוּ.

305. (2) Words and phrases used as Exclamations.

הָאֱלֹהִים by God! Ḥul. 54 a, &c. (late, and mostly in semi-Aram. passages).

בְּרִית by the Covenant! P^es. 38 b; t. Ḥal. 1.

גַּפָּה שֶׁל רוֹמִי by the Capitol of Rome, M^en. 44 a (in the mouth of a heathen).

חֲבָל alas! N^ed. 74 b; Sifre Deut. xviii. 12 (prob. Aram.).

חַס וְשָׁלוֹם May He have pity and grant peace!—God forbid 'Ed. v. 6; Ya. iii. 5.

הַמָּעוֹן הַזֶּה By this habitation (the Temple)! K^er. i. 7; vi. 3; K^et. ii. 9..

הָעֲבוֹדָה by the worship! B^er. 34 b; Y^eb. 32 b.

הַשָּׁמַיִם by Heaven, Ab. d^eRN. xxxviii. 3.

The following BH exclamations have been lost in MH: הָבָה, לְכָה, הִנֵּה.

PART III

SYNTAX

I. THE VERB

1. Tenses and Moods.

306. IN the use of the Tenses, MH has attained to a greater precision and exactness than BH. Generally in MH the perfect coincides with the present, the imperfect with the future, and the participle with the present. The perfect and the imperfect (and also the imperative) describe simple acts. Continuous, or repeated, or customary action is expressed by the participle alone for the present, by the participle with the perfect of הָיָה for the past, by the participle with the imperfect of הָיָה for the future, and by the participle with the imperative of הָיָה (= הֱוֵה) for the imperative.

It follows that the use of the perfect for the present in such expressions as אָהַבְתִּי, יָדַעְתִּי, צָדַקְתִּי, זָקַנְתִּי (Ges.-K., § 106 g), or the use of the perfect for actions that lie in the future (*Perfect of Confidence*, &c.; ib., § 106 m–n), is not admissible in MH. Likewise, the use of the imperfect to describe actions, whether simple or continuous, which lie in the past or even in the present (ib., § 107 b–h), is not tolerated in MH.

(1) THE PERFECT.

307. The perfect describes a single act or event that has already taken place, or that is conceived as having taken place. Hence the perfect is the tense of the past, e.g.: יוֹסֵף הַכֹּהֵן הֵבִיא בִיכּוּרִים Joseph the Priest brought first ripe fruits, Ḥal. iv. 2; מֹשֶׁה קִבֵּל

תּוֹרָה מִסִּינַי Moses received the Torah from Sinai, Ab. i. 1; לֹא קָרִינוּ אֶת שְׁמַע we have not read the Š^{e}ma', B^{e}r. i. 1.

308. In the absence of the imperfect consecutive in MH, the perfect serves also to describe a series of consecutive acts in the past: מְסָרוּהוּ . . . וְהֶעֱלוּהוּ (הוֹלִיכוּהוּ L) . . . הִשְׁבִּיעוּהוּ וְנִפְטְרוּ וְהָלְכוּ לָהֶם they delivered him . . . they brought him up . . . they adjured him, and departed, and went away, Yo. i. 5; הֵבִיאוּ אֶת הָאֲבָנִים וּבָנוּ אֶת הַמִּזְבֵּחַ וְסָדוּם בַּסִּיד וְכָתְבוּ עֲלֵיהֶם . . . וְנָטְלוּ אֶת הָאֲבָנִים וּבָאוּ וְלָנוּ בִמְקוֹמָן they brought the stones, and built the altar, and plastered them with plaster, and wrote on them . . . and took the stones, and came and lodged in their place, So. vii. 5.

309. The perf. also expresses an act which is anterior to another act in the past (pluperfect). Such a pluperfect is usually placed in a relative clause: רָחַץ בַּלַּיְלָה הָרִאשׁוֹן שֶׁמֵּתָה אִשְׁתּוֹ he bathed in the first night that his wife had died, B^{e}r. ii. 6; נִתְיַיחֵד עִמָּהּ אַחַר שֶׁכְּתָבוֹ he was alone with her after he had written it, 'Ed. iv. 7; וּכְשֶׁיָּצָא אָמַר and when he had gone forth he said, 'AZ. iii. 4; הֵבִיאוּ כָּל טָהֳרוֹת שֶׁטִּיהַר רַבִּי אֱלִיעֶזֶר they brought all the things which R. Eliezer had declared to be clean, B^{e}r. 19 a; וּבָאָה אִשָּׁה . . . שֶׁמָּלָה and there came a woman who had circumcised, Šab. 134 a.

310. The perf. is used in hypothetical sentences, with or without a conjunction, to express a single act conceived as already performed. English in such cases would often use the present, e.g. קָרָא וְלֹא דִקְדֵּק בְּאוֹתִיּוֹתֶיהָ . . . יָצָא if he has read (the Š^{e}ma'), but not pronounced its letters carefully . . . he has discharged his duty; קָרָא וְטָעָה יַחֲזוֹר . . . if he has read it, and made an error, let him return . . ., B^{e}r. ii. 3; פָּשַׁט הֶעָנִי אֶת יָדוֹ . . . וְנָתַן לְתוֹךְ יָדוֹ שֶׁל בַּעַל הַבַּיִת אוֹ שֶׁנָּטַל מִתּוֹכָהּ וְהוֹצִיא if the poor man puts forth his hand . . . and puts into the hand of the master of the house, or if he takes from it and brings forth, Šab. i. 1; אִם הֱבִיאוּהוּ לִידֵי מִיתָה . . . לֹא יְבִיאוּהוּ . . . if they bring him to death . . . should they not bring him . . ., K^er. iii. 1; אִם בָּאנוּ לִכְתּוֹב אֵין אָנוּ מַסְפִּיקִין if we came to write, we should not be capable, Šab. 13b; וְאִם כָּבְתָה כָּבְתָה if it is extinguished, let it be extinguished, ib. 120a; אִם שֶׁלָּנוּ הוּא הַפֶּסַח הַזֶּה יָדֶיךָ מְשׁוּכוֹת מִשֶּׁלָּךְ וְנִמְנֵיתָ עַל שֶׁלָּנוּ if ours be this Paschal lamb, then let thy hands be withdrawn from thine own, and thou art counted for ours, P^es. ix. 10.

311. In descriptions of continuous, or repeated, or customary actions in the past, for which the participle is regularly used, the perf. is sometimes found amidst a series of participles. In such cases the perfect usually has a temporal or hypothetical significance: הַקְּרוֹבִים מְבִיאִים . . . וְהַשּׁוֹר הוֹלֵךְ עִמָּהֶם . . . וְהֶחָלִיל מַכֶּה לִפְנֵיהֶם עַד שֶׁהֵן מַגִּיעִין קָרוֹב לִירוּשָׁלַיִם הִגִּיעוּ קָרוֹב לִירוּשָׁלַיִם שָׁלְחוּ לִפְנֵיהֶם וְעִיטְּרוּ אֶת בִּיכּוּרֵיהֶם וְהַפַּחוֹת יוֹצְאִין לִקְרָאתָם . . . those near bring . . ., and the ox goes with them . . ., and the flute strikes in front of them, until they reach near Jerusalem. When they have reached near Jerusalem, they send (messengers) in front of them, and they crown their first ripe fruits, and the rulers go forth to meet them . . ., Bik. iii. 3; הָיוּ מַכְנִיסִין אֶת הַשֵּׁנִי וּבוֹדְקִין אוֹתוֹ נִמְצְאוּ דִבְרֵיהֶם מְכֻוּוָנִים נוֹשְׂאִין וְנוֹתְנִין בַּדָּבָר . . . גָּמְרוּ אֶת הַדָּבָר הָיוּ מַכְנִיסִין they would bring in the second, and examine him. If their words were found to correspond, they discussed the matter . . . When they finished the matter, they would bring in . . ., San. iii. 6–7; v. 4–5; vi. 1. Sometimes the perf. is used in such cases without any apparent hypothetical or temporal significance: פּוֹשְׁטִים וּמְקַפְּלִים וּמַנִּיחִים . . . וּמִתְכַּסִּים . . . אֵירַע קֶרִי לְאֶחָד מֵהֶם יוֹצֵא וְהוֹלֵךְ לוֹ . . . יָרַד וְטָבַל עָלָה וְנִסְתַּפֵּג וְנִתְחַמֵּם . . . בָּא וְיָשַׁב אֵצֶל אֶחָיו . . . they undress and fold them and put them . . . and cover themselves . . . when an impurity happens to one of them he goes forth and departs . . . and goes down and dips himself, comes up and dries himself and warms himself . . . he comes and sits by the side of his brethren, Tam. i. 1; cf. also Yo. i. 1–5; Suk. iv. 5, 9; N^eg. xiv. 1–3; Pa. iii. 2–3, 7–8, f., &c.

312. Sometimes the act described by the perf. has just been performed, in which case English would use the present: עָקַרְתָּ מַה שֶּׁכָּתוּב בַּתּוֹרָה thou uprootest what is written in the Torah, Pes. vi. 1; מָה רָאִיתָ לְטַמֵּא what (reason) dost thou see to make it unclean? מָצִינוּ we find, 'Ed. vi. 3; קִיַּמְתָּ thou hast fulfilled, BQ iii. 9; נֵר שֶׁכָּבָה וְהוֹלֶכֶת אָדָם מַנִּיחַ אֶצְבָּעוֹ עָלֶיהָ מִיַּד כָּבְתָה a lamp which is gradually going out, when a man lays his hand upon it, immediately it is extinguished, Šab. 151 b. So also of single acts that may be performed at any time: נִכְנַס יַיִן יָצָא סוֹד when wine goes in, the secret goes out, 'Er. 65 a; הַכֹּל יוֹדְעִין כַּלָּה לָמָּה נִכְנְסָה לְחוּפָּה every body knows for what purpose a bride enters the bridal chamber, Ket. 8 b.

313. Finally, the perf. is found, though very rarely, also of a future act conceived as already performed: כְּשֵׁם שֶׁקִּבַּלְתִּי שָׂכָר עַל הַדְּרִישָׁה כָּךְ קִבַּלְתִּי שָׂכָר עַל הַפְּרִישָׁה just as I shall receive reward for expounding, so shall I receive reward for withdrawing (from expounding), Qid. 57 a.[1] So sometimes in a conditional sentence, as a *futurum exactum*, for which usually the participle or imperfect is used (cf. §§ 321, 486): אִם אֵחַרְתִּי שַׁחֲטוּ עָלַי if I shall have delayed, slay on my behalf, Pes. ix. 10; זֶה גִּטֵּךְ אִם מַתִּי . . . אִם לֹא בָאתִי this is thy bill of divorcement if I shall have died . . . if I shall not have come, Giṭ. vii. 3, 7–9.

(2) The Imperfect.

314. The imperf. describes a single act or event which has not yet taken place. It is, therefore, the tense of the future: אֲנִי אַחֲזִיר אֶת הַדִּינָר (L.) I shall restore the *dinar*, Ket. xi. 4; נִכְתּוֹב גֵּט let us write a bill of divorcement, Giṭ. vii. 1, 2. So in dependent clauses pointing to the future: עַד שֶׁיַּעֲלֶה עַמּוּד הַשַּׁחַר until dawn

[1] So in BQ 41 b. In Pes. 22 b; Bek. 6 b, the apodosis has a participle אֲנִי מְקַבֵּל.

rise, Bᵉr. i. 1; כְּדֵי שֶׁיְּהַבִּילוּ; אֶלָּא כְדֵי שֶׁיִּשּׁוֹרוּ, &c., except there be sufficient time that they be soaked, heated, &c., Šab. i. 5, 6; בַּקֵּשׁ עָלָיו רַחֲמִים וְיִחְיֶה seek for him (God's) mercy that he live, Bᵉr. 32 a. Also in questions: מַה יַּעֲשׂוּ what shall they do? Šab. 26 a; כַּמָּה יַרְחִיקוּ how far shall they go? Ṭoh. x. 2; וְלֹא אֶבְכֶּה shall I not weep? Bᵉr. 28 b; וְלֹא אֲקַיְּימֶנּוּ shall I not fulfil it? Yo. 19 b. So even of a past act: מָה אֶעֱשֶׂה וְרֻבּוּ עָלַי what can (could) I do, when they were a majority against me? (L, edd.: שֶׁחֲבֵרַי רַבּוּ עָלַי).

315. The futurity of an act is sometimes emphasized by periphrasis with עָתִיד שֶׁ־, especially in the later Agadic style: עֲתִידָה אִשָּׁה שֶׁתֵּלֵד a woman will bear; עֲתִידָה אֶרֶץ יִשְׂרָאֵל שֶׁתּוֹצִיא the land of Israel will bring forth, Šab. 30 b; עֲתִידָה תוֹרָה שֶׁתִּשְׁתַּכַּח the Torah will be forgotten, ib. 138 b.

316. The imperf. is used to describe a series of consecutive acts in the future, where BH would use the perf. consecutive: תָּחוּבוּ חוֹבַת גָּלוּת וְתִגְלוּ לִמְקוֹם הַמַּיִם הָרָעִים וְיִשְׁתּוּ הַתַּלְמִידִים . . . וְיָמוּתוּ you will incur the guilt of exile and you will be exiled to the place of the evil waters, and the disciples will drink and die, Ab. i. 9; אֵלֵךְ לְבֵיתִי וְאוֹכַל . . . וְאֶשְׁתֶּה . . . וְאִישַׁן וְאַחַר כָּךְ אֶקְרָא . . . וְאֶתְפַּלֵּל I shall go home and eat . . . and drink . . . and sleep and after that I shall read Šᵉma' and pray, Bᵉr. 4 b.

317. The imperf. is used of hypothetical acts, the performance of which lies in the future: לִכְשֶׁתָּבוֹא אֶצְלִי אֲזוּנָהּ I shall feed her when she comes to me, Kᵉt. xii. 1; אִם יִרְצֶה יִשְׂרָאֵל if the Israelite should wish, 'AZ. iv. 12; אִם תַּקְנִיטֵנִי if thou wilt provoke me, Šab. 17 a.

318. As a subjunctive: וְלֹא זָכִיתִי שֶׁתֵּאָמֵר I was not able to prove that it should be said, Bᵉr. i. 5; לֹא תִדְחֶה; לֹא יִדְחוּ should it not, should they not push away (override)? Pᵉs. vi. 2; מַה יַּעֲשֶׂה הַבֵּן שֶׁלֹּא יֶחֱטָא what can that son do that he might not sin? (he cannot hel committing sin), Bᵉr. 32 a.

319. The imperf. is used to express a wish or a prayer (Optative or Precative): מִי יְגַלֶּה עָפָר מֵעֵינֶיךָ Oh, who would uncover the dust from thine eyes, So. v. 2; יִכְבְּשׁוּ רַחֲמַי אֶת כַּעְסִי וְיִגּוֹלּוּ רַחֲמַי עַל כַּעְסִי וְאֶתְנַהֵג עִם בָּנַי בְּמִדַּת רַחֲמִים וְאֶכָּנֵס לָהֶם may my mercies suppress mine anger, and may my mercies roll themselves against mine anger, and may I conduct myself towards my children with the attribute of mercy, and may I enter for them . . ., B^e^r. 7 a; cf. ib. 16 b; 29 a; 60 b, &c. (§ 467).

320. To express a command that some act should or should not be performed (Jussive): תֵּדְעוּ know ye! B^e^r. 28 8; בָּעֶרֶב כָּל אָדָם יַטּוּ וְיִקְרוּ וּבַבֹּקֶר יַעַמְדוּ in the evening all men should incline and read, but in the morning they should stand, B^e^r. i. 3; אַל תְּרַצֶּה אֶת חֲבֵרְךָ . . . וְאַל תְּנַחֲמֶנּוּ . . . וְאַל תִּשְׁאַל לוֹ do not appease thy neighbour . . . and do not comfort him . . ., and do not ask of him . . ., Ab. iv. 18.

321. The imperf. expresses an act which must be performed prior to another act in the future (*Futurum Exactum*). Such an imperf. is put in a dependent clause introduced by שֶׁ־: כְּשֶׁאַגִּיעַ לוֹ אֲלַקְּטֶנּוּ I shall gather it when I shall have reached it, Kil. v. 6; אַל תָּדִין אֶת חֲבֵרְךָ עַד שֶׁתַּגִּיעַ לִמְקוֹמוֹ do not judge thy neighbour till thou hast reached his place, Ab. ii. 4; מֵאַחַר שֶׁיִּתָּלְשׁוּ after they shall have been plucked, Bik. iii. 1; לֹא יְכַסֶּנּוּ מִשֶּׁתֶּחְשַׁךְ he shall not cover it after it has become dark, Šab. iv. 2; cf. § 513.

(3) The Participle.

322. The participle has retained in MH its twofold character of noun and verb. Its primary function is to describe the subject as being in a state of activity or passivity. By emphasizing the state of the subject, the partic. becomes equivalent to a noun-adjective. By emphasizing the activity or the passivity of the subject, the partic. becomes equivalent to a verb. But as even in the latter case, the activity or passivity of the subject is expressed as a state, the partic. comes to describe an act as in the process of being performed. Hence the partic. becomes in MH the tense of the present. But is by no means confined to the present, even in its verbal character. It is also used, as in BH, of the past and the future to describe acts that are continuous, or repeated, or customary.

323. The partic. as present: עַל שְׁלֹשָׁה דְּבָרִים הָעוֹלָם עוֹמֵד the world stands on three things, Ab. i. 2; בַּעַל הַבַּיִת דּוֹחֵק the master presses, ib. ii. 15; הַחַזָּן רוֹאֶה הֵיכָן תִּינוֹקוֹת קוֹרְאִים the overseer may see where the children read, Šab. i. 3. With pronouns as subject: אֲנִי יוֹדֵעַ I know; אֵינִי יוֹדֵעַ I do not know, Ned. xi. 7; הוּא רוֹצֶה he is willing, BB vi. 6; קוֹבְלִין אָנוּ we complain, Ya. iv. 7; בְּנֵי אָדָם דּוֹמִים לְעִשְׂבֵי הַשָּׂדֶה הַלָּלוּ נוֹצְצִין וְהַלָּלוּ נוֹבְלִין human beings are like the herbs of the field, some sprout forth, others fade away, 'Er. 54 a.

324. The partic. as past, in a frequentative or iterative sense; usually with the perf. of היה as auxiliary to emphasize the tense: אֲנִי הָיִיתִי בָא בַּדֶּרֶךְ וְהִטֵּתִי I was coming by the road, and I inclined, Ber. i. 3; הָיִיתָ נוֹהֵג thou hast conducted thyself, Suk. ii. 7; הָיוּ אוֹמְרִין they used to say, Šebi. iv. 1; גִּילְּתָה אֶת רֹאשָׁהּ וְהָיְתָה מְטַפַּחַת וּמַנַּחַת . . . she uncovered her head, and kept on gathering it up with her hand and laying it, BQ viii. 6; especially in conditional sentences: אִילּוּ הָיִיתִי יוֹדֵעַ . . . לֹא הָיִיתִי נוֹדֵר if I had known it, I would not have vowed, Ned. ix. 2 ff.; אִילּוּ לִפְנֵי מֶלֶךְ בָּשָׂר וָדָם הָיוּ מוֹלִיכִין אוֹתִי . . . אַף עַל פִּי כֵן הָיִיתִי בוֹכֶה if they had led me into the presence of a human king . . ., I would, nevertheless, have wept, Ber. 28 b; 32 b (§§ 490, 494).

Often, however, the verb היה is omitted, when the context makes it clear that the reference is to the past: מְצָאוֹ שֶׁיּוֹשֵׁב he found that he was sitting, 'Er. 11 b; אִם הָיָה חָכָם דּוֹרֵשׁ וְאִם לָאו תַּלְמִידֵי חֲכָמִים דּוֹרְשִׁין לְפָנָיו if he was a scholar, he expounded, but if not, scholars expounded before him, Yo. i. 6; Bik. iii. 1; Suk. iv. 4, and other descriptive passages cited above, § 311.

325. The partic. as future, with or without היה: כְּשֶׁיִּהְיוּ בַּעֲלֵי הַדִּין עוֹמְדִין ... לְפָנֶיךָ ... וּכְשֶׁנִּפְטָרִין ... when the litigants will be standing before thee ... and when they will depart ..., Ab. i. 8; שֶׁמָּא אַתָּה מַחֲסִיר ... אַתָּה מְיַיתֵּר lest thou omit, lest thou add, 'Er. 13 a, for which the parallel passage in So. 20 a has the imperf.: תְּיַיתֵּר, תַּחְסִיר; מוּבְטָח אֲנִי בָזֶה שֶׁמּוֹרֶה הוֹרָאָה בְּיִשְׂרָאֵל I am sure of this one that he will teach doctrine (promulgate decisions) in Israel, Naz. 29 b; Giṭ. 58 a; אֲנִי מֵת I am going to die, Y^eb. xvi. 6; רָאָה שֶׁהוּא מִתְחַיֵּב he saw that he was going to be declared guilty, San. iii. 8. Also of single acts: מַה שֶּׁאַתְּ שׁוֹמַעַת what thou wilt hear, B^er. 18 b; אִם אֵין אַתָּה מְלַמְּדֵנִי אֲנִי אוֹמֵר לְיוֹחָא אַבָּא וּמוֹסֶרְךָ לַמַּלְכוּת if thou wilt not teach me, I shall tell my father Yoḥa, and he will deliver thee to the (Roman) authority, P^es. 112 a.

326. The partic. is used with the imperative הוה to command the performance of a frequentative or iterative act, as contrasted with the ordinary imperative which signifies the performance of a simple act: הֱוֵי מִתְאַבֵּק sit in the dust; הֱוֵי שׁוֹתֶה drink, Ab. i. 4; הֱוֵי מְקַבֵּל receive, ib. 15, viz. regularly and habitually, as opposed to עֲשֵׂה make; אֱמוֹר say, ib., which describe single acts.

327. The partic. is similarly used with the infinitive of היה in a frequentative and iterative sense: הַנּוֹטֵל שְׂכָרוֹ לִהְיוֹת רוֹאֶה he who takes wages to be examining, B^ek. iv. 5; הֶחָשׁוּד לִהְיוֹת מוֹכֵר he who is suspected to be selling, ib. ix; לִהְיוֹת מַפְרִישׁ to be separating (tithes), Git. iii. 7; הוּחְזְקוּ לִהְיוֹת גּוֹמְרִים they established the rule to finish, Y^eb. xii. 6; הוּחְזְקוּ לִהְיוֹת מַשִּׂיאִין to allow to marry, ib. xvi. 7. So with עָתִיד: עָתִיד לִהְיוֹת נָטוּעַ וְעוֹשֶׂה פֵּירוֹת it will be planted and bear fruit; עֲתִידִים לִהְיוֹת עוֹשִׂים they will make, Sifra (Weiss), 110 d; cf. below, § 349.

328. The auxiliary verb היה is sometimes omitted in the infin., as in the perf. and imperf. (§§ 324, 325), but only after certain expressions. Thus, after הִתְחִיל (= הֵחֵל): הִתְחִילוּ כָּל הָעָם שׂוֹרְפִין all the people began to burn (לִהְיוֹת שׂוֹרְפִין), P^e^s. i. 5; הִתְחִילוּ הַיְּחִידִים מִתְעַנִּין individuals began to fast (לִהְיוֹת מִתְעַ׳) Ta'a. i. 4; הֵחֵלּוּ מַעֲלִין they began to bring up, Tam. ii. 2, 3; הִתְחִיל מְרַבֵּד he began to spread out, ib. vi. 3.

After דֶּרֶךְ: בְּשָׁעָה שֶׁדֶּרֶךְ בְּנֵי אָדָם שׁוֹכְבִים . . . דֶּרֶךְ בְּנֵי אָדָם עוֹמְדִים at the hour when it is the custom of men to lie down . . . to rise up, B^e^r. i. 3 (לִהְיוֹת שׁוֹ׳); BB vi. 6; דֶּרֶךְ כָּל הַמּוּמָתִין מִתְוַדִּין it is the custom of all those about to be put to death to make a confession, San. vii. 2 (לִהְיוֹת מִתְוַדִּין); נוֹהֲגִין הָיוּ בֵּית אַבָּא נוֹתְנִין the house of father were accustomed to give, Pea ii. 4; Šab. i. 9 (L); לֹא נִמְנְעוּ עוֹשִׂין they did not shrink from preparing, Y^e^b. i. 4; 'Ed. iv. 8 (var.: לִהְיוֹת עוֹשִׂין); לֹא נֶחְשְׁדוּ חֲבֵרִים תּוֹרְמִין associates are not suspected of giving tithes . . ., t. Ma'a. ii. 5 (but var. לִתְרוֹם; so Ḥul. 7 a).

329. The partic. also expresses an act which is customary, without any reference to a particular time: הַכֹּהֲנִים נִכְנָסִין לֶאֱכוֹל the priests enter to eat, B^e^r. i. 1; יוֹרֵד אָדָם לְתוֹךְ שָׂדֵהוּ וְרוֹאֶה . . . a man goes down to his field and sees . . ., Bik. iii. 1; כְּשֶׁחוֹתְכִין . . . אֵין חוֹתְכִין אֶלָּא עַל גַּב הַשֻּׁלְחָן כְּשֶׁנּוֹשְׁקִין אֵין נוֹשְׁקִין אֶלָּא עַל גַּב הַיָּד וּכְשֶׁיּוֹעֲצִין אֵין יוֹעֲצִין אֶלָּא בַּשָּׂדֶה when they cut . . ., they do not cut but upon the table; when they kiss, they do not kiss but upon the hand; when they hold counsel they do not hold counsel but upon the field, B^e^r. 8 b. The subject is often omitted, and then the partic. has the force of an impersonal verb, which may usually be rendered in English by a passive: הַקּוֹרֵא אֶת שְׁמַע B^e^r. ii. 3. This is especially common in the plur.: כֵּיצַד מַפְרִישִׁין אֶת הַבִּכּוּרִים how are the first-ripe fruits separated? Bik. iii. 1; עַכְשָׁיו שֶׁמּוֹלִיכִים אוֹתִי now that I am led, B^e^r. 28 b; מִיַּד יוֹעֲצִים בַּאֲחִיתוֹפֶל וְנִמְלָכִים בְּסַנְהֶדְרִין וְשׁוֹאֲלִים בְּאוּרִים וְתוּמִּים immediately they take counsel with Ahitophel, and consult the Sanhedrin, and inquire of the oracle, ib. 3 b ; מְבִיאִין לוֹ עֲרִיבָה מְלֵאָה מַיִם a tub full of water was brought to him, Sab. 25 b. Cf. below, § 439.

330. Such participles often assume a somewhat jussive sense : מֵאֵימָתַי קוֹרִין אֶת שְׁמַע from when may the Šema' be read? Ber. i. 1 ; כָּל אָדָם קוֹרֵא כְּדַרְכּוֹ one may read in one's own way, as opposed to the preceding, יַטּוּ וְיִקְרְאוּ one must read in a bent position, ib. 3 ; שׁוֹאֵל ; מֵשִׁיב one may ask, answer, ib. ii. 1 ; מַשְׁאֶלֶת אִשָּׁה . . . וּבוֹרֶרֶת וְטוֹחֶנֶת וּמְרַקֶּדֶת a woman may lend . . . and pick and grind and sift . . . , Šebi. v. 9. The transition from this usage to a real jussive or imperative is easy : בּוֹדְקִין אֶת הֶחָמֵץ leaven must be searched, Pes. i. 1 ; הִתְקִינוּ שֶׁיְּהוּ אוֹמְרִין it was ordained that they should say ; שֶׁיְּהֵא אָדָם שׁוֹאֵל that one must ask, Ber. ix. 5. Particularly with a negative : אֵין עוֹמְדִין לְהִתְפַּלֵּל one must not stand up to pray, ib. v. 1 ; בַּמֶּה מַדְלִיקִין וּבַמָּה אֵין מַדְלִיקִין wherewith may one light, and wherewith may not one light? Šab. ii. 1 ; הִתְקִין רַבָּן גַּמְלִיאֵל שֶׁלֹּא יְהוּ עוֹשִׂין כֵּן Rabban Gamaliel ordained that one must not do so, Giṭ. iv. 2.

331. The partic. retains its verbal character even when it is apparently used as a noun : הַקּוֹרֵא אֶת שְׁמַע וְלֹא הִשְׁמִיעַ לְאָזְנָיו if one reads the Šema', but has not made it audible to his ears, Ber. ii. 3. Here the partic. takes the article like a noun, yet it also takes a direct object and is co-ordinated with a finite verb. Other examples are הַמִּתְפַּלֵּל וְטָעָה one who prays and makes a mistake, ib. v. 5 ; Šebi. x. 2 ; Ter. iii. 1, and often ; cf. also § 374.

332. As already stated in the treatment of the Verb (§§ 113, 127), in the passive forms the static significance of the partic. is predominant. The passive partic. of the Qal, and the participles Pu'al and Hoph'al are practically equivalent to adjectives. Thus, (לוּלָב) הַגָּזוּל that has been obtained by robbery, is parallel to הַיָּבֵשׁ a dry one, Suk. iv. 1 ; תָּלוּשׁ plucked from the ground ; מְחוּבָּר joined to the ground, are parallel to חָדָשׁ new ; יָשָׁן old, MŠ. v. 11 ; מְלוּבָּן whitened, washed, parallel to צוֹאִי dirty, Ḥul. xi. 2. So רָכוּב

BM i. 3; מְעוּמָּד, מְיוּשָּׁב Meg. 21 a, in a riding, standing, sitting posture, contrasted with the active forms רוֹכֵב, עוֹמֵד, יוֹשֵׁב.

333. These participles, viz. the passive of Qal, and the participles of Pu'al and Hoph'al, describe a more or less permanent state as the result of a verbal action. They thus differ from the participles of the corresponding reflexive-passive stems, which describe the verbal action as in the process of being performed. Thus פָּטוּר free, Šab. ii. 5; הַנִּפְטָר who frees himself—departs, MQ 29 a; שָׁחוּף consumptive; נִשְׁחָף wasting away, Sifra 111 c; מְבוּעָר cleared away; מִתְבַּעֲרִים being cleared away, MŠ. v. 6; מְעוּשָּׂרִין tithed (adjective); מִתְעַשְּׂרִין are tithed, Dam. iv. 1; ii. 1; מְחוּיָּב having an obligation, RH iv. 8; מִתְחַיֵּב incurring guilt, Ab. iii. 9; מְעוּנֶּה and מִתְעַנֶּה t. Ta'a. ii. 7.

334. The passive partic. sometimes has the significance of the Latin gerundive (cf. Ges.-K., § 116 e): שׁוֹר הַנִּסְקָל an ox that is to be stoned, Qid. ii. 9; שָׂעִיר הַמִּשְׁתַּלֵּחַ the goat that is to be sent away, Yo. vi. 1; זֵתִים הַנִּכְתָּשִׁין olives that are to be crushed; עֲנָבִים הַנִּדְרָכוֹת grapes that are to be trodden, Ter. i. 8; פָּרִים הַנִּשְׂרָפִים bulls that are to be burnt, Yo. vi. 7; כָּל הַמּוּמָתִין all that are to be put to death, San. vi. 2.[1]

335. The active partic. Qal is sometimes found in a middle sense which is equivalent to an English passive: חֲמוֹר טוֹעֶנֶת a loading—loaded ass, BM v. 4; פּוֹרֶקֶת unloading—unloaded, ib. vii. 4; קוֹטְעִין cut (ears of corn), Ma'a. i. 6; שׁוֹפְכִין pouring out—to be poured out, i.e. ill-smelling liquid, Šab. viii. 1.

336. The passive partic. Qal, being almost equivalent to an adjective, is found in an active sense in a few intransitive and transitive verbs. So already in BH, Ges.-K., § 50 f; also in Aram., and especially in Syriac, Nöldeke, *Syr. Gr.*, § 280; *Mand. Gr.*, § 380.

[1] The other examples cited by Albrecht, § 107 m, do not belong to this category.

The following is a fairly exhaustive list of such cases in MH.

(i) Intrans.: אֲבוּדָה lost, BM 22 b; מָתוּן cautious, Ab. i. 1; יָרוּד lowly, j. BM iv. 1; נְטוּפָה dripping, Pea vii. 1; סָבוּר thinking, Qid. iii. 5 (an Aramaism—סְבִיר); עֲסוּקִים occupied, Pa. iv 4 (L); רְבוּצִים lying down, Bek. ix. 7; רָכוּב riding, BM i. 3 (edd.; so BM 9 a, &c.); שָׁקוּד watchful, Ab. ii. 14; שְׁרוּיָה dwelling, ib. iii. 2.

(ii) Transitive: אֲחוּזַת הַדָּם holding in the blood, Ḥul. 58 b; אָרוּס betrothed male, masc. of אֲרוּסָה Ket. 13 b; זָכוּר remembering, Ket. ii. 10; חֲשׂוּכֵי בְגָדִים lacking garments, Kel. i. 2; טְבוּל יוֹם one who bathed by day, ṬY ii. 1; כְּפוּיֵי טוֹבָה repressing thanks, ungrateful, 'AZ 5 a; נָדוּר having vowed, t. Dam. ii. 23; נְשׂוּי שְׁתֵּי נָשִׁים married to two wives,[1] Ket. x. 1, 2; שֶׁלֹּא רָחוּץ יָדַיִם וְרַגְלָיִם not having washed the hands and feet,[2] Kel. i. 9; Pa. iv. 1; תְּפוּסֵי מַעֲשֵׂי אֲבוֹתֵיהֶם holding the acts of their fathers, Sifra 112 b.[3]

The following are only apparently active: חֲלוּצָה a woman that has received *ḥaliṣa*,[4] Yeb. ii. 3; טְעוּנָה burdened with—requiring, So. ii. 1; סָמוּךְ leaning on—near, Yo. i. 8 (cf. BH נִשְׁעָן); שָׁחוּל suspended—falling, Bek. vi. 7; שְׁלוּחִין stripped—olives dropping their kernels, 'AZ ii. 7; שָׁקוּל balanced—even, So. ix. 2; תָּלוּי hanged—hanging, ib.[5]

[1] As opposed to פָּנוּי unmarried, t. Qid. i. 1. Cf. the active and passive forms side by side: הַנְּשׂוּאִין אֶת הָאֲחָיוֹת נוֹשְׂאִין, those who are married to the sisters may marry . . ., t. 'Ed. ii. 9, the first expressing a state or condition, the second expressing an act.

[2] A standing phrase, derived from Exod. xxx. 21. Cf. t. Yo. i. 18; San. xiv. 6.

[3] Contrast אוֹחֲזִין מַעֲשֵׂי אֲבוֹתֵיהֶם, Ber. 7 a; San. 27 b.

[4] In Deut. xxv. 7–10 the woman is conceived as active (וְחָלְצָה, ver. 9), and the man as passive (חֲלוּץ הַנָּעַל, ver. 10); so also in MH: לֹא תַחֲלוֹץ, Yeb. iv. 10; חָלְצָה, ib. xii. 3. More often, however, the condition is reversed: the man is active, הַחוֹלֵץ, Yeb. iv. 1, 7; חֲלוֹץ, 5, 6; חָלַץ, v. 2 ff., and the woman is passive, חֲלוּצָה.

[5] The forms כְּתִיב written, Ab. vi. 10; שְׁכִיב מְרַע lying with disease, Pea iii. 7, &c., are pure Aramaisms.

337. In spite of the strong development of the verbal character of the participle in MH, the idiom has also retained in full the substantival usages of the partic. found in BH. Thus, the partic. is widely used as a noun, especially when determined by the article, e.g. הָעוֹמֵד what is standing; הַפָּרוּץ what is broken, Kil. iv. 4; הַנּוֹלָד what is born = the result of a action, Ab. ii. 9, &c. As an attribute, the partic. with the article often has the force of a relative clause, as in BH; cf. שׁוֹר הַנִּסְקָל and the other exx. in § 376.

338. The partic. often stands in the construct state: נְקוּבַת הַוֶּשֶׁט having a hole in the gullet; פְּסוּקַת הַגַּרְגֶּרֶת cut in the windpipe, Ḥul. iii. 1; מוּכַּת שְׁחִין struck with leprosy, Ket. iii. 5; חוֹתְמֵי בְרָכוֹת those who conclude the benedictions, Ber. ix. 5; cf. § 380.

339. In accordance with its substantival character, the partic. is regularly negatived by אֵין: אֵין מַדְלִיקִין Šab. ii. 1; cf. exx. above, §§ 329–30. Frequently, however, it is negatived by לֹא, but as a rule only when it is intended to impart a certain emphasis to the negation. This happens either when the negative follows immediately upon an affirmative, or when two or more negatives follow each other. In the first case, וְלֹא has the force of 'but not', in the second case לֹא . . . וְלֹא means 'neither . . . nor'. The participial clause negatived by לֹא contains, as a rule, no other words but the participle.

Exx. (i) יֵשׁ מְבִיאִין בִּכּוּרִים וְקוֹרִין מְבִיאִין וְלֹא קוֹרִין there are some who bring first-fruits and recite, some who bring but do not recite, Bik. i. 1, 3, 4; נִשְׁבָּעִין וְלֹא מְשַׁלְּמִין they take an oath, but do not pay, Šebu. vii. 1; cf. further, Šab. xi. 2; Yeb. iii. 1 f.; vi. 1; vii. 4; x. 8, 9; xi. 4, 6; So. 1, 2; San. vii. 5; Ḥul. i. 7.

(ii) תּוֹלִין לֹא אוֹכְלִין וְלֹא שׂוֹרְפִין they are in suspense: neither may they eat (the leavened bread), nor need they burn it, Pes. i. 5; Be. ii. 8; v. 2; Yeb. vii. 5; viii. 4, 5; לֹא חוֹלְצִים וְלֹא מְיַבְּמִים

neither do they give *ḥaliṣa*, nor do they marry (the deceased brother's childless wife), xi. 2. Contrast with 5, 7, where in similar cases the negative is אֵין, because the clauses are longer, and there is no particular emphasis on the negative; So. iv. 1 f.; Mak. iii. 13; 'Ed. v. 2; Ḥul. viii. 1; Tᵉm. iv. 1; M'il. iii. 1 ff. (contrast with 3); Nᵉg. x. 4: Nid. vi. 1.

(iii) The two cases side by side: כֹּהֵן גָּדוֹל מַקְרִיב אוֹנֵן וְלֹא אוֹכֵל וְהַהֶדְיוֹט לֹא מַקְרִיב וְלֹא אוֹכֵל the High Priest may offer sacrifices on the day of the death of a near kinsman, but may not eat of a sacrifice, while an ordinary priest may neither offer a sacrifice, nor eat of one, Hor. iii. 5; BB viii. 1; 'Ar. vii. 1; Oho. viii. 1; Miq. vii. 1; 'Uq. v. 5.

In longer clauses the partic. is negatived by אֵין, even in such cases as described above: אֵין מוֹעֲלִים בָּהֶם וְאֵין חַיָּבִים עֲלֵיהֶם מִשֵּׁם . . . one does not incur *mᵉ'ila* by using them, nor is one guilty in their case of . . . Mᵉ'il. i. 3; 'Ar. ii. 6; Kᵉt. v. 5.

340. There are, however, exceptions to the above rules, when the partic. is negatived by לֹא, where we would expect אֵין, especially in later texts; cf. Kᵉt. vii. 6; 'Ar. ii. 3; vii. 1, &c. But we also find in BH numerous examples of such an irregular construction,[1] e.g. Deut. xxviii. 61; Hab. i. 14; Job xii. 3; xxix. 12. Further, 2 Sam. iii. 34; Ezek. iv. 14, where the partic. is parallel to a finite verb.

341. The subject of a participial predicate is often placed after the partic., as in BH,[2] but as a rule only when a certain emphasis is intended on the predicate: בַּמֶּה בְהֵמָה יוֹצְאָה וּבַמָּה אֵינָהּ יוֹצְאָה יוֹצֵא הַגָּמָל wherewith may an animal go out, and wherewith may it

[1] All the examples in BH are collected and classified by E. Sellin, *Ueber die verbal-nominale Doppelnatur d. hebr. Participien u. Infinitive*, p. 27, and by J. Kahan in his dissertation with the same title, p. 19. Cf. also Ges.-K., § 152 d.

[2] Cf. Driver, *Tenses*, § 135 (4). So also in Phoenician: פָּעַל אנך, קֹרֵא אנך, Cooke, op. cit., No. 3, ll. 2, 3, and the note p. 21 f.

not go out? The camel may go out, Šab. v. 1. Contrast with 2: חֲמוֹר יוֹצֵא, זְכָרִים יוֹצְאִין, &c.; מִתְיַחֵד אָדָם a man may be alone, opposed to the preceding לֹא יִתְיַחֵד Qid. iv. 12; אוֹכֵל פּוֹעֵל a workman may eat, opposed to the following לֹא יֹאכַל פּוֹעֵל BM vii. 5, 6. So also with pronoun as subject: לֹא יִתֵּן לְתוֹכוֹ צוֹנֵן אֲבָל נוֹתֵן הוּא לְתוֹכוֹ one may not put into it cold water, but one may put into it . . ., Šab. iii. 5; מָה אָנוּ לֵירֵד . . . מוּתָּרִים אַתֶּם what are we in respect to going down? . . . you are permitted, 'Er. iv. 2.

Often, however, the emphasis is hardly noticeable: יוֹדֵעַ אֲנִי I know, Bᵉr. v. 5 (so Qoh. viii. 12); רוֹאֶה אֲנִי I prefer, Ab. ii. 9 (so Gen. xxxi. 5); זָכוּר אֲנִי I remember, Kᵉt. ii. 10 (זְכוּרַנִי, in Aram. fashion, Šab. 115 a, and often);[1] קוֹבֵעַ אַתָּה you rob, Yad. iv. 3; קוֹבְלִין אָנוּ we complain, ib. 6.

342. Similarly the auxiliary verb הָיָה sometimes follows the partic.: נוֹהֲגִין הָיוּ . . . my father's house were accustomed, Pea ii. 4, modifying the preceding statement; צוֹפֶה הָיִיתִי I was watching, Suk. iii. 9; אֲבָל אֲנוּסִים הָיִינוּ but we were forced, Kᵉt. ii. 3: פּוֹטְרוֹ הָיָה רַבִּי יְהוֹשֻׁעַ אַף . . . R. Joshua acquitted him even . . ., Kᵉr. iv. 2. So also in BH for the sake of emphasis: Exod. xxvii. 1; xxviii. 16; Deut. ix. 7, 22, 24; Joshua v. 5, &c. So in Aram.: Dan. ii. 31, 34; Ezra iv. 12, 22, &c., and often in the Targumim and other Aram. dialects.

343. Note. The construction of the partic. with היה in MH is of native origin, and is not borrowed from Aram. It is frequent in BH even where the partic. has a purely verbal force,[2] e.g. in the

[1] This contraction of אֲנִי with the partic., under Aram. influence, is common in the Midrashim and in late MH generally, but not in the Mishna. Where such forms occur in some texts of the Mishna they are due to the copyists, cf. e.g. Nᵉd. i. 1; RH ii. 9; Šab. xxii. 3; Yᵉb. xvi. 7; Ya. iv. 2 in edd. with L and N. The contraction of אָנוּ with the partic. is never found even in late MH, though common in Aram.; cf. Dalman, § 65; Nöldeke, *Syr. Gr.*, § 64; *Mand. Gr.*, § 175 a.

[2] Cf. Driver, *Tenses*, § 135 (5), and, with fuller lists, Sellin, op. cit., p. 35, and Kahan, p. 25.

past: Judges i. 7; 2 Sam. iii. 7; viii. 15; Jer. xxvi. 18, 20; 2 Kings xvii. 32, 33; of the future: Gen. i. 6; Deut. xxviii. 29; Isa. xxx. 20; with pass. partic.: Jer. xviii. 23; Ezek. xliv. 2; xlvi. 1; Zach. xiii. 1; especially in the later books: Neh. i. 4; ii. 13, 15; iii. 2; v. 18; vi. 14, 19; xiii. 5, 22; 2 Chron. xxx. 10; Dan. viii. 5, 7; x. 2; Esther ii. 7, 15, and with לִהְיוֹת (a genuine MH construction): i. 22; viii. 13; ix. 21.

On the other hand, it is worthy of note that, with perhaps one doubtful exception (cf. § 184 foot-note), the tenses are never found in MH combined with היה, as sometimes in the Targumim (e.g. דהוה חמידת, Gen. iv. 1 (Jer.); הוא נפיק Cant. i. 12), and very frequently in Syriac (Nöldeke, *Syr. Gr.*, §§ 263, 268), and in Arabic (Wright, *Arab. Gr.*[3], ii. § 3 (c)): also in Phoenician (כן נדר, Cooke, *NSI.*, No. 57, l. 5), evidently because there is nothing approaching such a construction in BH.

(4) The Infinitive.

344. Of the various constructions with the inf. in BH, MH has preserved only the gerundial use with ל to express the direction and purpose of a verb. In its use as a noun, the inf. has been supplanted in MH by the corresponding verbal nouns which are so numerous in MH (§ 217). For the BH inf. with the prepositions בְּ, כְּ, MH uses כְּשֶׁ־ with the finite verb, as often in BH (כַּאֲשֶׁר), and regularly in Aram. (כְּדִי Dan. vi. 10; כַּד).[1] Finally, the use of the inf. in its absolute form to emphasize a finite verb is never found in MH,[2] though this construction is very common in Aram.[3]

[1] The infin. with ב is frequent in the Targumim, e. g. Gen. xii. 4; xxiv. 6; xlviii. 7, &c., which proves that the construction was permissible in Aram.

[2] An exception is the liturgical passage: שַׂמֵּחַ תְּשַׂמַּח רֵעִים הָאֲהוּבִים (cf. Jer. xx. 15); שׂוֹשׂ תָּשִׂישׂ וְתָגֵל הָעֲקָרָה (cf. Isa. lxi. 10), Ket. 8 a; Singer, op cit., p. 299.

[3] Cf. Nöldeke, *Syr. Gr.*, § 295. In the Targumim the inf. absol. with

The loss of these infinitival constructions in MH is due to natural decay. They are already very scarce in the later books of the Bible. Thus, the combination of the inf. absolute with the finite verb is not found in Qoheleth, Canticles, Ezra, and Daniel, and is rare in Esther, Nehemiah, and Chronicles. So also the inf. with ב, and כ is rare in those books, and where found, it is not always used in a correct way.[1]

345. The use of the inf. with ל coincides generally with the BH inf. construct with ל. The pronominal suffixes attached to this inf. are, however, always of an objective force: לְזָרְעָהּ to sow it, Kil. ii. 3; לְנוֹטְעָהּ to plant it, ib. 4; לִפְדוֹתוֹ to redeem it, MŠ. iv. 6; לְאָכְלָן to eat them, Dam. iii. 3; לְהַחֲיוֹתְכֶם to revive you; לַהֲקִימְכֶם to raise you, Ber. 38 b.

346. After verbs of preventing, restraining, &c., either expressed or understood, the inf. takes the prepos. מִ־ before לְ־: אֲסוּרִין מִלִּזְרוֹעַ וּמִלְּקַיֵּים they are forbidden to be sown and to be kept, Kil. viii. 1; נִמְנְעוּ מִלְּהָבִיא they refrained from bringing, Ḥal. i. 7; Pes. i. 6; שַׁבָּת הִיא מִלִּזְעוֹק it is Sabbath, so that one must not cry, Šab. 15 a; נִשְׁתַּהוּ הָעֵדִים מִלָּבוֹא the witnesses delayed to come, RH iv. 4; cf. Ges.-K., § 119 x.

347. The inf. is sometimes used as a verbal noun with the לְ in the sense of 'with regard to': מָה אֲנִי לָבוֹא בַקָּהָל what am I with regard to entering the assembly (of Israel, cf. Deut. xxiii. 4)?—may I enter, &c., Ya. iv. 4; מָה אָנוּ לֵירֵד what are we with regard to going down—may we go down? 'Er. iv. 2; מַהוּ (= מַה + הוּא) לְהַזְכִּיר should one mention? Šab. 24 a.

348. The inf. sometimes expresses necessity, obligation, as in BH (Ges.-K., 114 i–l): הֲרֵי הוּא לְהַסְגִּיר behold, this is to be shut up, Neg. iv. 10; הֲרֵי הוּא לְהַחֲלִיט behold this is to be finally decided

finite verb is used almost always where the Hebrew text has it. Cf. also Winer, *Chald. Gr.* (1882), § 46, 4, 5.

[1] Cf. Driver, *Introd. to the Lit. of the OT.*[6], pp. 506, No. 12; 538, No. 37.

(as impure), ib. 11. The person upon whom the obligation rests is introduced by עַל with the appropriate suffix: הֲרֵי עָלַי לְשַׁלַּח פֶּרַע behold I must let (my hair) grow wild, Naz. i. 1; עָלֶיךָ . . . עָלָיו רְאָיָה לְלַמֵּד thou, he must teach (produce) the evidence, Ya. iv. 3.

349. When preceded by the adjective עָתִיד ready, the inf. expresses with certainty and emphasis the occurrence of an act or event in the future (*Periphrastic Future*): אִם עָתִיד לַחֲזוֹר if he is resolved, or going, to return, Meg. ii. 3; גָּמַר מִלִּמְסוֹק אֲבָל עָתִיד לִיקַּח גָּמַר מִלִּיקַּח אֲבָל עָתִיד לִלְווֹת he has finished gathering (the olives), but he is going to buy (more); he has finished buying, but he is going to borrow (more), Ṭoh. ix. 2; Dam. vii. 1; Ned. iii. 1; Šeq. vi. 3; Mid. ii. 6, 13 (הם עתידים להיות); Naz. v. 4; So. v. 2; BM iv. 2; San. x. 2; Ab. iii. 1; ʽUq. ii. 12 (a later addition).

These are all the passages in the Mishna where this construction occurs. But it becomes very common in the later Aggadic literature. Sometimes, however, עָתִיד is construed with the imperfect (cf. above, § 315). So also in the Targumim עָתִיד is found in both these constructions (e.g. Gen. iii. 15 in Jerus.; Isa. xl. 2). In Syriac ܥܬܝܕ is always followed by ܕ with the imperfect. In BH the construction is found only once, and in the primary sense of עָתִיד: הָעֲתִידִים עוֹרֵר (־לְעוֹרֵר) לִוְיָתָן Job iii. 8; cf. also Esther iii. 14; and עֲתִידוֹת the destined future, Deut. xxxii. 35.

350. The inf. expresses the certainty of a future action also when preceded by סוֹף: סוֹפוֹ לְהִשָּׁמַע it will eventually be understood, Ab. ii. 4; סוֹפוֹ לְקַיְּמָהּ: סוֹפוֹ לְבַטְּלָהּ he will eventually fulfil it, neglect it, ib. iv. 9; סוֹפוֹ לִיתֵּן he will eventually give, Mak. i. 1; סוֹפֵינוּ לִבְדּוֹק we shall certainly examine, San. iv. 5. Sometimes, however, the partic. is used, instead of the inf.: סוֹפוֹ יוֹרֵשׁ in the end he will inherit, Ab. i. 5; סוֹפָהּ בְּטֵלָה in the end it will cease, ib. ii. 2.

2. Government of the Verb.

(1) *Subordination of the Noun to the Verb as Accusative.*

351. The method in MH of marking the direct object of a transitive verb is exactly the same as in BH. As a rule, a determinate object is indicated by אֶת, an indeterminate object is left without any mark, e.g. אֵין חוֹפְרִין כּוּכִין . . . אֲבָל מְחַנְּכִין אֶת הַכּוּכִין one may not dig (new) sepulchres . . . but one may adapt the (old) sepulchres, MQ i. 6; קוֹרִין אֶת שְׁמַע read the 'Šᵉma'', Bᵉr. i. 1, &c. Sometimes, but not more frequently than in BH (Ges.-K., § 117 n), a determinate object is indicated by לְ, instead of אֶת: כַּפֶּר נָא לַעֲווֹנוֹת forgive, I pray, the iniquities, Yo. iii. 8; הַמְקַנֵּא לְאִשְׁתּוֹ one who suspects his wife (cf. Num. v. 14), So. i. 1. Often, however, a determinate object is found without the *nota accusativi*, whether ת or ל, especially when the object is determined by a possessive suffix: הִכְנִיס קְדֵרוֹתָיו, פֵּירוֹתָיו, שׁוֹרוֹ he brought in his pots, his fruit, his ox, BQ v. 2, 3; תַּרְבֶּה גְּבוּלֵנוּ . . . וְתַצְלִיחַ סוֹפֵנוּ . . . וְתָשִׂים חֶלְקֵנוּ mayest thou increase our border . . . prosper our end . . . put our portion, Bᵉr. 16 b. This omission may in many cases be due to scribal negligence, as is shown by the frequent disagreement of the texts: נָטְלוּ כְּסוּתוֹ they took his garment, BQ x. 2, L, but edd. את כס׳; הַמַּכִּיר כֵּלָיו if one recognizes his articles, edd., but L את כל׳ ib. 3, and often.

352. A nominative after a transitive verb is found in the expression יָבִיא הוּא וְלַחְמָהּ let him bring it and its bread, Mᵉn. vii. 8; יָבִיא הוּא וּנְסָכָיו let him bring it and its drink-offerings, ib. xiii. 7. The phrase may be an invariable technical expression, like אוֹתוֹ וְאֶת בְּנוֹ, § 275.

353. The accusative is found also after a passive verb: נִשְׂכָּר אֶת הַזָּוִיּוֹת gain the corners, 'Er. v. 1; לְהִפָּרַע אֶת שֶׁלָּךְ to be paid thine own, Kᵉt. xiii. 18; נִזְרַק אֶת דָּמוֹ its blood was sprinkled, Pᵉs. vii. 7 (L, edd. without את); cf. Ges.-K., § 121 a, b.

354. The double accusative is somewhat rarer in MH than in BH: לֹא יַעֲשֶׂה אָדָם אֶת סְלָעָיו דִּינְרֵי זָהָב one shall not make (change) his silver *sela'im* into gold *dinars*, MŠ. ii. 7; לֹא יְמַלֵּא אָדָם קְעָרָה שֶׁמֶן one shall not fill a dish with oil, Šab. ii. 4; מוֹצִיא אֶת הָרַבִּים יְדֵי חוֹבָתָן causing the public to discharge their duty, RH iv. 9; אוֹפִין אֶת פִּתָּן גְּרִיצוֹת baking their bread into thick loaves, Be. ii. 6; 'Ed. iii. 11.

More frequently the remoter object takes a preposition: הִלְבִּישׁוֹ בְּאוּנְקְלִי וַחֲגָרוֹ בְּצִילְצוּל he clothed him with a (woman's) tunic, and girded him with a (woman's) girdle, Mᵉn. 109 b. In the passive the verb is followed by the accusative of the remoter object: לָבוּשׁ לְבָנִים וְעָטוּף לְבָנִים clothed in white garments and wrapped in white garments, Yo. 39 b; Mᵉn. ib.; טָעוּן פִּשְׁתִּים laden with flax, BM. vi. 8; . . . טְעוּנָה הַפְשֵׁט requiring flaying, &c., Zᵉb. v. 4.

355. The accusative, but without the *nota accusativi*,[1] is also used to define the action of the verb in reference to time, especially to express duration of time: נֶאֶסְרָה עָלָיו שָׁעָה אַחַת she was prohibited to him for one hour, Yᵉb. iii. 7; אוֹר לְאַרְבָּעָה עָשָׂר בּוֹדְקִין on the eve of the fourteenth one must search, Pᵉs. i. 1; אוֹכְלִין כָּל אַרְבַּע וְתוֹלִים כָּל חָמֵשׁ וְשׂוֹרְפִין בִּתְחִלַּת שֵׁשׁ one may eat all the four (hours), and suspend all the fifth (hour), and burn at the beginning of the sixth (hour), ib. 4; עַרְבֵי פְסָחִים . . . לֹא יֹאכַל אָדָם on the eve of Passover one must not eat, ib. x. 1; נָדְרָה לֵילֵי שַׁבָּת she vowed on the night of the Sabbath, Šab. 157 a (but Nᵉd. x. 8: נ׳ בְּלֵילֵי שַׁבָּת). More often, the noun is introduced by a preposition, especially when it is intended to express a point of time, and not duration: בְּכָל יוֹם אָדָם מִתְפַּלֵּל every day a man prays, Bᵉr iv. 3; וְלַמַּשְׁכִּים הָיָה הַמְמוּנֶּה אוֹמֵר early in the morning the director would

[1] This accusative of time is found also with אֶת in the liturgical passage: הַחֲלִיצֵנוּ . . . אֶת יוֹם רֹאשׁ הַחֹדֶשׁ הַזֶּה fortify us on this day of the New Moon, 'Er. iii. 9.

say, Bik. iii. 2; לְשָׁנָה הָאַחֶרֶת הָלַךְ וְלָן the following year he went and spent the night, Ber. 18 b; cf. § 361 (viii).

356. The accusative also defines a verb as to the place: מָקוֹם שֶׁנָּהֲגוּ לַעֲשׂוֹת in the place where they have been accustomed to do, Pes. iv. 1; מָקוֹם שֶׁהוּא מַתְחִיל the place where he begins, Yo. v. 5; but more frequently with a preposition: נִכְנַס לְמָקוֹם שֶׁנִּכְנַס וְעָמַד בְּמָקוֹם שֶׁעָמַד he entered to the place where he has to enter, and stood in the place where he has to stand, ib. 3.

357. The accus. is often used to describe the mode or manner of a verb: הָעוֹשֶׂה עִיסָּתוֹ קַבִּים if one makes his dough by single *qabs*, Hal. ii. 4; מַכְנִיסָן זוּג זוּג he brings them in pair by pair; מְצָאָן צְבָתִים he found them in small bundles, 'Er. x. 1; קְרָאָהּ סֵירוּגִין he read it in alternate verses, Meg. ii. 2; לְעוֹלָם יִשְׁנֶה אָדָם לְתַלְמִידוֹ דֶּרֶךְ קְצָרָה one should always teach a disciple in a brief manner, Pes. 3 b; נָטוּעַ עִרְבּוּבְיָה planted in confusion, Kil. v. 1; especially with participles and adjectives: וְקוֹרֵא עוֹמֵד Yo. vii. 1; וְקוֹרֵא יוֹשֵׁב So. vii. 8; he reads standing, sitting; וְקוֹצָה חַלָּתָהּ עֲרוּמָה and she cuts her *ḥallah* naked, Ḥal. ii. 3; הַבָּא אֶל הַמִּקְדָּשׁ טָמֵא if one comes into the Temple when unclean, Mak. iii. 2; שְׁמָרָהּ עוֹמֶדֶת he watched her as she was standing, BQ viii. 6. Often, however, the partic. takes the prepos. בּ (בּ *essentiae*, § 360 (ii)): אוֹרְגִין בֵּין בְּעוֹמְדִין בֵּין בְּיוֹשְׁבִין they may weave whether standing or sitting, Zab. iii. 2; נִכְנַס ר״ט בְּלֹא מִתְכַּוֵּן R. Tarphon entered without intention, 'Er. iv. 4; or it is put in a relative clause with כְּ: אוֹכְלִין אוֹתוֹ כְּשֶׁהוּא חַי they eat it raw, Men. xi. 7; Qid. ii. 1 (כְּשֶׁהִיא נַעֲרָה, cf. Sirach xxx. 12 a: כְּשֶׁהוּא קָטָן); or, finally, it is put in a circumstantial clause: וְהֵם מְגוּלִּין when they are uncovered, Ma'a. v. 2; cf. below, § 479.

To this usage belongs also the adverbial use of nouns, such as כָּל עִיקָּר, סְתָם, תֵּכֶף, מָחָר, אֶמֶשׁ, or with prepositions: לְמָחָר, לְמַפְרֵעַ, בַּעֲלִיל, כַּתְּחִלָּה, בַּתְּחִלָּה, בְּיִיחוּד, מֵעוֹלָם, &c. Cf. § 299.

(2) *Subordination of the Noun to the Verb by means of Prepositions.*

358. As in BH, nouns can be governed by a verb also indirectly, by means of a preposition. Such nouns serve to define the verbal action in its various relations to time, place, manner, &c., but they may also represent the object of the verbal action in the same way as an accusative. The prepositions chiefly used for this purpose are: אֵצֶל, בְּ־, לְ־, מִ־, and עַל. These prepositions have preserved in MH the general characteristics of the meaning and usage which they have in BH. In the following sections some special constructions will be noted. (Cf. Ges.-K., § 119.)

359. אֵצֶל. This prepos. usually takes in MH the place of אֶל is BH (cf. § 301): מִי שֶׁשְּׁלָחֲךָ אֶצְלִי he who sent me to thee, Dam. iv. 6; גּוֹלְלוֹ אֶצְלוֹ he rolls it up towards himself, ʿEr. x. 2; נִכְנְסוּ אֶצְלוֹ חַכְמֵי יִשְׂרָאֵל the sages of Israel came in unto him, Ber. 3 b. Also in the old BH sense: מִתְאָרֵחַ אֵצֶל עַם הָאָרֶץ stays as a guest with an *ʿam ha-areṣ*, Dam. ii. 2.

360. בְּ־. (i) To introduce the object of a transitive verb:[1] שְׁנַיִם אוֹחֲזִין בְּטַלִּית two hold a cloak, BM i. 1; הֶחֱזִיק בָּהּ he took hold of it; זָכָה בָהּ he acquires it, ib. 2; הַחוֹבֵל בַּחֲבֵרוֹ if one injures his neighbour, BQ viii. 1; צָרַם בְּאָזְנוֹ he cut (or pulled) his ear; תָּלַשׁ בִּשְׂעָרוֹ he plucked his hair, ib. 8; הִתְרֵיתֶם בּוֹ have you warned him? San. v. 1; לָבַשׁ בְּחָלוּק he put on a shirt, Meʿil. v. 1. With a partitive sense: לַעֲשׂוֹת בְּצֶמֶר to work at wool, Ket. v. 6: אוֹכֵל בְּקָדָשִׁים eats of holy things, Naz. viii. 6; שׁוֹתֶה בְיַיִן drinks of wine, ib. iv. 3; מַרְבֶּה בִבְדִיקוֹת increases examinations, San. v. 2.

(ii) To describe the character of the subject or object in

[1] This use of a preposition to introduce a direct object is exactly parallel to the use of אֵת for the same purpose. In both cases, the preposition or the particle את is dependent on the verb as its accusative, and the noun is dependent on the preposition, or את, as its genitive.

relation to the verb, ב *essentiae*: נָדְרָה בְּנָזִיר she vowed as a Nazirite, Ned. iv. 3; נִכְנַס . . . בְּלֹא מִתְכַּוֵּן he entered without intention, 'Er. iv. 4; מַקְרִיב חֵלֶק בְּרֹאשׁ offers a portion as a chief; נוֹטֵל חֵלֶק בְּרֹאשׁ takes a portion as a chief—offers, takes the first portion, Yo. i. 2.

(iii) Expressing the instrument or means of an action: מַעֲגִיל בְּמַעֲגִילָה rolling with a roller; עוֹלֶה בְסוּלָּם ; יוֹרֵד בְּסוּלָּם going up, going down a ladder, Mak. ii. 1; בַּמֶּה מַדְלִיקִין wherewith may one kindle a light? Šab. ii. 1; or the price: לְשַׁלֵּם . . . בְּמֵיטַב הָאָרֶץ to pay with the best of his land, BQ i. 1; בְּכַמָּה חֵפֶץ זֶה for how much is this article, BM iv. 10; מַצִּילִין אוֹתָן בְּנַפְשָׁם one may deliver them at the cost of their lives, San. viii. 7; or the measure: הַטֶּבֶל אוֹסֵר . . . בְּנוֹתֵן טַעַם *Tebel* renders a food prohibited when it is sufficient to add a flavour, Ḥal. iii. 10; אוֹסֵר בְּכָל שֶׁהוּא prohibits by any quantity, 'AZ v. 8; נְקוּבָה בְכוֹנֵס מַשְׁקֶה bored with a hole large enough to take in liquid, Oh. v. 2; Kel. x. 8; cf. ib. iii. 1, 2. For BH cf. *BDB*, p. 90 b, iii. 8.

(iv). To define and limit the verb, in the sense of 'in respect to', 'in the case of': מוּתָּר בְּצָלוּי וּבְשָׁלוּק permitted as regards roast or seethed food: אָסוּר בְּמַעֲשֵׂה קְדֵרָה prohibited as regards food prepared in a pot, Ned. vi. 1; מוּתָּרִין בַּאֲכִילָה permitted to eat, Kil. viii. 1; לָמָּה לֹא אֲסָרוּהָ בְהֲנָאָה why did they not prohibit it as regards (indirect) profit? 'AZ ii. 5.

(v) Finally, in a local sense after a verb of motion: שׁוֹלְחִין בְּכָל הַמְּקוֹמוֹת they send to all places, San. xi. 4; הָיִיתִי בָא בַדֶּרֶךְ I was coming by the way, Ber. i. 3; הַמְהַלֵּךְ בַּדֶּרֶךְ if one walks by the way, Ab. iii. 4; הִילֵּךְ בָּהֶן he walked on them, Ḥul. ix. 2; נְתַתּוֹ בְּאַנְפּוּלֵי[1] thou hast put it into a bag, Šebu. vii. 6.

361. ל. (i) To introduce a direct object, like את; cf. above, § 351.

[1] Or אַמְפּוּלֵי *mappula*; cf. Kohut. i. 124 a.

(ii) To introduce an indirect object, the ל of the dative: נְתָנוּ לוֹ they gave him, 'Er. vi. 3.

(iii) The *dativus ethicus*: בָּא לוֹ he came, Yo. iii. 8; נָפַל לוֹ עָלֶיהָ he fell on it, Pe. iv. 2; הוֹלֵךְ לוֹ אֵצֶל יוֹחָנָן he goes to Johanan, Š^e^q. v. 4.

(iv) To introduce the genitive: belonging to, cf. below, § 384.

(v) To introduce the agent after a passive or reflexive verb: וְנֶאֱכָלִין . . . לְכָל אָדָם they are eaten by all men, Z^e^b. v. 6; מִי שֶׁנִּשְׁאַל לְחָכָם if one consults a sage, MQ iii. 2; הַמִּשְׁתַּתֵּף לוֹ he who joins him in partnership, B^e^k. ii. 1 (cf. Ges.-K., § 121 f). So also after an active verb: בּוֹדְקִין . . . לְאוֹר הַנֵּר one searches by the light of a candle, P^e^s. i. 1; שֶׁאֵינִי טוֹעֵם לָךְ, שֶׁאֵינִי אוֹכֵל לָךְ that I will not eat, taste, of thine, N^e^d. i. 1.

(vi) 'In respect to': מְבָרֵךְ לְעַצְמוֹ pronounces a benediction for himself, B^e^r. vi. 6; מוּעָד לְמִינוֹ forewarned in respect to his own kind, BQ iv. 2; פָּתוּחַ לִרְוָחָה open wide, Ab. i. 5; הַמַּשְׂכִּיר בַּיִת לְשָׁנָה . . . לֶחֳדָשִׁים if one lets a house for a year, for months, BM viii. 8.

(vii) In a local sense, after verbs of motion: 'into'—BH אֶל: הַכּוֹנֵס צֹאן לַדִּיר if one gathers sheep into a shed, BQ vi. 1; יוֹרְדִין לְשָׁם they go down there, Suk. iv. 5; cf. § 295; הוֹלַכְתָּם לְתוֹךְ בֵּיתֶךָ thou hast carried them to thine house, Š^e^bu. vii. 6; in a figurative sense: אֵין מַעֲלִין לִכְהוּנָּה one does not raise to the priesthood, K^e^t. ii. 8.

(viii) Of time: לְיָמִים הַרְבֵּה after many days, 'Ed. i. 1; לַמַּשְׁכִּים Bik. iii. 2; לְכַתְּחִילָּה at the beginning, Šab. 65 a; לְשַׁחֲרִית מְצָאוֹ ר״ג in the morning R. Gamaliel found him, P^e^s. 72 b; cf. §§ 296, 297, 301.

362. מִן. (i) Of place: עָבַר מִכְּנֶגֶד פָּנָיו he passed from before him, Naz. ix. 1; מֵחֶצְיוֹ וְלַחוּץ ; מֵחֶצְיוֹ וְלִפְנִים from the half of it and towards outside, inside, BM ii. 3; מִן הָאַרְכּוּבָה וּלְמַטָּה from the knee down, Y^e^b. xii. 1; cf. § 301.

(ii) Of time: מוּכָן מִבְּעוֹד יוֹם prepared from day-time, Be. i. 2; מִכָּאן וְעַד ג׳ שָׁנִים from now till three years, BM v. 3.

(iii) Partitive: שָׁמַע מִן הַנָּשִׁים אוֹמְרוֹת; שָׁמַע מִן הַתִּינוֹקוֹת אוֹמְרִים he heard some of the women, some of the children, say, Yeb. xvi. 5; מִיַּקִּירֵי יְרוּשָׁלַיִם of the notables of Jerusalem, Yo. vi. 6; גָּנַב מִשֶּׁל אָבִיו he stole of his father's, San. viii. 3; רָאִיתָ מִיָּמֶיךָ hast thou seen on any of thy days—ever? Qid. iv. 14; so מִיָּמָיו Suk. v. 1; מִיָּמֶיהָ (L); מִימֵיהֶם Pes. v. 7; i. 6 (cf. Ges.-K., § 119 w, foot-note 1); לְסַפֵּק סְלָתוֹת מֵאַרְבַּע עָמְדוּ מִשָּׁלֹש to supply flours at four (*seahs* per *sela'*) they stood at three (*seahs* per *sela'*), Šeq. iv. 9; so Kel. xvii. 11; Pa. i. 1, &c.

(iv) In a privative sense: 'away from'—not to, after verbs of preventing, restraining, &c.; לֹא הָיוּ מוֹנְעִין מִמֶּנּוּ they did not withhold from him, Yo. i. 4; cf. § 346.

(v) Introducing the source, cause, instrument of an action: לֹא מִפִּיהָ אָנוּ חַיִּין we do not live from her mouth—depend on her words, Ket. i. 6; נֵיאוֹתִין מִמֶּנּוּ make use of it, Šab. iii. 6; . . . שׂוֹרְפִין מֵעֲצֵי עַצְמָן they burn with their own wood, Pes. vii. 8; נָפַל לְפָנָיו מִקּוֹל הַכְּרִיָּיה he fell forward because of the noise of the digging, BQ v. 8. So with אֶל in a reflexive sense: מְנַגֵּן מֵאֵלָיו plays by itself, Ber. 3 b; cf. above, § 301, and below, § 432.

363. עַל. (i) To introduce the object: הִשְׁבִּיעַ עָלָיו he adjured him (parallel to מַשְׁבִּיעֲךָ), Šebu. v. 2; iv. 3; מַצִּיל עַל הַכֹּל protects everything, 'Ed. i. 14; כָּבַשׁ עָלָיו לְתוֹךְ הַמַּיִם he pressed him into the water, San. ix. 1; לְלַמֵּד עַל מַעֲשֵׂה הַקְּטֹרֶת to teach the work of making the incense, Yo. iii. 11.[1]

(ii) After verbs of going, standing, &c.: מְהַלְּכִין עַל כָּל הָאַחִין they go over all the brothers, Yeb. iv. 5; הָלְכָה לָהּ עַל לִבּוֹ it went

[1] Further examples of this unusual construction are: לְהַעֲבִיר עַל הַכֶּתֶם to remove a stain, Šab. ix. 5 (L and j.; edd. אֶת הכ׳); אֵין מְשַׁנִּין עַל הַמִּנְהָג one should not change the custom, j. BM vi. 4. So, perhaps, in BH: חוֹלֵשׁ עַל גּוֹיִם Isa. xiv. 12; cf. Exod. xvii. 13.

to his heart, San. ix. 2; יְחַזְּרוּ עַל הַפְּתָחִים (L יִשָּׁאֲלוּ), let them go about (beg) at the doors, Kᵉt. xiii. 3; עוֹמֵד עַל דְּבָרָיו stand on his words, refuse to change one's opinion, ʽEd. i. 4;[1] יָדוֹ עַל הָעֶלְיוֹנָה (L לְעֶלְ׳) to have an advantage, Šᵒq. iv. 9; עַל הַתַּחְתּוֹנָה (L לְתַחְ׳) to have a disadvantage, BM vi. 2; ג׳ עַל ג׳ עַל רוּם ג׳ three (cubits) by three by three high, Šᵉbi. iii. 5; אֶחָד יוֹשֵׁב עַל פֶּתַח one sits at the door . . ., San. xi. 2.

(iii) In the sense of 'in addition to': נוֹשְׂאִין עַל הָאֲנוּסָה וְעַל הַמְּפוּתָּה one may marry in addition to the woman that has been forced or seduced, Yᵉb. xi. 1; מוֹסִיף עָלָיו it adds unto it, Kᵉt. iii. 5; יְתֵרוֹת עַל הָרִאשׁוֹנוֹת exceed the first, Taʽa. i. 6; and so often to express the comparative degree of adjectives, § 391. So עַל יַד: יִקָּבֵר עַל יַד עוֹרוֹ let it be buried together with its skin, MŠ. i. 6; iii. 11; מְמַעֶטֶת עַל יַד . . . reduces by the side of . . ., Nid. i. 1; cf. *BDB*, p. 755, 4.

(iv) 'In respect to', 'concerning': אָמְרוּ לָהּ עַל בִּתָּהּ they told her about her daughter, Naz. vi. 11; הַשּׁוֹמֵעַ עַל מֵתוֹ if one hears concerning his dead, Pᵉs. 92 b; נִמְלָךְ עֲלֵיהֶן he changed his mind concerning them, BM. i. 7; שָׁחַט עָלֶיהָ he slew on her behalf, Pᵉs. viii. 1; cf. *BDB*, p. 754 b (g).

(v) To express the agent or cause: שֶׁלֹּא יִמָּחֶה עַל הַמָּיִם that it might not be blotted out by the water, So. i. 4; הַבָּנוֹת נִיזּוֹנוֹת עַל הַבָּנִים the daughters are maintained by the sons, BB. viii. 8; לֹא יִשְׁחוֹט עָלָיו he shall not slay (it) through it, Bᵉk. v. 2 ff.; נוֹטֵל נַפְשׁוֹ עָלֶיהָ his life is taken because of it, Mak. iii. 15; so: קְרָאָהּ עַל פֶּה he read it by mouth—by heart, Mᵉg. ii. 2; הַמְחַלֵּק נְכָסָיו עַל פִּיו if one divides his property by word of mouth, BB ix. 7.

(3) *Co-ordination of a Verb to another Verb as Auxiliary*

364. Certain verbs are used in an auxiliary character to give an adverbial definition to another verb with which they are

[1] Contrast עוֹמֵד בְּדִיבּוּרוֹ keeping his word, BM 47 b.

co-ordinated. Some of these, as in BH (Ges.-K., § 120 d), stand before the principal verb which they serve to define. Others stand after the principal verb.

(i) Before the principal verb.

דחק to press: דָּחַק וְנִכְנַס he entered by force, Ber. 31 b; Naz. 49 b; וַאֲנִי דָחַקְתִּי וְנִכְנַסְתִּי and I entered by pressing, San. 70 b.

חזר to return: חוֹזֵר וּמְחַלְּלָם he changes them again, MŠ ii. 6; חָזַר וְהוֹסִיף he added again; יַחֲזוֹר וְיִתְרוֹם let him tithe again, Ter. iv. 3. But also with inf.: חָזְרוּ לוֹמַר they said again, Giṭ. vi. 5, &c.

מִהֵר to hasten: מַהֲרוּ וְהוֹצִיאוּ bring forth quickly; מַהֲרוּ וַעֲשׂוּ do quickly, 'Er. vi. 1.

הִשְׁכִּים to rise early: מַשְׁכִּימִים וּבָאִין they come early in the morning, Suk. iii. 13; מַשְׁכִּים וְטוֹבֵל he immerses himself early, Tam. i. 2; הִשְׁכִּים וּמָצָא he found early, Ḥul. ii. 6; הַשְׁכֵּם וְצֵא הַעֲרֵב וְצֵא go forth early in the morning, go forth late in the evening, Ber. 62 a.

שנה to repeat: שׁוֹנִין וְאוֹמְרִין they say a second time (L שׁוֹנִין לוֹמַר), Suk. v. 4; שָׁנָה וְלִימֵּד he taught a second time, San. xi. 2.

שקד to be diligent; כָּל אוּמּוֹת שׁוֹקְדוֹת וּבָאוֹת all nations come diligently, Ber. 58 a.

365. (ii) After the principal verb.

בא to come: לֹא יְהֵא זוֹרֵעַ וּבָא he shall not sow on, Kil. ii. 5; אֲנִי מְרַקֵּד וּבָא I come on dancing, Ber. 51 a; הָיָה מוֹדֵד וּבָא he was measuring on, 'Er. 42 b; נִיזּוֹנוֹת וּבָאוֹת נִיזּוֹנִין וּבָאִין they are continued to be maintained, t. BB viii. 18, 19.

הלך to go: מוֹסִיף עָלָיו וְהוֹלֵךְ he goes on adding to it, Šebi. iii. 3; מִתְנַוְּנָה וְהוֹלֶכֶת she goes on decaying more and more, So. iii. 5; מְסַפֵּר וְהוֹלֵךְ he goes on relating, Ber. 13 a; הָיְתָה דוֹלֶקֶת וְהוֹלֶכֶת כָּל הַיּוֹם כּוּלּוֹ it was burning continually for the whole day, Šab. 23 a; מִתְמַעֲטִין וְהוֹלְכִין they may go on becoming fewer and fewer, Pes. 99 a; אוֹכֵל וְהוֹלֵךְ he may go on eating, ib. 99 b; 105 a.

ירד to go down: הִתְחִיל מְחַטֵּא וְיוֹרֵד he began to purify downwards, Yo. v. 5; מִתְגַּלְגֵּל וְיוֹרֵד it rolls downwards, ib. vi. 6; הָיָה חוֹתֵךְ וְיוֹרֵד he would cut downwards, Tam. iv. 3.

עלה to go up: הָיוּ הַמַּיִם צָפִין וְעוֹלִין לִקְרָאתוֹ the waters were floating upwards towards him, Ab. deRN. xx; הָיָה מִתַּמֵּר וְעוֹלֶה (the smoke) was going straight upwards (palm-like), ib. xxxv. 7; טוּמְאָה בוֹקַעַת וְעוֹלָה בּוֹקַעַת וְיוֹרֶדֶת the impurity breaks through upwards, downwards, Oh. vi. 6; מְטַפֵּס וְעוֹלֶה מְטַפֵּס וְיוֹרֵד climbing upwards, downwards, 'Er. 21 a; מַשְׁפִּיעַ וְעוֹלֶה מַשְׁפִּיעַ וְיוֹרֵד sloping upwards, downwards, ib. 43 b.

יצא to go forth: הָיָה מוֹשְׁכוֹ וְיוֹצֵא he was pulling it out, BQ vii. 6; מְבַצְבֵּץ וְיוֹצֵא bursting outwards, Pes. 13 a; מְפַכְפְּכִין וְיוֹצְאִין trickling forth, t. Šeq. iii. 2; גְּרָרוּם וְהוֹצִיאוּם they dragged them forth, ib. 1.

ישב to sit: הָיָה הִלֵּל כָּפוּף וְיוֹשֵׁב Hillel was sitting bowed, Šab. 17 a.

עמד to stand: מוּשְׁבָּע וְעוֹמֵד מֵהַר סִינַי he is under oath from Sinai, Ned. 8 a.

II. THE NOUN

1. Determination of the Gender.[1]

366. In the determination of the gender, MH follows the principles of BH. Thus, in the case of animate beings the gender agrees with the sex, whether the two sexes are distinguished by independent words, as אָב, אֵם; עֶבֶד, שִׁפְחָה; חָתָן, כַּלָּה; or the fem. is formed from the masc. as גְּדִיָּה, חֲמוֹרָה[2] (cf. § 277); טָלָה (L; edd. טְלָיָה) Men. xiii. 6; or one word serves for the two sexes, as נְמָלָה, יוֹנָה, אַרְנֶבֶת, צִפּוֹר, גָּמָל, בָּקָר.

MH shows some new fem. formations from the masc., especially in late texts. Thus, beside טָלָה, חֲמוֹרָה we find וְאֵבָה Est. R. i. 9; חֲזִירָה ib. iii. 1; חֲתוּלָה cat, j. Pea 17 d; כַּלְבָּה dog, j. San. 26 b;

[1] Cf. Ges.-K., § 122, and H. Rosenberg, *Das Geschlecht d. Hauptwörter in d. Mischna* (Berlin, 1908), especially pp. 73 ff.

[2] חֲמוֹר is also found as fem.: הָלְכָה חֲמוֹרְךָ thy ass is gone, Bek. iv. 4. אָתוֹן is not used in MH.

רְחֵלָה ewe, Ḥul. xi. 2; also בַּחוּרָה young woman; בַּחוּרוֹת Gen. R. 71; Num. R. 10; תְּאוֹמָה twin sister, BB 123 a; Gen. R. 22.

367. So also in the case of inanimate objects, MH follows generally the rules of BH. The following are construed as fem.

(i) Limbs or parts of the body, especially those in pairs: אֹזֶן, אֶצְבַּע, דּוֹפֶן side (and wall); חֹפֶן hollow of the hand; יָד, כַּף palm; יָרֵךְ, כָּבֵד, כָּנָף, כֶּרֶס (or כָּרֵס) belly; כֶּרַע knee; פָּנִים Ab. i. 13; צֵלָע rib; צִפּוֹרֶן nail (of finger or toe); קֶרֶן, רֶגֶל, שׁוֹק, שֵׁן. (For reff. cf. the Lexicons).

The following are of common gender: לָשׁוֹן, זָנָב; לְחִי and זָקָן are masc.

(ii) Names of tools, utensils, &c.: אֶבֶן, חֵמֶת, חֶרֶב, יָתֵד, כַּד, מַחַט needle; מַקֵּל, סַיִיף sword; סַכִּין, קֶלַע, רֵיחַיִם Be. ii. 9 (construed as sing. like the Aram. רֵיחְיָא).

(iii) Names of countries, towns, &c.: אֶרֶץ, יְרוּשָׁלַיִם, עִיר, שָׂדֶה BM i. 4.

(iv) Names denoting a circumscribed space: בְּאֵר, חָצֵר, יָצִיעַ, מֶרְחָץ bath, Šebi. viii. 11; קֵן. But גַּן, גּוֹרֶן, and דֶּרֶךְ are common.

Fem. are also: דְּיוֹ ink, Ab. iv. 25; סוּבִּין bran, Ter. xi. 5; פִּשְׁתָּן flax, BQ vi. 6; תִּלְתָּן fenugreek, MŠ ii. 3.

The following are common: אוּר fire; חַלּוֹן, כִּכָּר, Ya. ii. 4; מָעוֹת money, small change, MŠ iii. 5; iv. 9.

Fem. are names of abstract ideas: גְּדוּלָּה greatness; שְׂרָרָה dominion; מַחְלוֹקֶת controversy; רַבָּנוּת authority; also verbal nouns: אֲכִילָה eating; בַּטָּלָה idling; הַבְדָּלָה separating, &c.; cf. §§ 217, 272.

Further, certain collectives: בַּלֶּשֶׁת, נַמֶּלֶת, חַמֶּרֶת (§ 237); and most diminutives, § 276.

368. Some nouns change their gender when used in a derived sense: כַּף palm of hand, fem. Ab. ii. 8; כַּף spoon, masc. Tam. v. 4; סֶלַע rock, masc. BB vii. 1; סֶלַע *sela'* (weight, or coin), fem. MŠ ii. 10; רֶגֶל foot, fem. Oh. x. 2; רֶגֶל festival, masc. Pes. viii. 1.

369. The following fem. nouns which form the plur. in ם—ִ are construed in the plur. as masc: דְּלַעַת pumpkin, דְּלוּעִין Kil. iii. 7; Šebi. i. 7; כַּרְשִׁינָה leek, כַּרְשִׁינִין MŠ ii. 4; קִישּׁוּת cucumber, קִישּׁוּאִים Ter. iii. 1; Ber. 57 b; קַשְׂקֶשֶׂת scale (of fish), קַשְׂקַשִּׂין Ḥul. iii. 7; cf. § 289.

370. Certain nouns ending in ת— are fem., even when the ת is treated as a radical letter: אוֹת sign, letter of the alphabet, MQ iii. 4; Kil. ix. 10; אֶמֶת So. ix. 15; גַּת Ma'a. i. 7; זֶפֶת Kel. x. 5; עֵת Tam. i. 2; דָּת law, Ket. vii. 6; חֲבִתִּים wafers, Men. xi. 3; פַּת Ber. vi. 7; צְבַת tongs, Ab. v. 6; שַׁבָּת Dam. iv. 2; cf. also Nöldeke, *Syr. Gr.*, § 86.

371. A number of nouns are found both in the masc. and in the fem. form but with a difference in meaning: גַּן garden; גִּנָּה (or גִּינָּה) vegetable garden, Kil. ii. 2; דִּיר shed for animals, BQ vi. 1; דִּירָה dwelling for human beings, Ber. 77 b; חוֹב debt, BM i. 7; חוֹבָה duty, Pes. x. 4; חוֹל sand, Šab. viii. 5; חוֹלָה sand-dune, 'Ar. iii. 2; Sab. 31 a; חֶרֶב sword, So. viii. 5; חַרְבָּה knife, Šebi. viii. 6; צֵל shadow, Pes. 114 a; צִלָּה shade, protection from the sun, Suk. i. 1; קוֹר cold, BM 106 b; קוֹרָה cooling, satisfaction, Ab. iv. 17.

372. Gender of Greek and Latin nouns.

(i) Nouns ending in ס- (*-os*, *-us*) are construed as masc.: פָּנָס φανός, Kel. ii. 4; פּוֹלְמוֹס πόλεμος, So. ix. 14; פִּנְקָס πίναξ, Ab. iii. 16; סוּלְיָם *soleas*, Kel. xxvi. 4.

(ii) Nouns ending in ה—ָ, א—ָ, י— (*-α*, *-ια*, *-εια*, *-η*, *-a*) are fem.: טַבְלָה *tabula*, Yo. iii. 10; קַצְרָה *castra*, 'Ar. ix. 6; קְלוֹסְטְרָא κλεῖστρα (pl.), Kel. xi. 14; דְּיָיטִי δίαιτα, Šab. xi. 2.

(iii) Nouns ending in וֹן—, ן—ָ (*-ον*), are masc.: סִיקָרִיקוֹן σικαρικόν, Giṭ. v. 6; קְלָבוֹן κόλλυβος Šeq i. 6, but קִיטוֹן κοιτών is construed as fem., Mid. i. 6.[1]

(iv) Nouns ending in ין— are fem.: אִפּוּפוֹדִין ὑποπόδιον, Kel.

[1] This is not due to the plur. ending (קִיטוֹנוֹת פְּתוּחוֹת); cf. קִיטוֹן אַחַת, Exod. R. 33.

xxiv. 7; סַנְהֶדְרִין συνέδριον, San. i. 6; סוּדָרִין σουδάριον, ib. vii. 2 (L); but בִּיבָרִין (*vivarium*) is masc., Šab. xiii. 2; cf. further, Krauss, *Lehnwörter*, i, §§ 287–305.

2. The Use of the Article.

373. As in BH, so in MH nouns are either determinate by their nature, such as proper nouns and pronouns, or are rendered determinate by their grammatical connexion, viz. when followed by a determinate noun as genitive, or by a pronominal suffix, or when preceded by the article.

Only in the latter case does MH exhibit certain peculiarities which demand special treatment.

The MH article is identical with the BH article, both in form and in the general characteristics of its usage.

374 (i) The article is used whenever the noun is definite.

Thus with nouns which are definite by themselves: הַחַמָּה the sun; הָעוֹלָם the world; הַשַּׁחַר the dawn; הַשַּׁבָּת the Sabbath. With nouns that have been mentioned before: כּוּכִין, הַכּוּכִין, cf. above, § 351.

With nouns that are known or necessary in connexion with the subject treated: נוֹשְׂאֵי הַמִּטָּה the bearers of the bier, in connexion with a dead body, Ber. iii. 1; הַיּוֹם; הַיַּיִן, &c., in connexion with *Qiddus*, Ber. viii. 1 ff. So also with nouns that are definite in the mind of the speaker: הַצּוֹאָה dirt, Ber. iii. 5; הַחֲמוֹר ib. iv. 5; הַפֵּירוֹת ib. vi. 1, &c. This last usage is even more common in MH than in BH.[1]

(ii) The article is used with titles: הַמְּמוּנֶּה the overseer, Yo. ii. 1; הַסְּגָן the deputy High Priest, ib. vii. 1; אַגְרִיפּוּס הַמֶּלֶךְ King Agrippa, Bik. iii. 4 (but always כֹּהֵן גָּדוֹל the High Priest, even when definite, Yo. i. 1; cf. § 378).

[1] Cf. Ges.-K., § 126 q–t; Driver, *Notes on Samuel*, i. 4; xix. 13.

(iii) With the vocative: הַמָּעוֹן הַזֶּה; הָעֲבוֹדָה; הַמֶּלֶךְ O King! Sifre Deut. iii. 23; cf. § 305.

(iv) With names of material: הַצֶּמֶר wool, Šab. i. 6; הָעֵץ wood, ib. ii. 3; הַכֶּסֶף, הַזָּהָב silver, gold, BM iv. 1.

(v) With collectives: הַלּוּף וְהַשּׁוּם *lof* and garlic, &c., Ter. ix. 6; Kil. i. 1 f.

(vi) With abstracts: הַנּוֹי וְהַכֹּחַ וְהָעוֹשֶׁר וְהַכָּבוֹד beauty, strength, riches, glory, &c., Ab. vi. 8; BM iv. 3.

(vii) The article is used with participles in a somewhat demonstrative sense: he who . . ., she who . . ., &c., especially in conditional sentences: הַקּוֹרֵא אֶת שְׁמַע he who reads the *Šema'*, Ber. ii. 3; הַמִּתְפַּלֵּל וְטָעָה he who prays and commits an error, ib. v. 5; הַמּוֹצֵא תְּפִלִּין he who finds *tephillin*, 'Er. x. 1; cf. § 331.

So sometimes in BH: הַנּוֹגֵעַ Gen. xxvi. 11; הַמַּקְרִיב Lev. vii. 33; xiv. 46–7; xv. 6–10; xvi. 28. Contrast: . . . מַכֵּה Exod. xxi. 12; Prov. xv. 32; Qoh. x. 8, &c.

(viii) The article is prefixed to adjectives or participles when used substantivally, i. e. when the nouns to which they refer are omitted. In such cases the article serves to emphasize the substantival character of the adjective. When two such adjectives are contrasted, the article has a demonstrative force: that which. Exx.: טוֹל אַתָּה אֶת הַלַּח וַאֲנִי אֶת הַיָּבֵשׁ take thou the wet, and I (take) the dry, sc. חִטִּים mentioned before, or תְּבוּאָה Dam. vi. 9; . . . וְלֹא מִן הַתָּלוּשׁ עַל הַמְּחוּבָּר וְלֹא מִן הֶחָדָשׁ עַל הַיָּשָׁן nor from that which is loose upon that which is joined (to the soil) . . . nor from the new upon the old . . ., Ter. i. 5, 7; ii. 6; iv. 8; הַשּׁוֹחֵט הַמְסוּכֶּנֶת if one slays a beast afflicted with a fatal illness, Ḥul. ii. 6; iv. 2, &c.

375. The attribute of a determinate noun regularly takes the article in MH as in BH: הַיָּם הַגָּדוֹל the great sea, Ber. ix. 2; הַמָּעוֹת הָאֵלּוּ . . . הָהֵם these, those moneys, MŠ iii. 3, 4; בְּנוֹ וּבִתּוֹ הַגְּדוֹלִים his grown-up son and daughter, ib. iv. 4; כָּל הַכֵּלִים הַנִּיטָּלִים

all the vessels that may be handled, Šab. xvii. 5; שְׁבִיל הַיָּחִיד הַקָּבוּעַ a permanent private path, Pea ii. 1.

Where the noun has a preposition prefixed, the preposition may be pointed with *pataḥ* with the article elided: כַּמַּעְיָן הַנּוֹבֵעַ like the bubbling spring, BB x. 8; לַדָּבָר הָאָסוּר for a thing that is forbidden, Pe. vi. 5; בָּעוֹף הַדַּק in a small bird; בָּעוֹף הַגַּס in a big bird, Ḥul. iii. 1.

There are, however, important and numerous exceptions to this rule.

376. (*a*) The attribute (an adjective, or a participle) is found with the article, while the noun is without the article.

(i) When one attribute of a substantive is to be distinguished from another attribute of the same substantive. The article is then equivalent to a qualifying relative clause.[1]

נֶגֶר הַנִּגְרָר a bolt which is dragged to the ground by a string tied to the door, opposed to the following: וְהַמּוּנָּח one which lies loose, 'Er. x. 11; פֵּירוֹת הַתְּלוּשִׁין fruits which have been plucked, opposed to הַמְּחוּבָּרִין those which are fixed to the ground, Ket. viii. 3. נְכָסִים הַמְּיוּחָדִין property which is the possession of a special owner, opposed to נִכְסֵי הֶפְקֵר ownerless property, BQ i. 2; גִּזֵּי צֶמֶר הַבָּאוֹת מִמְּדִינָתָן fleece which comes from the country, opposed to הַלְּקוּחוֹת מִבֵּית הָאוּמָּן fleece which has been taken from the mechanic, BM ii. 1.

(ii) With one attribute only, where the chief emphasis is to be laid on the attribute, rather than on the substantive. Here, too, the article is virtually equivalent to a relative clause: גְּשָׁרִים הַמְּפוּלָּשִׁין covered bridges with an open passage; מָבוֹי הַמְּפוּלָּשׁ a covered entry with an open passage, 'Er. ix. 4; עֵצָה הַהוֹגֶנֶת לוֹ a counsel which is suitable (profitable) to him, Yeb. xii. 6; בְּהֵמָה הַמַּקְשָׁה לֵילֵד a beast which has hard labour in giving birth, Ḥul. ii. 1, 2, 4.

[1] The art. is never used in MH as a relative with a finite verb, as sometimes in BH; cf. Ges.-K., § 138 i, k.

(iii) With standing expressions which have acquired a technical sense: שַׁעַר הָעֶלְיוֹן the Upper Gate, Šeq. vi. 1; so Ezek. ix. 2; שָׂעִיר הַמִּשְׁתַּלֵּחַ the goat which is to be sent away, as opposed to שְׂעִיר הַחַטָּאת Yo. iv. 2; vi. 2 (cf. Lev. xvi. 10); שׁוֹר הַנִּסְקָל an ox condemned to stoning, Qid. ii. 2 (cf. Exod. xxi. 28); שׁוֹר הַמּוּעָד a goring ox, the owner of which has been forewarned, as opposed to שׁוֹר תָּם BQ i. 4 (cf. Exod. xxi. 29); נַעֲרָה הַמְאוֹרָסָה a betrothed maiden, San. vii. 4 (cf. Deut. xxii. 25, 27); כְּנֶסֶת הַגְּדוֹלָה the Great Synagogue, as distinguished from an ordinary כְּנֶסֶת Ab. i. 1.

(iv) In numerous other cases where no special emphasis can be detected: פּוֹל הַלָּבָן white beans, Ma'a. iv. 6; חוֹמֶץ הָאֲדוֹמִי Idumean vinegar, Pes. iii. 1; מַיִם הָרָעִים evil waters, Ab. i. 11; נֶפֶשׁ הַיָּפָה a good appetite, Ḥul. iv. 7; גָּמָל הָרַכָּה a tender camel, ib. ix. 2, and many more, especially in later texts. Many of these are, indeed, due to the negligence of copyists, as shown by a comparison of different texts. Thus, for שִׁפְחָה הַמְּשׁוּחְרֶרֶת a manumitted female slave, L has שׁ׳ מְשׁוּ׳, 'Ed. v. 6. So K has נַעֲרָה מְאוֹרָסָה for נ׳ המא׳ Ned. x. 1; שׁוֹר נִסְקָל for שׁ׳ הנ׳ San. i. 4, &c.[1] There still remain, however, a large number of genuine cases which exhibit a looseness in the observance of this rule. But this irregularity is also found in BH; cf. Ges.-K., § 126 w, x; Driver, *Tenses*, § 209. It was probably peculiar to popular speech even in the Biblical period.

377. (*b*) Conversely, cases are found where the substantive has the article, but not the attribute. In some of these cases the attribute has the force of a circumstantial clause: הַמַּאֲכִיל אֶת בָּנָיו קְטַנִּים וְאֶת עֲבָדָיו בֵּין גְּדוֹלִים וּבֵין קְטַנִּים one who gives to eat his sons when small, and his slaves whether grown up or small, Ter. vii. 3; הִכְנִיס ראשׁוֹ לַאֲוִיר הַתַּנּוּר טָהוֹר טִמְּאֵהוּ if he caused his head to enter into an oven which is clean, he has defiled it; הִכְנִיס ראשׁוֹ לַאֲוִיר הַתַּנּוּר טָמֵא נִטְמָא . . . an oven which is unclean, he becomes unclean, Kel. viii. 10. So also: נֶאֱמָנִין עַל הַיָּרָק חַי וְאֵין נֶאֱמָנִין

[1] Cf. Krauss, *MGWJ.*, li, p. 452.

עַל הַמְּבוּשָּׁל they are believed in the case of vegetables when raw, but they are not believed in the case of cooked (vegetables), Pea vii. 4.[1]

Other exx. do not allow of such an explanation, e.g. הַמַּעֲרָכָה גְּדוֹלָה the great pile, Tam. ii. 4; but for הַמַּעֲרָכָה שְׁנִיָּה ib. 5, L has המ' השנ'. So other cases rest on a textual error: הֶחָבִית מְרוּתַּחַת the foaming jar, L has חב' מר', while M reads הח' המר' ʻAZ iv. 10; הַמַּיִם שְׁאוּבִים drawn water, L מים שא'. N המ' הש' Tᵉm. i. 4; הַשֵּׂעָר צָהוֹב yellow hair, Nᵉg. x. 3, L; שער צהוב, and so elsewhere.

The article is sometimes omitted with a demonstrative attribute: הַכְּרִי זֶה this heap, Tᵉr. iii. 5; הַכִּיס זֶה this bag, Mᵉʻil. vi. 6.

For such irregularities in BH, cf. Ges.-K., § 126 y, and especially Koenig, *Syntax*, § 334 m, s.[2]

378. The article is always omitted with a number of common expressions, especially compounds, which are considered definite in themselves: תַּלְמוּד תּוֹרָה the study of the Torah, Pea i. 1; דֶּרֶךְ אֶרֶץ good manners, Ab. ii. 2; בַּעַל קֶרִי one with an issue, Miq. iii. 4; בַּעַל מוּם one with a blemish, ʻEd. iv. 1; יוֹם טוֹב a festival, ʻEr. vi. 6; כֹּהֵן גָּדוֹל High Priest, Yo. i. 1; יֵצֶר טוֹב the good inclination, Bᵉr. 5 a. Conversely, other nouns of the same character are only found with the article: בַּעַל הַבַּיִת the master of the house, Šab. i. 1; בֵּית הַמִּדְרָשׁ house of study, Šab. xvi. 1; בֵּית הַכְּנֶסֶת a synagogue, Mᵉg. iii. 1; but plur. is without the article: בַּעֲלֵי בָתִּים Kel. xvii. 1; בָּתֵּי מִדְרָשׁוֹת, בָּתֵּי כְנֵסִיּוֹת Tᵉr. xi. 10. Further, עַם הָאָרֶץ Dam. i. 3; plur. עַמֵּי הָאָרֶץ Ab. iii. 10

[1] L actually reads in the second clause עָלָיו מְבוּשָּׁל, which shows that חַי is an accusative of state, like הַזְּרֹעַ בְּשֵׁלָה, Num. vi. 19; cf. G. B. Gray's note, *ad loc.* M., however, reads הַחַי.

[2] Cf. also in Moabite and Phoenician, G. A. Cooke, *NSI.*, p. 26; Schroeder, op. cit., §§ 43, 58, and 61. Note also in BH בֵּית חֹרֹן תַּחְתּוֹן 1 Kings ix. 17, contrasted with ב' ח' הַתַּחְתּוֹן 2 Chron. viii. 5; also ירושלם קדשה on coins of Simon, beside the more usual י' הקדושה, Madden, *Coins of the Jews*, p. 67 f. Cf. also Nöldeke, *Syr. Gr.*, §§ 202, B. Rem., 203.

The article is always omitted with the genitive when introduced by שֶׁל, and preceded by an anticipatory suffix : יָדוֹ שֶׁל עָנִי the hand of the poor man, Šab. i. 1 ; cf. below, § 388.[1]

3. The Expression of the Genitive.

379. The genitive relationship between two nouns is expressed in MH, as in BH, by putting the first noun (*regens*) in the construct state, or by a circumlocution, in which the connexion between the two nouns is indicated by a special particle placed before the second noun (*rectum*). This latter method is much more frequent in MH than in BH. Nevertheless, the construct state still remains in MH the regular and prevailing method. Circumlocution is resorted to, at least in earlier MH, only when the grammatical form of the nouns, or the desire for lucidity makes the use of the construct impracticable. Thus, the use of the circumlocution in MH can be classified under certain logical and grammatical rules.

In Aram., on the other hand, the two constructions are used indiscriminately. Contrast Ezra v. 13 : מלכא די בבל, with vi. 14 : מלך פרס ; v. 14 : מאניא די בית with vi. 5 : מאני בית ; Dan. ii. 19 with iv. 2, 6 ; ii. 49 with iii. 12 ; iii. 1 with iii. 5, 7, &c. ; v. 5 with v. 24. This is especially the case in the *Targumim* ; cf. Winer, *op. cit.*, § 56. In the non-Jewish dialects of Aram. the construct state has been given up almost entirely, e. g. Syriac (Nöldeke, *Syr. Gr.*, § 205 B), Christian Palestinian Aram. (Nöldeke, *ZDMG.*, p. 507, § 36), and nearly so in Mandaic (Nöldeke, *Mand. Gr.*, § 221 f.).[2]

[1] Cf. further, *JQR.*, xx, pp. 653 ff. ; Barth, *Pronominalbildung*, p. 137.

[2] But in the old Aram. of the Zinjirli Inscriptions the constr. state alone is used ; cf. Cooke *NSI.*, Nos. 61–3. In the Aram. papyri of Assuan, however, the constr. is confined to 'the most common words where the relation is a close and natural one' (Cowley, *Introd.*, p. 19).

(1) *The Construct State.*

380. The construct state is especially common in the following cases:

(i) With *nomina actionis* as *regens*: מַגַּע טְרֵפָה touching of *ṭᵉrepha*, Ḥul. iv. 4; מַתַּן סָבִיב sprinkling of the blood round about the altar, Zᵉb. xiv. 10; שְׁבִירַת הָעֶצֶם breaking the bone, Pᵉs. vii. 12; יְדִיעוֹת הַטּוּמְאָה cases of knowledge of uncleanness, Šᵉbu. i. 1; בִּיטּוּל בֵּית הַמִּדְרָשׁ the neglect of the house of study, Šab. xvi. 1; עֵרוּבֵי תְחוּמִין *'erubim* of limits, 'Er. vii. 11; קִלְקוּלֵי הַמַּיִם the damaged receptacles of water, MQ i. 3; צִחְצוּחַ חֲרָבוֹת the glistening of swords, So. viii. 1; סַכָּנַת נְפָשׁוֹת danger of life, Ḥul. iii. 5; הֶפְסֵד מִצְוָה the loss by a commandment, Ab. ii. 1; הַדְלָקַת הַנֵּר kindling of the lamp, Šab. ii. 6; הוֹדָיַת הַמַּעֲשֵׂר the confession over the tithe, MŠ v. 15.

(ii) With *nomina agentis* as *regens*: חוֹתְמֵי בְרָכוֹת those that close benedictions, Bᵉr. ix. 3; עוֹלֵי בָבֶל those that came up from Babylon, Šᵉbi. vi. 1; שְׁלוּחֵי מִצְוָה those sent to perform a divine commandment, Suk. ii. 4; אֲנוּסַת אָבִיו a woman outraged by her father, Yᵉb. xi. 1; חַזַּן הַכְּנֶסֶת beadle of the Synagogue, So. vii. 7; חַיָּיבֵי חַטָּאוֹת those bound to bring sin-offerings, Šab. xi. 6. Further, adjectives: נְקִיֵּי הַדַּעַת men pure of mind, Giṭ. ix. 8; שְׁחוֹרֵי הָרֹאשׁ black-headed, Nᵉd. iii. 8.

(iii) Nouns of a common type; קֶשֶׁר מוֹכְסִין a knot of tax-gatherers, Šab. viii. 2; צָרְכֵי הַמֵּת the requirements of the dead, ib. xxiii. 5; וְלַד שִׁפְחָה a child of a female slave, Qid. iii. 12; שִׁגְגַת הַמַּעֲשֶׂה error of action, Hor. ii. 3; סְעוּדַת אֵירוּסִין a meal of betrothal, Pᵉs. iii. 7; תַּנְחוּמֵי אֲבֵלִים consolations of mourners, Mᵉg. iv. 3; תַּכְשִׁיטֵי נָשִׁים ornaments of women, Pᵉs. iii. 1; רְשׁוּת הָרַבִּים a public place, BQ iii. 1, &c.

381. The formation of the plur. of construct combinations follows the example of BH (cf. Ges.-K., § 124 p–r).

(i) The usual method is to attach the plur. termination to the *regens*: חוּטֵי צֶמֶר woollen threads, Šab. vi. 5; צוֹרְפֵי זָהָב goldsmiths, ib. viii. 4; פְּקִיעֵי עָמִיר bundles of sheaves, ib. xxiv. 2, &c.

(ii) Sometimes both nouns receive the plur. terminations Thus with בַּיִת: בָּתֵּי כְנֵסִיּוֹת וּבָתֵּי מִדְרָשׁוֹת synagogues and houses of study, Pes. iv. 4; בָּתֵּי הַבַּדִּים wine-presses, MS iii. 7; בָּתֵּי דִינִין courts of law, San. xi. 2; בָּתֵּי נִירִין meshes, Šab. vii. 2; בָּתֵּי דְשָׁנִין receptacles for ashes, Zeb. 104 b. With בַּעַל: בַּעֲלֵי אוּמָּנִיּוֹת artisans, Bik. iii. 3; בַּעֲלֵי דִינִים litigants, Ab. vii. 6; בַּעֲלֵי בָתִּים house-holders, Kel. xvii. 1, בַּעֲלֵי מוּמִים those with a blemish, Bek. vii. 6; בַּעֲלוֹת מוּמִים Tem. iv. 6 (L); בַּעֲלֵי קְרָיִין men with an issue, Miq. viii. 1; בַּעֲלֵי שֵׁיבוֹת greyheads, Ned. iii. 8. With רֹאשׁ: רָאשֵׁי חֳדָשִׁים New Moons, Pes. vii. 4; רָאשֵׁי שָׁנִים New Years, RH i. 1; רָאשֵׁי דְבָרִים chief points, ib. ii. 6. Further, עַרְבֵי פְסָחִים eves of the Passover, Pes. iv. 1; עַרְבֵי שַׁבָּתוֹת eves of the Sabbath, BM iv. 6; דִּינֵי מָמוֹנוֹת; דִּינֵי נְפָשׁוֹת civil, capital cases, San. iv. 1; עֵדֵי נְפָשׁוֹת witnesses in capital cases, ib. 5; חַיָּיבֵי חַטָּאוֹת; חַיָּיבֵי אֲשָׁמוֹת those bound to bring a sin-offering, a guilt-offering, Ker. vi. 4; חַיָּיבֵי מִיתוֹת men guilty of death, San. vii. 10, but חַיָּיבֵי עוֹלָה Tem. v. 1; גִּטֵּי נָשִׁים bills of divorce; שִׁחְרוּרֵי עֲבָדִים bills of manumission, Giṭ. i. 4.

(iii) The plur. termination is attached to the *rectum* alone, only with בַּיִת as *regens*: (טְהוֹרוֹת) בֵּית הָאֶצְבָּעוֹת gloves, Kel. xxvi. 3; בֵּית הַבַּדִּין wine-presses, BB iii. 1; בֵּית הַגִּיתּוֹת olive presses, t. Ter. iii. 1; בֵּית הַמִּשְׁתָּאוֹת banqueting houses, So. ix. 11; בֵּית הַטּוּמְאוֹת (מְטַמְּאִין) houses for menstruous women, Nid. vii. 4; בֵּית הַסְּתָרִים וּבֵית הַקְּמָטִים (אֵינָן) folds and hidden parts (of the body), Miq. viii. 5; בֵּית פְּרָסוֹת fields rendered unclean by dead bones from a ploughed grave, Oh. xviii. 2; בֵּית הַשְּׁוָוקִים market places, Makš. vi. 2.

382. A *nomen rectum* can itself become a *regens* to another *rectum*, but it can take only one *regens*. When one *rectum* has more than one *regens*, the second *regens* follows the *rectum*, and takes the appropriate possessive suffix, as in BH (Ges.-K., § 128 a): וְלָד תּוֹדָה וּתְמוּרָתָהּ the child and the exchange of a thank-offering, Men. vii. 4; זוֹמְמֵי בַּת כֹּהֵן וּבוֹעֲלָהּ the false witnesses against, and the paramour of, the daughter of a priest, San. xi. 1; מִבְּלָאֵי מִכְנְסֵי כֹהֲנִים וּמֵהֶמְיָינֵיהֶן from the worn-out breeches and girdles of the priests, Suk. v. 3.

383. The construct is not found in MH before a relative clause, except in stereotyped conjunctional expressions like כְּדֵי שֶׁ־, מִפְּנֵי שֶׁ־, כְּלַפֵּי שֶׁ־, &c. (§ 303). Also with חֲזָקָה state, assumption, which is very common in the constr. state before nouns (e.g. Ket. i. 6, 7; Naz. ix. 2; BB iii. 1 &c.): בְּחֶזְקַת שֶׁהוּא קַיָּים on the assumption that he is alive, Giṭ. iii. 3, 7, 8 (cf. 4); בְּחֶזְקַת שֶׁלֹּא נָתַן, בְּחֶזְקַת שֶׁנָּתַן, on the assumption that he has given . . . that he has not given, BB i. 4; בְּחֶזְקַת שֶׁנִּפְדָּה in the state of having been redeemed, Bek. viii. 6.

(2) *Simple Circumlocution of the Genitive.*

384. In addition to the constr. state, BH also indicates the genitival connexion between two nouns by the preposition לְ, prefixed to the *rectum* in apposition to the *regens* which remains in the absolute state (e.g. בֵּן לְיִשַׁי); or, further, by placing the *rectum* with this לְ in a relative clause אֲשֶׁר לְ־, so as to specify more clearly the subordinate relation of the *rectum* to the *regens* (e.g. הַצֹּאן אֲשֶׁר לְאָבִיהָ Ges.-K., § 129 a f.). This אֲשֶׁר לְ־ would become in colloquial speech שֶׁלְּ־, cf. § 77 f.

In MH circumlocution of the genitive by means of ל alone is extremely rare, and generally only when the ל may also be construed as a ל of the dative or of reference.[1] Exx.: הֲלָכָה לְמשֶׁה מִסִּינַי a law of Moses from Sinai (*sc.* שֶׁנִּיתְּנָה, Pea ii. 6); אוֹר לי״ד the eve of the fourteenth, Pes. i. 1; so אוֹר לפ״א Ker. i. 6, but

[1] So in Ethiopic; cf. Dillmann, *Aethiop. Gr.*, § 145, 6.

אור עִבּוּרוֹ the eve of its intercalation (the 30th day of the month), RH 22 b; רֹאשׁ הַשָּׁנָה לִמְלָכִים the New Year of Kings, RH. i. 1; זָנָב לָאֲרָיוֹת a tail of lions, Ab. iv. 15; אַלְפָּא לְסֹלֶת ἄλφα (the first, best) of fine flour, Men. viii. 1; and a few more.[1]

385. Much more common is the use of the relative clause in its colloquial form שֶׁל־. This particle is merely a prefix of the *rectum*, as in BH (Cant. iii. 7) and in older texts of MH. But it was gradually detached from its noun and given the appearance of an independent particle.

It follows from what has been said that the use of שֶׁל in MH is a genuine Hebraic construction derived from the BH use of אֲשֶׁר לְ־. שֶׁל is not an adaptation of the Aram. דִּי, דְּ־ which is merely equivalent to אֲשֶׁר, שֶׁ־ alone. On the contrary, the frequent use of דִּיל־, דְּל־ in Jewish Aram., instead of the more regular דִּי, or דִּיד (דְּיָד), must be ascribed to MH influence.[2]

386. The use of של for the genitive may be classified as follows.

(i) To express the material.[3]

סָדִין שֶׁל בּוּץ a sheet of fine linen, Yo. iii. 4; חָבִית שֶׁל זָהָב a jar of gold, Suk. iv. 10; also to express a quality: יָרָק שֶׁל תְּרוּמָה vegetables of *teruma*, 'Ed. ii. 2 and often. But the constr. is also common: כַּן הַזָּהָב base of gold, Yo. v. 2; Pes. v. 5; Tam. i. 4.

(ii) When more than one *regens* govern one *rectum*: תְּאֵנִים

[1] Cf further, *JQR.*, xx, pp. 725–6.

[2] In Phoenician the genitive is expressed by prefixing to the *rectum* ל, then by אשל, and finally by של. In late Phoenician, however, ש takes the place of של, evidently under Aram. influence. In MH we never find the use of שֶׁ־ for שֶׁל־. For possible cases in BH of אֲשֶׁר expressing the genitive, cf. *BDB.*, p. 83, and Koenig, *Syntax*, § 283.

[3] This construction is not found in BH, except, perhaps, Lev. xiii. 48; Ezra i. 11. It is regular in the Targum; cf. Gen. xxiv. 21, 53; Exod. ii. 2, 4 (but contrast vers. 21, 22, &c.), also Dan. v. 7; cf. Kautzsch, *Gr. d. Bib. Aram.*, § 81 c.

וַעֲנָבִים שֶׁל טֶבֶל figs and grapes of untithed produce, Ma'a. i. 7; זִכְרוֹן מַלְכוּת וְשׁוֹפָר שֶׁל פּוּרְעָנוּת verses of retribution containing the words 'remembering', 'king', and 'shofar', RH iv. 6; T^e^r. xi. 4; BM x. 1, &c. So in BH: Gen. xl. 5; Exod. xiv. 28; 2 Kings xi. 10; cf. Ges.-K., § 129 h.

(iii) When the *regens* consists of a construct combination: תְּרוּמַת מַעֲשֵׂר שֶׁל דְּמַאי Dam. iv. 1; מַעֲשֵׂר עָנִי שֶׁל דְּמַאי ib. 3, 4; פַּר עֲבוֹדַת הֶעְלֵם דָּבָר שֶׁל מָשִׁיחַ Sifre Num. viii. 3.

When the *rectum* is made up of such a compound expression: מַכְבֵּשׁ שֶׁל בַּעֲלֵי בָתִּים a press of householders, Šab. xx. 5; נְכָסִים שֶׁל בְּנֵי בְרִית property of sons of the Covenant, BQ i. 2; or both *regens* and *rectum* consist of compound expressions; תְּפִיסַת יָד שֶׁל בַּעַל הַבַּיִת holding of hand (right of access) by the householder, 'Er. viii. 4; כָּל יְדוֹת הַכֵּלִים שֶׁל יוֹם הַכִּפּוּרִים all the handles of the vessels of the Day of Atonement, Yo. iii. 10.

The constr. is also found in such cases, e. g. שִׂמְחַת בֵּית הַשּׁוֹאֵבָה the joy of the (celebration of) drawing of water, beside הֶחָלִיל שֶׁל בֵּית הַשּׁוֹאֵבָה the flute of . . ., Suk. v. 1. So in BH: Gen. xxv. 6; Num. xvi. 22; xxxi. 48, &c; Ges.-K., § 129 d, 2; cf. also Koenig, *Syntax*, § 281 l–m; § 282 e, f.

(iv) When an adjective intervenes between the *regens* and the *rectum*: יְסוֹד מַעֲרָבִי שֶׁל מִזְבֵּחַ the western base of the altar, Yo. v. 6; כּוֹר אֶחָד שֶׁל חִטִּים one *cor* of wheat, N^e^d. viii. 7; שׁוּרָה שֶׁל חֲמִשָּׁה גְפָנִים a row of five vines, Kil. iv. 5; עֶבֶד שֶׁל שְׁנֵי שׁוּתָּפִים a slave of two partners, P^e^s. viii. 1. So in BH: 1 Sam. xxii. 20; Ezek. xl. 40 b.

(v) Circumlocution is generally used with nouns borrowed from other languages, including Aram., which the language could not assimilate so thoroughly as to inflect them like native words: אִיסְטְרַטְיָא שֶׁל מֶלֶךְ the King's *στρατιά*, Qid. iv. 5; פּוּנְדְּקָאוֹת שֶׁל עכו"ם the *πανδοκεῖα* of the heathen, 'AZ ii. 1.

(vi) Generally when for one reason or another the *regens* or the *rectum* is to be emphasized, as when a noun is used in a secondary or derived sense: זוג שֶׁל סַפָּרִים shears of barbers, Kel. xiii. 1 (זוג סַפָּרִים may mean a pair of barbers); הַשֵּׁן שֶׁל מַעְדֵּר the tooth of a mattock, ib. 2; or in enumerating different cases which either agree with or differ from one another; טַבַּעַת שֶׁל מַתֶּכֶת טַבַּעַת שֶׁל אַלְמוּג . . ., a ring of metal . . . a ring of sandal wood, ib. 6; מַסְרֵק שֶׁל פִּשְׁתָּן וְשֶׁל צֶמֶר . . ., a comb for flax . . . and for wool, 8; xiv. 8; xv. 2, &c. Cf. in BH 2 Sam. iii. 2, 3.

Circumlocution is found also in many other cases which cannot be well brought under the above rules, especially in later MH under Aram. influence.

(3) *Circumlocution of the Genitive with Anticipation.*

387. The circumlocutory genitive is often anticipated in MH by a possessive suffix attached to the *regens*, e.g. יָדוֹ שֶׁל עָנִי the hand of the poor man, Šab. i. 1. The construction is only employed when the *regens* is a flexible noun, which is elsewhere found in the constr. state, as otherwise it could not take the suffix.

388. The *rectum* is almost always determinate, either by a suffix (תְּבוּאָתוֹ שֶׁל חֲבֵרוֹ his neighbour's produce, Kil. vii. 4) or by being a proper noun (תַּלְמִידָיו שֶׁל אַהֲרֹן Aaron's disciples, Ab. i. 12): a demonstrative pronoun (הֶפְשֵׁיטָן וְנִיתּוּחָן שֶׁל אֵלּוּ the flaying and cutting up of these, Yo. vii. 2); by having been mentioned before; or, finally, by being well known generally, or only in connexion with the subject treated in the context. Nevertheless, this determinate *rectum* never takes the article, except in such stereotyped expressions as הַקָּדוֹשׁ בָּרוּךְ הוּא, בַּעַל הַבַּיִת, and עַם הָאָרֶץ, which are never found without the article (cf. § 378). Cf. the following passages in which the *rectum* is mentioned previously with the article, but the article is dropped when the *rectum* stands in our construction: הֶעָנִי, but יָדוֹ שֶׁל עָנִי Šab. i. 1; הָעוּבָּר the embryo, but חֶלְקוֹ שֶׁל עוּבָּר the share of the embryo, Yᵉb. vii. 3;

הָעִיר but תְּחוּמָהּ שֶׁל עִיר the boundary of the city, Neď. vii. 5; הֶחָצֵר but אֲוִירָהּ שֶׁל חָצֵר the air of the courtyard, BB iv. 3; So. viii. 8 (עָם); Šebu. i. 7 (פָּר); Men. xi. 5 (שֻׁלְחָן); Oh. ii. 1 (מֵת); Neg. xiv. 1 (מְצוֹרָע).

Evidently, the *rectum* is regarded as having been determinated by the suffix of the *regens*, and, therefore, can as little take the article, as if the suffix had been attached to itself. Hence in Ethiopic, which has no article, this construction is regularly used for rendering a noun definite.[1]

In Aram., however, the *rectum* when standing in this construction is always in the emphatic state; cf. Dan. ii. 20, 44; iii. 26, and so in the *Targumim*.

389. This construction of anticipating the noun by a preceding pronominal suffix is widely used in MH to express the genitive. But it occurs also in other cases when the noun is introduced by a preposition.

With בְּ, only in the phrase בּוֹ בְיוֹם Ya. iv. 1, &c. Cf. in Aram.: Dan. iii. 6–8, 15; v. 11; Ezra v. 3.

With לְ: אָמְרוּ לוֹ לר״ג 'Er. iv. 2; הָיוּ לוֹ לְשַׁעַר Mid. iv. 2; so usually with דַּי: דַּיּוֹ לְיָחִיד sufficient for the private person, Men. xii. 4; דַּיָּהּ לְקוֹרָה sufficient for the beam, 'Er. i. 3; so also to express an object: אֵין מְקָרְבִין לוֹ לְאָדָם they do not draw a man near, Ab. ii. 3

With מִן (הֵימ־, cf. § 301), only in the expression: לֹא כָל הֵימֶנּוּ מִן הָרִאשׁוֹן everything does not depend on him, even on the first, Giṭ. viii. 8; cf. BQ x. 3.

With עַל: אָמְרוּ עָלָיו עַל רחב״ד they said of him, of R. Ḥanina . . .; Ber. v. 5; מָה עָלָיו עַל אָדָם what is there on a man, t. Ḥag. ii. 6.

390. This construction is, of course, very common in Aram., but it is also extensively used in Assyrian (Delitzsch, *Assyr. Gr.*, § 166), and in Ethiopic (Dillmann, *Aeth. Gr.*, § 172). It is also

[1] Cf. Dillmann, *Aeth. Gr.*, § 172 c.

found in BH. Thus, before the construct state: Jer. lii. 20 (לִנְחֻשְׁתָּם כָּל הַכֵּלִים); Ezek. x. 3 (בְּבֹאוֹ הָאִישׁ); xlii. 14 (בְּבֹאָם הַכֹּהֲנִים); xlvi. 22; Prov. xiii. 4 (נַפְשׁוֹ עָצֵל); Job xxix. 3 (בְּהִלּוֹ נֵרוֹ); Ezra ii. 62 (כְּתָבָם הַמִּתְיַחְשִׂים); iii. 12 (בְּיָסְדוֹ זֶה הַבַּיִת). With circumlocution, Cant. iii. 7 (מִטָּתוֹ שֶׁלִּשְׁלֹמֹה). With ל alone: Num. i. 21–43 (פְּקֻדֵיהֶם לְמַטֵּה); Ezra ix. 1 (כְּתוֹעֲבוֹתֵיהֶם לַכְּנַעֲנִי), &c. With the object: Exod. ii. 6 (וַתִּרְאֵהוּ אֶת); Deut. iii. 14 (וַיִּקְרָא אֹתָם . . . אֶת); 1 Kings xix. 21 (בִּשְּׁלָם הַבָּשָׂר); xxi. 13 (וַיְעִדֻהוּ . . . אֶת); 2 Kings xvi. 15 (וַיְצַוֵּהוּ . . . אֶת Kethib); 1 Sam. xxi. 14 (וַיְשַׁנּוֹ אֶת); Jer. ix. 14 (מַאֲכִילָם אֶת); Ps. lxxxiii. 12; Num. xxxii. 33 (וַיִּתֵּן לָהֶם . . . לִבְנֵי); Ezek. xxxiv. 2 (וְאָמַרְתָּ אֲלֵיהֶם לָרֹעִים); 1 Chron. v. 26; xxiii. 6; 2 Chron. xxv. 5, 10. Cf. further, Driver, *Tenses*, § 201; also Ges.-K., § 131 m, n.

It is, therefore, clear that the construction in MH is of native origin, but its somewhat extensive use, especially in late MH, may be due to Aram. influence.

4. Comparison of Adjectives.

391. The Comparative degree is expressed, as in BH, by מִן or מִ–, following the adject.: עָמוֹק מִכֵּן deeper than this, Nid. ii. 7; חַמָּתָהּ מְרוּבָּה מִצִּילָּתָהּ its sun is greater than its shade, Suk. i. 1; מְשׁוּנָּה מֵחַבְרוֹתֶיהָ different from its fellows, Šeq. vi. 2; יְתֵרָה מִכַּעֲדָשָׁה more than the measure of a lentil, Neg. vi. 4.

Very often יָתֵר is followed by עַל: יָתֵר עַל נ׳ סֶלַע more than 50 *sela'*, 'Ar. ii. 1; יְתֵרוֹת עַל הַבִּנְיָן exceeding the building, 'Er. i. 8, 9; יְתֵרוֹת עַל בְּנוֹת ג׳ . . . more than 3 years old, Ket. i. 4. Cf. in BH הָעוֹדְפִים עַל . . . Num. iii. 46; also Gen. xlviii. 22. See further above, § 363 (iii).

יוֹתֵר more, and פָּחוּת less, are often used adverbially to emphasize the comparison: עָנִי יוֹתֵר מֵהִלֵּל poorer than Hillel; עָשִׁיר יוֹתֵר מר״א richer than R. El'azer, Yo. 35 b; פָּחוּת מִכַּגְּרוֹגֶרֶת less than a dried fig, Šab. ix. 7. So after a verb יותר is sometimes omitted:

יִתְמָעֵט פָּחוּת מִשָּׁוֶה פְּרוּטָה it will become less than the value of a *pruṭa*, BQ ix. 7; רוֹאֶה אֲנִי אֶת דִּבְרֵי ראב״ע מִדִּבְרֵיכֶם I approve the words of . . . more than your words, Ab. ii. 13, 14.

392. The Superlative degree is expressed when the adjective is followed by a determinate noun, or by a pronoun, with the partitive ב prefixed, and introduced by the relative -שֶׁ. The adjective may take the article or not: הַיָּפָה שֶׁבָּהֶן the fairest (best) of them, Pes. ix. 8; הַגָּדוֹל שֶׁבַּדַּיָּנִין the greatest of the judges, San. iii. 7; קְטַנָּה שֶׁבַּבָּנוֹת the smallest of girls, Šab. viii. 4; בֵּיצָה קַלָּה שֶׁבַּבֵּיצִים the lightest of eggs, ib. 5; גְּדוֹלָה שֶׁבַּגְּדוֹלוֹת the oldest of the big ones; קְטַנָּה שֶׁבַּקְּטַנּוֹת the youngest of the little ones, Qid. iii. 8; טוֹב שֶׁבָּרוֹפְאִים the best of physicians; הַכָּשֵׁר שֶׁבַּטַּבָּחִים the worthiest of butchers, ib. iv. 14. Cf. in BH הַיָּפָה בַּנָּשִׁים Cant. vi. 1; Ges.-K., § 133 g.

393. The superlative idea is also expressed by the repetition of the adjective or the noun in the construct state, or, rarely, in the comparative: דַּקָּה מִן הַדַּקָּה thinnest, Yo. iv. 4; חַמֵּי חַמִּין exceedingly hot, Ber. 16 a; דַּלֵּי דַלּוּת the greatest poverty, Ker. 10 b; so חַדְרֵי חֲדָרִים the innermost chamber, Šab. 64 b (cf. 1 Kings xx. 30; xxii. 25: חֶדֶר בְּחֶדֶר); עֲדִי עֲדָיִים greatest ornament, ʻAZ 24 b (cf. Ezek. xvi. 7); further, לִפְנִים וְלִפְנֵי וְלִפְנִים within and right within, BM 16 a; Zeb. 52 a; 57 a (cf. 1 Kings vi. 17, 29). So also in BH; cf. קֹדֶשׁ הַקֳּדָשִׁים Exod. xxvi. 33; Ges.-K., § 133 i.

5. Numerals.

(1) Cardinals.

394. אֶחָד, אַחַת, follow the noun: מִין אֶחָד; פֵּאָה אַחַת Pea ii. 5; sometimes, with יָד, אַחַת precedes the noun: מֵאַחַת יָד from one place, Pea iii. 3; בְּאַחַת יָד Šebi. iii. 9; Pa. vii. 2, 3 (cf. Neh. iv. 11; Dan. viii. 13). All the other numerals when used as cardinals always precede the noun. שְׁתַּיִם, שְׁנַיִם are always in the construct state to the noun. The other numerals are usually in the absolute state, and in apposition to the noun. Sometimes, however, they are in the constr. state, thus: אַרְבַּעַת BB ii. 5; vi. 7; חֲמֵשֶׁת Ned. vii. 2; שִׁבְעַת Bik. i. 3; Yo. i. 1; עֲשֶׂרֶת San. x. 3, but the texts differ. The constr. is especially common in L: שְׁלֹשֶׁת, תְּשַׁעַת, BM iii. 7; שְׁמוֹנַת iv. 3, &c.

Some of the units take the pronominal suffixes. In addition to the BH שְׁנֵיהֶם, שְׁתֵּיהֶם, שְׁלָשְׁתָּם, and אַרְבַּעְתָּם, we also find חֲמִשְׁתָּן Men. xiii. 2; שִׁשְׁתָּן Mak. ii. 4; שִׁבְעָתָן Nid. ix. 8 (L, and so in citations, San. 49 b; Zeb. 95 b).

The number 2 is often expressed by the dual: קַבַּיִים two *qabs*, 'Ed. i. 2 (cf. § 293), but the dual is also found with the number, no doubt for the sake of emphasis שְׁנֵי כִכָּרַיִם Ṭoh. v. 6; שְׁתֵּי כִירַיִם Kel. vi. 3.

395. With the numerals 2–10, the object numbered takes the plur. In שְׁתֵּי כֶסֶף, אַרְבָּעָה כֶסֶף, שְׁמוֹנָה כֶסֶף BM iv. 3, 7, the name of a coin in the plur. (מָעוֹת) must be understood. So שְׁתֵּי הַלֶּחֶם, *sc.* חַלּוֹת Men. v. 1; xi. 1.

396. The numerals 11–19 also take the object numbered in the plur.: י״ב שְׁבָטִים, י״ב פָּרִים Hor. i. 5; י״ד כְּבָשִׂים Suk. v. 6; י״ד סְעוּדוֹת ib. ii. 6; ט״ו מַעֲלוֹת v. 4, &c. Certain nouns, however, that are in frequent use, remain in the sing.: י״ב מָנָה BM v. 2, י״ב זָהָב ib. viii. 8; י״ב חֹדֶשׁ Giṭ vii. 8; י״ד חֹדֶשׁ BB iii. 1; י״ד שָׁנָה Naz. iii. 6; ט״ו מָנָה Ket. vi. 3; ט״ז אַמָּה Kil. iv. 1; י״ח חֹדֶשׁ Giṭ. vii. 6.

397. Tens (20–90) and hundreds take the noun in the sing.: עֶשְׂרִים עִשָּׂרוֹן Men. vii. 1; ל׳ קַב ib. vii. 1; מ׳ זוג RH i. 6; נ׳ זוז BQ iv. 1 (but also נ׳ דִּיוֹרִים 50 dwellings, 'Er. v. 6); ס׳ לוֹג Men. ix. 3; ע׳ לָשׁוֹן Šeq. v. 1; פ׳ מַעֲשֵׂר Dam. vii. 7; צ׳ רִים Yo. vi. 4; ק׳ סְאָה Ter. iv. 11. (In מֵאָה חוּלִּין Dam. vii. 7, the noun has no sing. in that special technical sense), ק׳ שִׁפְחָה Ket. v. 5 (L; edd. שְׁפָחוֹת); but ק׳ עוֹפוֹת; ק׳ חַיּוֹת (L חַיָּיה) Ḥul. vi. 4; ק״כ לוֹג Suk. v. 2;

מָאתַיִם זוּז Ket. iv. 7; ד׳ מֵאוֹת זוּז BQ viii. 6; ג׳ מֵאוֹת שִׁיפָה 300 times rubbing; ה׳ מֵאוֹת בְּעִיטָה 500 times kicking (with the fist), Men. vi. 5; ז׳ מֵאוֹת זוּז BM ix. 10; but ג׳ מֵאוֹת כֹּהֲנִים Šeq. viii. 5; אֶלֶף דִּינָר Ket. vi. 3; אַלְפַּיִם אַמָּה ʻEr. iv. 3; אַרְבַּעַת אֲלָפִים אַמָּה ib. iv. 7.

But when units are added, the plur. is used: עֶשְׂרִים וְאַרְבָּעָה עֶשְׂרוֹנִים מִכ״ד סְאִין Men. vi. 6; כ״ד אַמּוֹת Kil. iv. 1; כ״ד חוּטִין Šeq. viii. 5; כ״ה שָׁנִים Ket. xii. 4; כ״ז אֲבָנִים Šebi. iii. 5; כ״ח קָנִים Men. xi. 6; מ״ה גְּפָנִים Kil. v. 5; ע״ב נִימִין 72 cords, Šeq. viii. 5[1]; מֵאָה וּשְׁנֵי חֲצָאִים 102 halves, Ter. iv. 13.

(2) Ordinals.

398. רִאשׁוֹן Yo. ii. 2; רִאשׁוֹנָה ib. i. 8; שֵׁנִי ii. 3; שְׁנִיָּה iv. 2 (with פַּעַם understood), Pea viii. 1; שְׁנִיִּים Hag. ii. 2; שְׁנִיּוֹת Taʻa. ii. 9; שְׁלִישִׁי Yo. ii. 4; שְׁלִישִׁית Kil. viii. 3; רְבִיעִי Yo. ii. 4; רְבִיעִית Ber. v. 2. Also with secondary forms: שְׁלָשִׁית רְבָעִי Pa. i. 1; חֲמִישִׁי Suk. v. 6; חֲמִישִׁית Meg. iii. 4, &c., as in BH.

399. Ordinals above ten are expressed by the corresponding cardinals, but with a noun always before the numeral, to distinguish them from the cardinals: לְיוֹם שְׁלֹשִׁים on the 30th day, Naz. iii. 1; יוֹם שְׁלֹשִׁים וְאֶחָד the 31st day, ib.; יוֹם שִׁשִּׁים the 60th; יוֹם שִׁשִּׁים וְאֶחָד the 61st; יוֹם שִׁשִּׁים חָסֵר אֶחָד the 60th less one—the 59th, ib. 2; יוֹם מֵאָה the 100th; יוֹם מֵאָה וְאֶחָד the 101st, ib. 4. Contrast this with the position of nouns with cardinals and ordinals in BH, Ges.-K., § 134 c, o, in which the difference between the two is not clear.

400. In counting the days of the month יוֹם is omitted: בְּאֶחָד בַּאֲדָר, בט״ו בּוֹ, בְּעֶשְׂרִים וַחֲמִשָּׁה the 1st, 15th, 25th of Adar,

[1] In שִׁבְעִים וּשְׁנַיִם זָקֵן Zeb. i. 3, the sing. is explained as indicating the complete unanimity of the assembled elders; cf. Zeb. 12 b with Rashi, *ad loc.* Some texts have also here the plur. זְקֵנִים.

Š^e^q. i. 1, 2; בִּשְׁנַיִם בַּחֹדֶשׁ the 2nd of the month, San. v. 3; בי״ז בְּתַמּוּז the 17th of Tammuz; בַּחֲמִשָּׁה עָשָׂר בְּאָב, בט׳ בְּאָב 9th, 15th of Ab, Ta'a. iv. 6, 8; Š^e^q. iii. 1, &c. In giving the time of the day שָׁעוֹת may be expressed or omitted: בִּשְׁתֵּי שָׁעוֹת, בְּשָׁלֹשׁ שָׁעוֹת, בְּחָמֵשׁ at 2, 3, 5 o'clock, San. v. 3; P^e^s. i. 4.

(3) Distributives.

401. The distributive is expressed by the repetition of the number without the copula:[1] אֶחָד אֶחָד; אַחַת אַחַת one by one, one at a time, Ma'a. iii. 2, 3; שְׁתֵּי חֲצֵרוֹת שֶׁל שְׁנֵי שְׁנֵי בָתִּים two courts with two houses each, 'Ar. ix. 7; שְׁנַיִם שְׁנַיִם Yo. ii. 6; שְׁלֹשָׁה שְׁלֹשָׁה ib. 7; שָׁלֹשׁ שָׁלֹשׁ Š^e^bi. iii. 3; Kil. v. 5; עֶשֶׂר שׁוּרוֹת שֶׁל עֶשֶׂר עֶשֶׂר כַּדֵּי יַיִן ten rows of ten jars of wine each, Dam. vii. 8; שֵׁשׁ עֶשְׂרֵה שֵׁשׁ עֶשְׂרֵה אַמָּה Kil. iv. 9.

(4) Fractions.

402. מֶחֱצָה half, Pea v. 5; חֲצִי קַב half a *qab*; קַב וַחֲצִי a *qab* and a half, ib. viii. 5; שְׁנֵי חֲצָאֵי זֵיתִים Oh. iii. 1; שְׁלִישׁ a third, Pea v. 5; שְׁנֵי שְׁלִישִׁים 'Er. 10 b; רְבִיעַ a quarter, Pea ib.; רְבִיעִית ib. viii. 5; רוֹבַע a quarter, Kil. ii. 1; רִבְעָתַיִם two quarters, K^e^r. i. 7; חֲמִשָּׁה רְבִיעִים קֶמַח Ḥal. ii. 6; חוֹמֶשׁ a fifth, Pea vii. 6; חֲמִשִּׁיּוֹת fifths, BQ 65 b; שְׁתּוּת[2] a sixth, T^e^r. iv. 7; שְׁמִין 1/8 of a *ma'ah*, j. Qid. i. 1; שְׁמִינִין Qid. 12^a^; שְׁמִינִית an eighth, Pea viii. 5; תְּשׁוּעַ a ninth, j. Dam. vii, and עִישּׂוּר a tenth, MŠ v. 9; אֶחָד מכ״ד 1/24, Kil. ii. 2; אֶחָד מִשְּׁלֹשִׁים וְשָׁלֹשׁ וּשְׁלִישׁ 1/33–1/3, Dam. v. 2; אֶחָד ממ״ח 1/48, Ḥal. ii. 7; אֶחָד מִמֵּאָה 1/100 Dam. v. 2; אֶחָד מֵרִבּוֹא 1/10,000, Pea iii. 8.

[1] But with כָּל, the copula is used: כָּל אֶחָד וְאֶחָד, כָּל אַחַת וְאַחַת, Pea iii. 1, 2.

[2] ת receives *dagesh* after שׁ to prevent the concurrence of two similar sounds; so in BH שְׁתַּיִם.

Sometimes אֶחָד is omitted : אֵין פּוֹחֲתִין . . . מִשִּׁשִּׁים one must not give less than 1/60, Pea i. 2 ; בְּמָאתַיִם by 1/200 Kil. v. 6.

403. (5) The following numerals are found in verbal forms : שְׁנַיִם : שָׁנוּ Pes. v. 2 ; שׁוֹנִין Suk. v. 4 ; נִשְׁנֵית San. 59 a ; שְׁלשָׁה : שִׁלֵּשׁוּ Pes. ib. ; יְשַׁלֵּשׁוּ : מְשׁוּלָּשִׁים BB x. 7 ; הִשְׁלִישׁ ib. 5 ; לְהִשְׁתַּלֵּשׁ Mak. iii. 11 ; אַרְבָּעָה : לְרַבְּעָהּ t. 'Er. ii. 1 ; vi. 10 ; מְרַבֵּעַ 'Er. 56 b ; מְרוּבַּעַת, מְרוּבָּע Oh. xii. 8 ; חֲמִשָּׁה : מְחוּמָּשׁוֹת BB 150 a ; תִּשְׁעָה : מִתּוּשָּׁעִים j. Š^e^bi. 33 b ; עֲשָׂרָה : יְעַשֵּׂר ; מְעוּשָּׂר Dam. iii. 1, 2 ; מִתְעַשֵּׂר Ma'a. iv. 3.

III. THE PRONOUN

1. The Personal Pronoun.

404. The personal pronoun is expressed with a finite verb, whenever it is desired to emphasize the subject : נָגַח הוּא if he gored, BQ v. 3 ; אֲבָל הוּא לֹא יִקְרָא but he himself must not read, Šab. i. 3 ; הֵם אָמְרוּ they said, Ab. i. 2 ; קְרָא אַתָּה read thou, Yo. i. 3 ; לְכִי אַתְּ go thou, B^e^r. 18 b ; אֲנִי הָיִיתִי בָא I was coming, B^e^r. i. 6 ; אִלּוּ אֲנִי פָּסַקְתִּי לְעַצְמִי if I had assigned by myself, Ket. xiii. 5. The emphasis is often strengthened by the addition of the particle אַף : אַף הוּא הֵעִיד he also testified, 'Ed. ii. 3 ; אַף הוּא עָשָׂה ; אַף הִיא עָשְׂתָה he, she also made, Yo. iii. 10 ; אַף הֵם אָמְרוּ they said, Suk. ii. 7 ; אַף אֲנִי לֹא אָמַרְתִּי Ta'a. i. 1 ; הָבֵא לְךָ אַף אָתָּה bring for thyself, Pes. iv. 2 ; אַף אַתָּה אַל תִּתְמַה neither shouldst thou be surprised, ib. vi. 2.

On the whole, MH uses the pronoun more sparingly than BH. It is omitted even with participles when the subject is understood : רוֹצָה הִיא . . . וּבוֹשָׁה מֵחֲתָנָהּ she desires . . . and is ashamed of her son-in-law, Dam. iii. 6.

405. The pronoun of the third person is regularly employed in noun clauses as the copula between subject and predicate : אַתָּה הוּא הִלֵּל art thou Hillel ? Šab. 31 a ; לֹא שָׂדֶה הִיא זוֹ is not this a field? 'Er. 53 a; אֵלּוּ הֵן הַמְמוּנִּים these are the overseers, Šeq. v. 1; הַפֶּה שֶׁאָסַר הוּא הַפֶּה שֶׁהִתִּיר the mouth that declared it forbidden is the mouth that declared it permitted, Dam. vi. 1; אֲנִי הוּא הַטָּמֵא I am the unclean, Naz. viii. 1. The pronoun is sometimes placed at the end for emphasis: אָדָם חָלוּל הוּא a man is hollow, Oh. xi. 3; הַיָּדַיִם עַסְקָנִיּוֹת הֵן the hands are busy, Šab. 14 a. Sometimes the pronoun stands before the subject in anticipation: שֶׁלָּנוּ הוּא הַפֶּסַח ours is the paschal sacrifice, &c., Pes. ix. 10; מְעוּבֶּרֶת הִיא צָרָתָהּ her rival is pregnant, Yeb. xvi. 1; עוֹמֵד הוּא הַטָּהוֹר the clean one may stand, Pa. x. 5; xii. 5. Cf. in BH Cant. vi. 9, and Driver's *Tenses*, § 201.

2. The Possessive Pronoun.

406. Possession is expressed by the pronominal suffixes attached to the noun in exactly the same way as in BH. MH, however, also makes wide use of the relative שֶׁ with the preposition ל (שֶׁל) as an independent possessive pronoun (cf. §§ 79, 385). It is used both in substantival and adjectival constructions.

(i) Substantival: שֶׁלִּי שֶׁלִּי וְשֶׁלְּךָ שֶׁלִּי mine is mine and thine is mine, Ab. v. 10; הַכֹּל שֶׁלּוֹ everything is his, ib. iv. 22; מֵפֵר אֶת שֶׁלָּהּ וְשֶׁלּוֹ קַיָּים he annuls hers but his remains in force, Naz. iv. 1; אֵלּוּ שֶׁלָּהֶן these are theirs, BM i. 5.

407. (ii) Adjectival, taking the place of the pronominal suffix.

This construction is used, at least in earlier MH works, only in the following cases.

(*a*) On grounds of grammar:

(1) With compound expressions which have become standing phrases are thus inseparable: מַעֲשֵׂר שֵׁנִי שֶׁלָּהֶם their Second Tithe, MŠ iii. 6; בֵּית קִיבּוּל שֶׁלָּהּ its receptacle, 'Ed. iii. 5; 'לֹא הוּדַע' שֶׁנָּהֶן (cf. Lev. iv. 28) Ker. i. 2.

(2) With a composite subject: כִּסֵּא וּסְמוּכוֹת שֶׁלּוֹ his seat and supports, Šab. vi. 8; הַפַּת וְהַשֶּׁמֶן שֶׁלָּהֶם their bread and oil, 'AZ ii. 6.

(3) With indeclinable nouns: בַּשְּׁמִינִי שֶׁלּוֹ; בַּשֵּׁנִי שֶׁלָּהּ Pes. viii. 5; רֵחַיִם שֶׁלָּהֶן their mill, 'Ed. iii. 12; חַמִּין שֶׁלּוֹ his hot water, t. Šab. iii. 3; שַׁעֲוָה שֶׁלָּהּ her wax, t. ib. xviii. 8; הָאַלְיָה שֶׁלָּהֶן their tail, Šab. v. 4; especially foreign nouns: הָאוּנְקְלִי שֶׁלָּהּ ἀγκύλη Kel. xiii. 7; מוּכְנִי שֶׁלָּהּ μηχανή, ib. xviii. 2; הַפִּיטְמָה שֶׁלָּהֶן their flower, 'Uq. i. 2.

408. (*b*) On grounds of style.

(i) With nouns used in a secondary or derived sense: הַתַּחְתּוֹן שֶׁלָּהּ its lower part, Šab. i. 10 (to distinguish from תַּחְתּוֹנָה, adjective); קַב שֶׁלּוֹ his artificial foot, ib. vi. 8 (not *qab*, measure); הַבֵּיצִים שֶׁלּוֹ *testes*, Y^eb. viii. 4; הָאֵם שֶׁלָּהּ the matrix, B^ek. iv. 4; הַפֶּרַח שֶׁלָּהּ the calyx of a candlestick, 'Oh. iv. 8.

Sometimes to emphasize specially the noun, rather than the possessor: אֲפִילּוּ הַחֶלְמוֹן שֶׁלָּהּ even its yolk, T^er. x. 12; חַפִּין שֶׁלָּהּ its teeth (of a key); חוֹתָם שֶׁלָּהּ its seal (of a ring), Kel. xiii. 6, in antithetical cases.

409. This construction is also frequent in BH, cf. מְעָרַת הַמַּכְפֵּלָה אֲשֶׁר לוֹ Gen. xxiii. 9; xli. 43; Exod. xxxviii. 30; Lev. ix. 8; xvi. 6, 11; הַנַּעַר אֲשֶׁר לוֹ 1 Sam. xx. 40; 2 Sam. xiv. 31; 1 Kings i. 33; iv. 2; Ruth ii. 21; כְּרֵעַ כְּאָח לִי Ps. xxxv. 14; cxx. 1; לְכִסֵּא לָךְ cxxxii. 11, 12; Lam. i. 10, &c.; cf. Koenig, *Syntax*, § 28 i, o.

So also in Phoenician (Punic), Schröder, § 69, and in modern Arabic, Spitta, §§ 77 c, 119 a, 120 c.

3. The Demonstrative Pronoun.

410. The demonstratives זֶה, זוֹ, אֵלּוּ, are used both substantively and adjectivally: זֶה אוֹמֵר . . . וְזֶה אוֹמֵר this one says . . . and this one says, BM i. 1; מַעַשְׂרוֹת זוֹ בְזוֹ the tithes of this one are in this one, Dam. vii. 6; אֵלּוּ וָאֵלּוּ מִתְעָרְבִין both these and these mingle, Yo. v. 6; or the noun follows as a predicate which is further defined by a relative clause : אֵלּוּ דְבָרִים שֶׁאֵין לָהֶם שִׁיעוּר these are the things which have no measure, Pea i. 1 ; Ber. vii. 1.

411. When used adjectivally the pronoun follows the noun : כִּכַּר זוֹ this loaf, Šebu. iii. 7 ; שׁוֹר זֶה this ox, Men. xiii. 9 ; הַמָּעוֹת הָאֵלּוּ this money, MŠ iii. 3. Sometimes, however, the pronoun precedes the noun in Aram. fashion : זֶה מִדְרָשׁ דָּרַשׁ ר״א this exposition, R. El'azar . . . expounded, Ket. iv. 6 ; זוֹ עֵדוּת הֵעִיד ר״פ R. Papias bore this testimony, Naz. iii. 2 ; v. 4 (but cf. below, § 477) ; עַל אֵלּוּ טוּמְאוֹת over these cases of uncleanness, ib. vii. 2. Cf. in BH, Ges.-K., § 136 d, foot-note 1.

412. Similarly, the stronger demonstratives הַלָּז, הַלָּלוּ, are used in both these ways : לַמָּקוֹם הַלָּז to that place, Ṭoh. iv. 3 ; vi. 5 ; בַּפֶּתַח הַזֶּה . . . בַּפֶּתַח הַלָּז in this entrance . . . in that entrance, ib. vi. 8 ; הַמּוּמִין הַלָּלוּ those blemishes, Ket. vii. 8 ; ג׳ דְּבָרִים הַלָּלוּ those three things, Ab. v. 19. On the other hand : הוֹצִיא הַלָּז אֶת רֹאשׁוֹ that one brought forth his head, Mak. ii. 2 ; וְתֵצֵא הַלֵּזוֹ and that one should go forth, Yeb. xiii. 7 ; הַלָּלוּ נוֹצְצִין, הַלָּלוּ נוֹבְלִין these sprout forth, these fade, 'Er. 54 a.

413. The shortened form הַלָּה is found only substantivally : וְהַלָּה אוֹמֵר and that one says, Šebu. vi. 7 ; הַלָּה מוּתָּר that one is permitted, Ned. iv. 8 ; v. 6 ; כֵּיצַד הַלָּה עוֹשֶׂה סְחוֹרָה how can that one make a business, BM iii. 2 ; San. vi. 1.

414. The pronoun of the third person is also used as a demonstrative : בִּזְמַן שֶׁאֵין לָהֶם אוּמָּנוּת אֶלָּא הִיא (L ; ed. הוּא) when they have no other trade but that one, San. iii. 3 ; so especially in contrast to the nearer demonstrative : חֲמוֹרְךָ זֶה . . . חֲמוֹרְךָ הוּא this ass, that ass, of thine, BB v. 2 ; הַפֵּירוֹת הָאֵלּוּ . . . הַפֵּירוֹת הָהֵם this fruit . . . that fruit ; הַמָּעוֹת הָאֵלּוּ . . . הַמָּעוֹת הָהֵם this, that money, MŠ iii. 4 ; but more frequently הַלָּה is found : . . . זֶה אוֹכֵל . . . וְהַלָּה עוֹשֶׂה this one eats . . . and that one does . . ., ib. 3. Cf. also the exx. above, § 74. הַלָּה is used also in contrast with הוּא : הוּא אוֹמֵר לוֹ . . . וְהַלָּה אוֹמֵר לוֹ San. vii. 10 ; Šebu, vii. 1.

415. The interrogative pronoun אֵיזֶה, אֵיזוֹ is used as a demonstrative to specify one out of a number of objects: מְבָרֵךְ עַל אֵיזֶה מֵהֶן שֶׁיִּרְצֶה he pronounces the benediction on whichever he likes, Bᵉr. vi. 4; Yᵉb. ii. 2; יָבִיא אֵיזוֹ שֶׁיִּרְצֶה he brings that one which he likes, Mᵉn. xiii. 1; אֵיזֶה שֶׁלָּקַח רִאשׁוֹן that one (of the two) who took first, Ḥul. v. 3.

416. MH also uses the particle אֶת as a demonstrative. The particle stands alone when introducing a clause: אֶת שֶׁיַּבֶּלֶת בְּעֵינוֹ the one which has a wart in its eye, Bᵉk. vi. 10; אֶת שֶׁהַגּוֹלֵל נִשְׁעָן עָלָיו that one on which the *golel* (the stone cover of a grave) is supported, Oh. ii. 4; Giṭ. ix. 5–7; Makš. i. 2; v. 2. So especially to introduce two alternate cases: אֶת שֶׁלִּפְנֵי הַמִּטָּה וְאֶת שֶׁלְּאַחַר הַמִּטָּה אֶת שֶׁלַּמִּטָּה צוֹרֶךְ בָּהֶן פְּטוּרִין אֶת שֶׁאֵין לַמִּטָּה צוֹרֶךְ בָּהֶן חַיָּיבִין both of those before the bier, and of those behind the bier: those of whom the bier has need are absolved, but those of whom the bier has no need are bound (to read the *Šᵉma'*), Bᵉr. iii. 1; 'Er. viii. 11; Šᵉq. viii. 7; BQ iv. 2, &c. Sometimes the particle is omitted before the second case: Nᵉd. x. 7; ṬY iii. 1; Ya. iii. 1.

417. When introducing a noun, את takes the appropriate pronominal suffix of the third person: אוֹתוֹ הַיּוֹם וְאוֹתוֹ הָאִישׁ that day and that man, 'AZ i. 3; אַנְשֵׁי אוֹתָהּ הָעִיר the men of that city, Be. v. 5; לְאוֹתוֹ הַמָּקוֹם to that place, 'AZ i. 4; בְּאוֹתָהּ שָׁעָה in that moment, Bᵉr. v. 3; אוֹתָן הַחוּלִּין those common things, Tᵉr. v. 1; אוֹתָן הַיָּמִים those days, Nᵉd. ix. 6; אוֹתָן שְׁתֵּי רוּחוֹת those two spirits, Bᵉr. 18 b.

The origin of this demonstrative use of את is to be found in the BH use of את before the nominative, in order to emphasize the noun, cf. Ges.-K., § 117 i; Koenig, *Syntax*, § 279 f.; *BDB*., p. 85, 3. An analogy to the MH use of את . . . את may be found in Ezek. xxxv. 10. Cf. also Barth, *Pronominalbildung*, p. 125.[1]

[1] This use of את (= יָת) is not found in Jewish Aram., or in the other

4. The Interrogative Pronoun.

418. מִי is only used substantivally : מִי יְגַלֶּה who would uncover ? So, v. 2 ; לְמִי מְשַׁלֵּם to whom does he pay ? BM iii. 1 ; מָה occurs in both the substantival and adjectival use : מָה הִפְסִיד what has he lost ? ib. v ; מַה מְטַמֵּא לוֹ what defiles him ? N^e^g. xii. 5 ; מָה הַלָּשׁוֹן אוֹמְרִים what expression do men say ? ib. x. 1 ; מַה קוֹל שָׁמַעְתָּ what voice hast thou heard ? B^e^r. 3 a ; מָה אֲנִי what am I ? Ya. iv. 4.

L often has מִי in a neuter sense in the frequent phrase בְּמִי דְבָרִים אֲמוּרִים in what case does the statement apply, e. g. Š^e^bi. iii. 7 ; Šab. xvii. 8 ; ʽEr. vii. 9, 11 ; x. 1. Conversely, מָה is found in L of persons : חוּץ מִמַּה שֶׁיֵּשׁ לוֹ except one whom he has, Y^e^b. ii. 5. Cf. in BH מִי שְׁמֶךָ Judges xiii. 17 ; *BDB.*, p. 566 a (a).

מִי is but rarely used to introduce an interrogative clause, e. g. מִי כָאן הִלֵּל is Hillel here ? Šab. 31 a.

419. אֵיזֶה, אֵיזוֹ, can be used both substantivally and adjectivally, e. g. בְּאֵיזֶה יוֹם ; בְּאֵיזוֹ שָׁעָה San. v. 1. When used substantivally, they are followed by the enclitic הוּא, הִיא, often spelt in one word, and without the final א : אֵיזֶהוּ דָבָר which is a thing that . . . ? T^e^r. ix. 6 ; אֵיזֶה הוּא בֶן זוּגוֹ which is its pair ? Šab. xii. 3 ; אֵיזוֹ הִיא שִׁכְחָה what is a forgotten sheaf? Pea vii. 8, 4 ; בְּאֵיזֶה ; בְּאֵיזוֹ שָׁנָה שָׁבוּעַ in which week, year, San. v. 1, &c.

So also the rare plur. form אֵילּוּ can be used in both ways : אֵלּוּ שֶׁהָפְכוּ וְאֵלּוּ שֶׁקָּדְמוּ t. N^e^g. ii. 7 ; אֵלּוּ הָאֲבָנִים which stones ? BM x. 1 ; cf. above, § 81.

Aram. dialects, except in Christian Palestinian Aram., and in Samaritan. Nöldeke's view that MH borrowed this usage from these two Aram. dialects (*ZDMG.*, xxii, p. 471) is improbable, in view of the great frequency of this usage in MH and its complete absence in Jewish Aram. It is more probable that Christian Palestinian Aram. and Samaritan borrowed this usage from MH. For other borrowings by the first-named dialect from MH, cf. Nöldeke, ib., pp. 513, 522.

5. The Relative Pronoun. The use of ־שֶׁ.

420. The particle שֶׁ is used to introduce a clause which serves to define a preceding noun or pronoun. It is then equivalent to the English relative 'who, which'. Thus, in the nominative: שׁוֹר שֶׁנָּגַח an ox which has gored, BQ iv. 1; אֵלּוּ שֶׁהֵם צְרִיכִים; אֵלּוּ שֶׁאֵינָם צְרִיכִים these that require, that do not require, Miq. x. 3, 4; חַטָּאת שֶׁקִּבֵּל דָּמָהּ a sin-offering, the blood of which he received, Zᵉb. viii. 12. Accusative: שָׂדֶה שֶׁקְּצָרוּהָ גוֹיִם a field which Gentiles have reaped, Pea ii. 7; אֲבָנִים שֶׁזִּעְזְעָתָן הַמַּחֲרֵישָׁה stones which the plough has moved, Šᵉbi. iii. 7. Usually, however, the retrospective pronominal suffix is omitted, as in BH (Ges.-K., § 138 b): שׁוֹרִי שֶׁגָּנַבְתָּ my ox which thou hast stolen, Šᵉbu. viii. 4; דֶּרֶךְ יְשָׁרָה שֶׁיָּבוֹר לוֹ הָאָדָם a straight road which a man should choose for himself, Ab. ii. 1; כָּל טָהֳרוֹת שֶׁטִּיהַר ר״א all things which R. Eli'ezer had declared clean, Bᵉr. 19 b.

421. Similarly, with nouns indicating place or time, when there is no risk of ambiguity, the retrospective preposition is omitted: מָקוֹם שֶׁנָּהֲגוּ לַעֲשׂוֹת a place where they are accustomed to do, Pᵉs. iv. 1; מִשָּׁעָה שֶׁהַכֹּהֲנִים נִכְנָסִין from the time when the priests enter; לְמָקוֹם שֶׁמַּיִם אַחֲרוֹנִים חוֹזְרִין to the place where the water for washing the hands after a meal returns, Bᵉr. 46 b. But more often the preposition is expressed: מָקוֹם שֶׁנַּעֲשׂוּ בוֹ נִסִּים a place where miracles were wrought; מָקוֹם שֶׁנֶּעֶקְרָה מִמֶּנּוּ a place from which idols have been uprooted, Bᵉr. ix. 1; הַמָּקוֹם שֶׁיָּצָא מִשָּׁם whence he came forth; הַמָּקוֹם שֶׁהָלַךְ לְשָׁם whither he went, Pᵉs. iv. 1; דְּבָרִים שֶׁאָדָם יוֹצֵא בָהֶן things with which one discharges one's duty, ib. ii. 4, 5; דְּבָרִים שֶׁאֵין נִשְׁבָּעִין עֲלֵיהֶם things on which one does not take an oath, Šᵉbu. vi. 5; מִי שֶׁהַפִּקָּדוֹן אֶצְלוֹ he with whom is the deposited article, ib. 7; כָּל שֶׁאֵין הַכֶּלֶב יָכוֹל לְחַפֵּשׂ אַחֲרָיו everything that a dog cannot search out, Pᵉs. ii. 2.

422. The original demonstrative significance of ־שֶׁ is still apparent in cases where the indefinite מִי, מָה stands as its antecedent (cf. § 436): מִי שֶׁהוֹצִיאוּהוּ; מִי שֶׁיָּצָא anyone whom they brought forth; who went forth, ʿEr. iv. 1, 3, 4, 5; מַה שֶּׁעָשָׂה עָשׂוּי what he has done is done, BB viii. 5. In BH אֲשֶׁר can stand in such cases without an antecedent, cf. Num. xxii. 6, &c.; Ges.-K., § 138 e. In MH -שׁ must always have an antecedent.

Sometimes, however, -שׁ is omitted after מִי, מָה: אֵין לוֹ מִי יַתִּירֶנּוּ he has no one who would make it permissible = שֶׁיַּתִּירֶנּוּ Men. iv. 3; אֵין לִי מָה אָשִׁיב I have nothing to reply = שֶׁאָשִׁיב Kel. xiii. 7. Cf. also § 477.

Likewise, the particle את can stand as antecedent to -שׁ, whether in the accusative or the nominative: מְעַשֵּׂר אֶת שֶׁהוּא אוֹכֵל וְאֶת שֶׁהוּא מוֹכֵר וְאֶת שֶׁהוּא לוֹקֵחַ he tithes what he eats, sells, buys, Dam. ii. 2; אֶת שֶׁהָעֵדִים נִקְרָאִין עִמּוֹ that one with which the witnesses can be read (i.e. their signatures following immediately), Giṭ. ix. 5–7; cf. above, § 416.

423. Like אֲשֶׁר, and especially כִּי in BH (Ges.-K., § 157), -שֶׁ also introduces a clause which serves as the object of a verb. -שֶׁ is then equivalent to a conjunction: לֹא לִמַּדְתָּנוּ . . . שֶׁחָתָן פָּטוּר didst thou not teach us that a bridegroom is absolved . . ., Ber. ii. 5; יוֹדֵעַ אֲנִי שֶׁהוּא מְקוּבָּל I know that he is accepted, ib. v. 5; סָבוּר שֶׁנָּדְרָה he thought that she had vowed, Ned. xi. 5; . . . לֵידַע שֶׁהוּא אֵל to know that He is God, AB iv. 22.

-שֶׁ often has as its antecedent a conjunction or a preposition: -אַחַר שֶׁ, -כְּשֶׁ, -מִשֶּׁ, &c.; cf. § 303. So אשר in BH, Ges.-K., § 104 b.

424. The use of -שֶׁ to introduce direct narration is rare and doubtful: הִיא כוֹתֶבֶת שֶׁנִּתְקַבַּלְתִּי she writes: I have received, Ket. v. 1 (L; edd. 'נתק); אָמַר לָהֶם שֶׁהַטְּהוֹרָה he said to them: the clean one, Ned. iv. 3; אָמַר לָהֶם שֶׁהַזֶּבַח Men. ii. 1 (but -שֶׁ in these cases may stand for -מִפְּנֵי שֶׁ because); after an oath: שְׁבוּעָה שֶׁאֵינִי יָשֵׁן שֶׁאֵינִי מְדַבֵּר an oath, that I will not sleep, speak, Ned. ii. 1, 2;

cf. below, §§ 456, 458 f. For similar use of אשר in BH, cf. Ges.-K., § 157 c.

425. שֶׁ־ is regularly used in adverbial expressions before לֹא: בְּטוֹבָה וְשֶׁלֹּא בְטוֹבָה with, and without thanks, Šebi. iv. 2; בְּבֵית דִּין וְשֶׁלֹּא בְבֵית דִּין at a court of law, and not at a court of law: בְּפָנָיו וְשֶׁלֹּא בְפָנָיו in his presence, and not in his presence, Yeb. xiii. 1; שֶׁלֹּא בִכְתוּבָּה without the marriage settlement, Ket. vii. 6. Rarely without שֶׁ־, as in BH בְּלֹא: בְּלֹא מִתְכַּוֵּן ʻEr. iv. 4; בְּלֹא מִסְפָּר Suk. v. 4.

426. שֶׁ־ is also often found before a verb introduced by אוֹ: אוֹ שֶׁנָּטַל or he took; אוֹ שֶׁנָּתַן or put, Šab. i. 1; אוֹ שֶׁהָיוּ or they were, Suk. iii. 2; הוּקְרוּ אוֹ שֶׁהוּזְלוּ they became dear or cheap, BB v. 8. Contrast, however, אוֹ מֵיאֲנוּ, &c. or repudiated, Yeb. i. 1, and often.

427. שֶׁ־ is also attached to a verb to lend it special emphasis in an antithesis: אָמַר לוֹ מֵת וְהוּא שֶׁנִּשְׁבַּר he said to him: it was dead, but it was really broken (injured); וְהוּא שֶׁמֵּת it was really dead, Šebu. viii. 2, 3, 5, 6; so in L וְהֵם שֶׁיּוֹדְעִין and they did really know, ib. iv. 11.

6. Reflexive and Reciprocal.

428. The expression of the reflexive by the simple pronominal suffix is rare in MH. Examples are: גּוֹלְלוֹ אֶצְלוֹ he rolls it up to himself, ʻEr. x. 3; הָאִישׁ מְקַדֵּשׁ בּוֹ וּבִשְׁלוּחוֹ a man can betroth by himself or by his messenger; הָאִשָּׁה מִתְקַדֶּשֶׁת בָּהּ a woman can be betrothed by herself . . ., Qid. ii. 1; הָאִשָּׁה כּוֹתֶבֶת אֶת גִּטָּהּ a woman may write her own *Get*, Giṭ. ii. 5; אֲבֵידָתוֹ וַאֲבֵידַת אָבִיו his own lost property and his father's lost property, &c., BM ii. 11.

429. Usually, a periphrasis is employed to express the reflexive idea. The most common noun used for this purpose is עֶצֶם with the appropriate suffix.

Nomin.: הַפְּרִי עַצְמוֹ the fruit itself, Šebi. viii. 7; (הַתָּמִיד) עַצְמוֹ בְּתִשְׁעָה itself by nine, Yo. ii. 5; הָאִשָּׁה עַצְמָהּ the woman herself, Giṭ. ii. 7; תְּמַהּ עַצְמְךָ wonder thyself, Makš. i. 3.

Genit.: עֲצֵי עַצְמָן their own wood, opposed to עֲצֵי הַמַּעֲרָכָה the wood of the pile, Pes. vii. 8; מַעֲשֵׂה עַצְמוֹ his own act, opposed to מַעֲשֵׂה שׁוֹרוֹ BQ iii. 9; דְּבָרִים שֶׁל עַצְמוֹ his own words, opposed to דְּבָרִים שֶׁל אֲחֵרִים Šebu. iii. 5; אֵין אָדָם מֵעִיד עַל יְדֵי עַצְמוֹ a man cannot give evidence for himself, Ket. ii. 9; כְּסוּת עַצְמָן their own garment, Tam. i. 1; בֵּינוֹ לְבֵין עַצְמוֹ privately, Bik. i. 4.

Accus., after transitive verbs, as a periphrasis of the reflexive stem: קוֹנָה אֶת עַצְמָהּ acquires herself, Qid. i. 1; אַל תַּעַשׂ עַצְמְךָ do not make thyself, Ab. i. 8; יָזֵמּוּ אֶת עַצְמָן refute themselves, Mak. i. 4 (L); אֵין אָדָם מֵשִׂים אֶת עַצְמוֹ רָשָׁע a man cannot make himself guilty, Yeb. 25 b.

With a preposition: זֶה בְּעַצְמוֹ וְזֶה בְעַצְמוֹ this by itself and this by itself, Šab. xix. 2; לָחוּב בְּעַצְמְךָ to be guilty against thyself, Ber. i. 3; בְּעַצְמוֹ שֶׁל כֹּהֵן by the priest himself, Sifra, 8 d; זוֹ לְעַצְמָהּ וְזוֹ לְעַצְמָהּ this for itself and this for itself, Pes. i. 2; אִם יָצְאוּ מֵעַצְמָן if they went forth of themselves, Šab. 143 b.

430. Sometimes, עֶצֶם is preceded by כָּל, for the sake of emphasis: כָּל עַצְמוֹ אֵינוֹ כּוֹתֵב altogether he only writes, So. ii. 3; כָּל עַצְמָן אָסוּר לְקַיֵּים they are altogether forbidden to preserve, t. Šab. iv. 9; כָּל עַצְמָהּ אֵינָהּ נַעֲשֵׂית the whole of it is not done, Sifra, 8 d; כָּל עַצְמָם שֶׁל מְלָכִים the kings themselves, Sifre, Deut. i. 1.

431. The use of עֶצֶם is peculiar to MH. The similar use of גֶּרֶם in late Aram. must be an imitation of MH.[1] In BH עֶצֶם is found in an analogous sense, but only in the construct state, and of things, not of persons: בְּעֶצֶם הַיּוֹם הַזֶּה Gen. vii. 13, and frequently; כְּעֶצֶם הַשָּׁמַיִם Exod. xxiv. 11; בְּעֶצֶם תֻּמּוֹ Job xxi. 23

[1] So perhaps also in BH: גֶּרֶם הַמַּעֲלוֹת 2 Kings ix. 13.

(Ges.-K., § 139 g). But it is obvious that a word meaning 'bone' must have been applied first to animate beings, and then only figuratively to inanimate objects. It is, therefore, clear that the expression must have been more commonly used in colloquial speech than appears in the literary remains of BH.

432. The BH נֶפֶשׁ is used rarely as a reflexive: תְּמַהּ נַפְשְׁךָ wonder thyself; מִתְחַיֵּב בְּנַפְשׁוֹ becomes guilty against himself, Ab. iii. 4.

So גּוּף: גּוּפָהּ שֶׁל מִנְחָה the meal offering itself, Sifra 25 b; גּוּפוֹ his own person, Ab. iv. 8.

Finally, the compound preposition מֵאֵל with the appropriate suffix sometimes expresses the reflexive idea: הָעוֹלֶה מֵאֵלָיו what springs up of itself, 'Or. i. 2; בָּאוּ מֵאֲלֵיהֶן they came of themselves, BM vii. 9; cf. § 301.

433. Reciprocity is expressed by such circumlocutions as the repetition of the demonstrative: שִׁחְרְרוּ זֶה אֶת זֶה they liberated each other, Y^e^b. xi. 5; רוֹאִין אֵלּוּ אֶת אֵלּוּ they see one another, Mak. i. 9; rarely רֵעַ . . . אִישׁ: לֹא יַכּוּ אִישׁ אֶת רֵעֵהוּ they should not strike one another, Pea iv. 4. Note also the use of חָבֵר, חֲבֶרֶת with inanimate objects: בֵּין פַּצִּים לַחֲבֵרוֹ between one beam and its fellow, Šab. viii. 7; מִסְּפִינָה לַחֲבֶרְתָּהּ from one ship to the other, ib. xi. 5; בֵּין שׁוּרָה לַחֲבֶרְתָּהּ between one row and the other, Kil. iii. 6; iv. 8; cf. § 139.

7. Indefinite.

434. Like BH, MH possesses no special indefinite pronouns. It employs certain nouns, and pronouns, and certain parts of the verb to express the indefinite subject, or object.

(i) אָדָם: שׁוֹאֵל אָדָם one may ask, Šab. xxiii. 1; מוֹנֶה אָדָם one may count, ib. 2; לֹא יָקוֹב אָדָם one may not bore, ib. ii. 4; שֶׁיָּבוֹר לוֹ הָאָדָם which one should choose for oneself, Ab. ii. 1; יְכַוֵּין אָדָם אֶת דַּעְתּוֹ לַשָּׁמַיִם one should direct one's mind towards heaven, M^e^n. xiii. 11. אָדָם is often strengthened by כָּל: כָּל אָדָם יָסֵב anyone must recline; כָּל אָדָם קוֹרֵא anyone may read . . ., B^e^r. i. 5; כָּל אָדָם מִיִּשְׂרָאֵל anyone in Israel, 'Ed. v. 6.

435. (ii) כָּל alone followed by a participle, or by -שֶׁ: כָּל הַשּׁוֹכֵחַ anyone who forgets, Šab. vii. 1, 5; כָּל הַמִּסְתַּכֵּל anyone who gazes, Ḥag. ii. 1; כָּל שֶׁאֵינוֹ יָכוֹל one who is not able, ib. i. 1; כָּל שֶׁעֲשָׂאָהּ one which he made, Suk. i. 1; . . . כָּל שֶׁיִּנָּטֵל one which when the tree be removed, ib. ii. 3; אָכַל כָּל מַאֲכָל he ate any food; שָׁתָה כָּל מַשְׁקִין he drank any drink, Zab. ii. 2. So especially with the pronoun of the third person: כָּל שֶׁהֵן, כָּל שֶׁהִיא, כָּל שֶׁהוּא somewhat, something, anything, Šab. i. 14; ix. 6; 'Er. ii. 2, &c.

This use of כָּל is also very frequent in BH; cf. *BDB.*, p. 482 a (e).

436. (iii) מִי: מִי לְחָשְׁךָ if anyone whispers to thee, Sifre, Deut. xi. 27; but usually with -שֶׁ and a relative clause, when מִי has a somewhat demonstrative force: מִי שֶׁאָכַל וְשָׁכַח if anyone ate and forgot, B^e^r. viii. 7; זָכָה מִי שֶׁזָּכָה he wins whoever wins, Tam. v. 2; מִי שֶׁלֹּא שָׁהֲתָה any woman who has not waited, Y^e^b. xi. 6; מִי שֶׁנִּתְחָרֵשׁ בַּעְלָהּ anyone whose husband became deaf mute, So. iv. 5.

So in BH: מִי אֲשֶׁר Exod. xxxii. 33; 2 Sam. xx. 11; cf. *BDB.*, p. 567 a (g).

מִי is often strengthened by כָּל: כָּל מִי שֶׁלֹּא רָאָה whoever has not seen, Suk. v. 1; כָּל מִי שֶׁאֵינוֹ צָרִיךְ whoever is not in need, Pea viii. 8; מַאֲכִיל לְכָל מִי שֶׁיִּרְצֶה he gives to eat to whomever he wishes, BB viii. 7.

So with מָה: מַה שֶּׁנָּתַן נָתַן whatever he gave, he gave, ib. vi. 7; טוֹל מַה שֶּׁהֵבֵאתָ take whatever thou hast brought, Ḥul. iv. 4; עַל מַה שֶּׁלֹּא שָׁמַע about what he has not heard, Ab. v. 7; מַה שֶּׁאַתְּ שׁוֹמַעַת whatever thou hearest, B^e^r. 18 b; cf. § 422. This usage is common in Qohelet, *e.g.* i. 9; iii. 15, 22, &c.; cf. *BDB.*, p. 553 a (e (b)); also col. b, 3; Ges.-K., § 137 c.

So especially with הוּא, הִיא, often written without א: מַשֶּׁהוּ,

מַשֶּׁהִי something, anything; אָדָם טוֹעֶה מַשֶּׁהוּ one errs somewhat, Pes. 11 b; אַחַד עָשָׂר וּמַשֶּׁהוּ eleven and something over, 'Er. 87 a; נָתַן מַשֶּׁהוּ שֶׁמֶן he gave a little oil, Men. 60 a.

437. (iv) כְּלוּם anything, equivalent to BH מְאוּמָה (from which it seems to be derived with the addition of כָּל, like the other indefinite nouns described above = כָּל + מְאוּם[1]), used as indefinite pronoun only with negatives: לֹא עָשָׂה כְלוּם he did nothing, Yo. v. 7; לֹא נִשְׁתַּיֵּיר הֵימֶנָּה כְּלוּם nothing was left of it, Ḥul. iii. 1; the negative is sometimes strengthened by the addition of וְלֹא: לֹא עָשָׂה וְלֹא כְלוּם he did nothing at all, Pes. 89 b. So מאומה in BH is usually found with negatives, Gen. xxii. 12; xxx. 31, &c.

(v) מִקְצָת some: נָטַל מִקְצַת פֵּיאָה he took some of the *Pea*, Pea iv. 2; מִקְצָתָן רוֹאִין some of them see, Ber. vii. 5; הָיוּ מִקְצַת הֶעָלִין some of the leaves were, Kil. i. 9.

(vi) פְּלוֹנִי, פְּלוֹנִית so and so, an unnamed one; אִישׁ פְּלוֹנִי בֶּן אִישׁ פְּלוֹנִי מִמָּקוֹם פְּלוֹנִי מֵת Yeb. xvi. 6; אֵינִי נוֹשֵׂא אֶת פְּלוֹנִית I will not marry so-and-so, Ned. ix. 3; עֲבֵרָה פְּלוֹנִית a certain transgression, San. vi. 1. So also כָּךְ וְכָךְ: שְׁנַת כָּךְ וְכָךְ, the year so-and-so, RH 18 b; כָּךְ וְכָךְ פּוֹעֲלִים so many labourers, Šab. 150 b.

438. (vii) An indefinite subject is also expressed by the cognate participle: מֵת לוֹ מֵת, if anyone died to him, San. ii. 3; סִילֵּק הַמְסַלֵּק וְהִטְמִין הַמַּטְמִין וְהִדְלִיק הַמַּדְלִיק he that has to remove removes, that has to hide hides, that has to light lights, Šab. 35 b; הַנִּכְנָס יִכָּנֵס וְהַיּוֹצֵא אַל יֵצֵא anyone may enter, but no one may go out, ib. 60 a; cf. BH Isa. xvi. 10; xxviii. 4, 24, &c.

439. (viii) More often the subject is omitted altogether, and the verb alone, in the third person, whether in the sing. or the plur., expresses the indefinite subject. Thus the participle שׁוֹאֵל . . . וּמֵשִׁיב one asks . . . one answers, Ber. ii. 1; especially with the article, used with a demonstrative force: הַקּוֹרֵא if one reads, ib. ii. 3;

[1] But it may, perhaps, be connected with the Arab. كلم, and equivalent to דָּבָר anything.

הַשּׁוֹחֵט if one slays, Šebi. x. 2; cf. above, §§ 329, 374 (vii). So in the plur., but without the article: קוֹרִין Ber. i. 1; מַזְכִּירִין ib. 8. So, particularly, when the subject is the Divine power: נִפְרָעִין מִמֶּנּוּ retribution is taken from him, Ab. iv. 5; מַסְפִּיקִין בְּיָדוֹ they enable him, ib. 6; הַבָּא לִיטַּהֵר מְסַיְּיעִין לוֹ הַבָּא לִיטַּמֵּא פּוֹתְחִין לוֹ if one comes to purify himself, they assist him; if one comes to defile himself, they open to him (an opportunity), Šab. 104 a.

So with the perfect: וְיִמֵּן לְבָנִים וּמָצָא שְׁחוֹרִים if one prepared white ones, and found black ones, Be. i. 5; מָזְגוּ לוֹ they poured out to him, Pes. x. 2; הֵבִיאוּ לְפָנָיו they brought before him, ib. 3; כִּירָה שֶׁהִסִּיקוּהָ . . . נוֹתְנִין עָלֶיהָ a hearth which has been heated . . . one may put on it . . ., Šab. iii. 1.

With the imperf.: לֹא יִתֵּן עַד שֶׁיִּגְרוֹף אוֹ עַד שֶׁיִּתֵּן אֶת הָאֵפֶר one may not put until one removes the coals, or until one puts on ashes, ib., &c. Cf. in BH, Ges.-K., § 144 d, g, i.

IV. SENTENCES AND CLAUSES

1. The Nominative Absolute.

440. The Nominative Absolute is very common in MH, as in BH and Aram.[1] In this construction the noun is placed at the head of the sentence for emphasis, and its proper grammatical relation is expressed later in the sentence by a resumptive pronoun.

441. (i) With a definite subject: פֵּאָה אֵין קוֹצְרִין אוֹתָהּ בְּמַגָּלוֹת וְאֵין עוֹקְרִין אוֹתָהּ בְּקַרְדּוּמּוֹת Pea[2]—they may not reap it with sickles, nor uproot it with axes, *Pea* iv. 4; הַנַּחְתּוֹמִין לֹא חִייְּבוּ אוֹתָם חֲכָמִים the bakers—the sages have not laid on them the obligation, Dam. ii. 4; הַתְּרוּמָה מֶה הָיוּ עוֹשִׂין בָּהּ the heave offering (of the

[1] Cf. Ges.-K., § 143; Nöldeke, *Syr. Gr.*, § 317; *Mand. Gr.*, § 275.

[2] The corn in the corner of a field which had to be left for the poor, Lev. xxiii. 22.

shekels)—what did they do with it, Šeq. iv. 1, 3 f.; הַדְּמַאי אֵין לוֹ חוֹמֶשׁ *Dammai*[1]—it has not the law of the fifth, Dam. i. 2; אַמַּת הַמַּיִם . . . אֵין מְמַלְּאִים הֵימֶנָּה a pool of water—one may not fill from it, ʿEr. viii. 7 ff.

442. (ii) With an indefinite subject (cf. §§ 435 f., 439). Such sentences are usually equivalent to a conditional sentence in English: הָאוֹמֵר . . . מְשַׁתְּקִין אוֹתוֹ if one says . . . they silence him, Ber. v. 3; הַקּוֹצֵר בַּלַּיְלָה וְהַמְעַמֵּר וְהַסּוּמָא יֵשׁ לָהֶם שִׁכְחָה if one reaps or binds sheaves by night, and the blind man—to them applies the law of a forgotten sheaf (Deut. xxiv. 19), Pea vi. 11; מִי שֶׁאֲחָזוֹ בּוּלְמוֹס מַאֲכִילִין אוֹתוֹ he whom faintness has seized—they make him eat, Yo. viii. 6, 7; מִי שֶׁאָבַד חוֹתָמוֹ מַמְתִּינִין לוֹ if anyone has lost his seal—they wait for him, Šeq. v. 5; מַה שֶּׁהוּא מְשַׁיֵּיר יַנִּיחֶנּוּ whatever he leaves—he must put it away, Pes. i. 3; כָּל שֶׁבָּא בְחַמִּין . . . שׁוֹרִין אוֹתוֹ whatever came into hot water—they may soak it, Šab. xxii. 2; כָּל הַמְקַבֵּל עָלָיו . . . מַעֲבִירִין מִמֶּנּוּ whoever receives upon himself . . . they remove from him, Ab. iii. 6.

443. To this construction belongs the frequent resumption of the subject by the graphic particle הֲרֵי with the demonstrative pronoun: הַחוֹלֵץ לִיבִמְתּוֹ הֲרֵי הוּא כְאֶחָד מִן הָאַחִים if one grants *haliṣa* to the childless widow of his deceased brother—lo, he is like one of the (other) brothers, Yeb. iv. 7. This happens, especially, when the subject is described by a more or less lengthy intervening clause, or when the subject is compound: מִי שֶׁיֵּשׁ לוֹ נ׳ זוּז וְהוּא נוֹשֵׂא וְנוֹתֵן בָּהֶם הֲרֵי זֶה לֹא יִטּוֹל if anyone has 50 *zuzim* with which he trades—lo, this one must not take, Pea viii. 9. Contrast with: מִי שֶׁיֵּשׁ לוֹ מָאתַיִם זוּז לֹא יִטּוֹל ib. 8; הָיָה עוֹשֶׂה בְיָדָיו אֲבָל . . . הֲרֵי זֶה אוֹכֵל if he worked with his hands, but not with his feet . . . lo, this one may eat, BM vii. 3. Contrast with the following: הָיָה עוֹשֶׂה בַתְּאֵנִים לֹא יֹאכַל בָּעֲנָבִים if he worked at figs, he must not

[1] Fruit about which there is a doubt whether it has been tithed or not.

eat of grapes. ג׳ אִילָנוֹת שֶׁל ג׳ בְּנֵי אָדָם הֲרֵי אֵלּוּ מִצְטָרְפִין 3 trees of 3 men—lo, these combine, Šᵉbi. i. 5; אֲבָנִים שֶׁזִּעְזְעָתָן הַמַּחֲרֵישָׁה אוֹ שֶׁהָיוּ מְכוּסּוֹת וְנִתְגַּלּוּ . . . הֲרֵי אֵלּוּ יִנָּטְלוּ stones which the plough has moved, or if they were covered and became uncovered . . .—lo, these may be taken away, ib. iii. 7; הַחִטִּים וְהַשְּׂעוֹרִים . . . הֲרֵי אֵלּוּ חַיָּיבִין בְּחַלָּה wheat, barley . . .—lo, these are liable to the law of *Ḥalla* (Num. xv. 20).

444. Such a nom. abs. often consists of a subject, qualified by a relative clause, which has been removed from a subordinate object clause, and placed before the principal sentence. This happens usually in the case of an object clause dependent on the verb אמר, where two or more opposing views are expressed by different sages. The position of the nom. abs. serves to direct attention to it as the subject of the discussion that follows. Exx.: בֵּיצָה שֶׁנּוֹלְדָה בְּיוֹם טוֹב בֵּית שַׁמַּאי אוֹמְרִים תֵּאָכֵל וּבֵית הִלֵּל אוֹמְרִים an egg born on a festival—the House of Šammai say, it may be eaten; but the House of Hillel say, it may not be eaten. This is equivalent to: בֵּית שַׁמַּאי אוֹמְרִים בֵּיצָה שֶׁנּוֹלְדָה בי״ט תֵּאָכֵל Be. i. 1; so ib. 2, 8. Contrast ib. 3–7, &c.: הַשּׁוּתָּפִין שֶׁתָּרְמוּ זֶה אַחַר זֶה ר׳ עֲקִיבָא אוֹמֵר תְּרוּמַת שְׁנֵיהֶם תְּרוּמָה וַחֲכָמִים אוֹמְרִים תְּרוּמַת הָרִאשׁוֹן . . . ר׳י אוֹמֵר . . . partners who tithed one after the other=R. Akiba says: the tithing of both is tithes; the sages say: the tithing of the first (alone) is tithes; R. Jose says . . .—ר׳ע אוֹמֵר הַשּׁוּתָּפִין שֶׁתָּרְמוּ . . . Tᵉr. iii. 3; so ib. 5; viii. 8, 9 (with the verb מוֹדֶה); מִי שֶׁלִּיקֵּט אֶת הַפֵּאָה וְאָמַר הֲרֵי זוֹ לְאִישׁ פְּלוֹנִי עָנִי ר׳ אֱלִיעֶזֶר אוֹמֵר זָכָה לוֹ וַחֲכָמִים אוֹמְרִים if anyone gathers *pea*, and says: lo, this shall be for a certain poor man—R. Eliezer says: he acquires it for him; but the sages say . . ., Pea iv. 9; BM iii. 12; Yᵉb. iv. 3 (with מוֹדִים).

445. Frequently, a nom. abs. is left suspended, and is not resumed again at all, but the predicate is attached to another implicit subject, whether mentioned expressly before, but in a dependent relation, or not mentioned expressly, but understood from the context. Here, again, the position of the nom. abs. is designed to give special emphasis to a particular circumstance in the case under discussion. This construction is very common in the Mishna and Tosefta, and is characteristic of their Halakic diction. Exx.: מָעוֹת חוּלִּין וּמָעוֹת מַעֲשֵׂר שֵׁנִי שֶׁנִּתְפַּזְּרוּ מַה שֶׁלִּיקֵּט לִיקֵּט לְמַעֲשֵׂר שֵׁנִי (viz. הַמְלַקֵּט) common money and money of the second tithe which have been scattered together—whatever he picks up, he picks it up for the second tithe, MŠ ii. 5; עוֹבֵד כּוֹכָבִים שֶׁשָּׁלַח עוֹלָתוֹ מִמְּדִינַת הַיָּם וְשָׁלַח עִמָּהּ נְסָכִים קְרֵיבִין (viz. הַנְּסָכִים) מִשֶּׁלּוֹ if a heathen has sent from the country across the sea his burnt-offering, and has (also) sent with it libations,—then they (the libations) are offered of his own; so further: ... גֵּר שֶׁמֵּת Šeq. vii. 6. With indefinite subject: הַמְקָרֶה סוּכָּתוֹ בְּשַׁפּוּדִין ... כְּשֵׁרָה (viz. הַסּוּכָּה) if anyone covers his tabernacle with spits ... it (the tabernacle) is fit, Suk. i. 8, 9, 11 (implicit object); ii. 2–4; הָאוֹמֵר לִשְׁלוּחוֹ צֵא וּתְרוֹם תּוֹרֵם (viz. הַשָּׁלִיחַ) כְּדַעְתּוֹ שֶׁל בַּעַל הַבַּיִת if anyone says to his messenger: go out and tithe—then he (the messenger) tithes in accordance with the mind of the householder (the sender), Ter. iv. 4; מִי שֶׁזִּימֵּן אֶצְלוֹ אוֹרְחִים לֹא יוֹלִיכוּ (viz. הָאוֹרְחִים) בְּיָדָם מָנוֹת if anyone invited to himself guests—then they (the guests) may not carry with them gifts, Be. v. 7, 6; Yeb. x. 4; Ket. xiii. 2.

446. The nom. abs. may consist even of a grammatically complete sentence (i. e. with a finite verb), which is yet dependent upon a following predicate, as is shown by the context: הָיָה רוֹכֵב עַל גַּבֵּי בְהֵמָה וְרָאָה אֶת הַמְּצִיאָה וְאָמַר לַחֲבֵרוֹ תְּנָה לִי נְטָלָהּ (viz. חֲבֵרוֹ) וְאָמַר (if) he rode upon an animal and saw a lost article and said to his neighbour: give it to me—he (the neighbour) took it and said ..., BM i. 3.

447. Sometimes, the new subject is expressly referred to by a demonstrative, especially with הֲרֵי: הָיְתָה בֵּין הַקְּבָרוֹת הֲרֵי זֶה לֹא

(הַמּוֹצֵא viz.) יִטַּמָּא לָהּ if it was among the graves—lo, he (the finder, if a priest) should not defile himself for it, BM ii. 10; כֹּהֶנֶת שֶׁנִּתְעָרֵב וְלָדָהּ בִּוְלַד שִׁפְחָתָהּ הֲרֵי אֵלּוּ אוֹכְלִין בִּתְרוּמָה the wife of a priest, whose child was mixed up with the child of her female slave—lo, these (the two children) eat of *teruma* (priestly tithes), Yeb. xi. 5, iii. 4, &c.

2. Agreement between Subject and Predicate.

448. Collective nouns as subject sometimes take the predicate in the sing., sometimes in the plur.: שֶׁיְּהֵא הַבָּקָר עוֹבֵר בְּכֵלָיו that the oxen may pass with their harness, Šebi. i. 5; נִטְמָא קָהָל the congregation became unclean, Pes. vii. 6; בַּלֶּשֶׁת שֶׁנִּכְנְסָה a troop that has entered, ʿAZ v. 6; לֹא הָיָה בֵּית דִּין . . . בָּקִי the court of law was not expert, San. vii. 2; but: הוֹרוּ בֵּית דִּין the court of law taught, Ho. i. 1; כְּשֶׁרָאוּ בֵּית דִּין . . . הִתְקִינוּ when the court of law saw . . . they ordained . . ., Yo. ii. 2. The two constructions may be found side by side, the sing. preceding the subject: כְּשֶׁגָּבְרָה מַלְכוּת . . . וּנְצָחוּם when the kingdom of the house of Hasmonai prevailed, and conquered them, Šab. 21 b; מִשְׁפָּחָה אַחַת הָיְתָה בִּירוּשָׁלַיִם שֶׁהָיוּ פְּסִיעוֹתֵיהֶן גַּסּוֹת there was a certain family in Jerusalem whose steps were big, ib. 63 b; further מַחֲנֶה הַיּוֹצֵאת . . . מוּתָּרִין a troop that goes forth . . . are permitted, ʿEr. 17 a.

449. So with a construct expression as subject; הָיוּ מִקְצַת הֶעָלִין מְגוּלִּין if a portion of the leaves were uncovered, Kil. i. 9; שְׁאָר נְכָסִים יִפְּלוּ the remainder of the property shall fall, Šeq. iv. 81; קִבְּלוּ רוֹב הַצִּבּוּר the majority of the public have received, ib. v. 2; but נִטְמָא מִעוּט הַקָּהָל the minority of the congregation became unclean, Pes. vii. 6; אֵין כָּל אָדָם חַיָּיבִין no man is guilty, Mak. ii. 7; sometimes the texts differ: כָּל אָדָם יַטֶּה וְיִקְרָא every man must incline and read; כָּל אָדָם קוֹרֵא כְּדַרְכּוֹ reads according to his own way, Ber. ii. 3 edd., but L: יַטּוּ וְיִקְרוּ; קוֹרִין כְּדַרְכָּן; so Sifre, Deut. vii. 7; יְהֵא כָּל אָדָם אוֹמֵר San. vi. 2, edd., but L: יְהוּא . . . אוֹמְרִין.

450. A compound subject, consisting of a masc. and a fem. noun, takes the predicate in the masc.: הַסֹּלֶת וְהַשֶּׁמֶן מְעַכְּבִין זֶה אֶת זֶה the fine flour and the oil keep back each other, Men. iii. 5. The masc. is used even with fem. nouns: אֵין אֲכִילָה וְהַקְטָרָה מִצְטָרְפִים eating and burning incense do not combine, Zeb. vi. 7 (end); מַחַט אוֹ טַבַּעַת . . . נִרְאִין . . . יוֹצְאִין a needle or a ring . . . are seen but do not protrude, Kel. ix. 1.

451. Sometimes the gender agrees strictly with the grammatical form of the noun, rather than with the sense: בַּלֶּשֶׁת שֶׁנִּכְנְסָה 'AZ v. 6; שְׁתֵּי כִתֵּי עֵדִים מְעִידוֹת two groups of witnesses, Naz. iii. 7; אוּמָּנִיּוֹת שׁוֹקְדוֹת handicrafts labour diligently, t. Ber. vii. 2. Sometimes the gender agrees with the sense, and not with the grammatical form; especially when removed from the noun: כָּל הָעֲיָירוֹת מִתְכַּנְּסוֹת . . . וְלָנִים . . . נִכְנָסִים all the towns assemble . . . and spend the night . . . enter . . ., Bik. iii. 2; עֲיָירוֹת גְּדוֹלוֹת קוֹרִין big towns read (*sc.* אַנְשֵׁי), Meg. i. 2; שָׁלֹשׁ אוּמָּנִיּוֹת עוֹשִׂין . . . הַחַיָּיטִין . . . three handicrafts may work . . . tailors . . ., Pes. iv. 6; בֵּית הַפַּרְוָה וּבַקֹּדֶשׁ הָיְתָה the house of Parva, and it was in the holy precincts (*sc.* לִשְׁכַּת), Yo. iii. 6.

452. When the verb precedes the noun it may, sometimes, be used in an impersonal sense without reference to the gender and number of the following subject: הוּתַּר מִקְצָתוֹ its portion was made permissible, Ned. ix. 6; הִגִּיעַ עֵת the time has reached, Ta. i. 4; הָיָה לָהּ שְׁעַת הַכּשֶׁר it had a time when it was fit, Zeb. xi. 2; but Ḥul. iv. 7: הָיְתָה לָהּ שְׁעַת; יִלָּקַח בּוֹ עוֹלוֹת burnt-offerings shall be bought with it, Šeq. vi. 6; נָפַל לְתוֹכוֹ מַיִם; נָפַל לְתוֹכוֹ מַשְׁקִין there fell into it water, liquids, &c.; Pa. ix. 1.

3. Sentences expressing an Oath or a Vow.

453. Sentences expressing an oath are introduced by an imprecation followed by אִם, which then assumes a negative force, and by אִם לֹא with an affirmative force, as in BH (Ges.-K.,

§ 149 d). The tense used is the perf. for the past, and the imperf. for the future.

Exx. יֵהָנֶה סַם הַמָּוֶת בְּאַחַד בָּנֶיהָ שֶׁל אוֹתָהּ אִשָּׁה אִם נֶהֱנֵתִי מִדִּינָרְךָ כְלוּם may poison have enjoyment of one of the children of that woman (the speaker's), if I have enjoyed anything of thy dinar, Giṭ. 35 a = I have not, &c.; אֲקַפֵּחַ אֶת בָּנַי אִם לֹא רָאִיתִי אֶת שִׁמְעוֹן[1] may I cut down my children if I have not seen Simeon, j. Yo. i. 1 (end) = I did see, &c. יָבוֹא עָלַי אִם רָאוּ קוֹרוֹת בֵּיתִי שַׂעֲרוֹת רֹאשִׁי may (some evil) come upon me if the rafters of my house have ever seen the hair of my head, j. Meg. i. 12 = they have never seen, &c.; יָבוֹא עָלַי אִם נִתְכַּוַּנְתִּי לְכָךְ . . . if I intended this, j. So. iii. 3 = I did not intend this. So even after a prayer for a blessing אִם לֹא still has an affirmative force, though really the opposite is meant by the speaker: אֶרְאֶה בְנֶחָמָה אִם לֹא הָרַגְתִּי עֵד זוֹמֵם may I behold the consolation (of Israel)! I have slain a false witness[2]; אֶרְאֶה בְנֶחָמָה אִם לֹא שָׁפַכְתָּ דָּם נָקִי may I behold the consolation! thou hast shed innocent blood, Mak. 5 b; San. 37 b; j. Mak. vii. 11.

454. So with the formula קוֹנָם:[3] (קוֹנָם) אִם אָכַלְתִּי, אִם שָׁתִיתִי *qonam*, I have not eaten, I have not drunk; קוֹנָם אִם לֹא רָאִיתִי . . . *q.*, I have seen . . ., Ned. iii. 2; [4](קוֹנָם) אִם אֶרְחַץ אִם לֹא אֶרְחַץ אִם אֶתְקַשֵּׁט אִם לֹא אֶתְקַשֵּׁט *q.*, I will not wash, I will wash; I will not adorn myself, I will adorn myself, ib. xi. 1. So ק׳ אִי (= אִם) אַתָּה נֶהֱנֶה לִי *q.*, thou wilt not benefit of mine, BQ ix. 10.[5]

[1] This particular oath was peculiar to R. Tarphon. Later generations disapproved of this form of oath, cf. BM 85a.

[2] This is probably a euphemism for a curse = לא אראה בנחמה; cf. above, בניה של אותה אשה, for בָּנַי; so איבי דוד 1 Sam. xx. 16; xxv. 22; see Driver's notes, *ad loc.*

[3] The origin and exact meaning of this word are obscure; cf. the Lexicons and Cooke, *N. Sem. Inscriptions*, pp. 33–4. Perhaps it is a popular word for curse.

[4] קוֹנָם is to be understood; cf. the paraphrase in the Talmud babli, Ned. 79 b.

[5] L has ק׳ שֶׁאַתְּ׳, so also in citation, Ned. 42 a: שֶׁאַתָּה. The emendation of Albrecht, § 15 a, is unnecessary.

455. So with the formula שְׁבוּעָה expressed or understood: מַשְׁבִּיעַ אֲנִי (שְׁבוּעָה) אִם לֹא רָאִיתִי (an oath), I have seen, Š^e^bu. iii. 8; מַשְׁבִּיעַ אֲנִי עֲלֵיכֶם אִם לֹא תָבוֹאוּ וּתְעִידוּנִי I adjure you to come and give evidence for me, ib. iv. 5 ff.

456. Often, however, such sentences are introduced by שֶׁ־, preceded by various formulae, and construed regularly (like כִּי in BH, e.g. 1 Sam. xiv. 44).

Exx.: נִשְׁבַּע אֲנִי בְּשִׁמְךָ הַגָּדוֹל שֶׁאֵינִי זָז I swear by thy great name: I will not move, Ta'a. iii. 10; נִשְׁבַּע הַקָּדוֹשׁ בָּרוּךְ הוּא שֶׁאֲנִי גוֹאֵל אֶתְכֶם the Holy One, blessed be He, swore I will redeem you, So. 13 a; מַשְׁבִּיעִין אָנוּ עָלֶיךָ . . . שֶׁלֹּא תְשַׁנֶּה דָבָר we adjure thee . . . that thou shalt not change anything, Yo. i. 3; אָמֵן שֶׁלֹּא נִטְמֵאתִי אָמֵן שֶׁלֹּא סָטִיתִי Amen, I have not been defiled; Amen, I have not gone astray, So. ii. 6; אֲקַפֵּחַ אֶת בָּנַי שֶׁזּוֹ הֲלָכָה מְקוּפַּחַת may I cut down my children: this is a mutilated *halaka*, Oh. xvi. 1; Šab. 116 a; with לֹא j. Yo. i. 1; הָעֲבוֹדָה שֶׁאֲגַלְּחֲךָ לַשָּׁמַיִם by the Service I will shave thee for heaven, N^e^d. 9 b; but more frequently הָעֲבוֹדָה is used as an exclamation in apposition, and without שֶׁ־: הָעֲבוֹדָה . . . לֹא חִסַּרְתֶּם וְלֹא הוֹתַרְתֶּם you have made it neither less nor more, B^e^r. 34 b; הָעֲבוֹדָה כָּךְ שָׁמַעְתִּי מֵרַבִּי . . . thus I heard from Rabbi, Y^e^b. 32 b.

457. So also are other formulae used in an asseveration as exclamations: הַמָּעוֹן הַזֶּה לֹא זָזָה יָדָהּ by this habitation (the Temple)! her hand did not move, K^e^t. ii. 9; בְּרִית הֵן הֵן הַדְּבָרִים שֶׁנֶּאֶמְרוּ לְמֹשֶׁה בְּסִינַי by the Covenant! these are the very words which were told to Moses on Sinai, P^e^s. 38 b; גַּפָּהּ שֶׁל רוֹמִי אֵינִי מַנִּיחֲךָ by the Capitol of Rome! I will not leave thee, M^e^n. 41 a; cf. § 305 חַיֶּיךָ וְחַיֵּי רֹאשְׁךָ לֹא שָׁעָה זוֹ בִּלְבַד by thy life and by the life of thy head! not this hour alone . . . B^e^r. 3 a.

458. Likewise, שְׁבוּעָה may be followed by שֶׁ־ with the regular construction: שְׁבוּעָה שֶׁאוֹכַל וְשֶׁלֹּא אוֹכַל שֶׁאָכַלְתִּי וְשֶׁלֹּא אָכַלְתִּי an oath. I will eat, I will not eat; I have eaten, I have not eaten, Š^e^bu.

iii. 1 ff.; but also without -שֶׁ: שְׁבוּעָה לֹא אוֹכַל לָךְ, beside שְׁבוּעָה שֶׁאוֹכַל לָךְ Ned. ii. 2. An affirmative after -שְׁבוּעָה שֶׁ can, however, also be intended to have a negative force: ש׳ שֶׁאוֹכַל לָךְ an oath, I will *not* eat of thine, ib. Cf. the explanation of Abbaye, Ned. 16 a; Šebu. 19 b, f. So . . . ש׳ שֶׁאֲנִי יָשֵׁן שֶׁאֲנִי מְדַבֵּר . . . that I will not sleep, that I will not speak, ib. 1, in L. In edd. שֶׁאֵינִי is probably a correction, cf. the comment of R. Nissim on this passage, Ned. 14 b.

So with the formula -קָרְבָּן שֶׁ, an affirmative is equivalent to a negative: קָרְבָּן שֶׁאוֹכַל לָךְ what I will eat of thine be *qorban* = I will not eat . . ., Ned. i. 4.

459. In expressing a vow, קוֹנָם, followed by an affirmative is equivalent to a negative. It is construed with a participial verb with the meaning of a future tense, and if the subject is a pronoun, it takes the introductory particle -שֶׁ: קוֹנָם שֶׁאֲנִי יָשֵׁן שֶׁאֲנִי מְדַבֵּר שֶׁאֲנִי מְהַלֵּךְ *qonam*, I will not sleep, speak, walk, Ned. ii. 1;[1] קוֹנָם שֶׁאַתָּה נֶהֱנֶה לִי *q.*, thou wilt not benefit of me, ib. viii. 7. The object is placed first, as usual in emphatic speech: קוֹנָם סוּכָּה שֶׁאֲנִי עוֹשֶׂה לוּלָב שֶׁאֲנִי נוֹטֵל *q.*, I will not make a tabernacle; I will not take a *lulab*, ii. 2; קוֹנָם יַיִן זֶה שֶׁאֲנִי טוֹעֵם *q.*, this wine that I will not taste, iv. 10; קוֹנָם לְבֵיתְךָ שֶׁאֲנִי נִכְנָס שָׂדְךָ שֶׁאֲנִי לוֹקֵחַ *q.*, that I will not enter thy house; that I will not buy thy field, v. 3. But without -שֶׁ when the subject is a noun: קוֹנָם ` פִּי מְדַבֵּר עִמָּךְ יָדִי עוֹשָׂה עִמָּךְ *q.*, that my mouth will not speak with thee, that my hand will not work with thee, i. 4; קוֹנָם אִשְׁתִּי וּבָנַי נֶהֱנִים לִי *q.*, that my wife and children will not benefit of me, iii. 5.

4. Interrogative Sentences.

460. A question is often expressed in MH, as in BH (Ges.-K., § 150 a), merely by the emphasis of the voice, and without any

[1] The reading in edd. שֶׁאֵינִי is an erroneous correction, as shown by the citation from viii. 7. Cf. also H. Laible, שאני *oder* שאיני, *MGWJ.* vol. lx, pp. 29–40.

special introductory particle: עַד שֶׁבְּחֶבְרוֹן as far as those in Hebron? Yo. iii. 1; הִתְרֵיתֶם בּוֹ did you warn him? San. v. 1; הָיִיתָ מַחֲזִיר לוֹ would'st thou have returned to him? Ber. 32 b; so with copulative וְ: וְלֹא אֶבְכֶּה shall I not weep? ib. 28 b. Especially in long argumentative questions: אִם הֶעֱלוּ חוּלִּים . . . תַּעֲלֶה תְרוּמָה . . . if common things raised . . . should *teruma* raise . . . ? Ter. v. 4; אִם אָמַרְתָּ בַּפֶּסַח . . . תֹּאמַר בִּזְבָחִים . . . if thou didst say it in case of the paschal offering . . . wilt thou say . . . ? Pes. vi. 5.

461. More frequently the interrogative sentence is introduced by a particle. The BH interrogative הֲ is rare in MH, e.g. הֲתַחְמִיר זוֹ מִן הַגֶּפֶן wilt thou make this more grave than the vine? Kil. iii. 7; הֲכָזֶה רָאִיתָ did you see like this? RH ii. 8. It is, however, common with לֹא, which is further strengthened by the copulative וְ used in an interrogative force (cf. last §; Ges.-K., § 150 a): וַהֲלֹא יֵשׁ שֶׁאֵינָן מוֹסְקִין but are not there some who do not gather their olives . . . ? Pea viii. 1; וַהֲלֹא מִסֵּפֶר כְּתוּבָּתָהּ נִלְמוֹד but do we not learn from the text of her marriage settlement? Yeb. xvi. 3; וַהֲלֹא ר׳ יְהוֹשֻׁעַ אָמַר but did not R. Joshua say? Ber. 27 b. But frequently the interrogative particle is omitted: לֹא לִמַּדְתָּנוּ didst thou not teach us? Ber. ii. 5; לֹא יַעֲלֶה וְיִטְּלֶנָּהּ should he not go up and take it? Ber. 53 b; לֹא שָׂדֶה הִיא זוֹ is not this a field? 'Er. 53 b.

462. The particle וְכִי, which is rare in BH as an interrogative (Isa. xxxvi. 19; Job xxxix. 27) is very common in MH as introducing a lively question: וְכִי יָדָיו שֶׁל מֹשֶׁה עוֹשׂוֹת מִלְחָמָה but was it the hands of Moses that made war? RH iii. 8; וְכִי מִפְּנֵי שֶׁהִיא אַחֲרוֹנָה נִשְׂכָּרָה but should she gain because she is last? Ket. x. 5; וְכִי כָל הָעֵצִים כְּשֵׁרִים but are all woods fit . . . ? Ta. ii. 3. Frequently וְכִי stands even before another interrogative particle to give it greater emphasis: וְכִי הֵיאַךְ הֶעָנִי הַזֶּה מַחֲלִיף but how can this poor man exchange? Pea v. 2; וְכִי מִפְּנֵי מָה אֵין מְמִירִים but wherefore may they not exchange . . . ? Tem. i. 1; וְכִי בְאֵיזוֹ שָׁעָה הַמְּמוּנֶּה בָא but at what hour does the overseer come? Tam. i. 2.

463. The interrogative adverb מָה is often used as an introductory particle in long argumentative questions (קַל וָחוֹמֶר): מָה אִם הַפֶּסַח . . . חַיָּיב הַזְּבָחִים . . . אֵינוֹ דִין שֶׁיְּהֵא חַיָּיב what! if the Passover offering . . . is it not justice that he should be liable . . .? Pes. vi. 5; מָה אִם עֶצֶם כִּשְׂעוֹרָה . . . אֵינוֹ דִין שֶׁיְּהֵא נָזִיר מְגַלֵּחַ what! if a bone like a barley . . ., is it not justice that the Nazirite should shave . . .? Naz. vii. 4; וּמָה אִילּוּ טָעָה . . . שֶׁמָּא עָשָׂה כְלוּם and what! if he had erred . . . has he done anything? ib. v. 3, &c.

464. In later MH (not in the Mishna), a question can also be introduced by כְּלוּם (§ 437): כְּלוּם שָׁתִינוּ have we drunk . . .? כְּלוּם הִכִּירְךָ ר׳ גַּמְלִיאֵל מֵעוֹלָם has Rabban Gamaliel ever known thee? ʽEr. 64 b; כְּלוּם יֵשׁ אָדָם שֶׁיּוֹדֵעַ is there anyone who controverts . . .? Ber. 27 b; כְּלוּם חָסֵר לְבֵית הַמֶּלֶךְ is anything needed for the king's house? כְּלוּם יֵשׁ סְעוּדָה בְּלֹא טוֹרַח is there a feast without effort? Šab. 153 a; 89 a; Pes. 66 a; 118 b; Ber. 10 a; ʽAr. 15 a, &c.

Further, שֶׁמָּא ('perhaps'): שֶׁמָּא אֵינוֹ צָרִיךְ לוֹמַר is it unnecessary to say? j. Giṭ. i. 1; שֶׁמָּא מְגוֹרֶשֶׁת הִיא is she perhaps divorced? ib. viii. 5; שֶׁמָּא כְלוּם הוּא is it anything? j. So. i. 1.

465. An indirect question is construed just like a direct question: הַחַזָּן רוֹאֶה הֵיכָן הַתִּינוֹקוֹת קוֹרִין the beadle sees where the children read, Šab. i. 3; בּוֹאוּ וְהָפִיסוּ מִי מַעֲלֶה . . . come and cast lots who should bring up . . ., Tam. v. 2; שָׁמִין אוֹתָהּ כַּמָּה הִיא רְאוּיָה לַעֲשׂוֹת they value it how much is it capable of producing, BM ix. 3

466. In a disjunctive question, the first is formed like an ordinary question, the second is introduced by אוֹ: וְכִי מֵרוֹב הָעֳמָרִים יוֹפִי כּוֹחוֹ שֶׁל בַּעַל הַבַּיִת אוֹ הוּרַע כּוֹחוֹ is the power of the owner improved because of the multitude of the sheaves, or is it worsened? Pea vi. 6; הַכָּזֶה רָאִיתָ אוֹ כָזֶה hast thou seen like this, or like this? RH ii. 8 (L has הֲבָוֶה after או); תְּפִלַּת עַרְבִית רְשׁוּת או חוֹבָה is evening prayer optional, or obligatory? Ber. 27 b.

An indirect disjunctive question is introduced by אִם in both clauses: אֵינִי יוֹדֵעַ אִם הֶחֱזַרְתִּי לָךְ אִם (L וְאִם) לֹא הֶחֱזַרְתִּי לָךְ I do not know whether I have restored to thee, or not, BQ x. 7; v. 1 וְאֵין יָדוּעַ אִם בֶּן ט׳ לָרִאשׁוֹן אִם (L וְאִם) בֶּן ז׳ לָאַחֲרוֹן; (L: אִם . . . וְאִם) it is not known whether it is a child of nine months of the first, or of seven months of the last, Yeb. xi. 6; נִיכַּר אִם תַּלְמִיד חָכָם הוּא אִם לָאו it is recognized whether he is a scholar, or not, Ber. 50 a; Pes. 61 a; 9 b. Rarely by אִם . . . או: אֵינוֹ יָדוּעַ אִם בְּלוּלוֹת הֵן או לְאַיִן נָפְלָה it is not known whether they are mixed, or where it fell, Ter. iv. 11.

5. Desiderative Sentences.

467. A wish may be expressed by the simple imperfect (§ 319): יַנִּיחַ לָנוּ ר״ט let R. Tarphon leave us alone, BM iv. 3; especially in prayers: וְנִהְיֶה כֻּלָּנוּ יוֹדְעֵי תוֹרָתֶךָ let us all be skilled in thy law, Ber. 11 b; הַמָּקוֹם יְמַלֵּא חֶסְרוֹנָךְ may the Omnipresent make good thy loss, ib. 16 b; בַּעַל הַגְּמוּל יְשַׁלֵּם לָכֶם may the Lord of requital pay you, Ket. 8 b.

468. More frequently the imperf. is preceded by the formula: יְהִי רָצוֹן שֶׁ־ may it be the (divine) will that . . .; יְהִי רָצוֹן שֶׁתֵּלֵד אִשְׁתִּי זָכָר may my wife bear a male; יְהִי רָצוֹן שֶׁלֹּא יְהוּ אֵלּוּ בְתוֹךְ בֵּיתִי may these not be in my house, Ber. ix. 3; or with the full formula: יְהִי רָצוֹן מִלְּפָנֶיךָ ה׳ אֱלֹהֵינוּ . . . שֶׁ־ Ab. v. 20; Ber. 16 b; 17 a, &c.; Singer, pp. 7, 14, &c.

469. A wish can also be expressed by מִי with the imperf., as in BH (Ges.-K., § 151 a, b): מִי יְגַלֶּה עָפָר מֵעֵינֶיךָ oh, that the dust may be removed from thine eyes, So. v. 2; מִי יִתֵּן לִי תֵּל זֶה; מִי יִתֵּן לִי חָרִיץ זֶה oh, that one would give me this heap, this trench, Meg. 14 a. It may be noted that מִי יִתֵּן is used in its literal sense. It is never found in MH in the derived BH sense: oh, would! (Ges.-K., § 151 b).

470. In later Aggadic diction a wish is also expressed by הַלְוַאי (= BH לוּ, § 304): הַלְוַאי אוֹתִי עָזָבוּ וְאֶת תּוֹרָתִי שָׁמָרוּ would, they had forsaken Me, and kept My Torah, j. Ḥag. i; הַלְוַאי יְהֵא חֶלְקִי בָּאָרֶץ הַזֹּאת oh, would that my portion were in this land, Gen. R. 39; הַלְוַאי תְּהֵא מַעֲלַת חֵן לְפָנַי oh, would that she were graceful before me, ib. 89. הַלְוַאי also stands at the end of the sentence as an exclamation: טוֹל אוֹתָהּ בְּחִנָּם וְהַלְוַאי take it for nothing, oh do! M^e^g. 14 a.

6. Negative Sentences.

471. The uses of the negative adverbs לֹא, אֵין, אַל follow the same rules as in BH. לֹא is used to negative verbal clauses, while אֵין is used to negative noun clauses. Sometimes, however, participles are negatived by לֹא; cf. above, §§ 339–40. אַל is only used with the imperfect to express a negative wish, an exhortation, or a mild prohibition. With ordinary prohibitions, as well as in negative statements with the perfect and imperfect, לֹא is used: אַל תִּהְיוּ כַעֲבָדִים be not like servants, Ab. i. 3; אַל תַּעַשׂ עַצְמְךָ make not thyself, ib. 8; לֹא יָקֵל אָדָם אֶת רֹאשׁוֹ one must not be light-headed (i.e. guilty of levity), B^e^r. ix. 5.

472. The form בַּל is found for לֹא in citations of Biblical prohibitions: הוּא עוֹבֵר עַל בַּל תִּגְרַע he transgresses (the command) 'thou shalt not diminish'; הוּא עוֹבֵר עַל בַּל תּוֹסִיף . . . 'thou shalt not add' (Deut. xiii. 1); לֹא נֶאֱמַר בַּל תּוֹסִיף לֹא נֶאֱמַר בַּל תִּגְרַע 'thou shalt not add', 'thou shalt not diminish' was not said, Z^e^b. viii. 10; כָּל שֶׁהוּא בְּבַל תָּשׁוּב all that is in (the category of) 'thou shalt not return' (Deut. xxiv. 19), Pea vi. 4 (L has בל for בבל); שֶׁמּוּזְהָרִים עָלָיו בְּבַל יֵרָאֶה וּבְבַל יִמָּצֵא about which one is prohibited: 'it shall not be seen', and 'it shall not be found' (Exod. xiii. 7; xii. 19); P^e^s. iii. 3 (L has וּבַל . . . בַּל); אָסוּר בְּבַל יֵרָאֶה וּבְבַל יִמָּצֵא

prohibited by (the command) 'thou . . .', ib. ix. 3. Contrast: הוּא בְּלֹא יָבוֹא he is in (the category of) 'he shall not come'), (Deut. xxiii. 3); Y^e^b. iv. 13; הֲרֵי זֶה בְּלֹא יַחֵל דְּבָרוֹ lo, this one is in (the category of) 'he shall not profane his word' (Num. xxx. 3); N^e^d. ii. 1 (L has בל for בלא). Perhaps בל, בבל is not a genuine grammatical form, but merely a scribal contraction for בלא = בל'.

473. The negative is sometimes repeated to add emphasis: אֵין לָהֶם לֹא כָךְ וְלֹא כָךְ they have not, either so or so, Šab. 26 a; לֹא עָשָׂה וְלֹא כְלוּם he has done nothing at all, Pes. 89 b; N^e^d. 7 b. Emphasis is also expressed by כָּל עִיקָּר at the end of the clause; אֵינוֹ מְעָרֵב כָּל עִיקָּר he does not make an *'erub* at all 'Er. iii. 6; אֵין מַשְׁגִּיחִין . . . כָּל עִיקָּר one must not observe . . . at all, Be. iii. 6.

474. In a series of parallel verbs, the negative is sometimes expressed only with the first verb, but its force is extended also to the following verbs, as in BH (cf. Ges.-K., § 152 z): לֹא יִקּוֹב אָדָם . . . וִימַלְּאֶנָּה . . . וְיִתְּנֶנָּה one must not perforate . . . and fill it . . . and place it . . ., Šab. ii. 4; לֹא יִקְשׁוֹר . . . וְיִמְשׁוֹךְ one must not bind . . . and draw, ib. v. 3; 'Er. x. 5, 6, 9; אֵין מַשְׁקִין וְשׁוֹחֲטִין one may not give to drink nor slay . . ., Be. v. 7.

475. שֶׁמָּא is used, like פֶּן in BH, to introduce a clause after a verb of fear or caution, expressed or implied, and is then equivalent to a negative: הָיָה יָרֵא שֶׁמָּא תִתְעַבֵּר he was afraid, lest it be intercalated (= שֶׁלֹּא), 'Er. iii. 7; הֱוֵי זָהִיר . . . שֶׁמָּא . . . יִלְמְדוּ לְשַׁקֵּר be careful . . . that they should not learn . . . to lie, Ab. i. 9, 11; הִזָּהֲרוּ שֶׁמָּא תִגְּעוּ take care that you touch not, Ḥag. iii. 8 (L; edd. שֶׁלֹּא); שֶׁמָּא יְקַלְקְלוּ (for fear) lest they spoil, Ḥul. i. 1; שֶׁמָּא יַקְדִּים קָנֶה לְוֶשֶׁט (for fear) lest the windpipe come before the gullet, Ta'a. 5 b.

476. Note.—In colloquial speech, viz. in vows, לֹא was sometimes joined with the following noun almost like a preposition: לֹא חוּלִּין = לְחוּלִּין N^e^d. i. 3; לֹא קָרְבָּן = לְקָרְבָּן ib. 4 (L has

לֹא חוּלִּין ,לֹא קָרְבָּן; but cf. the discussion in Ned. 11 a, b; 13 b, and the comment of R. Nissim on Ned. i. 3. In ii. 1, L also has לֹא חוּלִּין = לָחוּלִּין).

7. Relative Clauses.

477. The construction of relative clauses has already been described in the treatment of -שֶׁ (§ 420 f.). Here we may add that sometimes a relative clause stands in apposition to the noun it qualifies, and without -שֶׁ: לֹא זוֹ הִיא דֶרֶךְ מוֹצִיאַתּוּ מִידֵי עֲבֵרָה this is not the way that brings him out of the power of a transgression, Yeb. xv. 6, 7; יֵשׁ בּוֹ דְּרָכִים שָׁוֶוה לְחַיָּה it has ways in which it is like a (wild) animal, Bik. ii. 8; אֵין לוֹ מִי יַתִּירֶנּוּ it has none that will make it permissible, Men. iv. 3 (cf. § 422). Perhaps here belong also cases with the demonstrative before the noun when followed by a verb: זֶה מִדְרָשׁ דָּרַשׁ = שֶׁדָּרַשׁ; זוֹ עֵדוּת הֵעִיד = שֶׁהֵעִיד, cf. above, § 411.

8. Circumstantial Clauses.

478. The circumstances attending an action, or the subject or object of an action, are usually expressed by a dependent clause. Such a clause may be a simple relative clause, or, more frequently, a relative or other clause under the government of a preposition. Exx.: יוֹשְׁבִים שֶׁלֹּא מְסוּמָּכִים sitting without being supported, Kel. ii. 2; אֵין טוֹמְנִים . . . בַּעֲשָׂבִים בִּזְמַן שֶׁהֵם לַחִים one may not hide . . . in grass when it is moist, Šab. iv. 1; נוֹלַד כְּשֶׁהוּא מָהוּל he was born circumcized, Šab. 135 a; נִכְנַס ר"ט בְּלֹא מִתְכַּוֵּן R. Tarphon entered without intention, 'Er. iv. 4; חוֹלֵץ תְּפִלִּין בְּרָחוֹק ד' אַמּוֹת he removes the *tephillin* at a distance of four cubits, Ber. 23 a.

Sometimes a participle or adjective in apposition will express a circumstance: קוֹרֵא עוֹמֵד; קוֹצָה חַלָּתָהּ עֲרוּמָּה, cf. § 357.

479. More frequently, however, the circumstantial clause is co-ordinated with the principal clause either with the copulative וְ, or without.

(i) Without the copula: שְׂאוֹר . . . שֶׁנָּפְלוּ . . . לֹא בָזֶה כְּדֵי לְחַמֵּץ leaven . . . that fell . . . there not being sufficient to leaven, Or. ii. 11, 14, 15; הָיָה רָחוֹק . . . י׳ אַמּוֹת אוֹמְרִים לוֹ when he was 10 cubits distant . . . they would say to him, San. vi. 3; יָלְדָה עוֹדָהּ שִׁפְחָה she gave birth while still a slave, viii. 1; בָּא לוֹ . . . הַסְּגָן בִּימִינוֹ he came . . . the deputy at his right, Yo. iii. 9; so Šab. i. 1; Pes. viii. 1, &c.

(ii) With copula: בָּא לוֹ אֵצֶל פָּרוֹ וּפָרוֹ הָיָה עוֹמֵד he came to his bullock, the bullock standing, Yo. iii. 8; בֵּית הַפַּרְוָוה וּבַקֹּדֶשׁ הָיְתָה ib. 6; מְמָאֶנֶת וְהִיא קְטַנָּה she can repudiate while a minor, Yeb. xiii. 1; נָפְלָה עֲלֵיהֶם מַפּוֹלֶת וְהֵם מְגוּלִּים earth fell upon them while (the leaves) were bare, Ma'a. v. 2; מְכַסָּהּ וְעוֹדָהּ בְּבֵית אָבִיהָ he covers her while she is still in her father's house, Ket. vi. 5; vii. 8; Nid. x. 1; נוֹטֵל אָדָם אֶת בְּנוֹ וְהָאֶבֶן בְּיָדוֹ one may carry his son with a stone in his (the son's) hand, Šab. xxi. 1; חָלָב שֶׁחֲלָבוֹ גוֹי וְאֵין יִשְׂרָאֵל רוֹאֵהוּ milk which a heathen has milked without an Israelite watching him, 'AZ ii. 9, 10.

480. For the sake of emphasis, a circumstantial clause can precede its principal clause: עוֹדֵהוּ הַסַּל עַל כְּתֵפוֹ קוֹרֵא he reads while the basket is still on his shoulder, Bik. iii. 6; מַטָּהּ עַל צִדָּהּ וְהִיא נוֹפֶלֶת it falls off as he tilts it on its side, Šab. xxi. 2; iv. 2; הוּא נוֹטֵל אֶת הַגְּלָלִים וְהַחֲרָסִים נוֹפְלִים the potsherds fall, when he takes away the dung, Kel. iii. 4. Cf. in BH, Ges.-K., §§ 116 v, 142 e; Driver, *Tenses*, § 166 ff.

9. Causal Clauses.

481. A clause giving the reason of a preceding or following sentence can be introduced by a variety of conjunctions.

By the fossilized verb הוֹאִיל, followed by the copula (§ 302, note): הוֹאִיל וְנִרְאֶה כְּתַבְנִית הַכְּרָמִים הֲרֵי זֶה כֶּרֶם because it looks like the shape of a vineyard, it is a vineyard, Kil. v. 1; הוֹאִיל וְלֹא הָיְתָה כַּוָּנָתוֹ לְכָךְ since his intention was not for this, ʿEr. iv. 4.

482. By שֶׁ־, שֶׁאֵין, שֶׁלֹּא, לֹא שֶׁ־: שֶׁעַל הַיַּיִן הוּא אוֹמֵר for on wine he says, Bᵉr. vi. 1; שֶׁלֹּא נֶחְשְׁדוּ because they are not suspected, Šᵉbi. ix. i; שֶׁאֵינוֹ יָכוֹל לוֹמַר for he cannot say, Bik. i. 4; לֹא שֶׁהָיוּ צְרִיכִים לָהֶם not because they needed them, RH ii. 6.

By שֶׁ־ combined with other conjunctions: מִפְּנֵי שֶׁהוּא מְכַבֶּה because he extinguishes, Šab. iii. 6; מִפְּנֵי שֶׁהֵן לִירוֹקָה because they are for jaundice, ib. xiv. 3; מִפְּנֵי שֶׁלֹּא שָׁווּ because they are not equal, ib. vii. 4. Before a noun מִפְּנֵי stands as *regens* without שֶׁ־: מִפְּנֵי בִּיטּוּל בֵּית הַמִּדְרָשׁ because of the neglect of the house of study, ib. xvi. 1; מִפְּנֵי הַכָּתוּב בַּתּוֹרָה because of what is written in the Torah, Bik. i. 3.

לְפִי שֶׁ־: לְפִי שֶׁאֵינוֹ מִן הַמּוּכָן because it is not prepared, Šab. iii. 6; לְפִי שֶׁאֵינוֹ מַאֲכַל בְּרִיאִים because it is not the food of healthy persons, ib. xiv. 3.

מֵאַחַר שֶׁ־: מֵאַחַר שֶׁשְּׁנֵיהֶם יְכוֹלִים because both are able, BM x. 6; מֵאַחַר שֶׁהֵעַדְתָּ לָנוּ since thou hast testified to us, Yᵉb. vii. 3.

בִּשְׁבִיל שֶׁ־: בִּשְׁבִיל שֶׁאֲנִי זָכָר הִפְסַדְתִּי because I am a male should I lose! BB ix. 1; בִּשְׁבִיל שֶׁכְּנַעֲנִי זֶה הֶרְאָה בְאֶצְבָּעוֹ because this Canaanite has shown with his finger, So. 46 a.

עַל שֶׁ־: עַל שֶׁהָרַג אֶת הַנֶּפֶשׁ because he slew a person, ʿEd. vi. 1.

עַל שֵׁם שֶׁ־: עַל שֵׁם שֶׁפָּסַח הקב״ה because the Holy One, blessed be He, passed over, Pᵉs. x. 5; עַל שֵׁם שֶׁנִּגְאֲלוּ; עַל שֵׁם שֶׁמֵּרֵרוּ because they were redeemed, they embittered, ib.

מִשּׁוּם שֶׁ־: מִשּׁוּם שֶׁנֶּאֱמַר because it is said, Bik. i. 2.

10. Conditional Sentences.

483. The construction of conditional sentences in MH follows in the main the principles of similar sentences in BH (Ges.-K., § 159).

The great variety of these sentences may be classified under two heads: those without an introductory particle, and those with an introductory particle.

484. (i) Without an introductory particle.

The relation between the protasis and the apodosis can be expressed by mere juxtaposition. This happens only when the condition is conceived as already fulfilled. The verb in the protasis is always the perfect; in the apodosis it is usually a participle, but sometimes a perfect. But when a command or prohibition is implied, the apodosis takes the imperfect (cf. above, § 310).

Exx.: נִמְצָא הַגַּנָּב מְשַׁלֵּם תַּשְׁלוּמֵי כֶפֶל, טָבַח וּמָכַר מְשַׁלֵּם ד׳ וה׳ if the thief has been found, he pays a double payment; if he slew it, or sold it, he pays four- or five-fold, BM iii. 1; נִגְמַר הַדִּין מוֹצִיאִין אוֹתוֹ when the case is finished, they lead him forth, San. vi. 1; קָרָא וְלֹא דִקְדֵּק בְּאוֹתִיּוֹתֶיהָ . . . יָצָא if he read, but was not careful in (the enunciation of) its letters . . . he has discharged his duty, Bᵉr. ii. 3; קָרָא וְטָעָה יַחֲזוֹר if he read and made a mistake, he must return . . ., ib.; נִזְכַּר שֶׁהוּא בַעַל קֶרִי לֹא יַפְסִיק if he recollected that he had an issue, he should not stop, ib. iii. 5; לֹא כִיסָּהוּ מִבְּעוֹד יוֹם לֹא יְכַסֶּנּוּ מִשֶּׁתֶּחְשַׁךְ if he did not cover it while it was day, he must not cover it after it has become dark, Šab. iv. 2.

Here may be mentioned the sentences with an indefinite subject, such as a determinate participle, or מִי שֶׁ־, especially with Nominative Absolute, which are equivalent to a conditional sentence in English; cf. §§ 436, 442.

485. (ii) With an introductory particle.

אִם. אִם introduces a condition that has already been fulfilled in the past or that is capable of fulfilment in the present or future. In the first case, the protasis always takes the perfect, since the condition has already been fulfilled. The apodosis takes the perfect, if its act lies in the past; the participle, if the act lies in the present or the future, and the imperfect, if a command is implied.

Exx.: אִם כִּיוֵּן לִבּוֹ יָצָא if he directed his attention, he has discharged his duty, B^e^r. ii. 1; אִם נִתְרַפֵּא נִתְרַפֵּא if he was healed, he was healed (then it does not matter), Šab. xxii. 6; אִם מֵיאֲנָה מֵיאֲנָה if she has repudiated (her marriage), then it is a repudiation, Y^e^b. xiii. 7; אִם בָּא לְהוֹסִיף מוֹסִיף if he has come to add, he may add, Šab. 51 a; אִם לֹא עָלָה עַמּוּד הַשַּׁחַר חַיָּיבִין אַתֶּם if dawn has not risen, you are bound to . . . B^e^r. i. 1; with the apodosis first: חָתָן פָּטוּר . . . אִם לֹא עָשָׂה מַעֲשֶׂה a bridegroom is absolved . . . if he has not performed the act, ib. ii. 5; אִם לֹא הֵבִיא כְּלִי מֵעֶרֶב שַׁבָּת מְבִיאוֹ בַּשַּׁבָּת if he has not brought the instrument on the eve of the Sabbath, he may bring it on the Sabbath, Šab. xix. 1; אִם מֵת יַנִּיחוּהוּ if dead, they must leave him, Yo. viii. 7; אִם רָאִיתָ תַּלְמִיד חָכָם שֶׁעָבַר עֲבֵרָה . . . אַל תְּהַרְהֵר . . . if thou hast seen a scholar commit a transgression . . . do not think . . ., B^e^r. 19 a.

486. When the condition has not been fulfilled, but is capable of fulfilment in the present or the future, the protasis takes the participle, or, less frequently, an imperfect, or even a perfect in the sense of a *futurum exactum* (cf. § 313). The apodosis takes a participle, or an imperfect when a command is implied, or even an imperative.

Exx.: אִם רָצָה לִקְרוֹת קוֹרֵא if he wishes to read . . ., he may read, B^e^r. ii. 8; אִם יְכוֹלִין לְהַתְחִיל . . . יַתְחִילוּ if they are able to begin . . . let them begin, ib. iii. 2; אִם אֵינוֹ יָכוֹל לֵירֵד יְחַוֵּיר אֶת פָּנָיו if he cannot go down, then he should turn his face, ib. iv. 5; אִם תַּקְנִיטֵנִי גּוֹזְרַנִי if thou wilt provoke me, I shall decree . . ., Šab. 17 a; אִם אֵחַרְתִּי צְאוּ וְשַׁחֲטוּ עָלַי if I shall have been late, go forth and slay for me, P^e^s. ix. 9.

487. Both protasis and apodosis can consist of a noun clause, as in some of the examples above; further: אִם תָּרְמוּ אֵין תְּרוּמָתָם תְּרוּמָה if they did tithe, it is not *teruma*, T^e^r. i. 1; אִם אֵין רְצוֹנוֹ

בַּעֲבוֹדָה זָרָה מִפְּנֵי מָה אֵינוֹ מְבַטְּלָהּ if his wish is against idolatry, why does he not abolish it, 'AZ iv. 7.

488. The subject of the apodosis is sometimes resumed by הֲרֵי with the demonstrative (cf. § 443): אִם יֵשׁ לָהֶם עָלָיו מְזוֹנוֹת הֲרֵי אֵלּוּ לֹא יֹאכְלוּ if they have (to receive) from him food, lo, these shall not eat, Ma'a. iii. 1; וְאִם מִתְחַשֵּׁב הוּא הֲרֵי זֶה לֹא יִרְחוֹץ if he claims importance, lo, this one shall not wash, Šebi. viii. 11.

489. An alternative condition in the negative is expressed by וְאִם לָאו[1] but if not, without the repetition of the verb: אִם כִּיוֵּן לִבּוֹ יָצָא וְאִם לָאו לֹא יָצָא Ber. ii. 1; אִם יְכוֹלִין לְהַתְחִיל . . . וְאִם לָאו לֹא יַתְחִילוּ ib. iii. 2; אִם שְׁגוּרָה תְּפִלָּתִי בְּפִי . . . וְאִם לָאו יוֹדֵעַ אֲנִי if my prayer is fluent in my mouth . . . but if not, I know . . ., ib. v. 5.

490. אִילּוּ, אִילּוּ לֹא, if the condition is represented as not fulfilled. The protasis takes the perfect, the apodosis takes the perfect if the consequence lies in the past, and the imperfect, if the consequence lies in the future: אִילּוּ הָיִיתִי יוֹדֵעַ . . . לֹא הָיִיתִי נוֹדֵר if I had known . . . I would not have vowed, Ned. ix. 2, 4, 5; אִילּוּ הָיִיתָ עוֹמֵד . . . הָיִיתָ מַחֲזִיר לוֹ if thou hast been standing . . . wouldst thou have returned . . .? Ber. 32 b; אִילּוּ לֹא הָיְתָה שְׂרֵפָה חֲמוּרָה לֹא נִתְּנָה if burning had not been heavier, it would not have been given . . ., San. ix. 3; אִילּוּ אֲנִי פָּסַקְתִּי לְעַצְמִי אֵשֵׁב עַד שֶׁיַּלְבִּין רֹאשִׁי if I had fixed it for myself, then I would sit till my head has become white, Ket. xiii. 5.

491. אִלְמָלֵא (or אִלְמָלֵי), אִלְמָלֵא לֹא; אִילּוּלֵי in Palestinian texts (cf. § 302). Like אִילּוּ, these conjunctions introduce a condition that has not been fulfilled. The verb is in the perfect, both in the protasis and apodosis: אִלְמָלֵא הִטִּיחַ בֶּן זַכַּאי אֶת רֹאשׁוֹ . . . לֹא הָיוּ מַשְׁגִּיחִין בּוֹ if the son of Zakkai had shot his head . . ., they would have taken no notice of him, Ber. 34 b; אִלְמָלֵא לֹא נִתְּנָה תוֹרָה הָיִינוּ לְמֵדִין צְנִיעוּת if the Torah had not been given, we would have learnt

[1] Cf. BH ואם לא Gen. xxiv. 39; 1 Sam. ii. 16; ואם אין Gen. xxx. 1; Exod. xxxii. 32.

chastity, &c., ʿEr. 100 b; אִלְמָלֵא כָּעַסְתִּי לֹא נִשְׁתַּיֵּיר if I had been angry, there would not have remained . . ., Ber. 19 a; אִלְמָלֵא לֹא עָלִינוּ אֶלָּא לֶאֱכוֹל . . . דַּיֵּינוּ if we had come up only to eat . . . it would have been sufficient for us, Pes. 8 b. When introducing a noun clause, אִלְמָלֵא (or אִלְמָלֵי) has the sense of 'if not': אִלְמָלֵא (אִילוּלֵי L) מוֹרָאָהּ אִישׁ אֶת רֵעֵהוּ חַיִּים בְּלָעוּ if not the fear of it, they would have swallowed each other alive, Ab. ii. 2; אִלְמָלֵא אוֹהֲבִי זֶה . . . הֲרַגְתִּיךָ if not this my friend . . . I would have killed thee, Ber. 32 a; 58 b; אִלְמָלֵא חוֹנִי אַתָּה גּוֹזְרַנִי עָלֶיךָ if thou wert not Ḥoni I would have decreed against thee, Taʿa. 19 a; Pes. 53 a; אִלְמָלֵא הוּא נִגְנַז סֵפֶר יְחֶזְקֵאל if not for him, the book of Ezekiel would have been hidden away, Šab. 13 b; Yo. 20 b; Meg. 12 b; 24 b; אִלְמָלֵא (L אִילוּלֵי) הִיא לֹא בָרָא . . . but for it, he would not have created . . ., Ned. iii. 11 (end); San. 49 a; 63 a.[1]

492. Hypothetical sentences can also be introduced by other conjunctions. Thus, בִּזְמַן שֶׁ־: בִּזְמַן שֶׁאֵין לָהֶם עָלָיו מְזוֹנוֹת when (if) they have not to receive from him food, Maʿa. iii. 1; בִּזְמַן שֶׁהֵם לַחִים when (if) they are moist, Šab. iv. 1; כְּשֶׁ־: כְּשֶׁיִּהְיוּ בַּעֲלֵי הַדִּין עוֹמְדִים לְפָנֶיךָ יִהְיוּ when litigants stand before thee, let them be, Ab. i. 8; הֲרֵינִי נָזִיר כְּשֶׁיִּהְיֶה לִי בֵן lo, I am a Nazirite if I shall have a son, Naz. ii. 7; with אַף: אַף כְּשֶׁאָמְרוּ even when they said, ib. 1; אֲפִילוּ: יָכוֹל אֲפִילוּ תָקְפָה עָלָיו מִשְׁנָתוֹ even if his study was too hard for him, Ab. iii. 8; אֲפִילוּ צ״ט אוֹמְרִים even if 99 say to divide, Pea iv. 1.

11. Concessive Clauses.

493. A concessive clause can be introduced by the simple copula: נִשְׁבֵּתִי וּטְהוֹרָה אֲנִי I was taken captive, nevertheless I am pure, Ket. ii. 6, רָאִיתָ מִיָּמֶיךָ . . . וְהֵן מִתְפַּרְנְסִין hast ever seen . . . yet

[1] Against Tossaphot, Meg. 21 a, Kohut i, p. 98 f., who make a distinction between אִלְמָלֵא and אִלְמָלֵי. Cf. also Lambert, *RÉJ.*, ix, p. 273 ff.; Jastrow, *ibid*, xi, p. 151 f.; Ben Yehuda, *Thesaurus*, i, p. 250 f.

they maintain themselves, Qid. iv. 14; כַּמָּה תְּהֵא הַסֶּלַע חֲסֵרָה וְלֹא יְהֵא בָהּ אוֹנָאָה by how much may the *sela'* be deficient, and yet there may be no deceit in its use, BM iv. 5.

494. More commonly, concessive clauses are introduced by special conjunctions. These consist of combinations with אַף: אֲפִילוּ (= אַף + אִילוּ), אַף כְּשֶׁ־, אַף עַל פִּי, אַף עַל פִּי כֵן: אֲפִילוּ הַמֶּלֶךְ שׁוֹאֵל בִּשְׁלוֹמוֹ לֹא יְשִׁיבֶנּוּ even though a king greets him, he must not answer him, Bᵉr. v. 1; אֲפִילוּ נוֹטֵל אֶת נַפְשְׁךָ even though he takes thy life, ib. ix. 5; אַף כְּשֶׁאָמְרוּ even when they said, Naz. ii. 1, 2; אַף עַל פִּי שֶׁאֵין מְבִיאִין מוּגְמָר although perfumes are not brought in, Bᵉr. vi. 6; אַף עַל פִּי שֶׁאָמְרוּ although they have said, Pea i. 2; so before a participle, but without שֶׁ־: סִילוֹנוֹת אַף עַל פִּי כְפוּפִין אַף עַל פִּי מְקַבְּלִין pipes, though bent, though receiving, Kel. ii. 3; אַף עַל פִּי כֵן חוֹזֵר וְקוֹרֵא אוֹתָם nevertheless, he calls them again, Bik. iii. 1; אַף עַל פִּי כֵן יַד כּוּלָּן שָׁוָה nevertheless, they are all equal, Šᵉq. ii. 4; אַף עַל פִּי כֵן הָיִיתִי בוֹכֶה nevertheless, I would have wept, Bᵉr. 28 b.

12. Comparative Clauses.

495. As in BH, comparison is expressed by כְּ־. From the nature of its substantival origin, כְּ־ alone can stand only before a noun as its *regens*, e.g. תֶּבֶן כִּמְלוֹא פִּי פָרָה straw like the mouthful of a cow, Šab. vii. 4; דָּמוֹ טָעוּן כִּיסּוּי כְּדַם חַיָּה its blood requires covering like the blood of a beast, Bik. ii. 9; שׁוֹאֵל כְּעִנְיָן וּמֵשִׁיב כַּהֲלָכָה he asks according to the subject, and answers according to the law, Ab. v. 10. To introduce a clause, כְּ־ must combine with another word to form a conjunction. Thus, כְּאִילוּ: כְּאִילוּ עֲשָׂאָהּ בְּתוֹךְ הַבַּיִת as if he made it within the house, Suk. i. 2; כְּאִילוּ הִיא פְשׁוּטָה; כְּאִילוּ הִיא מְרוּבַּעַת as if it was straight, square, 'Er. i. 5; כַּיּוֹצֵא בוֹ, to introduce a new case similar to the preceding one; כַּיּוֹצֵא בוֹ הַמַּשְׂכִּיר בַּיִת לַחֲבֵרוֹ likewise, if one lets a house to his fellow, Šᵉbi, ix. 7; כַּיּוֹצֵא בוֹ רוֹצֵחַ שֶׁגָּלָה similarly, a murderer who went into exile, ib. x. 8; Ḥal. iii. 9.

496. A comparative clause is also introduced by כְּמוֹת שֶׁ־ (כְּמוֹ שֶׁ־): כְּמוֹת שֶׁהוּא לָמוּד as he is accustomed, T^e^r. iv. 3; כְּמוֹת שֶׁהַחֶנְוָנִי לוֹקֵחַ וְלֹא כְּמוֹת שֶׁהוּא מוֹכֵר as the shop-keeper buys, and not as he sells, MŠ iv. 2. By וְכֵן: וְכֵן חָבִית שֶׁל שֶׁמֶן שֶׁנִּשְׁפְּכָה likewise, a jar of oil that was spilled, T^e^r. xi. 7; וְכֵן כַּיּוֹצֵא בָהֶם בִּשְׁאָר שְׁנֵי שָׁבוּעַ and similarly in the other years of the Seven, Š^e^bi. iv. 8, 9.

497. A more complete agreement is expressed when the two members of the comparison are both introduced by correlative conjunctions. The following correlatives are found:

כְּ . . . כָּךְ: כְּזֵירוּדָה וּכְפִיסוּלָהּ שֶׁל חֲמִשִּׁית כָּךְ שֶׁל שִׁשִּׁית just like the thinning and trimming of the fifth, so of the sixth, Š^e^bi. ii. 3; כְּעוֹנָתָן לְמַעַשְׂרוֹת כָּךְ עוֹנָתָן לִשְׁבִיעִית as their season for tithes, so their season for the seventh year, ib. iv. 9. These correlatives are used with nouns only.

כְּשֵׁם שֶׁ־ . . . כָּךְ: כְּשֵׁם שֶׁאָמְרוּ לְהַחֲמִיר כָּךְ אָמְרוּ לְהָקֵל as they said to make it heavy, so they said to make it light, Kil. ii. 2; כְּשֵׁם שֶׁחוֹלְקִין בִּתְבוּאָה כָּךְ חוֹלְקִין בְּתֶבֶן just as they divide the produce, so do they divide the straw, BM ix. 1; כְּשֵׁם שֶׁהוֹצֵאתַנִי . . . כָּךְ תַּכְנִיסֵנִי just as thou hast brought me forth . . . so shalt thou bring me in, B^e^r. 48 b. Sometimes כָּךְ is omitted: כְּשֵׁם שֶׁדַּנְתַּנִי . . . הַמָּקוֹם יָדִין אוֹתָךְ as thou hast judged me . . . may the Almighty judge thee; כְּשֵׁם שֶׁדַּנְתּוּנִי . . . הַמָּקוֹם יָדִין אֶתְכֶם Šab. 127 b.

כְּשֵׁם שֶׁ־ . . . כֵּן: כְּשֵׁם שֶׁהוּא מֵדֵל בְּתוֹךְ שֶׁלּוֹ כֵּן הוּא מֵדֵל בְּשֶׁל עֲנִיִּים just as he thins out among his own, so he thins out of the poor, Pea vii. 5. After a long protasis, the comparison is resumed by means of the copula: כְּשֵׁם שֶׁאָמְרוּ הַפּוֹגֶמֶת כְּתוּבָּתָהּ לֹא תִפָּרַע . . . , וְכֵן יְתוֹמִים לֹא יִפָּרְעוּ just as they said (that) she who damages the bill of her marriage settlement shall not be paid . . . so orphans shall not be paid . . . , Š^e^bu. vii. 7.

כְּדֶרֶךְ שֶׁ־ . . . כָּךְ: כְּדֶרֶךְ שֶׁאֵין מְקַלְקְלִין בִּרְשׁוּת הָרַבִּים כָּךְ לֹא יְתַקֵּן just as one must not cause damage in a public thoroughfare, so must not one repair therein, Š^e^bi. iii 10.

כְּעִנְיָן שֶׁהוּא מְבָרֵךְ כָּךְ עוֹנִין אַחֲרָיו : כְּעִנְיָן שֶׁ־ . . . כָּךְ according as he pronounces the benediction, so they respond after him, Bᵉr. vii. 3.

498. The apodosis may come first for special emphasis, and then the protasis alone has the conjunction: חַיָּב אָדָם לְבָרֵךְ עַל הָרָעָה כְּשֵׁם שֶׁהוּא מְבָרֵךְ עַל הַטּוֹבָה one is bound to bless (God) for evil, as one blesses Him for good, Bᵉr. ix. 5; נוֹהֵג בִּתְרוּמָה כְּדֶרֶךְ שֶׁהוּא נוֹהֵג בְּחוּלִּין one behaves towards *teruma*, just as one behaves towards common things, Tᵉr. xi. 5; Šᵉbi. iv. 1.

499. An argument to prove a similarity between two cases is introduced by the exclamatory מָה in the protasis, and אַף in the apodosis: מָה הַטְּהוֹרָה עוֹלָה אַף הַטְּמֵאָה תַּעֲלֶה what! the pure rises, also the impure shall rise = just as . . . so . . ., Tᵉr. v. 4; מָה הַנִּדָּה מְטַמְּאָה בְּמַשָּׂא אַף עֲבוֹדָה זָרָה מְטַמְּאָה בְּמַשָּׂא what! the menstruous defiles by carrying, also the idol defiles by carrying, AZ iii. 6.

500. In an argument from the minor to the major (קַל וָחֹמֶר), the protasis is introduced by מָה אִם, the apodosis by דִּין הוּא: מָה אִם . . . מָקוֹם שֶׁאֵין כֹּהֵן הֶדְיוֹט מִטַּמֵּא . . . דִּין הוּא שֶׁלֹּא יְהֵא כֹהֵן גָּדוֹל מִטַּמֵּא what! if . . . where a private priest may not defile himself . . . it is justice that the High Priest should not defile himself, Sifre Num. vi. 6. But more often the apodosis is put in a rhetorical question in the negative: מָה אִם שְׁחִיטָה . . . דּוֹחָה אֶת הַשַּׁבָּת אֵלּוּ . . . לֹא יִדְחוּ אֶת הַשַּׁבָּת what! if slaughtering . . . overrides the Sabbath, these . . ., should they not override the Sabbath? Pᵉs. vi. 2; especially with אֵינוֹ דִּין: מָה אִם הַפֶּסַח . . . חַיָּב הַזְּבָחִים . . . אֵינוֹ דִּין שֶׁיְּהֵא חַיָּב what! if the Passover sacrifice . . . he is liable, the sacrifices . . ., is it not justice that he should be liable? ib. 5; Nᵉd. x. 6; Naz. vii. 4; So. vi. 3, &c. The apodosis may also take the phrase עַל אַחַת כַּמָּה וְכַמָּה before the predicate: מָה אִם הָעוֹבֵר עֲבֵרָה אַחַת . . . הָעוֹשֶׂה מִצְוָה אַחַת עַל אַחַת כַּמָּה וְכַמָּה שֶׁתִּנָּתֵן לוֹ נַפְשׁוֹ what! if one who commits one transgression . . ., one who performs one command, how much more so should his life be given to him?

Mak. iii. 15; וּמָה אִם הַדָּם . . . גָּזֵל וַעֲרָיוֹת . . . עַל אַחַת כַּמָּה וְכַמָּה שֶׁיִּזְכֶּה what! if blood . . . robbery and incest . . ., how much more so should he secure merit . . ., ib.; ib. i. 7; Ab. vi. 3, &c.; or, finally in later diction, by the rhetorical negative question, placed at the end as a predicate, לֹא כָל שֶׁכֵּן is not everything (in its favour) that it should be so? כְּשֶׁהוּא שָׂבֵעַ מְבָרֵךְ כְּשֶׁהוּא רָעֵב לֹא כָל שֶׁכֵּן if he blesses when he is full, when he is hungry all the more so, Ber. 48 b, &c.[1]

13. Disjunctive Clauses.

501. A clause giving an alternative case is co-ordinated with the preceding clause with or without the copula, but only in the case of very short clauses: נִקְלַף נִסְדַּק נִיקַּב וְחָסֵר כָּל שֶׁהוּא if it was peeled, or cracked, or perforated, or had something missing, Suk. iii. 6, 1, 2; גְּזַלְתִּיךָ וְהִלְוִיתַנִי וְהִפְקַדְתָּ אֶצְלִי I robbed thee, or thou didst lend me, or thou didst deposit with me, BQ x. 7; so with adjectives: בָּשָׂר צָלִי שָׁלוּק וּמְבוּשָּׁל roast, or seethed, or cooked meat, Pes. x. 4. But a longer clause is introduced by אוֹ: הָיוּ שְׁנַיִם רוֹכְבִין . . . אוֹ שֶׁהָיָה אֶחָד רוֹכֵב וְאֶחָד מַנְהִיג two were riding . . ., or one was riding and one leading, BM i. 2.

502. Two or more alternative cases may be introduced by correlative conjunctions, as follows:

אוֹ . . . אוֹ either . . . or: אוֹ חוֹלֶצֶת אוֹ מִתְיַבֶּמֶת she either takes *ḥaliṣa*, or she is married to her deceased husband's brother, Yeb. iii. 3; iv. 5, 6; אוֹ מְעָרֵב . . . אוֹ אֵינוֹ מְעָרֵב he either makes an *'erub* . . . or he does not make an *'erub*, 'Er. iii. 9; אוֹ לֶחִי אוֹ קוֹרָה either a board or a beam, ib. i. 2.

לֹא . . . וְלֹא neither . . . nor; לֹא אוֹכְלִין וְלֹא שׂוֹרְפִין they neither eat, nor burn, Pes. i. 5; Yeb. xi. 2; cf. § 339 (ii).

אִם . . . אִם whether . . . or; cf. § 466. אִם הַיּוֹם אִם לְמָחָר whether to-day or to-morrow, 'Er. iii. 9.

[1] Cf. Bacher, *Aelteste Terminologie*, p. 172 f.

אֶחָד שֶׁ־ . . . וְאֶחָד שֶׁ־ whether . . . or : אֶחָד שֶׁהֵן כֶּסֶף וְאֶחָד שֶׁהֵן פֵּירוֹת whether they are silver or whether they are fruit, MŠ v. 7. This is especially common before nominal forms without שֶׁ־: אֶחָד שׁוֹגֵג וְאֶחָד מֵזִיד whether in error or intentionally, Ab. iv. 4; אֶחָד הָאוֹכֵל וְאֶחָד הַשּׁוֹתֶה וְאֶחָד הַסָּךְ whether one eats, or drinks, or anoints, T^er. vi. 1. Sometimes אֶחָד is expressed before the first case only: אֶחָד הַחוֹפֵר בּוֹר שִׁיחַ וּמְעָרָה whether one digs a pit, or a ditch, or a cave, BQ v. 5.

בֵּין שֶׁ־ . . . בֵּין שֶׁ־ : בֵּין שֶׁיֵּשׁ בּוֹ . . . בֵּין שֶׁאֵין בּוֹ whether it has in it . . . or it has not in it . . . 'Or. ii. 6, 7; בֵּין שֶׁנִּרְאָה בַעֲלִיל וּבֵין שֶׁלֹּא נִרְאָה בַעֲלִיל whether it was seen clearly, or not, RH i. 5; with nominal forms without שֶׁ־, except before a negative (cf. § 425): בֵּין מִתּוֹכוֹ בֵּין מֵעַל גַּבָּיו whether within, or above, Šab. iii. 2; בֵּין עוֹשִׂין בֵּין שֶׁאֵינָן עוֹשִׂין whether they produce, or not, Š^ebi. i. 4.

פְּעָמִים שֶׁ־ . . . וּפְעָמִים שֶׁ־ sometimes . . . sometimes: פְּעָמִים שֶׁהוּא אִישׁ וּפְעָמִים שֶׁהוּא אִשָּׁה Bik. iv. 5; פְּעָמִים שֶׁאַתָּה מִתְעַלֵּם וּפְעָמִים שֶׁאֵין אַתָּה מִתְעַלֵּם sometimes thou mayest hide thyself, and sometimes not, BM 30 a. Before nominal forms without שֶׁ־: פְּעָמִים מְכוּרִים וּפְעָמִים אֵינָן מְכוּרִים sometimes they are sold, sometimes not, BB v. 2. Also פְּעָמִים שֶׁ־ . . . אוֹ: פְּעָמִים שֶׁהוּא בָא מִקְּרִיאַת הַגֶּבֶר אוֹ סָמוּךְ לוֹ sometimes he comes with the crowing of the cock, sometimes near it, Tam. i. 2.

14. Adversative, Exceptive, and Restrictive Clauses.

503. A clause expressing the antithesis to a preceding clause can be introduced by the simple copula: מֵת וְהוּא שֶׁנִּשְׁבַּר (he said) it had died, but really it was broken, Š^ebu. viii. 2 f., 6 ff.; הָעוֹף עוֹלֶה עִם הַגְּבִינָה . . . וְאֵינוֹ נֶאֱכָל the bird goes up with the cheese . . . but is not eaten, 'Ed. v. 2; מוּתָּרִין . . . וְהַשּׁוֹחֵט . . . חַיָּיב they are permitted . . ., but he who slays . . . is liable, P^es. vi. 5.

More frequently, an antithesis is introduced by אֲבָל or אֶלָּא.

אֲבָל introduces a co-ordinated sentence which contains a new case in opposition to the foregoing: לֹא יַתִּיר אֶת סוּכָּתוֹ אֲבָל מוֹרִיד הוּא אֶת הַכֵּלִים he must not undo his tabernacle, but he may take down the things, Suk. iv. 8; אֵין נוֹתְנִין לִתְלוּיָה בְּשַׁבָּת אֲבָל נוֹתְנִין לִתְלוּיָה בְּיוֹם טוֹב one may not put (wine) into a hanging (strainer) on the Sabbath, but one may put . . . on the Festival, Šab. xx. 1; יוֹדֵעַ אֲנִי שֶׁיֵּשׁ נְזִירוּת אֲבָל אֵינִי יוֹדֵעַ שֶׁהַנָּזִיר אָסוּר בְּיַיִן I know that there is the state of the Nazirite, but I do not know that the Nazirite is forbidden the use of wine, Naz. ii. 4; MŠ iii. 1; Ber. iii. 5; 'Er. ii. 3, &c.

504. אֶלָּא is but rarely used like אֲבָל to introduce an adversative sentence: כָּל כֹּהֵן שֶׁאֵינוֹ שׁוֹקֵל חוֹטֵא אֶלָּא שֶׁהַכֹּהֲנִים דּוֹרְשׁוּ . . . any priest that does not pay the shekel is a sinner; however, the priests expound . . ., Šeq. i. 4; הָיָה כִּדְבָרֶיךָ אֶלָּא אָמְרוּ חֲכָמִים it would be as thou sayest, but the sages have said, Bek. iii. 1; with a mild adversative (like וְ): עַל הַחֲדָשִׁים אָנוּ בוֹשִׁין אֶלָּא שֶׁאַתֶּם מְגַלְגְּלִין עָלֵינוּ אֶת הַיְשָׁנִים we are ashamed of the new ones, and you roll upon us also the old ones, Ket. viii. 1; BB ix. 10.

505. More often אֶלָּא introduces an exceptive or restrictive clause: כָּל הַזְּבָחִים . . . כְּשֵׁרִים אֶלָּא שֶׁלֹּא עָלוּ לַבְּעָלִים לְשֵׁם חוֹבָה all sacrifices . . . are proper, except that they do not rise for the owner to the category of a duty (discharged, &c.), Zeb. i. 1; Men. i. 1; הַמּוּרָם מֵהֶם כַּיּוֹצֵא בָהֶם אֶלָּא שֶׁהַמּוּרָם נֶאֱכָל what is lifted from them (for the priests) is like them, except that what is lifted may be eaten, Zeb. v. 6, 7; הֲרֵי אַתְּ מוּתֶּרֶת לְכָל אָדָם אֶלָּא לְאִישׁ פְּלוֹנִי lo, thou art free to marry any man, except so and so, Giṭ. ix. 1, 2.

506. In this exceptive or restrictive sense, אֶלָּא is very widely used after a negative (as in Aram. and כִּי אִם in BH, Ges.-K., § 163 a, f.).[1] The negative with אֶלָּא may usually be rendered in English by an affirmative with 'only': לֹא הָיוּ אֶלָּא שְׁנַיִם they had

[1] This use of אֶלָּא after a negative is already found in BH with אִם לֹא, the equivalent of אֶלָּא (§ 302), Gen. xxiv. 37–8; Ps. cxxxi. 1–2. Cf. also the French *ne . . . que*.

been only two, Yo. iii. 10; לֹא נִעְנְעוּ אֶלָּא בְּ־ they only shook at ..., Suk. iii. 9; אַף הִיא לֹא תִפָּרַע אֶלָּא בִשְׁבוּעָה she, too, shall be paid only by oath, K^e^t. x. 5; אֵין חוֹתְכִין אֶלָּא . . . אֵין נוֹשְׁקִין אֶלָּא . . . אֵין יוֹעֲצִין אֶלָּא . . . they only cut ...; they only kiss ...; they only consult ..., B^e^r. 8 b (§ 329).

507. אֶלָּא is sometimes strengthened by בִּלְבַד placed at the end of the sentence: אֵין מַדְלִיקִין אֶלָּא בְשֶׁמֶן זַיִת בִּלְבַד one may light only with olive oil alone, Šab. ii. 2; לֹא הָיוּ תוֹקְעִין אֶלָּא בְבֵית דִּין בִּלְבַד they only blew (the *shofar*) at the *Beth Din* alone, RH iv. 2.

508. אֶלָּא introduces a complete antithesis in the idiomatic expression לֹא כֵי אֶלָּא not so, but: לֹא כֵי אֶלָּא בְסֶלַע לָקָה not so, but he struck against a stone, BQ iii. 11; Š^e^q. i. 4; Y^e^b. viii. 3, 4; Š^e^bu. vi. 7; M^e^n. iv. 3. Cf. § 298.

So with כְּלוּם which is equivalent to a negative: כְּלוּם אָמַרְתָּ אֶלָּא מִפְּנֵי כְבוֹדִי thou only saidst it for my honour, N^e^d. viii. 7; כְּלוּם נָתַתִּי לְךָ גְּדוּלָה אֶלָּא בִשְׁבִיל יִשְׂרָאֵל I have only given thee greatness for the sake of Israel, B^e^r. 32 a.

509. Such a clause following אֶלָּא may have a conditional force: אֵין שׁוֹרִין אֶלָּא כְּדֵי שֶׁיִּשּׁוֹרוּ one may not soak . . . unless they can be soaked ..., Šab. i. 5–8, 10. If such a condition is introduced by אִם, the conditional particle is usually strengthened by כֵּן: אֵינוֹ מַפְסִיק אֶלָּא אִם כֵּן חָרַשׁ it does not separate, unless he ploughed it, Pea ii. 1; אֵין נוֹעֲלִים בָּהֶם אֶלָּא אִם כֵּן גְּבוֹהִים מִן הָאָרֶץ one must not shut with them, unless they are high above the ground, 'Er. x. 8; לֹא יִטּוֹל אֶלָּא אִם כֵּן נִעְנַע מִבְּעוֹד יוֹם he must not take unless he shook it while it was still day, Be. i. 3, 5; ii. 5; iii. 2.

510. The same construction is found with clauses introduced by עַד 'after'—viz. until the condition named has been fulfilled. The verb used is the imperfect (§ 321): אֵין מְעִידִין אֶלָּא עַד שֶׁתֵּצֵא נַפְשׁוֹ no evidence must be given, except after his soul is gone forth, Y^e^b. xvi. 3. But, usually, אֶלָּא is omitted in such a construction:

אֵינוֹ מֵת עַד שֶׁיִּצְטָרֵךְ לַבְּרִיּוֹת he will not die, until after he has become dependent on his fellow creatures = אֶלָּא עַד, Pea vii. 8; עַד שֶׁיְּפַרְנֵס אֲחֵרִים . . . until after he has fed others = אֶלָּא עַד ib.; אֵינוֹ חַיָּב עַד שֶׁיִּכְתּוֹב he is not liable until after he has written = אֶלָּא עַד, Mak. ii. 7. Sometimes the negative also is omitted: וַחֲכָמִים אוֹמְרִים עַד שֶׁיִּרְשׁוֹם . . . (No, except) if he mark, Be. iv. 7; עַד שֶׁתְּפַרְכֵּס (not, except) if it has moved convulsively, Ḥul. ii. 6.

511. The negative is also omitted before אֶלָּא in answer to a question: לָמָּה נֶאֱמַר . . . אֶלָּא בְשָׁעָה שֶׁדֶּרֶךְ why is it said . . . ? (not) except when it is the custom . . . (= לֹא נֶאֱמַר אֶלָּא), B^e^r. i. 3; וּמִי שׁוֹמֵעַ לוֹ שֶׁיִּדּוֹר בְּנָזִיר אֶלָּא מֵבִיא but who will listen to him to vow as a Nazirite? (no), but he brings . . ., Naz. viii. 1; מַה בֵּין שְׂדֵה אֲחוּזָּה לִשְׂדֵה מִקְנָה אֶלָּא שֶׁבִּשְׂדֵה אֲחוּזָּה what is the difference between an inherited field and a purchased field? (none) except that in a purchased field . . . (= אֵין בֵּין . . . אֶלָּא), 'Ar. iii. 2; מַה בֵּין נְדָרִים לִנְדָבוֹת אֶלָּא שֶׁהַנְּדָרִים what is the difference between vows and free-will offerings? (none) except that, Qin. i. 1. Cf. אֵין בֵּין שַׁבָּת לְיוֹם טוֹב אֶלָּא אוֹכֶל נֶפֶשׁ בִּלְבָד there is no difference between the Sabbath and the Festival except in the matter of food alone, M^e^g. i. 5–11.

Cf. the omission of the negative before כִּי אִם in BH, 1 Sam. xxvi. 10, &c., *BDB.*, p. 475 a.

512. Exceptive clauses are also introduced by וּבִלְבַד שֶׁ־: וּבִלְבַד שֶׁיּוֹדִיעֶנּוּ but only if he will make it known to him, Dam. iii. 3; וּבִלְבַד שֶׁיְּהֵא מַמָּשׁ בִּדְבָרָיו but only when there will be something real in his words, San. vi. 1; וּבִלְבַד שֶׁיִּתֵּן כְּנֶגֶד הַיְסוֹד but only if he will put it against the base, Z^e^b. v. 8.

By חוּץ מִ־ outside of: חוּץ מִשֶּׁנִּטְמְאָה except that which was defiled, MŠ. iii. 9; or without שֶׁ־ before nominal forms: חוּץ מִן הַיַּיִן; חוּץ מִן הַפַּת except wine, bread, B^e^r. vi. 1; חוּץ מֵאֶחָד מֵהֶם except one of them, Z^e^b. viii. 8. Sometimes strengthened by

חוּץ מִלֵּילֵי . . . הָרִאשׁוֹן בִּלְבַד : בִּלְבַד except the first night . . . alone, Suk ii. 6; חוּץ מִזּוֹ בִלְבַד except this alone, Yo. iii. 3.

15. Temporal Clauses.

513. The relation of time between two verbs is expressed by various conjunctions followed by -שֶׁ.

-כְּשֶׁ when: כְּשֶׁהָיוּ יִשְׂרָאֵל בַּמִּדְבָּר when the Israelites were in the wilderness, M^e^n. iv. 3; כְּשֶׁיָּצָא אָמַר when he had gone forth, he said (pluperfect, § 309), 'AZ. iii. 4; כְּשֶׁאַגִּיעַ לוֹ אֲלַקְּטֶנּוּ I shall gather it when I shall have reached it (*fut. exactum*, § 321), Kil. v. 6. In later MH often with -לְ prefixed: . . . לִכְשֶׁיִּבָּנֶה בֵּית הַמִּקְדָּשׁ when the Temple will be re-built, I will bring, Šab. 12 b. Cf. in BH, Ges.-K., § 164 d; *BDB*., p. 455.

-מִשֶּׁ after: מוֹכֵר הוּא מִשֶּׁיְּקַצֵּץ he may sell after he has cut down, 'AZ. i. 8; מִשֶּׁתֶּחְשַׁךְ after it has become dark, Šab. iv. 2; with pleonastic -כְּ: מִכְּשֶׁיָּצָאת הָאֶבֶן after the stone had gone forth, Mak. ii. 2. -מִשֶּׁ with the perfect is usually found only as correlative to -עַד שֶׁ, see next section. In BH this temporal use of מִן is only found with nouns: כְּמִשְׁלֹשׁ חֳדָשִׁים Gen. xxxviii. 24; cf. *BDB*., p. 581, 4 b.

-עַד שֶׁ until, before: עַד שֶׁיַּעֲלֶה עַמּוּד הַשַּׁחַר until dawn will rise, B^e^r. i. 1. After a negative, with אֶלָּא understood (§ 510): אַל תָּדִין אֶת חֲבֵרְךָ עַד שֶׁתַּגִּיעַ לִמְקוֹמוֹ judge not thy neighbour before thou shalt have reached his place, Ab. ii. 4 (§ 321); לֹא הָיָה מַגִּיעַ . . . עַד שֶׁנַּעֲשָׂה he did not reach . . . before he became, Yo. vi. 6 (cf. Aram.: לָא מְטוֹ . . . עַד דִּי שְׁלִטוּ Dan. vi. 25). Cf. BH: עַד שֶׁתֶּחְפָּץ Cant. ii. 7, עַד שֶׁיָּפוּחַ 17, &c.; *BDB*., p. 724 f.

עַד שֶׁלֹּא: עַד שֶׁלֹּא נִבְחֲרוּ before they had been chosen, Mak. ii. 4; so in BH עַד אֲשֶׁר לֹא יָבֹאוּ before they will come, Qoh. xii. 1, 2, 6.

So, especially, as correlative to -מִשֶּׁ: . . . עַד שֶׁלֹּא בָא לְעוֹנַת נְדָרִים מִשֶּׁבָּא before he had reached the season of vows . . . after he had reached . . . Tᵉr. i. 3 ; . . . מִשֶּׁהִגְרִיל . . . עַד שֶׁלֹּא הִגְרִיל before he had cast lots . . . after he had cast lots . . ., Yo. vi. 1 ; עַד שֶׁלֹּא נְגָחָהּ . . . מִשֶּׁנְּגָחָהּ before he had gored her . . . after he had gored her, BQ v. 1.

עַד כְּדֵי שֶׁ־ until : עַד כְּדֵי שֶׁיִּתְאַכֵּל הַמָּזוֹן until the food will be digested, Bᵉr. viii. 7 ; עַד כְּדֵי שֶׁיֵּדְעוּ בוֹ שְׁכֵנָיו until his neighbours will know of it, BM ii. 6. (But L has : עד שישמעו שכינים.)

בְּשָׁעָה שֶׁ־ when (a point of time) : בְּשָׁעָה שֶׁהַמְּלָכִים עוֹבְרִים when kings pass, ʻAZ iv. 6 ; כָּל שָׁעָה שֶׁ־ when (duration of time) : כָּל שָׁעָה שֶׁמּוּתָּר לֶאֱכוֹל when, as long as, he is allowed to eat, Pᵉs. ii. 1.

מִשָּׁעָה שֶׁ־ : מִשָּׁעָה שֶׁהַכֹּהֲנִים נִכְנָסִין from the time when the priests enter, Bᵉr. i. 1 ; מִשָּׁעָה שֶׁנִּפְסְקָה ʻOr. i. 5.

בִּזְמַן שֶׁ־ when, usually with a hypothetical force : בִּזְמַן שֶׁקָּנָה קַרְקַע אֲבָל בִּזְמַן שֶׁלֹּא קָנָה קַרְקַע when he bought land, but when he did not buy land, Maʻa. v. 5 ; cf. § 492.

כָּל זְמַן when, while (duration of time) : כָּל זְמַן שֶׁבְּנֵי אָדָם חוֹרְשִׁין while men plough, Šᵉbi. ii. 1 ; כָּל זְמַן שֶׁבִּכְּרוּ when they have ripened, ib. ix. 4.

אֵימָתַי שֶׁ־ whenever ; אֵימָתַי שֶׁתִּרְצֶה whenever thou wishest, BM v. 3 ; אֵימָתַי שֶׁיִּבָּנֶה בֵּית הַמִּקְדָּשׁ whenever the Temple will be re-built, MŠ v. 2.

כֵּיוָן שֶׁ־ as soon as : כֵּיוָן שֶׁהִגִּיעַ הַשָּׂעִיר as soon as the goat reached, Yo. vi. 8 ; כֵּיוָן שֶׁהִיא נוֹתֶנֶת אֶת הַמַּיִם as soon as she puts in the water, Ḥal. iii. 1.

קוֹדֶם שֶׁ־ before : קוֹדֶם שֶׁתִּתְאָרֵס before she was betrothed, So. ii. 6.

אַחַר שֶׁ־ after : אַחַר שֶׁכְּתָבוֹ לָהּ after he had written it for her, ʻEd. iv. 7 ; or with ל : לְאַחַר שֶׁהוֹדוּ after they had agreed, Tᵉr. v. 4.

עֵת שֶׁ־ when (rare) : עֵת שֶׁבָּאוּ אֲבוֹתֵינוּ when our fathers came, ʻOr. i. 2.

מִיַּד immediately : מִיַּד הָיָה עוֹמֵד וְעוֹסֵק בַּתּוֹרָה immediately he would arise and study the Torah; מִיַּד יוֹעֲצִים בַּאֲחִיתוֹפֶל immediately they would consult Ahitophel, Ber. 3 b; מִיַּד כָּבְתָה immediately it is extinguished, Šab. 151 b.

16. Final Clauses.

514. The purpose or aim of an action may be expressed by the infinitive with לְ־: נִכְנָסִין לֶאֱכוֹל they enter to eat, Ber. i. 1; הִטֵּיתִי לִקְרוֹת I inclined to read, ib. 3. In the negative: שֶׁלֹּא לְהַבְעִית not to frighten, Yo. v. 2; שֶׁלֹּא לְבַיֵּישׁ not to shame, Ta'a. iv. 8. After verbs of preventing, &c., the inf. takes מִן: לֹא נִמְנְעוּ מִלִּשְׂרוֹף . . . מִלְּהַדְלִיק they refrained not from burning . . . from kindling, Pes. i. 6; cf. § 346. The infin. can also be introduced by כְּדֵי: אָמְרוּ . . . כְּדֵי לְהַרְחִיק they said . . . in order to remove, Ber. i. 1 (L אֶלָּא לְהַרְחִיק). By עַל מְנָת: הַקּוֹרֵעַ עַל מְנָת לִתְפּוֹר if one tears in order to sew; הַמְקַלְקֵל עַל מְנָת לְתַקֵּן if one damages, in order to repair, Šab. xiii. 2, 3.

515. Clauses expressing purpose are introduced by שֶׁ־, שֶׁלֹּא: לֹא שֶׁיַּעֲלֶה אֶלָּא שֶׁלֹּא יוֹסִיף not that it may rise, but that it may not increase, Šab. xxiii. 5; שֶׁלֹּא יִהְיוּ מֵימָיו נִפְסָלִין that its water may not be disqualified, Yo. iii. 10.

כְּדֵי שֶׁ־, כְּדֵי שֶׁלֹּא: כְּדֵי שֶׁיְּהוּ רוֹאִין זֶה אֶת זֶה that they may see one another, San. iv. 3; כְּדֵי שֶׁלֹּא לְשַׁכֵּחַ אֶת הַתִּינוֹקוֹת not to make the children forget, 'Er. vii. 9.

בִּשְׁבִיל שֶׁ־, בִּשְׁבִיל שֶׁלֹּא: בִּשְׁבִיל שֶׁיִּצַּנּוּ; בִּשְׁבִיל שֶׁיֵּחַמּוּ in order that they may be cold, hot, Šab. xxii. 4; בִּשְׁבִיל שֶׁיִּתְמַיֵּן that he may last, ib. xxiii. 5; בִּשְׁבִיל שֶׁלֹּא תֵצֵא that it should not go out, ib. xv. 2; בִּשְׁבִיל שֶׁלֹּא יִמּוֹקוּ that they may not melt, Ta'a. iii. 8.

עַל מְנָת שֶׁ־: עַל מְנָת שֶׁיִּלְקוֹט בְּנוֹ on condition that his son may gather, Pea v. 6.

17. Consecutive Clauses.

516. Clauses expressing the consequence of an action may be introduced by the simple copula, especially in questions: כַּמָּה

יִבְנֶה וִיהֵא חַיָּיב how much should he build, so as to be liable? Šab. xxii. 1; כַּמָּה יִשְׁהוּ וְיִהְיוּ אֲסוּרִים how long should they abide, so as to become prohibited? T^{e}r. viii. 4; Š^{e}bi. iv. 10; Oh. xii. 8; מָתַי יָבוֹא לְיָדִי וַאֲקַיְּימֶנָּה when will it come to my hand that I may fulfil it? B^{e}r. 61 b; שֶׁלֹּא יְהֵא רַעַבְתָן וִיהֵא סוֹתֵם אֶת הַפֶּתַח בְּפָנָיו that he may not be a glutton, and so shut the door in his own face, BM vii. 5.

More often, consecutive clauses are introduced by כְּדֵי שֶׁ־, כְּדֵי שֶׁלֹּא: נוֹתֵן . . . כְּדֵי שֶׁיִּטּוֹל מִן הַמּוּקָף he gives . . . so that he may take from the nearest, Ḥal. ii. 8; קוֹצֵץ כְּדֵי שֶׁיְּהֵא גָמָל עוֹבֵר וְרוֹכְבוֹ he cuts off, so that a camel may pass with its rider, BB ii. 14; יִתְחַלְּקוּ . . . כְּדֵי שֶׁלֹּא יְהֵא בְּמָקוֹם אֶחָד כְּבֵיצָה they shall be divided, so that there be not in one place as much as an egg, T^{e}r. v. 1.

517. Consecutive sentences, as distinguished from consecutive clauses, are introduced by לְפִיכָךְ: לְפִיכָךְ אִם אֵירַע בָּהֶן פְּסוּל therefore, if a disqualification occurred in them, P^{e}s. viii. 6; לְפִיכָךְ אָנוּ חַיָּיבִין therefore, we are bound to, ib. x. 4; לְפִיכָךְ נִבְרָא אָדָם therefore, was man created, San. iv. 5.

INDEX OF BIBLICAL PASSAGES

(The references are to sections. n. = foot-note.)

GENESIS.

i. 6	343
28	2.6
xii. 13	431
xxii. 12	437
xxiii. 9	409
xxiv. 37–38	506 n.
xxiv. 39	489
xxv. 6	386
xxvi. 11	374
28	295
xxvii. 1	153 n.
29	312
xxx. 1	489 n.
31	437
39	153 n.
xxxi. 5	341
xli. 43	409
xlviii. 22	391

EXODUS.

ii. 6	390
xii. 19	472
xiii. 7	472
xvii. 1	342
3	363 n.
xxi. 12	374
28	376
29	376
xxii. 30	142
32	489 n.
xxiv. 6	43 n.
11	431
xxv. 29	271 n.
xxviii. 16	342
xxxii. 33	436
xxxviii. 30	409

LEVITICUS.

ii. 21	252
iv. 28	407
vii. 33	374
ix. 8	409
xiii. 48	386 n.
xiv. 46–7	374
xv. 6–10	374
xvi. 6	409
10	376
11	409
28	374
xix. 23	222
xx. 7	224
xxii. 28	275
37	275
xxvi. 33	153 n.
xxvii. 8	251

NUMBERS.

i. 24–43	390
iii. 46	391
iv. 19	377 n.
v. 14	351
xv. 31	116
38	60
xvi. 22	386
xxii. 6	422
xxviii. 3	291
xxx. 3	472
15	301
xxxi. 48	385
xxxii. 33	390

DEUTERONOMY.

iii. 14	290
vi. 4	3

DEUTERONOMY.
ix. 7 . . . 342
22 . . . 342
24 . . . 342
xi. 5 . . . 60
xiii. 1 . . . 472
xx. 3-4 . . . 3
xxi. 3 . . . 77
8 . . . 133 n
xxii. 25 . . . 376
27 . . . 376
xxiii. 3 . . . 275
3 . . . 472
16 . . . 228
xxiv. 10 . . . 133
19 . . . 472
xxv. 5 . . . 74 n.
9 . . . 3
7 . . . 336 n.
10 . . . 336 n.
xxvi. 3-10 . . . 3
xxvii. 15-26 . . . 3
xxviii. 29 . . . 343
61 . . . 340
xxxii. 35 . . . 349

JOSHUA.
vii. 7 . . . 302 n.

JUDGES.
i. 7 . . . 343
v. 16 . . . 228
vi. 20 . . . 74
viii. 1 . . . 199
xiii. 17 . . . 418
xvi. 10 . . . 196
xxi. 21 . . . 153 n.

1 SAMUEL.
ii. 26 . . . 489 n.
iii. 2 . . . 153 n.
viii. 19 . . . 298 n.
ix. 18 . . . 82
xiii. 21 . . . 228
xiv. 44 . . . 456
xv. 23 . . . 251
xvii. 4 . . . 295
xix. 10 . . . 119 n.
xx. 16 . . . 453 n.

1 SAMUEL.
40 . . . 409
xxi. 14 . . . 390
xxii. 20 . . . 386
xxv. 22 . . . 453 n.
23 . . . 301
xxvi. 10 . . . 511

2 SAMUEL.
iii. 2 . . . 286
3 . . . 286
7 . . . 343
34 . . . 340
vi. 9 . . . 43 n.
vii. 29 . . . 302 n.
viii. 15 . . . 343
xiv. 31 . . . 409
xv. 2 . . . 80
xix. 10 . . . 177
xx. 11 . . . 436

1 KINGS.
i. 6 . . . 297
33 . . . 409
iv. 2 . . . 409
vi. 17 . . . 269
17 . . . 393
19 . . . 169
29 . . . 293
ix. 17 . . . 377 n.
xvii. 14 . . . 169
xix. 8 . . . 228
21 . . . 390
xx. 30 . . . 393
xxi. 13 . . . 390
xxii. 25 . . . 393

2 KINGS.
ii. 20 . . . 271 n.
iii. 8 . . . 82
iv. 25 . . . 74 n.
v. 19 . . . 72
ix. 13 . . . 431 n.
xvi. 15 . . . 390
xvii. 32 . . . 343
33 . . . 343
xxi. 13 . . . 271 n.

ISAIAH.

i. 22	43 n.
iii. 9	252
19	54 n.
vii. 25	77
viii. 7	41
xiv. 12	363 n.
23	251
xvi. 4	212
10	438
xxv. 28	252
xxvi. 19	462
xxviii. 4	438
24	438
xxx. 20	343
xxxiii. 17	153 n.
lxi. 10	344 n.

JEREMIAH.

i. 10	170
v. 2	80
vi. 29	235
xviii. 23	343
ix. 14	390
xx. 15	344
xxvi. 18	343
20	343
xxxviii. 11	288
12	288
xlvi. 20	245
lii. 20	390

EZEKIEL.

iv. 14	340
vii. 4	235
viii. 5	228
x. 2	390
xvi. 7	393
xxiii. 48	133 n.
xxxiv. 2	390
xxxv. 10	417
xl. 40	385
45	72
xlii. 14	390
xliv. 2	343
xlvi. 1	343
22	393

JOEL.

ii. 17	301

JONAH.

i. 8	80

MICAH.

vi. 8	252
16	140

HABAKKUK.

i. 4	340

ZACHARIAH.

xiii. 1	343

PSALMS.

xii. 7	299 n.
xvii. 2	153 n.
xix. 3	228
xxxii. 1	199
xxxv. 14	409
lxiii. 12	390
cvi. 11	156
cxix. 61	180
cxx. 1	409
cxxxi. 1–2	506 n.
cxxxii. 11	409
12	409
12	72
cxxxvii. 9	235

PROVERBS.

vi. 5	296
xiii. 4	390
11	296
xv. 32	374
xxiii. 16	153 n.
xxviii. 23	269
xxxi. 30	140

JOB.

iii. 8	349
xii. 3	340
xv. 7	61
xxi. 23	431
xxiv. 24	197 n.
xxv. 2	251
xxix. 3	390
xxxix. 27	462

CANTICLES.
ii. 7 . . . 153 n.
7 . . . 513
17 . . . 513
iii. 5 . . . 153 n.
7 . . . 385
7 . . . 390
11 . . . 153 n.
iv. 11 . . . 153 n.
v. 8 . . . 153 n.
vi. 1 . . . 392
9 . . . 153 n.
9 . . . 405
viii. 4 . . . 153 n.

RUTH.
ii. 21 . . . 409

LAMENTATIONS.
i. 10 . . . 409
iii. 63 . . . 228

QOHELET.
i. 9 . . . 436
ii. 3 . . . 82
22 . . . 212
iii. 11 . . . 78 n.
15 . . . 436
22 . . . 436
iv. 10 . . . 304
viii. 10 . . . 140
xx. 1, 2, 6 . . . 513

ESTHER.
i. 22 . . . 343
ii. 7 . . . 343
15 . . . 343
18 . . . 252
23 . . . 156
iii. 14 . . . 349
iv. 14 . . . 252
viii. 13 . . . 343
ix. 21 . . . 343

DANIEL.
i. 10 . . . 180
16 . . . 268
ii. 9 . . . 134
15 . . . 296

DANIEL.
19 . . . 379
49 . . . 379
31 . . . 342
34 . . . 342
iii. 1 . . . 379
5 . . . 379
7 . . . 379
12 . . . 379
iv. 2 . . . 379
6 . . . 379
v. 5 . . . 379
7 . . . 386 n.
vi. 25 . . . 513
viii. 5 . . . 343
7 . . . 343
13 . . . 394
x. 2 . . . 343
7 . . . 43 n.
xi. 45 . . . 48

EZRA.
i. 11 . . . 386 n.
ii. 62 . . . 390
iii. 5 . . . 137
12 . . . 390
iv. 12 . . . 342
22 . . . 342
iv. 24 . . . 24
v. 2 . . . 24
16 . . . 24
13 . . . 379
14 . . . 379
vi. 5 . . . 379
14 . . . 379
12 . . . 24
18 . . . 24
23 . . . 24
ix. 1 . . . 390
x. 16 . . . 156

NEHEMIAH.
i. 2 . . . 343
ii. 13 . . . 343
15 . . . 343
iii. 2 . . . 343
iv. 11 . . . 394
v. 18 . . . 343
vi. 4 . . . 343
6 . . . 212

NEHEMIAH.
vi. 19 . . . 343
ix. 2 . . . 156
xiii. 5 . . . 343
12 . . . 343

1 CHRONICLES.
v. 26 . . . 390
xiii. 12 . . . 43 n.
xxiii. 6 . . . 390
xxix. 17 . . . 137

2 CHRONICLES.
viii. 5 . . . 377 n.
xxv. 5 . . . 390
10 . . . 390
xxviii. 23 . . . 82
xxx. 7 . . . 228
10 . . . 343
xxxv. 13 . . . 271 n.

SIRACH.
v. 25 . . . 149
xi. 3 . . . 273 n.
21 . . . 180
xiv. 14 . . . 241
xvi. 25 . . . 252
xxx. 2 . . . 181
12 . . . 357
19 . . . 120 n.
xxxii. 1 . . . 241
3 . . . 252
xxxv. 10 . . . 252
xxxviii. 16 . . . 228
25 . . . 228
26 . . . 228
17 . . . 298 n.
xl. 2 . . . 194 n.
29 . . . 241
xli. 17 . . . 252
28 . . . 241
xliv. 20 . . . 241
li. 24 . . . 72